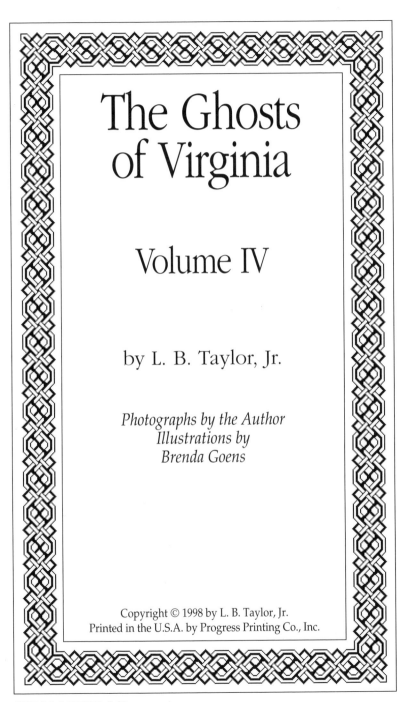

The Ghosts of Virginia

Volume IV

by L. B. Taylor, Jr.

Photographs by the Author
Illustrations by
Brenda Goens

ISBN 0-9628271-0-X

Contents

THE SHENANDOAH VALLEY

RICHMOND AND CENTRAL VIRGINIA

ROANOKE AND SOUTHWEST VIRGINIA

This book is for
Emily Megan Willis,
my granddaughter.

Author's Note

I know, I know!

I should know better by now. Every time I complete one of these books on Virginia ghosts, I am convinced I have exhausted the subject matter. And every time I get proven wrong! I said it: after "The Ghosts of Virginia, Volume I" (1993); after Volume II (1994); after "Civil War Ghosts of Virginia," (1995); and emphatically after Volume III (December 1996). I used every scrap of data I had in the files. I even delayed the publication of III to cram in last minute material. The cupboard was bare. Then it happened again. Before I could even get Volume III off the presses, "new" ghost lore and legends began to surface. I got phone calls. I got letters. Wherever I gave talks around the commonwealth, invariably people would come up to me afterwards and tell me of yet another interesting or historic encounter I had not heard before. Absolutely amazing.

A neighbor of mine in Williamsburg, Kathleen ("Kappy") Simpson, showed me an old, long forgotten pamphlet on "The Mystery of the Female Stranger," which put an entirely new twist, and intriguing turn to a chapter I had written about years ago. Francine Rosenberg, whose incredible photographs I ran in Volume III, came to Williamsburg for a visit and showed me her portfolio of even more incredible pictures. An officer at the Powhatan Correctional Facility west of Richmond called me about the strange phenomena which have been occurring where he works. He sent a notebook full of inexplicable incidents.

My dear late cousin Vance Lewis, who lived in Dahlgren, set up an interview for me with a charming couple in Dogue, Virginia, whose 200+ year old house is haunted. Bill Guerrant, who now lives in Florida, left me a note to call, and told me about a colorful spirit named Sookie Short in Pittsylvania County. I gave a talk to the Roanoke Historical Museum members in October 1996. Afterwards, as I was signing books, a man came up and left a manuscript with me. He asked me to read it when I had time. His name was Richard Raymond and the text was a lifetime work of poetry devoted to ghostly topics.

Around Halloween 1996, I went out to Sherwood Forest, as part of their annual Hauntings Tour, to sign books. Stephen Harriman, travel editor of the Norfolk Pilot newspaper, interviewed me and wrote a long article which appeared in a Sunday edition. At the end of the article, he told readers with ghost experiences to call or write me. I received a barrage of calls and letters.

And so it went. I began to build yet another new file. And it was a good file. I have always maintained that if the material was not good, different, interesting and/or historical, I would not continue. You can, after all, only write about so many footsteps without quickly becoming boringly repetitive. But the cases were good; the phenomena were unusual; and a good deal of it was historical.

Volume IV includes coverage of: Theodosia Burr, Aaron Burr's daughter; Stephen Decatur, the great American naval hero; William Byrd, II, the brilliant colonist; and James Monroe, fifth President of the United States. Famous houses include: Sherwood Forest, home of John Tyler, 10th President of the U.S.; the Adam Thoroughgood House in Virginia Beach; the Carlyle House in Alexandria; and an actual residential house in Petersburg built entirely of Civil War tombstones!

As the lore began accumulating, I went back to the stacks — back to the archives of libraries across the commonwealth. I had pretty much exhausted books on ghosts and psychic phenomena, as well as city and county histories, in my past searches. This time I looked in old tomes on family histories. Surprisingly, I found several new hauntings. I pored through bound volumes of such magazines as "Harper's Monthly," and "The Southern Literary Messenger," some dating back more than 150 years. And again I was rewarded with a few precious selections, such as "The Miser's Curse." In old, yellowed newspaper files from Gloucester County came two accounts of ghosts in plantation homes I had not uncovered before. I frequented, once more, used and rare bookshops. In Charlottesville, for example, I found a chapter on "The Trueheart Ghost" in an 1882 book written by Marion Harland, a.k.a. Mary Elizabeth Terhune. In a book published in the 1860s, I discovered yet more supernatural happenings relating to the Civil War.

It is difficult for me to describe the thrill I get whenever I come across such ancient and obscure passages relating to ghostly activity in Virginia. I am also pleased and somewhat pleasantly surprised by what seems to be the fast-growing popularity of this subject. There are now ghost tours, some nightly, some seasonal around Halloween — in Williamsburg, Petersburg, Richmond, Portsmouth, Norfolk, Fredericksburg, Alexandria, Springfield, Roanoke, and in Southwest Virginia. Thousands of people are taking these tours, and having a hauntingly good time. I love it. And I have found that many of the staid old talks accompanying historic homes and plantations, now include references to resident spirits. Such was rarely the case when I first began writing about the subject 15 years ago.

Ghosts are "in."

I would be remiss not to acknowledge the terrific help I have received during the publication of the now ten volumes in this series from my printer, Progress Printing of Lynchburg. In particular, I have been exceptionally supported and encouraged by Danny Thornton, sales vice president, and by Sara Adams, all-around person extraordinaire. Without them, I couldn't have done it.

On a personal note, I gave a talk at a book signing at the Borders Book Store in northern Virginia in October 1996. In the audience was: my daughter and fellow author, Cindy; my son-in-law, Joe Myers, and my granddaughter, Emily, then six years old. I talked about what experts think ghosts are, how and why they appear, and then I related several case histories of hauntings. When I called for questions afterward, a tiny hand shot up. It was Emily. "How do you know all that stuff?" she asked. I could only laugh.

Whenever and wherever I speak, people continue to ask if I have seen a ghost. I still haven't. I am still trying, as the great poet Percy Shelley did. He wrote:

"While yet a boy I sought for ghosts, and sped
Through many a listening chamber, cave and ruin,
And starlit wood, with fearful steps pursuing
Hopes of high talk with the departed dead."

And to the next question I am often asked, "Do I believe in ghosts?" — I reply as I always have. I began this venture with, hopefully an open and journalistically objective mind. I cannot personally attest to the existence of ghosts, because I have not personally experienced one. I do believe — deeply believe — that the people I have interviewed, hundreds of them, believe they have had such an experience. I believe in their sincerity. And I have also come to believe that there are many things which happen for which we do not have rational or scientific explanations. Maybe someday we will.

And, finally, let me say a word about the rewards of producing ten volumes on this ever-fascinating subject:

I have learned so much about the rich history of our great

commonwealth.

I have met so many interesting and wonderful people.

I have encountered so many compelling and absorbing instances of inexplicable phenomena.

I have been profoundly gratified at the nice calls, letters and comments I receive, unsolicited, from all over; letters, for example, from mothers and fathers telling me their children are reading, and learning history for the first time through my books. Nothing could be more gratifying to a writer.

I have been dedicated this past decade and a half to keeping alive a part of our heritage that is rapidly being swallowed in the glow and clutter of our high-tech, televised age. These are heirlooms of our history that we must not lose. Perhaps Margaret DuPont Lee summed up my feelings best in the preface to her classic 1930 book, "Virginia Ghosts." Mrs. Lee wrote, "My desire is to preserve to a posterity, destined to be much more fully persuaded of the reality of psychic phenomena than are we, these appearings to Virginians and in Virginia homes."

She added a line as follows, "In no instance has elaboration colored the material furnished me in an endeavor to create an interesting story." Neither have I found the need to stretch or embellish. No elaboration is necessary.

Mrs. Lee also said, "I am very appreciative of the interest extended to my little adventure by many friends, known and unknown. Their assistance alone made it possible."

I couldn't have said it better.

Enjoy!

Introduction

The origin of the word "ghost" is said to come from the German word "geist," an expression derived from the old Norse, "geisa," which meant "rage," or "fury," which, in turn, came out in Early Gothic as "us-gais-jan," meaning to terrify.

What exactly is a ghost? In the previous nine books in this series on Virginia ghosts, dozens of possible definitions have been offered. Here are some more:

* "Ghosts are spirits of some kind — spirits of dead humans who continue to resemble their earthly forms in appearance, dress and sound."

* In the fourth century, B.C., Plato wrote of "the soul which survives the body," wrapped "in an earthy covering, which makes it heavy and visible and drags it down to the visible region."

* Physicist Sir Oliver Lodge said, "Violent emotions might somehow imprint themselves on their environment for later transmission to people sensitive enough to tune them in."

* Some experts believe that the soul leaves the body at death, and that, under certain circumstances, this spirit may *tarry* on earth instead of proceeding to the "other side," and thus may be observed as a ghost.

* The great English author, Daniel Defoe once said, "Apparitions are the invisible inhabitants of the unknown world, affecting human shapes or other shapes, and showing themselves visibly to us."

* An anonymous writer offered, "Ghosts are in a spiritual halfway house."

* A more scientific point of view? "A ghost is the spirit of a person who has died, but remains entrapped in the vibrational force field of the earth."

* Perhaps the most common definition is that a ghost is, "The disembodied spirit of a person who has died but is unaware of his or her death."

* Some parapsychologists have even attempted to break ghosts down into separate categories:

1. There is the "haunting" ghost, which reappears from time to time — always in the same location.
2. The "crisis" ghost is one that emerges to help a friend or

family member in time of trouble.

3. The "after death" ghost manifests itself at the moment of death, or immediately afterward, in effect, to say goodbye to loved ones.

One can choose from any of these explanations, or from scores of others. The fact is, no one really knows exactly what a ghost — if there are such things as ghosts — is.

Henry Price of Oxford University may have summed it up best when he said, "Ghosts exist in a dimension or dimensions unknown to us."

If there are ghosts, why do ghosts exist?

This book, of course, is about Virginia ghosts. Since this is the tenth book in the series, the logical question is why are there so many ghosts in the commonwealth?

— There is so much history here.

— There are so many existing old homes; so many cemeteries, burial grounds, and other sites rife for hauntings.

— There has been so much tragedy and trauma on Virginia soil. So many, before their time, have died — in Indian massacres, and in the Revolutionary and Civil Wars.

— And there is so much tradition.

Again, the choice of why ghosts is broad: to seek vengeance from some type of injustice or unspeakable deed which may have occurred in their mortal life; to warn; to "look over the shoulder" of those left behind on earth; to complete something left undone in life, such as provide a will; to let others know they, (the departed spirits), are "okay."

Do ghosts exist? It is an ageless question that has been debated continuously throughout civilized history. Some believe, some don't.

Sir Walter Scott wrote: "Enthusiastic feelings of an impressive and solemn nature occur . . . which seem to add testimony to an intercourse betwixt earth and the world beyond it. For example, the son who has been lately deprived of his father feels a sudden crisis approach, in which he is anxious to have recourse to his sagacious advice . . . or, to use a darker yet very common instance, the wretched man who has dipped his hand in his fellow creature's blood, is haunted by the apprehension that the phantom of the slain stands by the bedside of his murderer.

"In all or any of these cases, who shall doubt that imagination, favoured by circumstances, has power to summon up to the organ of sight — specters which only exist in the mind of those by whom their apparition seems to be witnessed?"

Adding to this point, a writer in the January 1851 issue of "The Southern Literary Messenger" said, "When one has spent a lonely hour at midnight, in devouring some well wrought narrative of supernatural and tragic mystery, nerves are strung up to a pitch of morbid acuteness; imagination rules with irresistible, if not undisputed, sway. Logic and common sense are summoned to no purpose — they fleet at the first symptom of an appearance. The flap of a shutter, the rustle of a curtain makes one start as if a specter has already been seen."

Parapsychologist Dr. William Roll says the mind may create an apparition it perceives. "Stored psychic traces from the past can evoke apparitions," but in many cases, a person's mental state "plays an active role, unconsciously creating haunting phenomena to satisfy emotional needs."

Such theories may explain most instances of suspected ghostly activity, but can they explain *all* of them? Likely not. Some instances seem to defy logical explanation.

As ghost expert and author Hans Holzer has said: "That the incidence of mysterious happenings exceeds the laws of probability — and that their sheer number establishes that there *is* something to investigate — is beyond dispute."

American author H. P. Lovecraft adds: "It is an unfortunate fact that the bulk of humanity is too limited in its mental vision to weigh — with patience and intelligence — those isolated phenomena, seen and felt by a psychologically sensitive few, which lie outside its common experience."

Are not the arguments against the existence of ghosts locked within the present and limited boundaries of human understanding? Who can dare say, for sure, whether or not there is a psychic world that still lurks in the dark recesses of the unknown, the key to which may still be somewhere in the future?

Margaret DuPont Lee, author of "Virginia Ghosts," published in 1930, may have summed it up best when she inscribed one of her books this way: "Go little book on joyous wing! To each, and all, a message bring. Tell of a life beyond our day, just out of sight a little way."

Dr. Samuel Johnson, the eminent Englishman said: "It is wonderful that 5,000 years have now elapsed since the creation of the world, and still it is undecided whether or not there has ever been an instance of the spirit of any person appearing after death. All argument is against it, but all belief is for it."

So, it's okay to believe. It's okay not to believe. And it's certainly all right to be undecided.

There is an old story that two men find themselves alone together down a long darkened hallway in a near deserted museum. One turns to the other and says, "spooky, isn't it?" He then is asked if he believes in ghosts and he says, "no." Then he asks the other man if he believes in ghosts. The man says "yes" . . . and then vanishes!

Whatever one believes, ghosts constitute a most excellent subject for intellectual exercise and debate, and although the argument may never be fully resolved, they should form an important field for scientific inquiry.

What can be agreed upon, by believers and skeptics alike, is that the public fascination with ghosts has never waned through the centuries. This was summed up in a passage in the book, "Great American Folklore:" "However modern we might think we have become, the supernatural has a sure hold on our imagination. Wherever we pass an abandoned house or a graveyard at night, we feel the ripple along our spine."

A writer in the November 1871 issue of "The Southern Magazine," put it this way: "Everywhere, the human mind, in its rude and uncultivated state, is prone to a belief in the supernatural . . . we all remember how in our childhood we shuddered at the creations of our own fancy when sent to bed alone in a dark room."

The intent of this book is not to resolve the timeless debate on whether or not ghosts exist. That cannot be done. The intent rather is to present some examples through Virginia's rich history of what may be described as "inexplicable occurrences." The accounts are not fictional. Some are folklorian in nature — legends handed down, generation to generation, by families in the commonwealth. Many are direct reports, through interviews, of incidents which happened to living persons. All are part of our heritage. One does not have to be a believer, or a non-believer, to enjoy them. The purpose is to entertain. As in past volumes, some of the cases have historical significance, which, the author feels, is a bonus.

Enjoy!

A word about the organization of the book.

We begin with a conglomerate chapter on ghosts, and follow with hauntings in northern Virginia, running down the Shenandoah Valley, through the central part of the state, to Roanoke and the southwestern sector, and the southside, back up to Tidewater, the Northern Neck and Fredericksburg, interspersed between some of the regional sectors, are specialized sections, such as Psychic Dreams, Letters from the Author's Mailbag, Civil War Spirits, Vignettes, Miscellaneous, and "Some Ghosts that Weren't," and, finally, a chapter on Psychic Roses.

Let the journey begin.

Clocks That Strike Death!

Old superstition: If there is a death in a house, all the clocks in that house must be stopped at once. Otherwise if one strikes while a corpse still lies in the house, it is striking another member out of the family. Also, the "time cycle," which culminated in the death of a person, must be broken so that further deaths do not occur. If clocks are stopped, then time must wait; it cannot continue its destruction.

* * * * *

(Author's note: There is a prophetic line in the famous German folk song, "My Grandfather's Clock," that goes "it stopped short, never to run again, when the old man died." It is prophetic because in the annals of recorded psychic phenomena, there are scores of instances where the sudden stopping of a clock or watch has, in fact, signaled the death of its owner or someone close to the owner. Many of these strange cases have been documented by the Duke University Parapsychology Laboratory. Following are some accounts of time-keeping-related deaths in Virginia. The first of these is from the legendary James Taylor Adams collection of oral histories collected during the Great Depression years by Virginia writers. It is reprinted here with the permission of Clinch Valley College and the Blue Ridge Institute.)

THE DAY TIME RAN OUT
(Wise)

his experience was related to interviewer James M. Hylton on September 25, 1941 by Elmar Morgan. It had been passed down to Morgan by his father, and the events involved his grandmother. In the preface of his interview Hylton wrote an intriguing and mysterious passage. He noted that Grandma Morgan "believed in witchcraft and in conjuring up things of that sort," and then said, "she is the one in which the outlaws put too much faith to keep her mouth shut and caused them to be taken by the law through the medium of sulphur being burned on paper and mentioning some unknown words. He (Elmar Morgan) related this incident in the words of his father, and they think it had a lot to do with her death and leaving them in someway they cannot explain." While the details of this — whatever it means — have been lost in the sands of time, here is what Elmar told Hylton in 1941, with slight editorial corrections for clarification:

"We had an old 'regulator' clock made by a firm in Kaintuckey in our old home when Ma (the grandmother) was with us in life, and she always saw to it that it was running and keeping the best of time. She thought a lot of that old clock and it seemed it was a part of her life, too. I've gone in the room when she'd be settin' in the old rocker she had that she always set in, and she'd rock herself to sleep in, and that old clock would be tickin' along making a sound you could hear all over the whole place. Well, she'd look 'bout that old clock no matter what else they was to do 'bout the house, the clock come first thing in the morning.

"A few months before she died, the old clock stopped one day and she was settin' in the old chair and most asleep when it stopped. She jumped up, old as she was, and I thought something was wrong with her, but she'd noticed that old clock stopped a tickin' as near as she was asleep. (We) looked at it to see what was wrong. It was not run down but must have got some little something in the wheel, for I turned one or two and it started going then all right.

"But that evening after supper, Ma felt bad and had a spell with her heart, and we thought sure she'd die bustin' her lungs for air as she seemed to be losin' breath. But she was all right the next day, outside of being a little weak. She never done much more work 'round the place though after that until she died a few months later. Anyway, that old clock started losin' time and seemed to get weaker, too, and if you didn't wind her up in the morning, and again in the evening late, it would stop altogether sure.

"Well, we never thought so much about it at the time, but one late evening about two months later Ma'd not been feein' so well, and laid down on the bed to rest. My wife was out in the yard dryin' some apples to put away for winter when Ralph, my boy, went in to get her some paper to spread them on. He thought he d see what time it was and went into the room where (the clock) was and noticed it had stopped again.

"Sometime later we went in with the apples. I thought about the time and went to the door of the room where it (the clock) was, and seed that it had stopped, and looked over at Ma and noticed she was mighty quiet-like. I went over to the bed and then I saw she was dead. (Later) we was all talking about it when Ralph spoke up and said one day he had passed the door of the room a short time after the clock had stopped the first time and Ma was standing in front of the mantel talkin' to the clock like it was somebody, and saying some mighty funny words, and making some motions with her hands. She said (to Ralph) she'd bewitched it and when it would die and stop tickin' for good, she would die, too.

"The clock must have stopped about the same time Ma died, too, for it couldn't have been but a few minutes difference anyway . . . Ma was always telling fortunes and things. I know more than one case where she predicted something and it would happen just as she'd say, too. She'd been taught by her parents before her how to conjure up things and just what to say. She'd take off warts and the likes, and sometimes moles that had been on people for years and years. After we all was talking about this all, we then saw how close to Ma that old clock had been, and we hadn't thought to wind it since she'd died.

"We went and took it down again, and it was wound tight and the big drum wouldn't budge an inch after we turned wheels and things for a half hour or more. We got a feller down in town (Wise) to fix it, but I went back in a day or so to get it and he told me there wasn't anything he could do for it, it had just wore itself out, he said, and died. He never knowed, 'course, how it had played such a part in my Ma s life and death though. Anyway, we got the clock and had it polished and it's in our home now on the mantel just as we always kept it, but it never has, and never will run again I don't guess. Several fellers in the watch tinkerin' business has looked at it but said they'd never be able to make it run again.

"We'll keep it though to remember Ma by. I never look up there at it but what I think of how she'd been talkin' to the clock in the hall that day and said it was part of her life, and when it would die, she'd die, too."

* * * * *

THE DREADED WATCH OF THE MINES
(Southwestern Virginia)

(Author's note: The following account has been passed down generation to generation in the coal mining communities of Southwestern Virginia, and has been reported in anthologies of Southern and American folklore. The exact location and time period is uncertain, although it is likely it occurred near the Kentucky border, and probably early in the 20th century.)

The legend's origins began when a miner slipped into a mine one night to steal some coal to heat his house. He was buried alive under an avalanche of coal. It was known that this particular miner, whenever he was working, had a habit of always taking off his watch and hanging it on a nearby timber. But rescue workers never found the watch and assumed it had been buried with the man.

4

But over the next several months, a very strange thing seemed to happen. Men would hear what they said was the sound of a watch ticking in various areas of the mines. And whenever the sound was experienced, a terrible accident would befall the person working in that area. It was said that the ticking was louder than that of an ordinary watch, but no one was ever able to find the source. In one written account of the phenomenon, it was noted that the watch "eluded all measures of force and merely mocked men's curses." It was as inevitable as death itself. There were stretches of weeks or months when it kept silent. Then, with the suddenness of a fall of top rock, there would come the fateful tick-tock . . .

In the already-superstitious minds of the miners, the threat of hearing the ticking created stark fear throughout the community, especially after several accidents, some fatal, closely followed the discovery of the sound.

Then one night the fire boss, on his usual inspection rounds, heard the watch himself. He said it sounded weird and awesome in the empty mine. He immediately left the area. The next morning, he was waiting at the entrance of the mine when one of his workers, a man named Jim Kelly, approached. The fire boss told Kelly he had heard the dreaded ticking in his work area, and told him to take the day off. "Otherwise, you'll be killed," he warned Kelly.

The miner turned pale. He needed the work badly because he had a large family to feed, but the curse of the ticking watch was so strong he heeded the advice and headed home. As it was early in the morning, Kelly thought that if he went straight home and changed his clothes he still might make the 8 o'clock mass at the church. He hurried to his house, changed, and started down the road. When he got to a railroad crossing, the guard gates were down, but he was in a hurry, so he ran onto the tracks.

At 7:55 a.m., the fast-moving flyer train killed him on the spot!

* * * * *

THE HOUSE WHERE TIME STOPPED STILL
(Williamsburg)

 wenty years ago, Russell Simons moved into a boarding house on Lafayette Street in

Williamsburg with the intent of finding a job in the colonial town. Simons was sound asleep one night when something suddenly woke him. When he opened his eyes he saw what he described as an apparitional woman standing about 10 feet from his bed. It was a smallish woman with dark hair and a "kindly face." He said she was staring at him and appeared to be "floating" a few inches above the floor. He added that the figure seemed to be transparent, because he could see, by moonlight streaming through a window, the window frame and curtains *through* the apparition.

While most people would be terrified at such a sight, Simons said he inexplicably felt completely at peace, and had the strong impression that the woman meant no harm to him. In fact, he went back to sleep, although he emphasized that he definitely was not asleep when the vision appeared to him.

The next morning when he awoke, he noticed that his electric alarm clock had stopped during the night, and he could not get it to start running again. Later, when he mentioned to his landlord that the clock had stopped and he needed to purchase another one, the man said not to waste his money.

The landlord then told him that when his wife had died, every clock in the house except one had stopped at the precise moment of her death. He told Simons that he had gone out and bought some new clocks, but they had all stopped, too. He then opened a desk drawer and showed Simons several clocks. They had all stopped at the same time as Simons had. The landlord then pointed to a very old clock hanging over the mantel. He said it was more than 150 years old and had been in his wife's family for generations. For some unknown reason, this was the only clock which would work in the house.

Also in the room was an old photograph of a woman. The landlord said it was a picture of his wife. Simons was astounded! It was the same woman he had seen in apparitional form in his room! Simons had been sleeping in her room.

Simons stayed in the house for a few more days and then moved into new quarters. He plugged in his alarm clock. It worked perfectly!

* * * * *

THE CLOCK THAT TOLLED FOR THEE
(King and Queen County)

Built in the first half of the 18th century, mighty Woodlawn stood proud for more than 200 years as a landmark wooden home in King and Queen County about 20 miles from Tappahannock. This is not to be confused with Woodlawn Plantation, which is adjacent to Mount Vernon.

The Thomas Gresham family lived here in the early 1800s. Fearing an attack by the British during the War of 1812, the Greshams moved to a second plantation, Pigeon Hill, for a short time. When the threat of invasion was over, the family moved back to Woodlawn.

One victim of the transfer of furniture from one house to another was a clock that was set in an oblong case four and a half feet high and six inches wide. The front of the clock was set into three sections; a large mirror with openings at the top for the face, and at the bottom to display the pendulum. Colored pictures of houses and trees were painted around the face.

The clock did not survive the journey, over rutted roads, back to Woodlawn. It stood mute.

However, according to Mrs. Ella Haile of Tappahannock, granddaughter of Thomas Gresham, the old clock signaled a death in the household. She told this in a letter to Margaret DuPont Lee who wrote about it in her 1930 book, "Virginia Ghosts."

Such an ominous signal was heard on three separate occasions. Mrs. Haile said when her uncle was brought into the house, the clock suddenly struck. He died soon after of consumption. Six years later the clock sounded again, and Mrs. Haile's grandmother died within hours. The third time the chimes were heard, a servant's child was scalded to death while playing on the kitchen floor.

After this, Mrs. Haile's father, calling the clock "Such a source of superstitious dread," had the works removed. These were "thrown into the woodshed where the children often used them as playthings. The case of the clock was moved upstairs.

There were no more soundings of a death knell.

* * * * *

7

THE CLOCK THAT REALLY DID STRIKE DEATH!
(Newport News)

Eunice Anderson of Vinton, Virginia, tells of an electrifying experience her mother once had when she was 13 years old. It happened in a residential area near where the Mariner's Museum stands today at her sister's house. It occurred about 1937.

"She has told the story many times," Eunice says. "It is something I'm sure she will never forget. It scared her at the time and I'm sure it must scare her still today when she recalls it."

Eunice says her mother was babysitting for her sister one night, when all of a sudden an old clock, which hadn't worked in years began to strike. It struck five times. Helen had never heard it strike before. She became petrified. She grabbed the child she was babysitting and ran out of the house.

Shortly afterwards, when she had gone back into the house, the telephone rang. Helen was told that there had been a bad accident. Her brother and five others, including his fiancee and her mother, had been struck in their car by a train. Her brother had survived, but the five other people had all been killed. It was later revealed that the accident had occurred at the same time the old clock had struck! And it had tolled exactly five times — one for each fatality.

"My mother was always afraid of that clock after that," Eunice says.

* * * * *

THE CLOCK THAT STRUCK 79 TIMES!
(Winchester)

Waverley is a rambling old stone house, shaded by giant sycamores, that sits on land that once (1735) belonged to a prominent Quaker Scotsman named Alexander Ross. At one time (1826) Waverley, about five miles from Winchester, was owned by George Fayette Washington, a great nephew of George Washington. During the Civil War, upon entering the old mansion, a Yankee soldier impulsively fired a bullet through the forehead of a woman in a portrait, causing the owners to have a blue ribbon painted there to "hide the scar."

According to Margaret DuPont Lee, a number of ghostly manifestations took place at Waverley in the years after the Civil War. Once, for example, a neighbor, Lily Jolliffe, was invited to spend the night in the house. She was in the guest chamber over the parlor. Sometime around midnight she was awakened by the sound of steps on the stairs. She assumed it was her hostess, Mrs. Burwell Byrd Washington.

Before she could get out of bed, however, the door to the room opened and "the gray figure of a man" entered. He walked over to the window and looked out, then he stepped up to the foot of the bed and stared down at the now-terrified Miss Jolliffe. After a few seconds, he turned and left the room, bolting the door.

The next day she told what happened to her father. He then told her that he, too, had had an other-worldly experience in that very room. Mrs. Lee quoted him: "One night Byrd Washington and myself, with two other men, were playing cards. We had four candles lighted. In the middle of the game the door opened; a man entered and blew out the candles! I can tell you, we four left the cards and ran!"

When Miss Jolliffe related her encounter to Mrs. Dabney Harrison of Winchester, she said she had seen the same ghost. She said she had been sleeping in the haunted guest room one night with her dog at the foot of the bed. She was awakened when the dog, trembling all over, sprang up near her. "Opening my eyes, I saw the ghost standing at the foot of the bed," she related. One other woman later told Miss Jolliffe that she had seen the apparition in that room in broad daylight!

The Dabney Harrisons lived at Waverley for 19 years. They reported a most curious incident involving an old grandfather clock which stood in the hall. At the time, Dabney's grandfather was nearing his 79th birthday, and had never been sick a day in his life. One evening the family was gathered in the dining room when the old clock began to strike. Everyone was startled. The clock had not run for years.

It struck 79 times!

When Dabney's grandfather reached the age of 79, he died!

As Mrs. Lee wrote: "Possibly the spirit of the old Quaker entered the room to rebuke the card players, and possibly by the striking of the clock, announced to the tenant at Waverley that his lease had expired."

CHAPTER 2

Possession!!!

s there such a thing as demonic possession? The question has been asked, and largely been unanswered, for centuries. Debates on just about every aspect of this subject rage on today. It is, in fact, even difficult to arrive at a consensus definition. Webster's Dictionary calls possession, "Domination by something (as an evil spirit) . . . A psychological state in which an individual's normal personality is replaced by another."

Some experts have defined possession as a state in which individuals believed that their physical and mental functions had been "invaded" and were being controlled by either a demon, or the spirit of someone dead.

A general religious interpretation of possession involves the entrance into the soul of the concerned individual of an "outside force, generally evil, i.e., demonic possession. The inference here is that a living entity has entered the body of the victim.

Many in the medical profession are of the belief that the person inflicted is suffering from a mental or psychological disorder, such as schizophrenia.

Some parapsychologists, however, subscribe to the inclination that it may well be the spirit of a dead person which takes over the body of someone living. For example, Hans Holzer, the noted parapsychologist and author, has said, "The relationship between a deceased mind and a living mind may be contrary to orthodox views, but the evidence points strongly in the direction that such a relationship does, in fact, exist."

He adds that, "The overwhelming majority of cases involve possession of a living person by the spirit of a dead individual."

Most spiritualists, who are convinced that possession does occur, contend that such spirits infest living bodies because they are in need of "further expression."

And there are some skeptics, including respected professionals in paranormal activities, who believe most cases of suspected possession can actually be explained as poltergeist activities, and may even be caused by psychokinesis, especially in incidents involving adolescents.

Edgar Cayce, arguably the greatest psychic of the 20th century, (see "The Ghosts of Virginia, Volume I") called possession "the most startling concept" in all the realm of the unexplained. "The old fashioned sense of the word means that a human being has been 'taken over' by the spirit of some discarnate entity."

Cayce's son, Hugh Lynn Cayce, once wrote, "Is insanity sometimes caused by discarnate (dead) people interfering with the living? Do such cases provide evidence for discarnate existence, life after death?" To this, he could only answer, "The rooms of the unconscious are surely vaster and darker than is generally known."

So what, exactly, is possession? There are still more questions than answers. Perhaps each individual case is different, maybe involving some, or all, of the above. More likely, possession, like ghosts themselves, exists in a dimension still largely unknown.

What is known is that possession has been the root cause for centuries of misconception, misinformation, misunderstanding, and a world of superstition all its own.

Even the origins of possession are confused. A popular conception, for instance, is that the demoniacal form of possession began in the earliest days of Christianity. This may be because references in the Bible tell of Jesus Christ exorcising demons.

In one instance, Jesus was confronted with a man in Gerasenes; a man whose strange behavior had caused the townspeople to banish him from the town, and to live among tombs of the dead. Jesus said, "Come out of the man, unclean spirit. What is your name?" The man answered "Legion, for there are many of us (evil spirits). Jesus exorcised the spirits. Another example came when Christ was met by a man who said his son was possessed by "a dumb spirit," which prevented the boy from speaking. Further, the man added, his son was subject to fits in which he would tremble and fall to the ground, and also, at times, to become rigid and grind his teeth. When the boy appeared before Jesus, he convulsed, writhed on the ground, and foamed at the mouth. Jesus then said, "Deaf and dumb spirit, I command you; come out of him and never enter him again. After a moment of more convulsions, the boy lay so still on the ground that onlookers thought he might be dead. But Jesus helped the boy up and took him into his house. Jesus later told his disciples that this type of spirit could only be removed by prayer.

In actuality, some of the earliest civilizations on earth believed that physical and spiritual disorders were caused by the invasion of the body by demons. This was true, too, in ancient Egypt. The Bible tells of Jewish religious leaders roaming the desert and casting devils out of possessed people.

In the Middle Ages, as fears and superstitions grew, it became a common occurrence to torture those suspected of being possessed. The prevailing theory was to literally beat the devil out of victims. If the person afflicted died in the process — and many did — than it was thought that the evil spirit had won out.

In the 12th and 13th centuries possession was considered the work of Satan, and thousands were thrown into dungeons, all but forgotten by society. Such beliefs created stark fear among the general population, rising to the point where even the touch of one possessed was thought to be poisonous and to be avoided at all costs.

While the recognition and treatment of possession has progressed through the centuries, there is still much unknown. To this day the thought or mention of a person possessed can create terror.

THE SYMPTOMS

While there is still considerable disagreement of many aspects of possession, most experts seem to more or less agree on how manifestations of the affliction are recognized. Some of these are very similar to ghostly functions. Often, inexplicable sounds are heard, such as rappings on the walls or ceilings. These can be ear-banging loud at times. Certain objects, from small ones up to large pieces of furniture are heard, and sometimes seen, being moved about by unseen hands.

At times, terrible, stomach-wrenching stenches are experienced by witnesses. There are documented reports of beds, in which the victims are lying, being dramatically shaken, bounced, and, in rare instances, levitated off the floor. In one famous case, two boys, Joseph and Thiebaut Burner, ages eight and ten, were witnessed "lying on their backs and suddenly whirling like tops with the utmost rapidity." Some of these manifestations are similar to those associated with instances of poltergeist activity.

But there are distinct differences in the occurrences ascribed to possessed persons also. Almost always, there is a dramatic personality change in the victim. This can take many forms. The soft voices of young girls, for example, may, in a flash, become deep, gutteral utterings. Facial features may twist and contort to become frightening masks, barely recognizable to those present.

One of the most compelling manifestations is that the victim speaks in languages, or tongues, and tells of facts that he, or she have absolutely no way of knowing. There are cases on file of persons possessed who have spoken in ancient and long forgotten languages. Others have spoken of complex or little known issues far beyond their ages or education.

THE WATSEKA WONDER

One of the most startling examples of this occurred in the town of Watseka, Illinois, in 1876. It involved two girls. One, Mary Roff, died at the age of 18 in 1862. The other girl, Lurancy Vennum, was then two-years-old. Twelve years later, when Lurancy was 14, the spirit of Mary Roff apparently took possession of Lurancy's body!

Lurancy's demeanor and personality seemed to take a sharp and immediate transformation. She did not recognize members of her own family or her friends. And, she begged to be taken "home." What was incredible about the incident — and what led expert observers to believe this was a true example of possession — was the fact that Lurancy did recognize Mary Roff's family and friends, and *remembered details of events which had taken place in the life of the dead girl!* These were facts that Lurancy had no way of knowing.

The possession lasted a period of 14 weeks, and then Lurancy returned to her "own self," and the spirit, or possession, of Mary Roff disappeared altogether.

Cases such as this have led such experts as Holzer, and others, to conclude that possession involves the transference of a dead person into the body of a living person.

Here is another incident that lends credence to this theory.

A 'MOMENTARY' POSSESSION

In all of the hundreds of interviews the author has conducted with Virginians over the past decade and a half, one of the most astounding was included in a chapter titled, "Evil in the English Basement," and published in "The Ghosts of Charlottesville and Lynchburg," (1992), and reprinted in "The Ghosts of Virginia, Volume I," (1993).

It involved a woman named Sue Anne Elmore, who in 1982, with her husband, Jim, had moved into an old house known as Tufton, which was on property that had once been part of Thomas Jefferson's Monticello estate. The house dated to the 1820s. It has more than 5,000 square feet of living space, with huge rooms on two floors plus a large attic. The Elmores experienced a wide variety of psychic activity almost from the moment they moved in, including strange sounds, and the sighting of an amber-colored apparition of a male entity.

The possession occurred one day to Sue Anne. Her description: "I was alone in the house one day. I remember it was very hot, and I was carrying a load of clothes up the stairs. There was no air conditioning. About half way up the stairs I stopped, leaned against the wall, and shut my eyes for a moment. I felt a very strong presence. I mean *very* strong!

"I don't know how to put it in words. This may sound crazy, but it was as if I had slipped into a time warp, and I *became* that presence; I became another person!

"It was the presence of a young girl, a servant or a slave. I think she was either white or mulatto. She was wearing an old muslin type dress. It was gray and had no buttons. It wasn't fancy at all, maybe like a uniform, with a fitted bodice and long sleeves.

"It was like a feeling of regression, like I had gone back in time and assumed this person's body. Although she was young, I felt that she was worn out. She had had too many children, and she had been worked too hard. I felt the total sadness and tiredness of that young woman. I felt her smallness and her utter fatigue, so much so, in fact, that I didn't have the strength to carry the clothes upstairs. I don't know how long I stood there on the stairs. It might have been four or five minutes. And then the feeling lifted, and I was back in present time again. I had a feeling of astonishment. It was so real!"

By far the best known account of a case of possession was "The Exorcist," written more than 25 years ago by William Peter Blatty. The book was made into a movie that scared millions of people. The book was fictionalized, but it is not widely known that Blatty based his premise on an actual case that occurred in the northern Virginia-Washington D.C.-Maryland area in 1949.

In "The Exorcist," the victim is a young girl, Regan, and where the author took liberties with the facts are in the manifestations the girl exhibited: levitation; a deep, harsh voice uttering obscenities in various languages, and even speaking backwards; spurting vomit onto people across a room; visible welts, sometimes spelling words, rising on her chest; displays of superhuman power; and, the most shocking, swiveling her head completely around on her neck. Most of these incredible manifestations have never been documented in actual instances of possession.

In the book, and movie, two exorcists from the Catholic Church are called in to remove the demon from Regan's body. One is young and idealistic; the other is old and experienced. During the course of the long exorcism procedure, the older priest, suffering from the strain, dies, and the younger one is thrown through an upstairs window to his death on the ground below. Well, it made a good story line.

Much in the book, however, was factual, or based on fact, such as the exorcism itself. According to Holzer, the Catholic Church retains the rite of exorcism in its scriptures. Practice of the rite is rare today.

The ceremony known as exorcism today probably dates back a thousand years or more. It is based on a set of general instructions, but these can be adapted to meet the circumstances of individual cases. According to experts, the person performing the exorcism must have permission from a bishop of the church, and must be a person of piety and integrity. The ritual is begun by invoking protection from God for the priest-exorcist, his assistants, and the possessed person. This is done by making the sign of the cross, sprinkling holy water, and reciting a prayer asking for deliverance from sin for all of humanity. Excerpts from the Bible regarding Jesus' teachings on the power of God over the devil are read. The exorcist then addresses the evil spirit directly, and commands it to leave the body of the possessed. At the end of the ceremony, Satan is commanded to leave. This is followed by readings of more religious texts, and a prayer of thanks. Although exorcisms were originally performed in Latin, they may be done in any language. Often, one run-through of the ritual may not be enough. The exercise may be repeated many times before the possessed person is at peace.

The actual case of possession, upon which the book and movie were based, involved a 14-year-old boy, who lived with his family in a Washington suburb. As with Blatty's book, the initial sign of something supernatural was strange noises, this time coming from the boy's room. His parents suspected natural causes at first, possibly mice, but gradually the disturbances became more violent. Heavy furniture was inexplicably moved about, household items fell, apparently on their own, from shelves, and pictures came off walls. The boy's bed was seen visible shaking.

As the activities escalated, the boy's parents called in friends and neighbors, and they, too, witnessed the absorbing phenomena. The minister of their church spent one night in the boy's room in February 1949, and reported hearing scraping noises coming from the wall and seeing the bed shake. He asked the boy to move from the bed to an armchair. When he did, the chair began moving about the room. Then it rocked back and forth, shoving the boy to the floor. The minister next asked the boy to lay on the floor. When he did, he began sliding around the room. The minister, a skeptic, then believed he had witnessed something he had no way of explaining.

The parents had their son examined, both by physicians and a psychiatrist. They found nothing. The manifestations continued. In desperation, a Catholic priest was called in and asked to perform an exorcism.

The details of this extremely rare procedure were covered in 1993 in a book written by Thomas B. Allen. It was titled "Possessed — the True Story of an Exorcism." Allen based the bulk of his findings on a 26-page single spaced diary which had been kept during the period in 1949 by a priest who was supporting the exorcist. The diary was sealed for more than 40 years, but a copy was finally made available to Allen.

According to him, the actual manifestations of the boy were preceded by extensive sessions of "playing" with an Ouija board with one of his aunts. This occurred in January 1949. On the 26th of that month the aunt died and the boy was devastated. It was said he then spent endless hours with the board. Some believed he was trying to make contact with his recently departed aunt, who had told him such communications with the dead were possible.

This was about the time the strange sounds began. Scratchings behind the walls were heard by a number of witnesses. They were described as "if claws were scraping across wood." The boy's father had floor and wall boards torn up, but no logical source for the sounds was ever found. Curious, too, was the fact that the noise only occurred in the evenings, generally between 7 p.m. and midnight.

As time went on, the phenomena increased. Most of it

occurred in the boy's house, specifically in his bedroom. But there were manifestations elsewhere as well. One day at school, his desk began spinning wildly. Everyone thought he was somehow causing the movement, but he protested he wasn't. One evening, before several witnesses, a heavy stuffed chair in which the boy was sitting, rose up off the floor, then flipped over, sending him sprawling to the floor. At a friend's house the rocking chair in which the boy was sitting suddenly began spinning around like a top.

Each evening when he went to bed, he would violently thrash around, flailing his arms and legs, as if they were uncontrollable. The bed itself would shake and sometimes lift completely off the floor. His personality went through an abrupt change during these periods. While he seemed perfectly normal during the day, he became withdrawn and morose, at times violent, at night. He eventually had to drop out of school.

That was when the boy's parents called in a priest to consider doing an exorcism. At first the priest left some holy water and candles in the house. When the boy began his spasms that evening, his mother sprinkled him with the holy water. The bottle then seemed to lift up by itself and then smashed to the floor. When she lit a candle, she said the flames shot straight up to the ceiling, causing her to quickly extinguish it. A telephone table smashed into "a thousand pieces."

The priest came one evening to read prayers. The boy, inexplicably, began speaking in Latin, a language he had no conscious knowledge of. He reportedly said, in Latin, "Oh priest of Christ, you know that I am the devil. Why do you keep bothering me?"

One of the most compelling manifestations was the appearance of blood-colored scratches or welts on the boy's body. They would periodically show up over the next several weeks. Observers said there was no way the boy was causing this by scraping his fingernails over his body. At times the scratches would spell out letters and numbers, such as the words "spite," "Christ," and "hell."

It was now felt that the boy might indeed be possessed. He was taken to Georgetown Hospital for further examination. Although he lay restrained in bed, he somehow managed to work one hand loose, tore out a bedspring, and slashed a priest's arm from the shoulder to the wrist. It required more than 100 stitches to sew it up. Although the boy weighed less than 100 pounds, there were occasions where two or more full grown men had their hands full keeping him restrained in his bed.

In March another priest was called in to perform an exorcism. He would spend the next two months in intensive sessions with the boy. The ritual is long and complex and requires hours of prayer and readings. It also is exhausting. Some nights the priest and his helpers, other priests, would work for hours, until two or three in the morning. Often the readings would have to be done while the boy was physically held down. Finally, he would lapse into a deep sleep, and the ordeal would be over until the next evening.

As the exorcism progressed, the priests in attendance suffered considerably. The boy, with his eyes tightly closed, would spit great globs in their faces. He would cause incredible, overpowering stenches. He spoke and swore in a deep guttural voice, and his appearance would become grotesquely distorted. The exorcism was a long, grueling and punishing exercise, both for the boy and the priests.

More than two months after the exorcism had begun, suddenly it was over. One day, while the boy lay restrained on a hospital bed, a loud explosion was heard throughout the building. It was like a gun shot. Following this, the boy sat up, smiling. He said the spirit, devil, or whatever it was, had left his now-frail body.

Although the entire ritual had been shrouded in secrecy, somehow word of the successful exorcism leaked out and was extensively covered in the press, particularly in Washington. While the priests involved and the church would not officially comment on the case, a short notice was published in a church newspaper, "The

Catholic Review." It stated: "A 14-year-old Washington boy whose history of diabolical possession was widely reported in the press, was successfully exorcised by a priest after being received into the Catholic Church, it was learned here.

"The priest involved refused to discuss the case in any way. However, it is known that several attempts had been made to free the boy of the manifestations."

It was this notice, and the other media reports, that inspired Blatty to write his best selling novel, "The Exorcist." The actual details of the story, contained in a priest's diary, remained under lock and key for more than four decades, until they were revealed to author Thomas Allen.

Throughout the several months of suspected possession, none of the more bizarre occurrences such as the head swiveling around, described by Blatty in "The Exorcist, surfaced. This has led some experts, including author Daniel Cohen, who wrote about the case in his book "The Encyclopedia of Ghosts," to the possibility that the manifestations were caused either by poltergeist activity, or by the boy himself, through psychokinesis.

Proponents of spontaneous psychokinesis, or RSPK, believe that such things as flying objects and unexplained loud noises, are, in reality, caused by human beings rather than ghosts, generally adolescent youth. The focus of investigations into such disturbances is on the individual or individuals at the center of the action — in this case, the 14-year-old boy. Some scientists believe that RSPK activity is triggered by tension of certain neurological features.

They believe that ideal RSPK "agents," especially children from the ages of eight or nine until or through early teenage, fit into a set pattern. They may exhibit a built-up hostility that is being repressed from consciousness. Such persons have a deep feeling of hostility and frustration, and have great difficulty expressing such feelings. Thus the feelings are somehow manifested in the movement of objects. Just how they do this, how they have such ability, remains a dark mystery.

Was the case of the teenage boy one of possession, a poltergeist, or psychokinesis. It may never be known.

Since it happened nearly a half century ago, witnesses are either dead or are still reluctant to speak of it. The boy's true identity has never been revealed.

Is there such a thing as demonic possession? The mystery lives on.

C H A P T E R 3

Ghostly Notes from a Family History

(Leesburg)

(Author's note: A good source for ghost material can sometimes be found in little-known family histories. Some of these are
published publicly and some privately. A century ago it was not
uncommon for a family to put together such a history and limit
production from a few copies up to a few hundred for internal dis-
tribution. Some of these journals were well researched, consequently they, at times, painted a graphic picture of the eras in
which they were done.

Such was the case with a book I stumbled upon one day deep
in the archive recesses at the Colonial Williamsburg Library. There
is here a wonderful collection of books on Virginiana, and I have
spent untold hours riffling through them. Imagine my surprise
when I came across an obscure volume titled, "Old Virginia Days
and Ways." The subtitle was "Reminiscences of Mrs. Sally McCarty
Pleasants, edited by her daughter Lucy Lee Pleasants." It was published in 1916. Since a considerable amount of the reminiscences
covered events in Mrs. Pleasants' childhood and early life, they
date back to Civil War days and the latter half of the 19th century.

In perusing the table of contents, I found there was an entire
chapter on "ghosts." Following are some excerpted quotes from
that chapter, which not only are of interest on their own merit, but
also give an unusual insight into how people perceived the spirit
world in those days.)

he isolation of the plantations, superstition, tales and traditions transplanted from the old world — all fostered a belief in the supernatural," Mrs. Pleasants wrote. "Sometimes I have fancied that there might have been actual foundation for some of these stories and that ghosts did continue to manifest themselves in the South long after they had ceased to be welcome in more frequented parts of the earth. As rats driven from one place repair to another, so the poor discredited apparitions.

". . . If anybody had one, nobody ever said anything about it. Moreover, if you had more confidence in the veracity of the people who saw the ghosts than you had in your own, how could you help believing?

* * * * *

REAPPEARANCE

 y brother James was killed at the age of 17 by the accidental discharge of his gun while hunting. He was very fond of his cousin, Virginia Bronaugh, and loved to hear her play. At the very hour of the fatal shot, as she was practicing, she looked up from her music and saw him, leaning in his accustomed attitude upon the piano. 'Why, James McCarty,' she explained, 'I didn't see you come in.'

"To her surprise he made no reply but turned and passed into the adjoining room where her mother and sisters sat with their sewing. She sprang up and followed him.

"'You can't hide from me,' she cried (they were always romping together and playing tricks on each other); 'I saw you!'

"'Why, Virginia,' said her mother, 'what are you talking about?'

"'James McCarty came in here a minute ago. He is in this room somewhere now. I know you are hiding him from me.'

"'Virginia, you are crazy,' they cried. 'James McCarty hasn't been here.' But she would not be convinced until she had looked behind the curtains and under the furniture. Later in the day a messenger brought the dreadful tidings. Then she knew that she had been privileged to see her beloved cousin at the moment of his passing."

THE HARBINGER OF DEATH

t Contention, the home of Governor Pleasants, there was an apparently well-founded belief that when one of the family was about to die, a wagon loaded with boards to make the coffin would be driven into the yard and its burden dumped at the door. Fancy, if you can, the scene! The sufferer, with burning cheeks and glazing eyes, tossing, picking at the sheets, the wind roaring in the chimney and rattling the windows, then the creaking and rumbling of the invisible wagon driving round the circle in the lawn and the awful thud of spectral planks thrown out at the door!"

* * * * *

THE MESSENGER OF DEATH

relation of my husband had a little daughter named Rosy, a child so utterly lovely that few people saw her without declaring that she was too sweet to live. One day she came to her mother and said, 'Mother, I have seen a spirit."

" 'Did you, dearest?' said the mother, alarmed but fearing to frighten the child by showing what she felt. 'Yes, Mother, and he spoke to me. He said 'How d'y do, Rosy?' and I said 'how d'y do, Spirit?' Then he said, 'I'm coming for you tonight, Rosy.' Is he, Mother? Is he coming for me tonight?' 'Hush, hush, my darling, of course he isn't. Mother will keep you safe with her.'

"That night, towards the small hours, the baby was seized with a frightful attack of croup and died before morning."

* * * * *

INVISIBLE SOLDIERS

ne winter night several years after the war (the Civil War), two of our neighbors went coon-hunting. The moon shone bright, the air had a frosty stillness and the ground was frozen hard. The men bagged their game and were returning home about midnight when they distinctly heard a sound which had grown familiar during the years of conflict, the sound of clanking sabres and of thudding hoofs. So vivid was the impression, so certain were they that a squad of cavalry was coming down the road, that involuntarily, by a common impulse, they both stepped aside to let it pass. It passed! The invisible host went by, the rush of whose riding stirred their hair! Terror-striken, they looked into each other's eyes and each murmured in the breath the one word, 'Yankees!' Then, as they told me in relating the experience, they took to their heels and ran home as fast as if the Yankees were really pursuing them."

* * * * *

A PROPHETIC DREAM

he one noteworthy thing in the way of visions or warnings that ever came to my personal knowledge was a dream that visited my roommate when we were at boarding school. She awoke one morning disturbed and unhappy. She had dreamed that her guardian, with whom she lived, was dead and that she had seen him carried through the streets for burial in his armchair, robed in a dressing gown that he habitually wore. The dream haunted her all the morning.

"About noon she was summoned from the classroom. A messenger had come for her with the tidings that her guardian was dead. While sitting in his arm-chair in his library, he had committed suicide by cutting his throat."

* * * * *

THE 'GHOSTS' WHO WERE MORTAL

nother, and more agreeable incident, illustrating the relations between master and slave, occurred in the family of my husband's grandmother, Mrs. Eustace of Staffordshire. The estate was heavily encumbered and the number of Negroes out of all proportion to the size of the plantation. To remedy the situation my grandmother's lawyer advised her to 'hire' out as many of the slaves as possible, and a dozen or more of the likeliest were sent to work in the coal pits in Chesterfield County.

"Among them, amid tears and lamentations, went Castor and Pollux, the twin sons of Mammy Lily, Mrs. Eustace's cook and factotum. Mammy Lily was six feet tall and possessed a vigor of mind in keeping with the size of her body. She ruled everything in the household; no one dreamed of disputing her sway.

"A few weeks after the departure of Castor and Pollux, rumors were heard that they were receiving harsh treatment in the coal pit. My husband, a little boy at the time, remembers that Mammy Lily cried and that his grandmother spent many hours in prayer. Then came the news that Castor and Pollux had run away. A large reward was offered for their apprehension and the country round Mrs. Eustace's plantation soon swarmed with people searching for the fugitives, it being conjectured that their devotion to their home would bring them back to it. A searching party that actually invaded the Eustace kitchen was driven off by Mammy Lily with blows and abuse.

"My husband says that about this time strange noises would be heard late at night and that when he had to go on an errand in the evening, the fear of ghosts would send him flying across the dark passages. One morning the ghosts turned into very substantial flesh and blood when Mammy Lily threw open the dining room door and dramatically announcing, 'Mistis, here's your Negroes,' ushered in the delinquent Castor and Pollux who had been concealed for a week or more in the closet under the stairs.

"They were not sent back to work in the coal pits in Chesterfield."

Return of the Vengeful Slave?

(Leesburg)

(Author's note: There is, according to sources at the Loudoun County Museum, a passel of ghosts in Leesburg, Virginia. So many, in fact, that the town now has an annual ghost tour every October. In 1996, for example, it ran for four nights and was very well attended. How could one resist the brochure copy: "Ghosts live year round in Leesburg, but come to life especially at this time of year during our annual hauntings tours." Costumed interpreters tell the spirited tales. The event was conceived by Loudoun Museum board president Joe Holbert. Reservations can be made by calling 703-777-0099. The museum itself is worth a visit. Located at 14-16 Loudoun Street, it includes items from the county's rich heritage, dating from Indian migrations and settlement in the early 1700s to the present.

I had heard of several snippets of spectral legends in the town: the apparition of a soldier who fought in the Battle of Ball's Bluff during the Civil War is said to appear at the Glenfiddich House on North King Street; another feisty spirit moves items about and is occasionally glimpsed in the basement or on the stairwells of a stately Victorian house on North King Street. And there allegedly are even supernatural happenings — in the forms of unexplained stompings and slammed doors — in the Loudoun Museum log cabin gift shop.

Leesburg, by the way, was first known as Georgetown, in

honor of King George, II, of England. But its name was changed in recognition of Francis Lightfoot Lee, signer of the Declaration of Independence, who owned property nearby.

After reading about the tours, I called the museum's executive director, Tracy Gillespie, and inquired. She, in turn, sent me some material on perhaps the best known haunting in Leesburg, and one of the centerpieces of the tours — the Loudoun County Courthouse. This is a somewhat ornate red brick structure with white Corinthian columns supporting a pediment cupola with clock and belfry. A Confederate Memorial on the courthouse lawn features "a handsome and alert soldier" on a block of roughhewn granite. The courthouse was built in 1894.)

To understand the prevalent legend of Leesburg, one must go back more than 200 years. Loudoun County was formed in 1757. In these years there was a major fear, both in Loudoun and throughout the Virginia colony, that the increasing slave population would try to rebel against their white masters and fight for their freedom. Consequently, slaves were treated very harshly. Runaways were brutally whipped, or beaten. They were rarely killed for trying to escape because they were of monetary value. The beatings were severe, often leaving scars for life, to, in the minds of the plantation owners, set an example for others; to discourage others from attempts to flee.

Black criminals were treated even worse. For an assault, especially on a white person, or murder, the penalty was often death by hanging, either after a trial in which there inevitably was little or no hope for the defendant, or by lynching without even the semblance of a trial. And, at times, the body would be desecrated and displayed in public — again as a graphic example of what would happen to any potential perpetrators.

Such was the case, on July 28, 1768, when a Negro slave named Mercer, "belonging to Samuel Selden of the County of Stafford," was brought to the Loudoun County Courthouse to be tried for murder. Following is an excerpt from the actual transcript of that trial: "The said Mercer, being led to the Bar and publicly arraigned and asked whether of the Offence for which he stood charged, he was Guilty thereof or not Guilty, says that he is guilty of the Murder aforesaid of which he is charged.

"Therefore, it is considered by the Court that the said Mercer for his Offence be hanged by the Neck until he be dead, and that the Sheriff on Friday the twelfth day of August next drag the said Mercer to the Gallows and there hang him pursuant to the aforesaid Judgment and then sever his head from his body and place the same on a pole near the said Gallows, and also set up his four Quarters Vis-a-Vis one at Thompson Mason, Esq. his Mill, another at the forks of the Road at John Griffiths, one other at the place where the Ox road leaves Alexandria Road below Goose creek, and the last at the Fork of the Roads at Moss' and Sorrells. And the Court Values the said Slave at Seventy pounds current money and ordered that the Clerk so certify the same to the General Assembly."

Now *that's* punishment! Apparently, however, the powers that be may have had second thoughts and considered the post-hanging treatment to be excessive, for there is a handwritten note on a court document which states, "This sentence was mitigated as thinking it might prove (too extreme), and his head only to be severed and set on a pole near the gallows."

Mercer was hanged, and his head was placed on a pole for all to see; to act as a grisly deterrent to others who may have been contemplating mayhem. What effect this had is not known.

However, there are many today who believe the mutilated slave returns in ghostly form at the site of the old courthouse, either seeking his severed head or justice, or both. For the tour guides each Halloween stop in front of the courthouse and tell viewers the present structure, built in 1894, replaced an earlier building, which in turn was erected over the original edifice dating to the mid-18th century. The guide then says, "Little remains of this first county courthouse, except, perhaps, there lingers the spirit of one who was tried, sentenced and hanged here by the royal court back in the 18th century. . ." The prepared script goes on: "As you can imagine, today many people say that Mercer's spirit still haunts the courthouse grounds. Several members of the court staff tell of hearing strange sounds, and some people even report seeing a face staring out the courtroom windows."

"That's true," says Alice Alkire, administrative assistant to Judge Thomas Horne. "We do hear sounds. We first noticed it about five years ago. Everyone in the courthouse has experienced it at one time or another. I never dreamed I would be saying this. I don't believe in ghosts. But there is a definite presence."

Alice says voices are heard whispering, in the courtroom and in the judge's offices. "We hear papers being moved around and voices, but whenever we go to check it out, there is no one there." There are other manifestations: the sounds of someone working the keyboard of a word processor; toilets flushing when no one is in the rest room; books and papers being shuffled; mysterious footsteps on the stairs; doors opening and shutting by themselves.

"It almost always occurs at dusk, or at night," Alice says. "No one wants to work late in the building. The main courtroom has a balcony. One night a young law clerk was working up there and heard a noise under the balcony. She said it sounded like a 'whoosh.' She thought at first another law clerk was playing a trick on her, but he wasn't in the building. She was alone. When she realized this, she raced out of the building.

"Sometimes when I come in to work on the weekend, I bring my two dogs with me — a Brittany and a Yellow Lab. They won't go in the building. They freeze. Their ears go back against their necks and their tails tuck between their legs."

Alice says the phenomena seem to come in waves. Things will be quiet for two or three months, and then a rash of inexplicable happenings occur.

"If I could relate it to a specific case, I would, but so much has happened here over the years," she adds. "They used to hang people from large trees in the jail yard near here."

Could it be these victims who return? Could it be lawyers of years past who come back to retry cases they lost? Could it be repentant judges?

Or could it be, as many believe, the ghost of Mercer, still seeking vengeance for the dismemberment of his body more than 200 years ago?

Whatever, this is one stop on the October ghost tours in Leesburg where the building really *is* haunted.

A Tale Only Poe Could Devise

(Author's note: I have written about the possible surfacing of Edgar Allan Poe's spirit twice in this series. First was a report, "The Raven's Last Reading," in "The Ghosts of Richmond," (1985). And, in "The Ghosts of Virginia, Volume III," there was a chapter titled, "The Ghosts of Edgar Allan Poe." Rummaging through a flea market several months ago, I came across yet another reference of the great writer's possible return. Although this was published as a "true account," the details are somewhat sketchy, and the premise stretches credibility somewhat. However, since Poe allegedly was involved, I include it.)

pparently, in 1849, the year Poe died, medical school anatomy classes in the Baltimore area were having a difficult time finding enough corpses for study. It was said that three young students, Jonas Kallen, Harold Forster, and Maxim Hurd thus decided to earn some tuition money by robbing graves.

According to this particular account, the three either dug up Poe's coffin, or one near his, one night. Whether it was in fact Poe is doubtful, but the three men nevertheless, thought it was his body they had uncovered. As they carried the coffin out of the cemetery, a strange thing happened — one that proved to be a tragic omen for the three young men. The bell in a nearby church tower began ringing. Strange, because this church had been abandoned for some years.

The Edgar Allan Poe atatue in Richmond's capitol park

Then, as they loaded the coffin onto a cart, a wispy apparition appeared, or seemed to appear, in the form of a man resembling Poe. It warned the three students that they would all die by "the very rope that sounds the knell" (of the church bell.) Then the apparition faded away. The students tried to persuade each other that what they had seen was caused by overactive imaginations, coupled with guilt feelings. Still, the vision seemed to gnaw at them in the weeks that followed. It especially affected Jonas Kallen.

It wasn't long after that that Kallen graduated with a degree as doctor of medicine, magna cum laude. For some unknown reason, whether to celebrate, or to taunt the curse which had been declared upon him, Kallen returned to the cemetery on graduation night, alone, and ascended the old church tower. It is thought that he must have believed by ringing the bell he would prove the curse false.

Neighbors upon hearing the bell ringing, called the police. They arrived, climbed to the tower, and found young Jonas Kallen on the floor. He was dead! Police could only speculate that he had tripped and fell over a chair in the dark and accidentally got tangled in the bell rope. He had snapped one of his vertebrae!

When word reached his two friends, they became frightened. Maxim Hurd tried to convince Harold Forster that Kallen's death had just been a dreadful coincidence, but Forster couldn't be shaken from his belief that the curse had taken effect. It disturbed him so much that one night shortly after Kallen had been buried, he slipped out to the cemetery to the spot where they had dug up the corpse, and "apologized."

It was then that something must have spooked him, because he ran across the muddy graveyard to the bell tower. The bell tolled again, and investigators found Forster's body on the tower floor. They guessed that in his panic he had stumbled over the rope, fell, and fractured his skull!

Now petrified, Maxim Hurd decided to take action into his own hands. Since the curse had involved the bell rope, he went to the tower one night and cut it down. Then, he took a rowboat out into the Chesapeake Bay, tied it to a large rock, and flung it over the side. His foot, however, became entangled in the rope and it pulled him down into the dark waters. He drowned!

It was said that when this happened, peals from the ropeless bell in the abandoned church tower were heard throughout the town.

* * * * *

A CLUE TO POE'S DEATH

here is today still much mystery as to how Edgar Allan Poe died. He was found in a bar on Lombard Street in Baltimore in October 1849 in soiled and ill fitting clothes. He was delirious. Many thought he was drunk or on drugs. He was taken to the Washington College Hospital, and died a few days later. It was also widely thought that foul play had been involved, since Poe had left Richmond earlier that month with $1,500. In Baltimore, he was penniless.

Now there is a theory that Poe had not been drunk or drugged; that he died, instead, of rabies! This surfaced in an Associated Press article published in September 1996. It quoted Dr. R. Michael Benitez, a cardiologist, who, oddly, practices within a block of Poe's grave. Writing in the September 1996 issue of the Maryland Medical Journal, Dr. Benitez described the poet's last days as a "medical horror story as dramatic as the writer's most gruesome tales." He noted that Poe entered the hospital comatose, but by the next day he was perspiring heavily, hallucinating, and shouting at imaginary companions. The day after that, he seemed better and was quiet, although he couldn't remember falling ill. On his fourth day, Poe was again confused and belligerent.

"That's a classic case of rabies," Benitez reported. He said that during the brief periods when Poe was calm and awake, he refused alcohol and could drink water only with great difficulty Rabies victims, Benitez noted, frequently exhibit hydrophobia of water, because it is painful for them to swallow.

The doctor added that rabies, especially in the 19th century, was a swift and brutal killer. Most patients died within a few days of being bitten by a rabid animal. Another expert, Dr. Henry Wilde, said Poe "had all the features of encephalitic rabies."

Jeff Jerome, curator of the Edgar Allan Poe House and Museum in Baltimore, welcomed this explanation. He said that over the years he had heard dozens of "wild tales" as to just how Poe had succumbed. Jerome added that he was almost certain Poe did not die of alcohol poisoning or withdrawal. He said that while Poe had garnered a reputation as a heavy drinker in his early days, he shunned strong drink in later years. In fact, he was so sensitive to alcohol that a mere glass of wine would render him violently ill for days afterward.

And so it goes. Like the man in life, Poe's death remains cloaked in dark mystery.

* * * * *

BEHIND THE CASK OF AMONTILLADO

(Author's note: The following material, excerpted and rephrased, first appeared in the April 1997 issue of Fate Magazine in an article titled "A Terrible Revenge," by Daemon Magus. It appears here with the approval of FATE Magazine.)

 ieutenant Robert F. Massie of Virginia was stationed at Fort Independence, Massachusetts in 1817. He was a popular young officer. One evening, however, following an argument over a card game, Massie was challenged to a duel. He was ill-equipped to fight such a duel with a master swordsman, and he was killed in an attempt to defend his honor. He was buried on Castle Island.

The man who killed him was in turn despised by his fellow officers and they plotted to do him in. He mysteriously disappeared. Ten years later, in May 1827, a young man who went by the name of Edgar A. Perry enlisted in the Army and was sent to Castle Island. Upon viewing Massie's grave, Perry inquired about his death and what had happened to his killer.

He was told about the duel and about what happened afterward. One night a group of officers got the survivor drunk. They then took him down to the lowest dungeon in the fort, forced him into a small casement, shackled him to the floor, and walled up the narrow opening to the windowless casement.

In 1905, while repairing the fortress, workmen broke open a wall and found a skeleton, covered with fragments of an old Army uniform dating to the 1820s.

Meanwhile, Massie's body was moved in 1892 to Governor's Island, and moved again in 1908 to Deer Island when Boston's Logan International Airport was being built. His remains were disinterred once again in 1939, and taken to Fort Devens in Ayer, Massachusetts. Finally, some time later, a group of "concerned southern citizens had his body exhumed and sent back to Virginia where he now rests. He had been disturbed so much that his remains became known as the "Bouncing Body of Boston Bay," as reported in Edward Rowe Snow's book, "Legends, Maps, and Stories of Boston and New England." One would think Massie had good reason to return for a ghostly protest, but there are no accounts of his reappearance.

The officer who had killed him, and then met his own terrible death by being walled up alive in the dank dungeon, however, turned out to be the real-life inspiration for one of the greatest horror stories in American fiction. It was he who the young man named Edgar A. Perry wrote about when he penned
"The Cask of Amontillado."

Edgar A. Perry, you see, was the Army enlistment name used by Edgar Allan Poe.

("A Terrible Revenge," FATE Magazine, April 1997. FATE Magazine, P.O. Box 64383, St. Paul, MN, 55164-0303, U.S.A. Reprinted by permission.)

CHAPTER 6

The Most Cantankerous Ghost in Town

(Washington, D.C.)

(Author's note: Sometimes the story tells itself. Such was the case when the following article appeared in an 1871 edition of the old Washington Star. It was headlined, "Washington's Haunted House," and sub-titled "The Ghost of a Wicked Marine — He Makes Things Lively in His Old House.")

The neighborhood of 9th Street, between G and H Streets Southeast, has been the scene of great excitement this week, in consequence of stories in circulation that a two-story house in the rear of the garrison, occupied by a family named Bonehart, is haunted by the ghost of a former occupant, a marine by the name of Howard. He was the owner of the house, and died there some eight or nine months since.

"He is represented to have been a fearfully wicked man, who abused his family and all around him, and finally died blaspheming his Maker and cursing his wife and children. His widow and children soon moved from the premises, not being able to sleep on account of hearing strange noises in the house, and they rented it to the Boneharts, who took possession about two months since, not hearing anything about the house being haunted. This family, soon after moving in, became very uncomfortable; they could not sleep at night and all became very nervous.

"They alledge that strange noises were heard every night,

which they could not account for. Doors would be found open which had previously been locked. When the family were on the lower floor, loud rappings would be heard upstairs, and when the family were in upper rooms, the rappings would appear to be below, as if someone was striking a table with a rattan stick. The back door would be found open after it had been carefully bolted, and when it was closed loud knocks were sometimes heard on the outside, making it shake.

"This was at first thought to be done by someone on the outside, but during its continuance the family would look out from an upper window immediately above, and nothing could be seen, although the knocking would continue. A blind door connecting with the next house, and which had been securely fastened up for years, was on several occasions found wide open, and no one could account for that.

"On Tuesday night last, a colored girl living with the Boneharts retired to bed in an upper room at rather a late hour, and when almost asleep she suddenly heard steps softly, ascending the stairs, and saw the reflection of what was apparently a lighted lamp, but believing it was some member of the family, she did not trouble her mind about it, until, hearing a heavy groan by the door, which stood ajar, she raised up in bed, and says she saw the ghost of old Howard.

"The light in his lamp was at once extinguished, and blue and red streaks of light shot through the room. At one bound she was up and raising a frightful scream, which roused the whole house. She bolted downstairs and left the house in her night clothes, the entire family following her. The colored girl could not be induced to return to the house, but Bonehart and his family did, and after they retired they heard terrible groaning from upstairs. Bonehart persuaded his wife that it was the window shutters swinging in the wind, although he did not believe it himself.

"Very soon the bed in which they were laying began to move out into the middle of the room, and loud groans came from underneath it. This so frightened them that they left the house, and Bonehart went to the station house, where he told his story. Officer O'Hare at once repaired to the house, and found the family running away from the house. He examined the premises throughout, but could find nothing wrong, and persuaded them to return, promising that he would watch in the house.

"After they had retired, he heard the noises and rapping and thought someone was at the back door, as the knob moved very perceptively. He kept the family quiet, however, until morning and left them. The next night these scenes were enacted over again, and on being notified, O'Hare and his partner, Shelton, stayed there again until about 12 o'clock, when nothing further being heard, the officers advised the family to go to bed, which they did, and the officers then left.

"After they left, the most unearthly noises were again heard, much worse than ever, and the family became so much frightened that they left the premises and took shelter in the house of Mr. De Neal, a neighbor. Yesterday morning Bonehart was seeking another house in which to move, declaring that he would not stay there another night.

"The neighborhood is greatly excited over the strange manifestations. We have told the story just as it is related by the Boneharts, their neighbors, and the policemen."

C H A P T E R   7

Virginia's Angelic Photographer

(Alexandria)

(Author's note: In "The Ghosts of Virginia, Volume III," published late in 1996, I included a short piece on the amazing photography of a woman named Francine Rosenberg of Alexandria. She is the one who takes photos of ordinary things, and sometimes, when the film is developed, there are inexplicable images on them. The images are generally whitish in nature and often bell shaped. Francine believes they are angelic symbols. At other times, mysterious faces appear "hidden" in the pictures. In Volume III, I ran two of these. One was taken in the Abraham Lincoln box in Ford's Theatre in Washington. The face of a black officer in the uniform of the Civil War appeared in it.

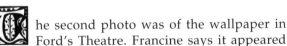he second photo was of the wallpaper in Ford's Theatre. Francine says it appeared interesting to her. When this was developed, there is, if one looks at it right, the clear outlined image of the face of what appears to be a handsome man, with dark curly hair and a mustache. She feels it bears a good resemblance to John Wilkes Booth, Lincoln's assassin. And I agree.

But here I must make an embarrassing admission. In Volume III, the picture was printed upside down! Horrors! Francine attended a book signing I did in December 1996 at the Borders Book Store at Tyson's Corner. The book had just come out. I had sent her an

Unexplained image on Polaroid photo at the Fort Washington jail

advance copy. When I asked her how she liked the photos, she told me the one of the wallpaper with Booth's face was *upside down*! To say that I was chagrined is a gross understatement. I told her I would reprint it the first chance I got, and so, I do it in this chapter — right side up. There is another curious point about this particular photo. Francine says it definitely looks better in the print in the book, than it did in the actual photograph.

I told Francine, after I had first seen the photos that were printed in Volume III, that if she had others, I would be interested in them. I met her for the first time in the fall of 1996 when she came to Williamsburg, my home, on a visit. She brought a whole album of pictures. As we sat in Merchant's Square in the historic section of Colonial Williamsburg, I was both intrigued and excited with what she showed me. There were some of the most unusual photographs I had ever seen. In fact, I had never seen anything like

Apparitional-type image on photo, taken with a Minolta 35 mm camera at Gunston Hall in northern Virginia

them before or since. I include a selection of them here, with, I hope, appropriate captions.

As I have written before, Francine believes the angelic images look amazingly like the ones painted by the well-known California artist, Andy Lakey. His paintings of angels are widely acclaimed, and Francine told me that he once had an out-of-body experience in which these figures, seven of them, appeared at his feet.

Francine does not know, for sure, why the images are on her photos. She knows there are no double exposures, and it is not from faulty film or cameras. In point of fact — and I find this to be truly incredible — she has gotten the same shaped figures on her photos with five different cameras! This has included three differ- ent Polaroids, and two different 35 millimeters — a Minolta and a Nikon. She has shown her unusual collection to parapsychologists, priests and professional photographers, but no one has been able to come up with a plausible answer.

"I think maybe it's a gift," she says, "to help ease the pain I have suffered the past few years." The pain was caused by the unexpected death of her son in 1991. The phenomena began in 1995. One of the first incidents occurred when she took some pic-

Bell-shaped "angelic" image taken at Woodlawn Plantation

tures in historic Pohick Church in northern Virginia. When she had them developed, she was astonished to see a filmy image in one of the series. It was the image of her son's face! On another early photo there appeared a serpentine form. She feels it is one shape of a human entity, perhaps the development of a spirit.

As I reported, since then, at right up to the present, she continues to record these incredible images. It doesn't happen every time she clicks the cameras. She doesn't know when or why they will appear. She doesn't see the images when she is focusing a camera. They do not appear to her naked eye. But she says she seems to "get a feeling" sometimes to take a picture.

For example, she went to the Vietnam Wall Monument in Washington in February 1997, and took several photos, but she didn't have any strong feelings. Nothing unusual came out on these prints. But later that day as she was approaching her house, she saw her two cats outside, with a wooded area in the background. She thought to herself that this would make a good picture. The feeling. When that photo was developed there was a clear image of a dove on it.

Francine says these feelings, like the images themselves, seem

"Angelic" figure taken above Gearge Washington's chair at Pohick Church in northern Virginia

to come to her intermittently. But they come often enough to bring hard questions to even the most severe skeptic. How do you explain them? The photos have drawn such interest that she has had an exhibit of them at the Washington Center for Photographic Art.

Some of the more curious ones include a series of shots she took with a Polaroid camera. In three of the pictures, initials can be seen — the initials "J," "A," and "R." *These are the initials of her dead son!*

Images on photo taken at the Stone House, Manassas National Battlefield Park. Francine Rosenberg believes them to be "the images of angels guiding lost spirits to the light."

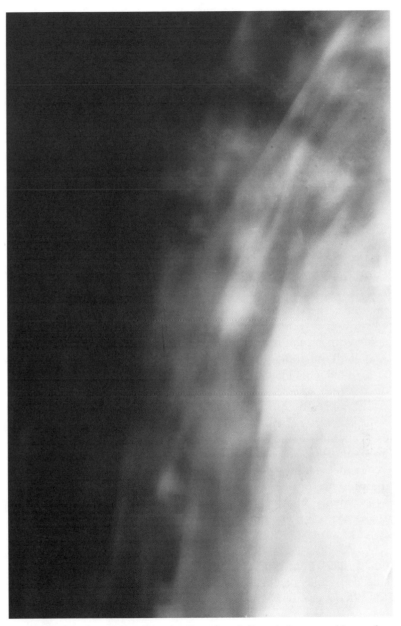

Image of the face of what Francine Rosenberg believes to be a resemblance of John Wilkes Booth, taken of the wallpaper at Ford's Theater in Washington, D.C.

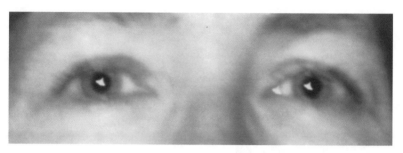

In this self portrait closeup, "angelic" images appear in the lens of Francine Rosenberg's eyes

Some believe her work to be of an unexplained but highly artistic quality. Francine has had some of these angelic images printed in a series of cards. If you are interested, you can obtain a set by writing her, Francine Rosenberg, Angel Connection, P.O. Box 6443, Alexandria, Virginia, 22306. Francine has been surprised that the cards, distributed in book stores and gift shops, have elicited quite a response. "People are sending me photos they have taken with similar images on them," she says.

Of all the photos, possibly the most fascinating is one Francine took of herself. "I just took it as an experiment. When it was developed, and I must say it was a very unflattering picture, I didn't really notice anything different about it. Then one day a friend of mine called my attention to my eyes. I was astonished." In the lens of Francine's eyes, there appears the same bell-shaped angelic image that she gets on her photos! Bizarre!

Francine thinks that maybe certain areas are more conducive to the presence of possible spirits. Some are of historic sites, such as Woodlawn Plantation, next to Mount Vernon, the old Stone House at the Manassas National Battlefield Park, and, in particular, the Pohick Church. "There must be a vortex or something in the area where George Washington's chair is," she says. I took photos in other places in the church and didn't get anything. But where the chair is — this must be a place where spirits can penetrate."

Whatever. The photographs speak for themselves.

The Enduring Mystery of the Female Stranger

(Alexandria)

(Author's note: In "The Ghosts of Virginia, Volume I, (1993), I wrote a short piece on Gadsby's Tavern in Old Town Alexandria. This included the legend of a beautiful yet most mysterious woman who came to the tavern in 1816. She died within a few days of arriving, and has been reported seen, in spectral form, ever since. The mystique was heightened by the fact that her husband demanded that all who attended the lady in her final days swear to never reveal her true identity.

As I wrote, "Speculative theories about who the woman was abounded in the city for years. Some believed her be the daughter of Aaron Burr, the man who shot Alexander Hamilton in a duel. Another version is that she was a ward of an English nobleman who had fallen in love with her. He was 75, and she but 23. . . Her husband walked into the garden of an undisclosed location one day and found her in the arms of a British officer. The old man reacted violently, and when he attacked the lover, he was pushed hard, fell, hit his head and died. The frightened couple then got on a ship and sailed to Alexandria, although she took sick enroute and never recovered.

"Yet still others subscribed to the tale that she was one of four orphaned children who were separated from each other at a young age. Many years later, she unknowingly married her own brother, and they didn't want the horrible secret to be known."

So which version is correct? As William McNamara, then president of Gadsby's Tavern and City Hotel, Inc., once said, "the mystery . . . is still one of the most fascinating traditions (of the tavern)."

In my continuing research covering Virginia's historic past, I came across an obscure and long out of date pamphlet titled, "The Story of the Female Stranger. I became absorbed in the text, which was based on the narrative of a man named John Trust. He presents a strong case for the latter of the theories involving the 1816 incident — that of the lady being one of four orphans. Following are edited excerpts from Trust's fascinating account.)

I am an old man now, and I feel the icy hand of death grasping colder and colder about my heart," he begins. "I long to lay this weary body in its mother earth, and to let my jaded spirit, worn with a life struggle, sleep for awhile, beside the eternal fountains. Yet before I go forth to judgment, I would write with faltering hand the story . . . of the spirits of the buried hopes and loves that were the companions of my young existence."

Trust says that he was born in England, and that his mother died in "the alms house at Truro in Cornwall, having shortly before given me life and a twin sister. Thus bequeathed by poverty . . . I never knew the warmth of a father's kiss nor caught the soft light of a mother's smile. . . We, little children as we were, loved no one, and no one loved us."

When he was four years old, Trust was adopted by "a French gentleman," who brought him to Alexandria, where they took up residence in "a mansion built of stone." John Trust grew up here and was given the best education money could buy. But he went through a sad and lonely adolescence. "I soon perceived," he said, "that he (his guardian) did not love me. It was, he added, "a joyless childhood."

Years later, Trust and his foster father moved back to Europe and travelled extensively. Eventually, they journeyed to Calcutta, India, and there Trust met a man named Dr. Wroe, who "had a reputation for familiarity with the occult sciences." They soon became fast friends.

Trust then moved to Paris, and although gifted with a superior intellect, believed himself to be a failure in life; an unloved failure as well. He contemplated suicide. "I was just about to drop quietly into the Seine (river) and slip away from life it was just a bore — when my Indian friend, Dr. Wroe, left his card at my hotel. We renewed our intimacy, and I found that he had learned from the Indian Brahmins an art similar to what is now called animal magnetism, or mesmerism, and that he was a most thorough master of it."

Wroe, Trust learned, was English by birth like himself and also had been adopted at an early age. He, too, had been separated from a sister and had lost contact with her. When Napoleon fell, Trust and Wroe left Paris and wound up on the isle of Martinique.

Gadsby's Tavern in Alexandria

It was here, Trust says, that "events happened which changed the whole tenor of our lives."

It was here that John Trust fell deeply in love. When he first met the young lady, he says, "I stood spellbound..... entranced. . . I was in the presence of majesty! . . . She seemed, indeed, the mold of form, the union of elegance and grace before undreamed of. Her eye, a diamond when she listened, flashed like a sword when she spoke . . . Her hair lay in its raven brilliancy.

"Her name was Blanche Fordan. "She shall be mine," Trust said to himself. "For weeks Blanche filled my soul," he wrote. She apparently loved him, too, as they courted. But there was an unexpected complication: Wroe had also succumbed to Blanche's charms. He told Trust that his love "was beyond his reason. He must have Blanche or death."

And then one morning, Trust awoke to learn, to his horror, that Blanche and Wroe had fled the island during the night; that they had sailed for America. "I had lost the only prize on which I ever set my heart," he said.

Trust next was summoned to London by his guardian, and there, for the first time, learned the story of his background. His mother had had four children. John Trust had a brother, a sister, and a twin sister. His twin had married an older portrait painter named Lorentz, and in her efforts to trace Trust, had found that he had lived in Alexandria, Virginia. She and Lorentz moved there. When Trust discovered this, he sailed to America and headed to Alexandria. There, he tracked down his twin sister and they were reunited. Trust was ecstatic.

Several years passed. Then one day Trust went to a park-like resort area near Alexandria then known as Bromilaw (or Broomlawn). There, to his astonishment, he saw Wroe. Wroe did not recognize him. Trust then followed Wroe and they entered "precincts sacred beyond all searching, because wasted flesh and moldering frames wait there to see God." Wroe climbed an iron trellis, then Trust said, "I heard moans, as of sorrow, and sounds of mourning." Although insatiably curious, Trust did not confront Wroe and went home, even though, as he said, "what I had seen excited me strangely. . . Ghosts of dead hopes, half memories and half dreams haunted me."

Unable to sleep, Trust went back to the cemetery. "I had nearly reached the place," he wrote, "when a figure, which at a glance I knew, (Wroe) merged from the shadows. He betrayed considerable agitation, and came forward, exclaiming: 'Dead or living, I fear you not, John Trust.' I knew he did fear me, and that he believed he saw a specter, for his voice was choked and tremulous, and the arm he raised, as though to threaten, shook like an aspen." Trust then said, "John Trust is not dead and you have no cause to fear him living."

It was then that Trust verified his darkest suspicions. They were there at the gravesite of his beloved Blanche. The tombstone read: "To the memory of a Female Stranger, whose mortal sufferings terminated on the 14th day of October 1816, aged 23 years and eight months. This stone is placed here by her disconsolate husband in whose arms she sighed out her latest breath and who under God did his utmost even to soothe the cold dead fear of death.

"How loved, how honor'd once avails the not,
    To whom related or by whom begot.
A heap of dust remains of thee
    'This all thou are, and all the proud should be."

Then Wroe made a surprising confession. "Madly as I loved her," he told Trust, "she did not love me. . . She loved you — you only — I'll tell all the truth." Wroe then told how Blanche had spurned his love and professed her love for Trust. Unable to accept this, Wroe had mesmerized her with his hypnotic powers, forced her onto a ship bound for America, and married her, while she was still under his spell, aboard the ship.

Wroe then told how "the glow of fever grew upon her cheek," as they sailed across the ocean. "For days her life hung lightly balanced on the eternal shore."

A description of their landing at the old port in Alexandria is detailed in the book, "Seaport in Virginia," by Gay Montague Moore, published in 1949. Moore wrote: "On a day in early autumn of 1816, a ship docked at the wharf in Alexandria, purported to have come from the West Indies. Down the ways came a striking couple. Luxuriously apparelled, they presented figures of great elegance. The handsome young 'milord' was all tender solicitude for the fragile beauty clinging weakly to his arm in a state of collapse.

"Bystanders were considerably intrigued and greatly impressed by the distinguished strangers. Unquestionably they were rich, and certainly noble. It was indeed curious that such important people had no attendants, neither manservant nor maidservant, and the young lady sadly in need of assistance. Even while the sailors were busy with the great ropes and anchors, the hand-some stranger was making arrogant inquiries for the best tavern in the town and demanding a carriage for transporting the lady there with the least delay.

"Naturally the strangers were directed to the best the town afforded and to 'Mr. Gadsby's City Hotel' the young people came looking for rooms. The gentleman evidently took mine host into his confidence and was provided with the most elegant accommo-dations. The young woman was put to bed and a physician ordered in attendance. She was truly very ill. . . The husband proved himself devoted and fairly daft with anxiety, and 'twas said rarely left the bedside. The young woman grew rapidly worse."

Here, the Trust narrative picks up: When they reached Alexandria, and entered Gadsby's Tavern, "her feeble frame had imbibed . . . the seeds of death . . . and hourly she grew nearer heaven." On her death bed, she told Wroe, "I shall soon be away, far from living fears and evil tongues." And then she implored Wroe to someday find John Trust and tell him that it was he who she had really loved. As Wroe leaned to kiss her, "death came between the bridegroom and the bride . . . Blanche was dead."

And then a most strange thing happened. As author Moore told it: "The doctors and volunteer nurses were asked to take an oath before ever they entered the sick chamber, and swore never to reveal aught that they heard, saw, or learned. That oath they kept. The young woman's name, her destination, her former habitation, have never been revealed, and her secrets lie buried with her."

Incredibly, Trust forgave Wroe, who had stolen his one love in life from him, and the two again became intimate friends. They plunged deeply into the study of the occult arts. As time passed, Trust came to believe that Wroe, "meditated evil," and that he would try, as he had done with Blanche, to place Trust's sister under his power. This, eventually, Trust believed, would lead to her death. He became obsessed with the idea. Under this delusion, he plotted to kill Wroe.

Thus, one day he hid in the woods skirting Alexandria at a spot where he knew Wroe often walked, and waited for his prey. He saw Wroe approaching, and got ready to fire. Wroe disap-peared behind some thick bushes. Trust waited. When a figure emerged from the other side of the brush, he fired. The figure dropped in his tracks, face down. When Trust knelt down over the fallen man he noticed there was a locket beneath him. He picked it up, hid the body, and then fled.

It was after this that Trust experienced a strange and vivid image, one which haunted him whenever he closed his eyes. "I saw my sister," he said. "She was at repose upon a couch clothed in white. . . An amazing glow filled the room in which she lay. All her attendants had retired, but she was not alone, for as I looked I saw angels, one on each hand. For awhile she seemed in pain; but soon a sweet expression fixed itself upon her face, and at the same moment a weird light rose from her forehead, taking quickly the form of a dome of strange beauty; as I still gazed, her breathing grew laborious, and the dome rising drew out into the exact image of her head, made as it were of pure light, and glowing in transfigured beauty, with an immortal loveliness.

"It startled me to see a careworn, weary face below, and its bright counterpart smiling above; but while I thought she labored for breath, with yet greater energy, up rose the head upon a well-defined neck and shoulders, as if rising from the dying body below, until the whole form stood at full length with arms uplifted. Can that be her pure soul issuing from its mortal tenement? My thought scarcely framed the question when there was a convulsive sob — the bright soul figure darted upward attended by its two companions like a flash of light — the mortal hands fell motionless, the mortal eyes were glazed forevermore.

"I had a presentiment that my dream was true."

Trust was right. His sister had died!

Later, Trust examined the locket he had taken from the dead man. Lorenz, the husband of Trust's sister, told him that his (Lorenz's) brother had painted the portraits in the locket many years ago in England. They were portraits of Trust's mother and father! Trust could not believe his eyes. His mother bore the exact image of Blanche! And his father looked exactly like Wroe! Extraordinary!

Then Trust received another shock. He got a letter from Wroe. It was dated *the day after* he thought he had killed him. *Wroe was alive!* Trust had mistakenly killed someone else!

He was thunderstruck as he read the letter.

"This note will be the punishment of your crime," Wroe wrote. . . . "You sought to steal from me, by murder, a glorious future which I valued most, because I could share it with you." Wroe told of how, while walking behind the brush, he dropped the locket. Realizing this, he doubled back, while out of Trust's sight, to retrieve it. Another man, however, had come along, picked up the locket, and proceeded along the path, and that was who Trust had shot and killed. Wroe said that the locket contained pictures of his mother and father!

Then John Trust read the line in Wroe's letter which stunned him almost to the point of fainting. "In my despairing travels," Wroe wrote, "after my wife's death, I met, in England, people, and learned circumstances which showed that *you were my long lost brother*. But for my unstrung nerves and wandering faculties, at our first meeting, beside the grave, I would have made myself known . . . You were unworthy, you were morose, suspicious; at last, jealous of my success, you laid in ambush to murder me."

Wroe then revealed how psychic phenomena may have spared his life. "My father watched over me, and his image (in the locket), by dropping from my breast, and causing me to go back in a fruitless search, saved one son from becoming the assassin of another. I saw the (other man) fall and watched you hide your dreadful burden, but wretch as you are I cannot consign to the gallows, my brother.

Wroe then closed his letter: "Go! ingrate wretch! Cain! The world is wide enough for us both, but remember when triumphs cluster around me that they would have been for you — MURDERER."

Trust then said, "My first impulse (after overcoming the shock of Wroe's disclosure) was to seek my new found brother, confess my guilt, implore his pardon, and begin again, at his side, the pursuit (into the occult arts) which had proved my undoing. But stronger than the fear of his hatred, which I even now believe I could have overcome, my promise to my dead sister interposed, and I dashed the thought aside as a temptation from the evil one.

"Then my thoughts turned again upon the locket. I opened it once more. . . That was my father, and I bedewed his picture with reverential tears; and this — my poor mother! Again, the striking resemblance to Blanche pressed itself upon me with a deadening conviction that no one but my mother's daughter could be so like her, and that she, too, was my sister."

Trust spent the better part of the rest of his life, seeking the full truth about himself, his sisters and his brother, Wroe. He was to learn that indeed, his older sister and brother had been separated in their youth, one to India, and the other to the French Islands, and had, in fact, grown up under the names of John Wroe and Blanche Forden. In Martinique, he found out that Blanche had told of being one of four children and that she had a brother in the

East Indies.

"This is all I have ever been able to gather of her history, he wrote. "Yet I feel in my heart, with the confidence of intimate knowledge, that she was my sister — the second of that band of orphans of whose fate this narrative is a partial record. The rest is soon told. My search for memorials of Blanche, vain! my sister dead! my brother estranged! what remained for me but the quiet coolness of death to soothe and still the restless fever that still beat at my heart and cooled itself life."

In his last days, John Trust became a Christian and took up residence in a monastery in Honduras. It was here that, shortly before his death, he wrote his confession in "The Story of the Female Stranger."

It is little wonder then that when the mysterious couple (Wroe and Blanche) sailed into Alexandria in 1816, and took a room at Gadsby's Tavern, that they sought to cloak their activities in secrecy. They were a married couple — brother and sister. And when Blanche died a few days later, it was hoped that the secret would be buried with her. Perhaps it was, until John Trust's narrative confession was published, years later.

This particular version of the Female Stranger may also yield a telling clue as to why the spirit of Blanche has sometimes manifested at the old tavern.

Her most notable appearance allegedly came one evening several years ago when a man said he saw her figure in the tavern ballroom. He followed her upstairs to what had been her bedroom. There, the figure disappeared. It was dark, but in the corner of the room was a lit candle in a hurricane lamp. He picked it up and searched the premises but found nothing. Then it dawned on him; what was a lit candle doing in the deserted room? He raced downstairs and got the tavern manager to go back up with him. When they got there, the candle was not only not lit, the wick was still white, as if it had never been lit! The manager thought the man was either seeing things, or had imbibed too much alcohol that night.

As he left the room, the man who had witnessed the apparition felt the lamp. It burned his fingers!

One might ask, was this the ghost of Blanche Fordan? And if so, did she return seeking her long lost love — John Trust?

The mystery endures.

CHAPTER 9

The Legend of Theodosia Burr

(Author's note: As incredible a tale as "The Enduring Mystery of the Female Stranger" is, it is perhaps matched by another saga — that of Theodosia Burr Alston, the legendary daughter of Aaron Burr. Remember, one of the speculative theories involving the enigmatic woman who landed in Alexandria in 1816, died at Gadsby's Tavern, and was buried under the most curious circumstances, was that the young woman was Theodosia. While there is no basis in fact to support such a supposition — whether or not there is even a shred of validity to it — it does, nevertheless, present an interesting concept.

For the life of this beautiful young woman was indeed shrouded in mystique and tragedy, and therein lies another tale of dark intrigue which includes her possible ghostly return along the beach fronts of southeastern Virginia and northeastern North Carolina.

Aaron Burr himself is a monumental tortured figure in the annals of American history. A brilliant young lawyer, he arose to the highest rank of national politics at the turn of the 19th century. Indeed, it is a little-known fact that he came whisker-close to unseating Thomas Jefferson in 1801 and becoming the third President of the United States! The vote ended in a tie in the electoral college and Jefferson won when the outcome was thrown to the House of Representatives — on the 36th ballot! Burr did become Jefferson's Vice President.

Burr achieved ever-lasting notoriety on July 11, 1804, when he killed, in a pistol duel, his long-time political adversary — Alexander Hamilton. This for all intents and purposes, ended

Burr's career in disgrace. From here, things got hazy. He traveled to New Orleans and fell into the wrong crowd. There were accusations that he was behind a revolutionary plot to eventually overthrow the government. But even though he was brought to Richmond and tried for treason, these were mostly conspired and trumped up charges, and he was acquitted under the gavel of Chief Justice John Marshall. Still, Burr became a bitter, disillusioned and beaten man. Such sometimes are the cruel vicissitudes of life.

Eventually, he retreated to New York. His one solace during these troubled times was his daughter, Theodosia. He adored her. She cherished him. In a biography of Burr by J. Parton, published in 1858, it states: "Theodosia was a nearly complete realization of her father's idea of a woman. With a great deal of wit, spirit, and talent, and possessing the elegant vivacity of manner which he so much admired, and a face strikingly beautiful, and strikingly peculiar, she also inherited all that a daughter could inherit of her father's courage and fortitude. In both solid and elegant accomplishments, she was very far superior to the ladies of her time. After shining in the circles of New York, she led the society of South Carolina, until the time of her father's misfortunes, when she shared his ostracism in both places, and was proud to share it.

"Her love for her father was more like passion than filial affection. Her faith in his honor and in his worth was absolute and entire. Immovable in that faith, she could cheerfully have braved the scorn, the derision of a world. . . No father ever more loved a child, nor more laboriously proved his love, than Aaron Burr. No child ever repaid a father's care and tenderness, with a love more constant and devoted than Theodosia.

It is at this point that our story begins.)

heodosia had married Joseph Alston, who became Governor of South Carolina. In the spring of 1812, she began making plans to travel north to New York and visit her father, with the intent of cheering him up. But then, in June of that year, her small son, Aaron Burr Alston, was felled by fever and died. This plunged Theodosia into a deep depression which lasted for months.

As time passed, she eventually recovered, buoyed by the thought of seeing her father. And so, in December 1812, she boarded the schooner "Patriot" at Georgetown, South Carolina, to begin

Theodosia Burr

a voyage that would end in tragedy. She carried with her a striking
oil portrait of herself, which she had had specially commissioned.

The portrait has been described as an oil painting on polished
mahogany, 20 inches in length and enclosed in a frame richly
gilded. The face is patrician and refined; the expression of the dark
eyes, proud and haughty; the hair dark auburn, curling and abun-
dant. A white bodice cut low in the neck and richly adorned with
lace, revealed a glimpse of the drooping shoulders, and the snowy

bust, unconfined by corset."

The painting was to be a gift for her father. Since America was then at war with Great Britain, Governor Alston had given his wife a letter explaining her mission in case the ship was challenged at sea by the British. Theodosia was accompanied by her faithful maid.

Sure enough, not long into the voyage, the Patriot was stopped at sea by a British man-of-war, and when its officers were shown the letter they allowed the ship to pass through their blockade without even inspecting it. Next came rough weather. For two days the winds howled and the seas swelled, almost as if they were presenting an omen of darker things to come. The ship passed off Cape Hatteras as it plodded northward.

It was sometime after this that mystery shrouded the ill-fated voyage. There are varying accounts of what happened next. According to one version, the Patriot was somewhere off the coast between Sandbridge, Virginia, and the upper Outer Banks of North Carolina. No one is quite sure of just where. The captain seemed to have lost his bearings. According to the 1858 biography of Burr, the author wrote, "A few days after she left Charleston, a storm of extreme violence raged along the whole coast; during which, in all probability, the vessel with all on board went down . . ."

When the Patriot did not appear in New York, as the days and weeks passed, "The agonies of suspense endured by the husband and the father, the eager letters written by each to tell the other she had not arrived, the weary waiting for the mail, the daily hope, the daily despair, the thousand conjectures that arose to give a moment s relief - all this can neither be imagined nor described."

Burr lost hope. He told a friend, "Were she alive, all the prisons in the world could not keep her from her father. When I realized the truth of her death, the world became a blank to me, and life had then lost all its value." For a long time, Theodosia was a name banished from the vocabulary in his house.

Still rumors ran rampant. In one version, a light appeared out of the darkness during the storm and the captain gave the order to sail toward it, in hopes of finding his location. As they neared the light, they realized, too late, that it was on the shore and the Patriot ran aground. Worse, the light, or lights, were from a pirate encampment on the beach. The wind snapped the ship's masts, and the crew and passengers looked on in horror as small boatloads of cutthroat pirates oared their way to the Patriot.

What occurred next is conjecture. Some believe the pirates

boarded the ship, forced everyone to "walk the plank" to their deaths, either by drowning, or at the mercy of sharks, then plundered everything on board. If so, then this is how Theodosia died.

But there is another account. This one holds that Theodosia was spared. Everyone else was thrust into the surging seas. At the sight of all this, coupled with her son's death and her father's shame, which had plagued her mind for months, she went mad. The pirates seemed somehow to respect her insanity, and instead of killing her, took her to shore where it is alleged that she lived with them.

Amidst the booty was the oil painting of her. It was placed over the mantel in one of the cottages that dotted the shore. It was said that she would stand and stare at the portrait at times, as if trying to piece things together and climb out of her dementia. But she was never able to. How long she lived in this disturbed state is not known.

Then, in the 1860s, Dr. William G. Pool (also spelled Poole) entered the scene. And here again there are differing and confusing remembrances. One says that he came to the area to treat an old woman who was, in fact, Theodosia. Another says he came to treat an old woman, but she wasn't Theodosia. It is agreed that Dr. Pool, a respected and prominent physician, treated someone.

In either case, there was no money to pay him. If it was not Theodosia, he was offered, as payment, the oil portrait which he had often admired. He accepted it. If it was Theodosia, there is a very different story. He was offered the portrait by someone else, and Theodosia became incensed. She leaped out of her bed, snatched the picture, and screamed, "It is mine. It is mine. You know I am going to visit my father in New York and this is to be his picture!"

She then grasped the portrait to her breast, ran out of the house in the darkness, in the midst of a storm, and raced toward the pounding surf. The startled doctor and others ran after her, but she was lost in the driving mist and spray of the raging storm. They never saw her again.

The next day, however, they found the portrait a short distance from the high tide mark. Whichever version is correct, the painting then became the possession of Dr. Pool. The year was 1869.

Some time later, bits of the mystery of Theodosia were uncovered. Before being executed in Norfolk for unspecified crimes, two men testified that they had been part of the pirate crew which had boarded the Patriot in 1812, and that everyone aboard had been forced to walk the plant. Another of the pirates, on his death bed in an almshouse in Michigan, independently said the same thing, adding that he would never forget the beautiful face of the young woman. She had, he said, pleaded for her life, but "went to her doom with so dauntless and calm a spirit, that even the most hardened pirates were touched."

Those are the two accounts, each ending in stark tragedy.

From here, the threads are more recognizable. Dr. Pool was reading an old magazine one day. He came upon an article and a picture of Aaron Burr. He was immediately struck by the similarity between that picture and the portrait of the young woman. Could it be Theodosia? He did some research, compared dates and facts, and became convinced it was. He sent photographs of the painting to Burr family members. They agreed without exception that it bore a striking resemblance to Theodosia. Some of the descendants came down to view the picture. They said both the features and the likeness were identical to Theodosia.

At last, the mystery of what happened to her was put to rest. Whether or not she had survived that awful night when the pirates boarded the ship, she had likely died by drowning. The question of whether or not this dreadful fate was decided by the pirates, or was placed in her own hands likely will remain unsolved for eternity.

Dr. Pool kept the portrait for the rest of his life. At his death it was inherited by his granddaughter. Today it hangs for all to see in the Macbeth Art Gallery in New York City. Theodosia has finally completed her journey.

But does Theodosia's spirit know this? Perhaps not. For it is said that if one walks today along the sandy beaches near the Virginia-North Carolina state line, when the sky is dark and overcast and the wind is whining, the willowy figure of a woman can sometimes be glimpsed walking along the beach. It is, say old-timers in the area, the figure of Theodosia Burr Alston, searching for the portrait she wants her father to have.

The Duellist's Date with Doom

(Washington, D.C.)

(Author's note: The following account did not happen in Virginia. It happened across the state line in Washington, D.C. I include it here, however, because: it is so close to Virginia; it has historical significance; it is similar in some respects to the previous two chapters, on the Female Stranger in Alexandria, and the Legend of Theodosia Burr; it also includes a famous spectral dueling ground in nearby Maryland; and there is a Virginia tie-in.)

This is the legend behind the Decatur House in Washington's Lafayette Square, and the man for whom the house was named — American naval hero Stephen Decatur. Born near Berlin, Maryland, in 1779, Decatur initially rose to fame during the Tripolitan War, when, in 1804, he led a brazen attack into Tripoli Harbor and destroyed a ship. The daring feat earned him a promotion to Captain in the U.S. Navy. Later, he won enduring fame in the War of 1812. He was known for his reckless bravery and stubborn patriotism, and is perhaps best remembered in American history for his proud toast: "Our country! In her intercourse with foreign nations, may she always be in the right; but our country, right or wrong!"

Decatur was young, dashing, and handsome. He sailed often in and out of the port of Norfolk, and married the beautiful Susan Wheeler, the daughter of the mayor of Norfolk. He seemed, when he moved to Washington, to have everything: the adulation of the nation, and a loving wife he cherished. But he had made one enemy, and this was, in years to come, to prove catastrophic, leading not only to his death before his time, but also his return in spectral form.

His adversary's name was James Barron, a high ranking naval officer. Barron had been court-marshalled in 1807 for an unauthorized provocative attack on a British frigate. He was suspended from the navy for five years. Decatur had sat on the commission which recommended the suspension, and, ironically, had been given command of the ship which Barron had previously captained. Rightly or wrongly, Barron held Decatur personally responsible for his punishment. Although he was later reinstated in the

Stephen Decatur

Navy, his career was forever limited, and he developed a deep hatred of Decatur.

He mounted numerous personal attacks on Decatur, which, eventually, could not be further ignored. In those days, in the early 1800s, the accustomed manner of settling such disputes and animosities, was the "gentleman's" art of duelling. A match between the two was arranged for March 14, 1820.

On the eve of that occasion, Stephen and Susan Decatur gave a party in their house. Guests were to recollect later that their host seemed preoccupied. In fact, he appeared depressed, as one said, "as though he sensed his imminent death." He was seen staring out "gloomily" over his estate.

The next morning he arose well before dawn, and, with his friend, William Bainbridge, went off for the ill-fated date to a field near Bladensburg, Maryland, just across the D.C. line. This site already had a sinister reputation. According to the "National Directory for Haunted Places," "more than 50 bloody pistol duels were fought here, and a number of corpse-like ghosts are said to walk the grounds. The ghosts appear as 'dark but not transparent' forms that disappear at the slightest sound." (One notable ghost is said to be that of Daniel Key, son of Francis Scott Key, author of America's national anthem. Key was killed at age 20 in a senseless duel with a fellow student at the Annapolis Naval Academy. The two had argued over which of two steamboats was the fastest.)

In his excellent book on Washington area ghosts, author John Alexander wrote: "Death seemed to hover permanently over Bladensburg, and often to seriously scar even the survivors. The duellists who walked away from those bloody grounds had seen death, and often their lives were drastically changed." Alexander told of "wispy corpses seen walking in a trance-like state over the old dueling ground."

It was amidst this eerie backdrop that Stephen Decatur arrived on that fateful morning. At first light, the two men squared off, aimed, and fired at the uncommon close range of eight paces. At the count of two, a pair of shots rang out. Barron was struck in the hip and fell immediately. Decatur stood for a moment and then fell also. He had been shot in the side. Barron's wound was painful but not serious. Many argued that Decatur, a crack shot, had purposely aimed to wound, not kill, his opponent. Decatur's wound, however, was fatal. He was carried home where he died, saying "If it were in the cause of my country, it would be nothing." It was said that his wife, Susan, was so paralyzed with shock, she couldn't bring herself to even see her dying husband.

Thousands mourned. Flags flew at half-mast as the funeral cortege passed through the streets of Washington. Decatur was buried with full military honors.

His ghost was to appear a year later. According to a reference in "The Encyclopedia of Ghosts," members of the household staff saw the wraith-like form of the slain hero standing at the very window he had stood brooding at on the night before his death. The window was walled up, but this did not deter the spirit. A Washington reporter once wrote of the recurring appearance of Decatur at the house. Over a period of years, a number of witnesses vouched that they saw "a transparent form" — at the walled up window, and also silently slipping out the back door in the predawn hours, just as Decatur had done on his way to his doom. Some said the figure they saw was carrying a black pistol box under his arm.

Today, the house is a museum. And while Decatur's ghost has not been seen for some years, there are the sounds of perhaps another spirit. A woman is occasionally heard weeping in the house. Is it Susan Decatur of Norfolk, grieving for her lost love?

Perhaps.

The House of Unspeakable Tragedies

(Alexandria)

ach Halloween week hundreds of visitors are treated to an "Historic Alexandria Hauntings" walking tour in the old city. One of the most interesting stops is at the venerable Carlyle House at 121 North Fairfax Street. Much has been written about this historic landmark. It was built in 1752 by John Carlyle, a Scottish merchant who had come to America 12 years earlier. A young Colonel George Washington was here in 1755, for a military strategy session during the French and Indian wars.

Says the Virginia Landmarks Register: "Like many Scottish houses of the period, the Carlyle House is built of stone and employs a somewhat austere classicism." A description of the building written more than 50 years ago states, "Along the garden side spreads a wide terrace. On the west front a long flight of stone steps leads to the double door with an elliptical fanlight and stone arch. . . the interior is distinguished by fine paneled woodwork. From the transverse hall, the stairway ascends gracefully in one continuous curve." The house was made into a museum in 1914, and contains "an extensive collection of early American furniture."

More historic background can be found in the old book, "Seaport in Virginia," by Gay Montague Moore. She wrote that Carlyle was at one time "the leading citizen" of Alexandria, and was, in fact, one of the town's incorporators. The Carlyle House "stands high above the river and so strong and thick are the foundations that tradition has it they were early fortifications against the Indians." Moore also noted that the mansion was "the social and political center of Alexandria. Such men as Aaron Burr, John Paul Jones, John Marshall, Thomas Jefferson, George Mason, George Washington and the two Fairfaxes are but a few of those who gathered here for good food, good wine, and better talk. Any visitor of importance was entertained at 'coffee;' the house was often filled with music, and 'balls' were common."

In writing of the colorful history of the house, Moore hints that one may wander upon a spirit from the past. "Perchance," she said, "Major John Carlyle, clad in Saxon green laced with silver, will be wandering up and down his box-bordered paths with his first love, Sarah Fairfax, watching the moon light up the rigging of Carlyle & Dalton's great ships at anchor just at the foot of the garden."

She also cites an event that may have laid the foundation for the Carlyle House's tradition of tragedies, which has survived for more than 150 years. She tells of John Carlyle's dying wish to see that his only son, George William Carlyle, get the best education money can buy. "Alas, for the plans of men! The lad, fired by the talk of his father and friends, was serving in Lee's Legion in 1781 (during the Revolutionary War), and ere John Carlyle was moldering in his grave this boy of seventeen years, spirited, brave, heir to large estates, great fortune and honorable name, and to the title of Lord Carlyle, was dead at Eutaw Springs, led by that boy hardly older than himself 'Light Horse Harry' Lee."

Eighty-three years later, the first of the "unspeakable tragedies" occurred. It was covered some years ago in a memorable paper authored by T. Michael Miller. "Halloween," he wrote, "is a time when departed spirits rise from their graves and haunt the scenes of their early demise. One such haunt may be found on the lovely pruned grounds of the Carlyle House. . . It was here that three men died mysteriously in a series of bizarre episodes."

The first of these, Moore said, took place at the Old Green Mansion House Hotel which fronted the Carlyle House on the west. It had been built in 1848 and was said to be "one of the premier hostelries on the east coast." As Moore related it, "During the Civil War, the hotel was confiscated by federal authorities and served as the largest hospital in Alexandria. In March 1864, a tragic accident occurred at this facility. One of the patients, who was insane, managed to get through a window in his ward and caught hold of the eaves of the building. There he hung for a short time and finally fell upon the balustrade of the hotel below, injuring himself so seriously as to die in a few hours."

The second "accident" was reported by the Alexandria Gazette on August 7, 1905. "Late yesterday evening Samuel D. Markell, a well-known Alexandrian, fell from an upper story platform of the Braddock House (the name of the Green Mansion House Hotel in the 1880s) into the court, a distance of 15 feet, and was instantly killed. The unfortunate man struck upon his head, breaking his neck.

"Late in the evening he was seen by certain inmates of the Braddock House lying in the court, and they, supposing he was asleep, made no mention of the matter. This morning, however, he was discovered to be dead, and the fact was reported to the station house, when officer Sherwood made an investigation and found that Markell had been dead for about 12 hours. The remains were removed to Mr. B. Wheatley's undertaking establishment.

"It was supposed that the deceased was sitting on the railing of a platform or bridge which leads from the old Mansion House to the Carlyle House, when he began to doze, and, falling, landed upon his head. It was first suggested that he might have been robbed of his watch and thrown into the area, but Chief Webster later ascertained that the timepiece had been found, and that Markell's death was due to the circumstances given above. He was about 50-years-old. He was a turner and cabinet-maker by trade."

The third "weird happening," according to Miller, involved Patrick Buckley, Alexandria's "celebrated Boy Guide." Miller: "Buckley had first come into prominence in Alexandria when he was 13 years of age. During the late 1890s, Alexandria was overrun with young boys who met trains and boats and offered for a fee to guide tourists around the town's historic sites. The guides became so numerous and annoyed visitors to such an extent that in 1900 the City Council was compelled to pass an ordinance which mandated that tour guides take out a license and pay an annual fee of $5.00. Buckley, 'a rosy-cheeked youngster with an attractive face and agreeable manner, was the only one who had sufficient nerve to apply for the license.'

" . . . All did not augur well for Pat Buckley, however. On November 16, 1912, accompanied by his brothers, Buckley had a night out on the town. After becoming inebriated, he was thrown out of several bars along King Street during which interval he had his face cut and his coat torn. Buckley then left his friends and started to the Braddock House. He entered the building from the

Cameron Street side and went to the window at the end of a hall on the fourth floor. Here he removed his long overcoat and hat and placed them on the floor, and stepped out on an iron fire escape."

According to an account in the Alexandria Gazette on November 18, 1912, "It was from here that he fell, his body being found on the brick pavement directly beneath it. Near the body was found the heel of one of his shoes which had been torn off, and the police think his heel caught in the iron bars of the fire escape, causing him to lose his balance.

"W. W. Simpson, proprietor of the Braddock House, heard Buckley enter the building and yelled to him to stop making so much noise. He did not know who it was at the time and said yesterday morning if he had known it was Buckley he would have stopped him from entering the building."

Miller states that "Buckley's body was found about 6:50 in the morning near the present entrance to the Carlyle House by another roomer. Chief of Police Goods found the young man, lying on his back, with his skull crushed, his face cut in several places and his coat covered with blood. . . At first it had been thought that Buckley had been murdered but the police later ruled that he fell from the fourth story of the building and that the plunge was accidental."

To these strange accounts, Miller footnotes, "On Halloween night, stalk to the old Carlyle House and peer across the brick wall as the moon illuminates the old edifice. If you look carefully, perhaps you may see three fleeting lights in the yard as the spirits of the insane soldier, Markell, and young Buckley return to the scene of their tragic deaths."

The Librarian Who Will Not Leave

(Purcellville, Loudoun County)

urcellville, population about 2,200, is located right at the northern tip of the commonwealth, directly east of Winchester and 12 miles west of Leesburg. In "Virginia, A Guide to the Old Dominion," published more than half a century ago, the entry for the town, then with a population of 700, says, "Purcellville, with rather standoffish houses behind hedge-bound lawns, is a marketing center with a crowded little block of stores." Just north of the town is the little hamlet of Hillsboro, the birthplace, in 1831, of Susan Koerner, the mother of Orville and Wilbur Wright.

Whether or not the good citizens here are still archly conservative in their politics and lifestyle is not known, but apparently they were quite so a couple of generations ago. And one could well argue that the staunchest guardian of such conservatism was a stern, strong-willed woman named Gertrude Robey. She was austere to the extreme — in both appearance and manner. As one example, she always dressed in black, sometimes wearing a broad-brimmed black hat, which she called her "emancipation hat." She could be spotted walking down the street from several blocks away.

Sometime in the early 1930s she persuaded area residents to build a town library which would double as a cultural center. As chief librarian, she had a piano put in the building and recitals and readings were commonly held there for a number of years.

Ms. Robey also took it upon herself to determine what was readable and what was not for her patrons. Anything in the romance vein with even a hint of eroticism was absolutely banned from her shelves. But she went further than that. Many classics were also deemed unworthy of presentation, and some of these were not sex-oriented, but of historical significance. Apparently, Ms. Robey was a southern sympathizer who recognized that feelings about the Civil War were still touchy. Thusly, one of the volumes she "hid" was Harriet Beecher Stowe's masterpiece, "Uncle Tom's Cabin." Hid, because when workmen were building an addition to the library in 1991, 25 years after Ms. Robey had died, they found a number of books walled up in an old chimney. Stowe's book was among them.

Although it now has been more than three decades since she passed on, her presence is still very much felt at the library, both figuratively and literally. "She's still here," declares present librarian Susie Shackleford. "We get reminders all the time."

One of the most dramatic manifestations comes in the form of a continued rejection of anything even faintly considered "off color." Such well-known authors as Anais Nin and the popular Judith Krantz are considered (by the spirit of Ms. Robey) to be in this category. Consequently, at infrequent intervals, such books are chucked off the shelves by unseen hands!

"They don't fall off onto the floor," says Susie Shackleford. "They leap out into the middle of the aisles. There is power behind them." There are a number of people, browsers and employees alike, who have witnessed this ghostly expression of distaste. And it only happens to certain books and specific authors. "It's Gertrude Robey, still letting us know she's around and watching out for what we display," Susie says. "Sometimes she also puts books back on the shelves. We've had workers say they hear the sound of books being replaced in the stacks, but when they look to see who is doing it, there is no one there. Such reshelving, however, does not include romance novels.

More recently, the critic-spirit has given present personnel fits over door locks. "I think she does it just to aggravate us," Susie notes. "We have a lot of trouble with the locks. I mean one of us will go and unlock a conference room door for say a library board meeting, and when the board members go to the room the door will suddenly be locked. I can't explain it."

This particular trouble began a few years ago when Ms. Robey's portrait was removed from its customary place in the

Gertrude Robey in her "Emancipation Hat"

library. It had been above a mantel, but when a series of rain storms began to cause leaks, a staff member moved the painting, or tried to, to safer quarters. She took it upstairs to a reference room, but the door was unaccountably locked. She then tried the fire doors, which are never locked, but they too were sealed shut. She went to get the key, but even that wouldn't work. The staffer then became unnerved when, she said, the eyes of Ms. Robey in the portrait were staring holes through her. Finally, a locksmith had to be called.

Others have reported seeing "a shadow" in the lounge area during hours when the library is closed and no one is in the building.

"My favorite is about the electric clock," Susie says. "This happened about eight years ago. The power went out. Gertrude had an old electric clock. It was about 18 inches in diameter. Well, it just kept running. Even after I unplugged it and took it down from the wall, it kept on running. An electric clock!"

Ms. Robey also made her presence felt in 1991 during the building renovations. Apparently, she didn't like what the workmen were doing, or how they were doing it. In fact, her disagreements with construction contractors go back more than 60 years. During the original work on the building, she was constantly badgering the crews. One day, in fact, she fell from some scaffolding and broke her leg. She sued the foreman for not forcing her to stay *off* the scaffolding.

So when an addition was being added in 1991, she continued her tight vigilance. The contractor said he couldn't get any of his men to work in the facility after dark. "They said they kept hearing footsteps above them on the second floor," Susie says. "Of course there was no one up there."

Then, when the cache of forbidden books was found, workers said when they picked them up, their fingers were burned!

"I never knew her in life," Susie says. "An older lady here, who used to mend books for her for 25 cents an hour said she had a very strong personality. She was right. Gertrude ruled this library for over 40 years and was judge and jury as to what books she felt the public should read. She pretty much is still in charge and likes to remind us of it from time to time."

Revelations of
Psychic Dreams

(Various sites)

(Author's note: To sleep, perchance to dream. Dreams have been inexorably intertwined with psychic phenomena and ghostly activity since time immemorial. "Dreams," said Hugh Lynn Cayce, son of the great psychic Edgar Cayce, "are the language of the unconscious." Sigmund Freud called dreams the "Via Regia," the royal road to the unconscious. According to Edgar Cayce, who gave more than 600 dream-interpretation-readings during his lifetime, virtually everything is dreamed before it happens. He put it, "Any condition is first dreamed before becoming reality." As one example, he told of one woman who dreamed everything that was going to happen to her — before it did. This included the breakup of her marriage, the departure of her husband, a reunion for her with a former lover, and the death of her mother.

Cayce said, "To every normal body with a developing mind, conditions are often presented through the subconscious forces during the sleeping state, wherein truths are given; visions are seen of things to be warned or taken advantage of; conditions shown in which would be brought advantages to the body — physically, mentally, morally, spiritually, and financially.

To this, Hugh Lynn Cayce has added, "In every man there exists a vast expanse, unfamiliar and unexplored, which sometimes appears in the guise of an angel, other times a monster. This is man's unconscious mind, and the language we call dreams." Hugh Lynn Cayce also believed that dreams are excellent "source material" for the study of all kinds of psychic experiences, including what appears to be telepathy, clairvoyance, precognition, communication with the dead, and memory of past lives, among other things.

There are, for instance, countless cases where dreams have foretold disaster, death, or serious injuries, often to loved ones of the dreamer. This includes incidents of precognition. In his book, "Venture Inward," Hugh Lynn Cayce described one which occurred on October 4, 1934. That night a coal miner's wife dreamed that her husband had come home from work with blood streaming down his cheek. She was terribly frightened because the dream had been so real, but when she told her husband about it, he just laughed. The next day, when he came home after his shift was over, there *was* blood streaming down his face. There had been an accident in the mines!

In past books in this series on Virginia ghosts, I have written about several other occurrences involving psychic revelations from dreams. In the chapter on Sherwood Forest, President John Tyler's home, in this book, there is a striking dream of the premonition of Tyler's death by his wife, Julia, in which she envisioned the room in which her husband was to die. It was so vivid, she even described details of the furniture in the room, although she had never been there. He died in such a room shortly after the dream.

In "The Ghosts of Virginia, Volume I" (1993), I wrote about a dream a farmer had in Buckingham County in 1909, in which he envisioned the murder of two reclusive brothers. Details of the dream were so precise that it led, eventually, to the arrests of the men who had committed the murder. And, in "The Ghosts of Virginia, Volume III," (1996), I told of how a murdered daughter appeared to her mother in a dream and told her who killed her and how — which led to the conviction of the husband-murderer.

And, of course, perhaps the most famous dream in American history was that of Abraham Lincoln, in which he envisioned his own death at the hands of an assassin.

With all this as background, here are a few more incredible dream accounts involving Virginians.)

* * * * *

A PRELUDE TO WORLD WAR II
(Virginia Beach)

In 1932, seven years before the outbreak of the second World War, a Virginia woman described an ominous dream she had to Edgar Cayce in Virginia Beach. "My husband and I," she said, "seemed to be in a large dwelling, and looking out toward the sky we saw large black circles floating through the air. We thought this very strange, and soon discovered that the circles looked like black auto tires or large truck tires. Suddenly, out of the sky a big black machine, resembling the large caterpillar machines used during the (first) World War, came down to earth.

"We said we had better get out of the place, for we realized it was the intention of this machine to crush people to death. Too, we realized that it meant troublous times, so we tried to get out of its way as quickly as possible. We walked down to the river front, and there saw a British ship tied up at the wharf. Someone said it had fired on the lone watchman while in his office on the wharf, but found out later that the watchman had fired on the British ship . . . We realized there were troublous times in the making, and I was much afraid. We walked further down the long wharf, and saw many more British ships."

Cayce, and others, interpreted this dark dream as foretelling the rise to power of Adolf Hitler, the opening of World War II, and the stout and heroic resistance of Great Britain as the other countries in Europe caved in.

* * * * *

DREAMS OF WINNING NUMBERS
(Norfolk)

The date is not specified, probably sometime in the 1920s or 1930s — A Norfolk housewife with a history of having precognitive dreams (she had envisioned a girl friend's divorce and a relative's problems with the police, etc.) dreamed that her home was burning, and after the fire all that was left was the number 912. She had no idea of the significance of that number. The day after the dream she walked into a dry cleaners to pick up a dress, and told the owner of the shop about her dream and the number. He was astounded. The number 912 had won an illegal lottery that day! Then he got irate. He told the woman if she had come in a day earlier, when her dress had been ready to pick up, he would have won thousands of dollars.

Even more compelling was the incredible account of a dream by another Norfolk woman, Mrs. Sally Coty, the proprietress of a tavern then on Mulberry Street known as "Gigi's." She, too, had had a number of precognitive dreams. She was in a state of physical and emotional stress because she had to go into a hospital for major surgery, which would cost about $1,000, and had just learned that her insurance did not cover such an operation.

One night before she entered the hospital she dreamed of the numbers 4-11-66, but had no clue as to what they meant. The next day, by chance, she saw a friend, who happened to be a numbers runner (another illegal lottery). She gave him three dollars to play the numbers she had envisioned, and then she went into the hospital. While there, she got a phone call from her brother. He told her that the numbers she had dreamed, 4-11-66, had won that week. She was richer by $1,500!

* * * * *

SOME COLONIAL PREMONITIONS
(Charles City County)

illiam Byrd, II, was, by virtually all accounts, one of the most extraordinary men of his time (1674-1744). He was a brilliant colonist who owned Westover Plantation in Charles City County. He had a beautiful daughter, Evelyn Byrd, who allegedly died at a tender age of a broken heart when her father wouldn't let her marry the man she loved. She is said to return in ghostly form in and around the plantation (See "The Ghosts of Williamsburg and Nearby Environs," 1983).

William Byrd, II, could speak and read several languages, including Hebrew, Latin and Greek; had the best library of the times in Virginia; was a charismatic leader and public servant; and certainly one of the most educated and intelligent men of his era. Yet, he also seemed to have a sense for psychic activity. In the introduction to his book, "The Secret Diary of William Byrd of Westover," it states, "Although Byrd was in most respects a typical

18th century rationalist, he had a vein of superstition that comes out in his attitude toward dreams."

In this particular diary, one of three different volumes, the period of 1709 to 1712 is covered. Here are a few entries concerning dreams:

* April 8, 1709: "The Indian woman died this evening, according to a dream I had last night about her."

* July 15, 1709: "I had a bad dream this morning which seemed to foretell the death of some of my family. I thought I saw my yard full of people and when I came into the house I could not find my wife."

* March 31, 1710: "Mrs. Burwell dreamed this night that she saw a person with money scales, weighed time, and declared that there was no more than 18 pennies worth of time to come, which seems to be a dream with some significance either concerning the world or a sick person."

* April 10, 1710: "I sent early to inquire after Mr. Harrison (of neighboring Berkeley Plantation) and received word that he died about 4 o'clock this morning which completed the 18th day of his sickness, according to Mrs. Burwell's dream exactly. Just before his death he was sensible and desired (a woman in attendance), with importunity, to open the door because he wanted to go out and could not go till the door was open, and as soon as the door was opened he died."

* June 18, 1710: "In the afternoon my wife told me a dream she had two nights. She thought she saw a scroll in the sky in the form of a light cloud with writing on it. It ran extremely fast from west to east with great swiftness. The writing she could not read but there was a woman before her that told her there would be a great dearth because of want of rain and after that a pestilence for that the seasons were changed and time inverted."

* June 21, 1710: "About five nights since I dreamed I saw a flaming star in the air at which I was much frightened and called some others to see it but when they came it disappeared. I fear this portends some judgment to this country or at least to myself."

* July 21, 1710: "About eight nights ago I dreamed that several of my Negroes lay sick on the floor and one Indian among the rest, and now it came exactly to pass."

* December 31, 1710: "Some night this month I dreamed that I saw a flaming sword in the sky and called some company to see it but before they could come it disappeared, and about a week after my wife and I were walking and we discovered in the clouds a

shining cloud exactly in the shape of a dart and seemed to be over my plantation but it soon disappeared likewise. Both these appearances seemed to foretell some misfortune to me which afterwards came to pass in the death of several of my Negroes after a very unusual manner.

"My wife about two months since dreamed she saw an angel in the shape of a big woman who told her the time was altered and the seasons were changed and that several calamities would follow that confusion. God avert his judgment from this poor country."

* January 6, 1711: "Poor old (name undeciphered) died this night to make up the number of the dead."

* January 16, 1712: "I dreamed a coffin was brought into my house and thrown into the hall."

* January 19, 1712: "I dreamed a mourning coach drove into my garden and stopped at the house door."

It is noted that two of William Byrd's four children by his first wife, Lucy Parke Byrd, did not survive infancy, and Lucy herself died at an early age in 1716.

* * * * *

FULFILLMENT OF A NEED TO KNOW

Can dreams warn of impending tragedies? Elizabeth Henderson of Falls Church believes they can, and she has a personal experience to support her feelings. Her grandmother died in 1966 after a brief illness. Two years later, Elizabeth had a startling dream. She was walking down a street in her home town when a storm approached. "Somehow," she says, "out of the storm clouds, a telephone rang and it was my grandmother calling me. She told me not to worry, that she had little David (my older son, who was eight at the time) with her, that she would take care of him, and that everything would be all right. When I awoke the next morning, I wrote down the dream because I couldn't understand it, for certainly David was alive and well. I put the dream away and forgot about it."

Two years later, David was killed in an accident on the street in front of their home. Elizabeth says, "the year following his death was a time of extreme mental and emotional struggle for me and one in which I had to do a tremendous amount of soul searching. I had always been rather atheistic and skeptical in spiritual matters.

"One day, about a year after David's death, I was sitting at my desk daydreaming when I began to wonder about David, where he might be, and whether anything really does happen after death. I began to experience a 'scene' which unfolded before my eyes. it was as though I had been removed from my surroundings. I no longer seemed to be sitting at my desk.

"It was as if I were looking into another dimension, a level of existence in which there seemed to be no time and no space, Elizabeth continues. "I was standing by the edge of a river and across the bank from me, almost close enough to reach out and touch, was David. He was standing between my grandparents and the three of them were smiling and waving at me. My grandparents looked to be in the prime of life, happy and healthy, and somehow the words came to me that they were dressed in their Easter best. As I approached closer to the river's edge, the scene began to draw away until they gradually disappeared into the distance, all the while smiling and waving. Then suddenly I found myself sitting back at my desk again, just as I had been before.

"For those in need of reassurance that their loved ones are well and happy, a dream-telepathy or a clairvoyant experience such as the preceding might be just what is required . . . In my case, it was just what was needed, filling within me a deep gap and a longing to know."

* * * * *

AN EXPERIENCE MOST STRANGE

t historic Belle Ville, a 340-year-old house on the North River in Gloucester County, a most singular example of what the experts call a "crisis apparition" occurred to a young man named Warner Taliaferro sometime in the 1870s. He had been deeply concerned about the serious illness of a close friend, the wife of Dr. Tabb, his neighbor who lived just across a nearby inlet. Tired, Taliaferro fell asleep on a settle on the porch leading to the garden.

Late at night he dreamed that he was awakened by a touch, or he actually *was* awakened by a touch. In either case, he looked up and was startled to see the figure of Mrs. Tabb upon the steps leading down into the garden. There was, he said later, no mistaking her identity. Since he knew she had been very ill and bed ridden, he assumed that she had somehow eluded those who stood watch by her bedside. Taliaferro got up and followed her, believing her to be wandering in delirium.

From the steps, the figure moved swiftly down the box- bordered walk, and crossed a wide lawn. She then disappeared into a "summer house." Taliaferro retraced her steps and when he reached the little cottage and entered, he was stunned. There was no one inside! She had vanished.

He ran back to the main house, awakened his wife, and told her of his experience. She said he must have been dreaming. He replied, "feel my clothes." They were drenched with dew from the tall grass.

The next morning a messenger brought news that Mrs. Tabb had died that night — at the time Taliaferro had seen the vision.

* * * * *

REALIZATION OF A PYSCHIC'S DREAM
(Floyd County)

(Author's note: Louise Loveland is psychic. I met her in October 1996, when she invited me to give a lecture at the Roanoke Historical Museum. It was part of a Halloween week of activities in the area. Louise had developed a script, based on interviews she and others conducted, on ghosts in and around Roanoke. A few months later, I talked with Louise about the hauntings, and during the conversation she revealed to me an extraordinary occurrence which happened to her in the early 1990s. Here is what happened, in Louise's words:)

I t was sometime in 1990 or 1991, that I was to have a meeting with a man in a nearby town the next day. That night I had a most unusual dream. In the dream I was to meet the man, but not in his office as I was supposed to. Rather, (in the dream) he had given me written instructions to meet at a house out in a remote section of the county. Well, as dreams go, everything seemed to happen. While driving out there with my husband, we had a flat tire. Then we got lost, and we couldn't find a quarter to make a phone call. We ended up being four hours late getting to the house. Finally, we drove up to this old house, it was like a log cabin, and I went up and knocked on the front door.

"A child opened the door. When I looked inside, there seemed to be children everywhere. They were playing. And there were a lot of dogs and cats. It was all so real to me. In fact, it was so real, that I later drew a complete picture of the floor plan of the house, and where all the interior furnishings were. I carried a box into the house, and when I walked into the kitchen a small boy opened the box. It was full of poisonous snakes! They went slithering all over the place, but for some strange reason, the boy didn't seem fazed at all. The snakes were crawling around all over the floor, but he stepped right through them and walked out the back door. I had a particularly vivid vision of that kitchen. I saw where every pot and pan hung. I later drew a detailed picture of the kitchen. That was the dream.

"Well, the following summer, exactly a year after I had the dream, my husband and I were driving out in Floyd County. We were going to a friend's house. My friend had asked me to house-sit there for a week or two while they went on a trip. When we arrived, there was no one home. So I said to my husband, let's drive on down the road and see what's there while we wait for my friends to return. So we did.

"It was way out in the country, and we drove on. As we approached a curve in the road, suddenly all my hair stuck straight out, and I got the eeriest feeling. There was something familiar about everything I saw. There was an old barn nearby that looked familiar. When we got to the end of the road, I looked over to one side and got the shock of my life. There was the house — the exact house that I had envisioned in my dream!

"We drove back to my friend's house, and later I told them what had happened. I told them about my dream and then about seeing the exact same house down the road. They encouraged me to go down there to the house, but I felt too uncomfortable. I couldn't bring myself to do it. They told me a widow lived in the house, and that it was very old.

"A few days later, I was in my friend's house when the pump broke. Here I was, out in the sticks, with no car and no water. Then a woman came to the back door. I invited her in. She asked if I needed anything, and when I told her the pump had broken, she said I could come to her house with her and fill up some water jugs. We got in her car and she drove down to the end of the road.

She lived in the house! The house I had dreamed about.

"I told her I knew all about her house; that I had been there before. I then sketched a copy of the floor plan of the house before I went inside. Then we went inside. I walked down the hall and found my way to the kitchen. I stood amazed. It was precisely how I had envisioned it. This was in the oldest part of the house. The only thing missing was the door where the little boy had gone out after he opened the box of snakes. The door wasn't there.

"I said to the lady, didn't there used to be a door right over here, and she smiled and acknowledged that there had once been a door there, but previous owners had closed it off to add another room. She then told me that several tenants had moved out of the house contending they had seen ghosts there.

"Then there was another odd revelation. I found out that the man I was supposed to meet the year before, had once lived in this very house! Somehow, I knew that.

"I still get goosebumps when I think about that old house. Could I have been there in another life? I have to admit the idea of having lived there in another life has occurred to me. And what about the children I had seen in the dream? Could this have once been an orphanage? I plan to go to the Floyd County Courthouse and do some research. And what about the snakes? The lady who lived in the house said there were poisonous snakes all over the place. But I guess there always will be some questions unanswered. How does one explain the man I was supposed to meet, and the fact that he had once lived in the house? What's the connection? Maybe someday I'll find the answers."

* * * * *

A VISION OF DEATH

There apparently has been precedent for cases similar to the one Louise Loveland experienced. One of the most famous, and most documented, occurred in 1878, and while the site was across the state line, in Tennessee, it is of such intrigue that it is included here. The incident happened to Dr. A. S. Wiltse, a well-known, and respected, psychic of his day. But instead of a dream, it was a vision which appeared to him while he was awake. In the spring of that year, he and his wife were visiting her mother and step-father, Mr. and Mrs. Todd, on their farm.

One evening, after his wife had gone to bed, Dr. Wiltse was up late, talking with the Todds, when, suddenly, a scene appeared to him, not unlike a slide projection several feet across on a screen. It was a scene of a landscape. He described it in detail to the Todds. It disappeared for a few seconds, then materialized again, this time showing a log cabin in the picture. Neither of the Todds saw anything, but when Dr. Wiltse detailed the house, they immediately recognized it as being the Cass Davis House, located only about a mile away from their farm, across a river. Dr. Wiltse had never been there before and had no way of knowing what the house looked like.

Then the image changed. It zoomed in closer on the house, with the door closed. Dr. Wiltse then said he heard what sounded like a muffled gun shot, and in the image he was still seeing, a man opened the door of the house, and, obviously frightened, ran out. Mr. Todd thought Dr. Wiltse was playing some kind of trick on them, but the doctor declared he wasn't. He said the image was like if one breathed on a mirror and then stood back to look at it. The view would be shadowy and dim, but still recognizable.

He then told the Todds that through the open door in the house he could see a man staggering toward it with blood running from his mouth. The man leaned against the door, leaving a handprint in his own blood. Dr. Wiltse said this image disappeared and another reappeared, much as if one slide were flicked onto a screen after another. In this one, a man was lying on the ground and several people, with hoes and mattocks in their hands had gathered around him. It appeared that the man was dead. Then the image vanished.

Dr. Wiltse asked the Todds if they were sure of the identity of the house, and they said from the description that he had given them they were certain. He then asked them if they knew of any past tragedy at the house. They said no. The doctor then said that what he had seen had either occurred at the house at some time, or was about to occur. "If it is past we may never know it; if it is to come, we may see," he said.

A few days later, Mr. Todd and Dr. Wiltse were on their way to a nearby town when they met Cass Davis, the owner of the house the doctor had seen in his vision. Davis asked them if they had heard that Henderson Whittaker had killed himself. They asked him what happened. Davis said that Whittaker had gone into (the Davis) house the day before and asked a Mr. Haun, who was in the house, if he might borrow his rifle to go hunting. Haun had said okay, but he didn't know if the gun was loaded or not.

Whittaker then took the rifle, put his mouth over the muzzle to blow into the gun, pushing back the hammer with his foot. His foot slipped off and the gun exploded into his mouth. Haun ran out into the field for help. When the hands from the field arrived, they found Whittaker sprawled on the ground. He was dead. And on the door frame was a bloody handprint.

Everything had occurred precisely as Dr. Wiltse had envisioned it, a few days before!

* * * * *

THE SHIP CAPTAIN'S 'EXTRA' MATE
(Off the Virginia Coast)

(Author's note: One of my favorite places to browse is at the library of the Association for Research and Enlightenment (A.R.E.) at 67th Street and Atlantic Avenue in Virginia Beach. This is the organization founded by the legendary psychic Edgar Cayce. On the second floor of the main building is one of the most extensive libraries on psychic phenomena in the world. In this collection are scores of books directly relating to ghostly activities, as well as pamphlets, booklets, manuscripts, documents, and magazine and newspaper articles. (All this in addition to the 14,000-plus recorded readings Edgar Cayce gave during his lifetime.

I have scanned the ghost collection a number of times, and each time I do, it seems something new catches my attention. Enroute to a talk I gave in March 1997 to the Hampton Roads Civil War Roundtable, for example, I had an hour or so to spare, so I dropped by the A.R.E. In thumbing through a volume titled, "Phantasms of the Dead, or True Ghost Stories," by Hereward Carrington, published in 1920, I came across a chapter headed, "Heave the Lead!" I have paraphrased and excerpted it as follows:)

 n 1664, Captain Thomas Rogers was commanding a ship called "The Society," on a voyage from England to Virginia. He was enroute to pick up a load of tobacco. As they neared their destination, as was the custom, the mates and officers each day would bring their books and cast up their reckonings with the captain to see how near they were to the American coast. One day they all agreed they were roughly 100 leagues (240 to 460 statute miles) from the capes of Virginia. From their measurements they determined they were in waters more than 100 fathoms deep.

The weather was fine one evening when the captain turned in for the night. He fell asleep for about three hours. He was awakened when he heard his second mate turn out and relieve the watch. He called to his first mate and asked him how things were. The mate said that all was well. They were running at a good rate of speed, there was a fair wind and it was a clear night.

Captain Rogers fell asleep again. Then he had a strange and vivid dream. He dreamed that someone had pulled him, and bade him turn out and look abroad. He experienced this effect several times during the night. Finally, the vision spoke. It said, rather emphatically, "Turn out and look abroad." The captain lay in a state of uneasiness for some time, then, unable to go back to sleep, he "felt compelled" to put on his great coat and go on deck. All appeared to be fine. The night was clear and calm. The ship was sailing southwest by south.

The captain was about to return to his cabin when something stood by him and said, "Heave the lead." He was startled, but saw nothing. He turned to the second mate and asked: "When did you heave the lead? What water have you?"

"About an hour ago, sir," replied the mate. "Sixty fathoms."

"Heave again," the captain commanded. The mate didn't understand the need for such an order, but he did as he was told. This time when the lead was cast, ground was at only 11 fathoms. This shocked the captain and crew. A few minutes later they cast again, and this time they were in only seven fathoms of water.

Alarmed, the captain immediately bid his men to "put the helm alee, and about ship, all hands ordered to back the sails." The ship came about, but before the sails filled they were down to just four and a half fathoms. Heading back out to sea, they soon again reached a depth of 20 fathoms.

When daybreak came, "the capes of Virginia were in fair view under their stern, and but a few leagues distant." Had they maintained their previous course during the night "but one cable-length further, they would have run aground, and certainly lost their ship, if not their lives — all through the erroneous reckonings of the day before."

Of this most strange occurrence, author Carrington wrote: "Who or what was it that waked the captain and bade him save the ship?

"That he has never been able to tell!"

CHAPTER 14

The Foreboding Phantom at Pheasant Hill

(Near Winchester)

n 1925, a country doctor who visited patients in the foothill villages around Winchester, told of seeing the apparitions of two women at various times. The sightings were always in the vicinity of Old Rag Mountain. Others in the area supported the doctor's claims, saying they, too, had seen the phantom women. One was described as an older woman, fashionably dressed. The other was younger. They appeared walking across a clearing that bordered a road through the woods near the mountain. It was believed, at the time, that the figures were the ethereal spirits of Marie d'Contreville Carwell, and her daughter, Lucy.

If so, this surely represents one of the strangest, most bizarre episodes in the history of the northern Shenandoah Valley. It dates back to pre-Civil War days, and was recorded in James Reynolds' 1965 book, "Gallery of Ghosts," among other sources. Marie was from the bayous of Louisiana. She married Gaines Carwell and they moved into a large manor house near Winchester known as Pheasant Hill. They had two children, Lucy, and Dulany Carwell.

When the Civil War came, Dulany and his foster brother, Bart Danvers, who also lived at Pheasant Hill, joined the Confederacy. Two months after the war ended in April 1865, Dulany returned home, walking from Luray. He was exhausted when he finally arrived. There, he learned that his mother, Marie, had been shot and killed by a Yankee soldier under most peculiar circumstances.

She had long adored a portrait of Dulany and his father, which had been painted when the boy was about four years old. It hung prominently in the sitting room of the house. One day a detachment of Union soldiers rode into the Carwell yard. Marie, perhaps in panic, raced into the room, unhooked the portrait and started to carry it out of the house through the back way. A soldier, entering through the front door, in the pale shadows, saw her and yelled for her to halt. She kept on and he fired. She fell dead, the portrait landing on top of her.

The house was ransacked, but the soldiers left Lucy alone. She sat all night on the floor, cradling her mother's head in her arms. The servants, who had fled, found Lucy and her mother the next morning when they returned. After Dulany had recovered from his fatiguing trip home, he asked his sister where the painting was now. It had been retrieved, she told him, and was hanging in Marie's sitting room.

At this point Bart took Dulany outside and told him that he thought the horrifying incident had adversely affected Lucy's mind. She had not been the same since. He said she would tell him that her mother was calling her, and she would enter the sitting room and conversations could be heard from it.

A few days later Dulany was walking by the sitting room — the door was closed — when he heard voices coming from inside. He slowly opened the door, but could see nothing, it was so dark inside. He started to open the curtains when he heard a familiar voice say, "No, do not let in the light." It was the voice of his dead mother! "We do not like the light," she said. "We sit and talk in the dark. It is pleasanter."

Clearly shaken by the experience, Dulany asked, "Mother, whom do you mean by 'we'?" "You have spoiled it," the voice answered. "I talk with my husband, Gaines Carwell (who also was dead), and my little son, Dulany." Then there was a laugh.

Dulany later told Bart what had happened, and Bart said that he also had heard conversations in the sitting room when only Lucy was in there. Bart said that one day as he was walking by the room he heard some furniture being moved about inside. He opened the door and saw the ghost of Marie Carwell standing on a chair. He told Dulany that she appeared to be trying to unhook the portrait she had been carrying when she was shot.

The months passed. As they did, Lucy seemed to slip more and more into a state of mental depression. She would spend long hours in the sitting room, apparently conversing with her mother.

Then one night Dulany was awakened by some sounds outside. He peered out his bedroom window and caught a glimpse of a shadow moving off from the springhouse. It looked like a young woman in a dark coat or cape. Dulany thought it might be a field hand and he went back to bed.

The next morning Lucy was missing. They searched for months but never found a trace of her. Two years later, Bart married and left Pheasant Hill. Bart tried to encourage Dulany to go

with him, but Dulany told him he couldn't leave because his mother was still there. He, too, seemed to have succumbed to the spell of Marie's spirit.

In the dark solitude of the old house Marie's voice was heard every night. Dulany would always hear her in the sitting room, talking to the portrait. It was driving him crazy. In desperation, he took the painting down one night and moved it to a room at the top of the attic stairs. That way, he reasoned, if she continued to talk to it, at least he wouldn't hear it.

Several days later, when Dulany heard the high winds banging a shutter in the sitting room, he went inside to fasten it. He was shocked to see the portrait back in its accustomed place. How had it gotten there? He had no idea. And there, in front of it, was the image of his mother, in "flowing hoops of pale gray-white misty material." She looked at the painting and said "Gaines, tell Dulany he must behave himself."

He moved the portrait twice more to different rooms. Each time it would resurface in the sitting room. Sometimes he would envision his mother entering the dining room when he ate alone.

In near madness, Dulany burned the portrait one day. That night he heard the door to the sitting room open and close, followed by the distinct sound of footsteps. It sounded like someone was going from room to room searching for something. Then he heard the footsteps going up the stairs to the upper hall. He followed them. Near the top of the stairs, Dulany heard a terrible, tortured scream. It came from very close to him. Suddenly, an unseen fist slammed into his chest with such force that he lost his balance and toppled over backwards, He tried to grab the railing, but it was rotten at the base and gave way. Dulany fell backwards down the stairs. He broke his neck.

By the time Mammy Effen, his servant-cook reached him he was dead!

Not long after that Pheasant Hill burned to the ground. But possibly the spirit of Marie Carwell, Dulany's mother, did not perish in the flames. It was conjectured, some years later, that Dulany's sister, Lucy, who had so mysteriously disappeared and had never been heard from, had, in fact, moved to a shack hidden in the woods near Old Rag Mountain. She lived as a hermit there for 20 or more years, no one knows for sure.

And so, some believe, it was the ghostly figures of Lucy, joined by her mother, Marie, who the country doctor and others saw in 1925.

CHAPTER 15

The Silent Sentinels at Guard Hill House

(Front Royal)

(Author's note: One of the more pleasant things about the month of April is the annual Historic Garden Week, sponsored by the member organizations of the Garden Club of Virginia. During this period one can visit many historic houses which are not normally open to the public. The Garden Club publishes a book each year featuring the homes open during the week, plus material on other interesting sites throughout the commonwealth. The book is a treasure house of information, with small-print details about scores of houses, mansions and plantations

I anxiously scan every edition. Sometimes there is a clue to the possible presence of a ghost. In reviewing the 1997 book (216 pages), however, I was disappointed in not finding any new leads — that is until I was almost finished. When I got to the "W's," I was pleasantly surprised to find not one, but two, references to possible entities from the beyond. Both were in the Front Royal area in Warren County. Subsequent interviews with the present owners, plus some additional research, led to the following two chapters.)

Warren County was created in 1836 from portions of Frederick and Shenandoah Counties. It was named for General Joseph Warren, the first general officer killed at Bunker Hill at the beginning of the

Revolutionary War. The area, lying at the top entrance to the Skyline Drive, had been explored as early as 1670. Front Royal was once known as Helltown, so named because of the frequent frontier brawls which took place at the early taverns and inns. It was incorporated in 1788, and there is some debate as to how Front Royal got its name. One version says that during the French and Indian War, a local drill master of the militia would command his men on the village common drill field to "front the royal oak." Another tradition holds that during this same period whenever a stranger approached, the sentry would call out "Front!" And the accepted passwords were "Royal Oak."

Whatever, it today is a pleasant, rustic town with many houses of rough-hewn stone which has maintained much of its 19th century flavor. Front Royal was an important point during the Civil War. The battles here in May 1862, and the following day at nearby Cedarville are reputed to be among Stonewall Jackson's most brilliant campaigns. It was here, so the legend goes, that the famous Confederate spy, Belle Boyd, operated, dashing through Yankee lines to pass along important strategic information to Jackson. Her cottage, on High Street, is open to the public. It was also in this area that John Singleton Mosby, the elusive "Grey Ghost of the Confederacy," ran his guerrilla attacks on the Union forces. Five of

Guard Hill House

his men were publicly executed as outlaws in Front Royal.

Across the Shenandoah River from town stands Guard Hill House. It was built in 1824 by Isaac Longacre. He was said to have had tuberculosis and chose the site because it was on a high hill. He designed his house to take full advantage of the cross breezes and the magnificent view of the river below.

The structure itself is almost like a fortress. The walls are 14 to 18 inches thick and the handmade bricks were shipped from England. Many of the hand-blown glass windows remain. The English kitchen and dining room are entered at the back of the house from ground level. On the main level are double parlors. Steep pine steps lead upstairs to the master suite which includes three rooms and a bath.

A natural wood dutch door dating from the 1700s leads from the kitchen through the lanai to a cottage addition which was added in the 1950s. It is used as a guest house. The Thomas Kenner family owned Guard Hill house for more than 90 years. Kenner operated a ferry. During the Civil War he moved his family to Strasburg for safety, but would sneak back, often through enemy lines, to check on his homestead. Both Union and Confederate troops occupied the house during the war, and it was used as a hospital, prison, and observation post.

There are two interesting portraits here. One is of Colonel Mosby, who captured 66 horses during a skirmish at Guard Hill House. The other painting is of Captain John Brock, Abraham Lincoln's cousin, and the great-great grandfather of present owner, retired U.S. Marine Corps Colonel William Hammack.

According to the 1997 Garden Club book entry, the house and cottage are "haunted by playful ghosts who like to pull pranks by doing such things as locking the cottage, hiding small objects and making short visits upon sleeping guests. Guests claim to hear marching and cadence late at night. Col. Hammack feels that Mr. Kenner continues to check upon the house as he did during the Civil War."

"Yes, that's basically true," Col. Hammack says today. "Such things have been reported to have happened here. I can tell you this. I was a skeptic when I moved here in May 1994, but I am a believer now." He then told of several specific incidents which helped changed his mind.

** "My former wife's parents were visiting once, staying in the cottage. One day we heard them arguing as they were coming out of the cottage. She had accused her husband of blocking her exit out of the door. He said he hadn't done any such thing. Somehow, and I can't explain how, the hook, apparently by itself, had fallen into the eye on the screen door, locking her inside. I told them not to worry, I would take the hinge off the door and take the door down. When I did this, the hinge dropped down on the concrete floor, and do you know we couldn't find that hinge. We looked everywhere. There was no place for it to go. But we couldn't find it. I never have found it. The door has been off ever since. I thought that was kind of unusual.

** "And there were other things that happened in the cottage that we couldn't explain. Guests staying in the cottage would sometimes bring gifts, and these gifts would mysteriously disappear.

** "Then there was this 'thing' about corks. It happened to my wife a number of times. She would drop a cork on the floor and we could never find it. It was like 'something' had a fascination with corks. It never happened to me, only to my wife. When she left here it didn't happen again.

** "I guess I became convinced right after we moved in. My wife and I were sitting at a large butcher table. I was looking out the window. Let me tell you what I saw. I saw some lower bodies of men, say from the pelvis down to the middle calf — four legs, two men. They were wearing gray pants with yellow stripes going down them. They appeared to be the pants of Confederate cavalry men. Of course, when I went out to look there was nothing there. But you know it was right here that Mosby captured a bunch of Yankee soldiers and their horses. They had been outside drinking and carousing when Mosby's men took them. Captain Michael Auer of the New York 15th Cavalry was the commander. He was sitting right here in the house when he heard the noise outside. He ran out in his underwear and they captured him, too. They dishonorably discharged him from the army, but Lincoln later reinstated him. Maybe it was the spirit of some of Mosby's men that I saw. I don't know. Or maybe it was Thomas Kenner, who owned the house then. He was always lurking about, keeping an eye on things. Maybe he still is. It could be the five men under Mosby who were hanged in the area. Some people have said they were executed right here, but I don't think so. I think if was a little further south. It was near where a bed and breakfast is today. I was even shown the walnut tree where they allegedly were strung up.

** "I'll tell you another thing," Col. Hammack continues. "My wife and I were sitting at a table one evening when a paper clip came flying through the air from the dining room and struck her on the cheek. There was no one else in the house. She accused me of doing it, but I didn't do it. How did that happen? You tell me! We separated last fall, and since she left, the 'activities' have quieted down. I think she was more sensitive to such phenomena. But seeing those striped pants out the window that day, and seeing that paper clip hit her, that was enough to make a believer out of me."

CHAPTER 16

The Ever Watchful Eye of Miss Lucy Buck

(Front Royal)

he second house mentioned in the Garden Club book is Bel Air on Happy Creek Road. In the write-up was this intriguing passage: "According to the present owners, Lucy (Buck) still resides in Bel Air and makes her presence known from time to time by rearranging the porch furniture and banging on the hot water pipes. She does this usually when they undertake a redecorating project in 'her' part of the house."

Bel Air is steeped in history. Construction began in 1795 after Captain Thomas Buck bought land from William LeHew, the son of Peter LeHew, founding father of Front Royal. Captain Buck led a group known as "Buck's Minute Men" during the Revolutionary War, and was a friend of Lafayette.

Bel Air is the oldest masonry house in Warren County. A number of additions have been made over the years, and the house contains many interesting features. In the breakfast room, for example, are stained-glass windows from the former Front Royal Presbyterian Church. The second floor Hunt Room contains many racehorse trophies and fox hunting photographs. The present owner, Larry LeHew (an eighth generation LeHew) for many years has been Master of the Fox Hounds for the Rappahannock Hunt. On the third floor is a Signature Room, where Union and Confederate soldiers signed the walls and ceilings during the Civil War. One who signed was General Robert E. Lee, but his name is missing.

Pam LeHew at Bel Air

It was removed by a worker who kept it as a souvenir. Another visitor at that time was Belle Boyd, the Confederate spy.

But perhaps the most interesting resident of Bel Air over the past 200 years was a woman named Lucy Rebecca Buck, the granddaughter of Captain Thomas Buck. Among other things, Lucy wrote a lengthy diary of her Civil War days in the house. It is titled, "Sad Earth, Sweet Heaven." In it, she describes, in poignant detail, her love for the house and the land, and her intense dislike of the Union forces who threatened both the house and her very own existence. Following are a few eloquent entries on these points:

Of the view from her home, she wrote, in the winter of 1861, before the land was invaded: "The evening was lovely and I turned to look on the landscape spread before me. In the foreground the smooth, lawn-like meadows and the little happy creek like a silver thread meandering through them. Then the quiet village (Front Royal) with the crimsom sunset on its undulating hill — and in the distance like a fitting frame to this sweet picture stretched the blue mountains all with a cloudless heaven overhead, painted with the sunset pencils."

As the Civil War waged on, Front Royal was occupied by alternating forces of the Union and the Confederacy. It changed hands several times. Once, when Lucy and her family had to abandon her home for safety, she wrote: "Dear old Bel Air! I looked at it after leaving there and wondered if I should ever again recross its threshold or stand by the old hearthstone. It would almost break my heart to lose the old place of mine nativity, the place hallowed by the recollection that the sweetest, most precious hours that I ever knew or will know were spent within its precinct, that the dearest ties of our lives have been formed there, the best loved friends grew with me there. Dear, dear old home!"

Lucy's deep feelings about the house, the land, and the coming invasion from the dreaded Yankees prompted her to pen: "So tranquil did everything seem that I could scarce persuade myself of the fact that just beyond those mountain barriers lay the encampments of an invading foe cruel and relentless, who had come with avowed purpose of deluging this beautiful land with the blood of the noblest and best of its sons. They were our enemies who would fain see the sun-cloud of the battlefield or the somber smoke from our pillaged burning homes ascending to the blackened heavens instead of the sweet Sabbath atmosphere which pervaded the scene now. Those who would ensanguine that little stream with human gore, those who would mar and devastate the face of the earth that they might thus blot out from remembrance everything of beauty from our now beautiful Virginia."

After the first full year of the war, Lucy eloquently summed up her feelings: "I saw the proud mansions that were wont to be glad with mirth and music as each New Year sped on with fleet wings, now shrouded in gloom and darkness. I thought how the warm light had died out from the hearthstones and from the eyes that had beamed brightly around them. I thought of the sad silences of those ancestral halls that erst rang with the music of footfalls that would stray on earth never more now. (I thought) of the maiden who glistened and thrilled as she listened to the vows of love from lips stilled in death ere the burning words grew cold upon them.

"I thought of the hardships endured, the cold and hunger and the harshness to the brave and noble young Southerners whose cradle had been rocked in luxury — who knew of nothing but gentle words and loving smiles in the dear home far away. I thought of the delicate forms of the boys tenderly nurtured now rent with anguish resting on the loathsome hospital couches, no gentle hands to minister to their wants, no dear voice to whisper comfort and cheer when the dark shadows from the valley of death closed about them, none to smooth the pillow, none to drop a tear when that wasted form was borne off to the stranger's rude grave.

Of Yankee occupation, Lucy wrote: "And now — oh, the change! Our country overrun by our remorseless foes there we sat, completely in the power of our implacable enemies . . . enemies who would pillage and destroy our homes, imprison or exile all our natural protectors and leave us poor females and children defenseless, without the means of subsistence and at the mercy of these St. Bartholomew assassins. Oh, it was all so terrible and everything seemed so much darker than ever before."

Lucy Buck persevered, however. She survived the war and, in fact, lived until 1918, although she and her sisters never married. She was buried in the same cemetery she visited so many times during her lifetime, Prospect Hill in Front Royal.

And, perhaps, her spirit has never really left the home she so cherished — Bel Air.

"We think she is still here," says Pam LeHew, Larry's wife. "It's like she's checking up on us and overlooking what we do, especially if we change things." The manifestations seem to come mostly in sounds. Pam says they sometimes hear furniture being moved around in the house. But the most frequent and consistent phenomena come in the form of banging radiators. "Radiators do make noise on their own when you turn them on or off," Pam says. "But they aren't this loud! It happens a lot when we go in the bedroom that used to be hers. It can be real quiet in the house, but when you walk in that one room, the radiators seem to bang real loud. Then when you leave the room, all is silent again. It's like she is venting her displeasure that you may be disturbing her. I don't think I would want to see her, but I'm not afraid. She loved this house so much I'm sure she wouldn't be harmful. I really do think she's here."

Larry agrees. He has lived at Bel Air since 1975. "Oh, she's here," he says. "She plays all kinds of tricks. She knocks lamps over, pushes furniture around, all kinds of things. Lights get turned on and off by themselves. It happens mostly upstairs in 'her' part of the house. Let me tell you what happened when we changed the wallpaper in her room. Lucy evidently didn't like it. There are hardwood floors in that room. They are beautiful. When the wallpapering was done the floors buckled up. The workmen said they didn't spill a drop of anything on the floors, but they were buckled up an inch or two. Then, over the next couple of weeks, the floors returned to their original fine finish. There was no sign of the buckling. We try to leave her room alone now. She doesn't like anyone messing with it.

"Like Pam said, as you enter Lucy's room, things are quiet as a mouse. Then it gets noisy as hell. It sounds like someone is pounding on the radiators with a sledgehammer. Then, when you leave, it gets quiet again," Larry says. "One time Pam and I came home. It was hot, but we keep Lucy's bedroom closed off, and it generally is cooler in there. I said to Pam, let's go in there. We went in the room and I swear, you would have thought the whole house was falling down. It was bedlam. The radiators were banging so loudly we had to cover our ears. We left the room and it stopped immediately."

Larry says his children told him they had once seen Lucy's apparition, but they couldn't describe it, because as soon as it appeared they fled. "They were scared to death. They didn't even want to talk about it."

Larry says there are four or five rocking chairs on the porch, and that Lucy is always turning one of the chairs around to face the window looking in. "I think she does it to see what is going on. We'll go out on the porch and there is that one chair turned around. Sometimes, for meanness, I'll turn it back around, but later we'll find it facing inward again. I guess she was used to having her way."

Lucy Buck's bedroom

Phantasmal Entities in Fauquier County

(Author's note: The following accounts were recorded a quarter century or so ago in a book titled, "The Foothills of The Blue Ridge in Fauquier County, Virginia." The work was compiled and edited by Clara S. McCarty. She included a section on "Our Ghosts.")

THE HORSEBACK HITCHHIKER

In a 19th century version of the ghostly hitch-hiker legend, Dr. James Brady recalled an incident which he swore to be true. It seems a local "swain" was returning home on horseback after an evening of courting. At about midnight he approached the Emmanuel Church graveyard, and, there, received the shock of his life. He was suddenly confronted by a lady standing amidst the tombstones. She asked him for a ride. Terrified, the man stuttered something about his horse would not carry double, whereupon he lashed his steed and "galloped up the road at a furious pace."

Some time and distance further, as he reached Cool Spring, the same apparitional lady appeared again and once more asked for a ride. The man spurred his horse and flew off again, as did Ichabod Crane in Washington Irving's masterpiece, "The Legend of Sleepy Hollow." This time he did not stop until he reached home, where he slung his saddle and bridle across the porch and raced to his bedroom.

* * * * *

THE HAUNTED MAPLE TREE

 n 1945, Dr. W. H. K. Pendleton, who grew up at The Grove near Delaplane, wrote the following:

"The Rector place, near Marshall, was said to be in my day fairly saturated with ghost stories and tales of ancient tragedy.

"Old Mrs. Hume told me with her own lips the story of the tragedy of her grandfather's death. He married a lady from the Valley who brought her slaves with her. The slaves did not like their new home and thought that if the master were dead, the mistress, with them, would return to the Valley of Virginia. A bear was reported to be terrorizing the Negroes from the loft of one of their cabins. The master immediately rode over to the cabin, climbed fearlessly into the loft, and was struck down by a strong Negro with a hoe.

"The horse returned riderless. Search followed without result until at length his dog took station by an uprooted maple tree near the house. Here his body was found as the dog kept vigil. It had been loaded on a wagon with a load of fodder and drawn right by the house to the place of concealment at the roots of the old maple tree.

"Two Negroes were found to be involved." One escaped, but the other one was caught and hanged by a chain to the big tree. Although the chain was removed afterward, according to Dr. Pendleton, "The chains were said to rustle and clank in the wind long after the execution." Here, the editor adds a footnote: "This must be true, for have I not heard them often when I passed half scared to death under that tree at night?

* * * * *

A CASE OF UNREQUITED LOVE

lsie R. McCarty tells one episode from her own memory: "Back in the 1840s, when travel and communication were difficult in this area even between adjoining counties, a young cousin, Elizabeth, was sent by her father from Clarke County to visit Dr. Robert Stribling of Mountain View, whose daughter Mildred (my grandmother) was about the same age.

"The girl was despondent, her father said, because he would not countenance a marriage to a penniless young Episcopal minister with whom she was very much in love. He did not tell the doctor, however, that she had recently been ill; maybe he felt guilty over the apparent reason for her disorder and did not wish that the extent of her distress be known. He hoped the change of scenery and companions would restore her spirits, and that she would form a new attachment and would forget her young minister.

"Her Fauquier kinfolk were delighted with their cousin, and there followed a round of parties in her honor. She seemed as gay and happy as a much-sought-after, beautiful young lady should be until one night after an especially festive evening at Morven.

"The girls were occupying the bedroom in the east wing. Just after Mildred had blown out the light, Elizabeth clutched her saying, 'Oh, Millie, I'm lost!' From that time on, she was never herself again. Back at Mountain View, Dr. Stribling decided that she had 'brain fever,' sent a message to her parents and did everything he could for her.

"In her delirium she would get up from her bed and feel the faces of those about her as if searching for someone, and after a short time, she died.

"Some time afterward, a young clergyman who had come to hold services at Leeds Church spent the night at Morven. The next morning at breakfast, Major Ambler asked if he had had a restful night. He replied, 'It is strange but as soon as I put out the lamp, I felt there was someone in the room, and suddenly a hand passed over my face feeling my features; then it seemed to disappear up the chimney!' Major Ambler expressed concern, but decided in silence that the young man had been dreaming.

"Some months later, however, a second young clergyman who was entirely unaware of the other's story also reported at breakfast that he had experienced the same strange feeling of a presence just as the lamp went out, followed by a woman's hand over his face. This time his host was impressed and thereafter whenever there was a visiting minister assigned to Morven, he was always put in the same east-wing guest room and never told that it was the ghost room, or that young preachers had had unusual experiences there.

"In the morning, to the usual inquiry about the night's rest, there was always a repetition of the others' story. Years later, my father, just graduated from the Seminary, saw and felt the woman's hand. When we children asked him about it, he was very serious and said, 'I cannot explain it; but it was not my imagination'."

* * * * *

THE DOOR THAT WAS NAILED SHUT

An account by Emily Glascock Ramey: "Shaded by towering locust trees near the road in Rectortown, one of the older houses has a door on the side next to the village that has been nailed shut for many years.

"Legend has it that the owner, Sam Jackson, used to visit the grog shop, or tavern, at the foot of the hill, as did many of his neighbors and friends, among them a man named Yates.

"(One night) after a lengthy session, an argument grew violent, tempers flared, and someone threw a brick through the window. There was a fight outside where Yates and Jackson were trying to settle their differences.

"The next morning Yates' frozen body was found. He was buried in a 'goods box' in the cemetery.

"From that time on, Jackson would be wakened several times at night by the ghost of his departed friend coming through the door towards the village. After several such alarming apparitions, the door was nailed shut, as it remains today, and Jackson slept more peacefully for the short time he continued to live there. He soon moved to the neighboring county of Culpeper but lived only a short time longer, and several others who had been at the grog shop on the night of the fight died in the next few years."

CHAPTER 18

Historic Spirits (?) at Swift Run Gap

(The Blue Ridge Mountains near Elkton)

f the ghosts of wayfarers . . . could be assembled and endowed with speech, what stories they might tell!" So wrote John Wayland a couple of decades ago in his book "Twenty-Five Chapters on the Shenandoah Valley." In the book is a chapter on "Ghosts of Swift Run Gap." This is perhaps the most famous pass in the entire mountain range. It crosses the Blue Ridge a few miles southeast of Elkton, roughly halfway between Culpeper and Harrisonburg.

The first definitive account of passage through this gap was recorded in September 1716 by the Frenchman John Fontaine, one of the men who accompanied Alexander Spotswood during his legendary journey of the Knights of the Golden Horseshoe. Spotswood had gathered up a group of "convivial gentlemen" and set out to explore the Blue Ridge Mountains at a time when Virginia colonists knew very little about them.

The expedition — the first such attempted by Englishmen — included 63 men, 74 horses, an assortment of dogs, and a "vast quantity of alcoholic beverages." They fought off mosquitoes, hornets and rattlesnakes, shot bear and deer for their suppers, and generally had a grand old time.

After reaching what they perceived to be the top of the mountains, they came down into the valley through what historians believe is Swift Run Gap, camped beside a river, and decided it was time to celebrate their accomplishment.

Fontaine, who recorded the adventure, wrote: "We had a good dinner, and after we got the men together and loaded all their arms, and we drank the King's health in champagne and fired a volley, and all the rest of the Royal Family and fired a volley — the Princess' health in Burgundy, and fired a volley, and all the rest of the Royal family in claret, and fired a volley. We drank (to) the Governor's health, and fired another volley. We had several sorts of liquors, viz., Virginia red wine and white, Irish usquebaugh, brandy, shrub, two sorts of rum, champagne, canary, cherry punch, water, cider, etc." Now that's celebrating!

While this was the first "official" crossing at Swift Run Gap, or at least the first one documented, it is possible that a few other explorer-types may have been there before. One was John Lederer, from Tidewater, who ascended the Blue Ridge 47 years earlier, in 1669, although it is believed he reached the mountains in the vicinity of Stanardsville.

General George Washington crossed here on horseback on September 30, 1784, traveling from Brock's Gap. He said, in his diary, "I set off very early from Mr. Lewis' who accompanied me to the foot of the Blue Ridge at Swift Run Gap, 10 miles, where I proceeded over the mountain."

There were more distinguished visitors through here during the Civil War. A young Confederate soldier named Kyd Douglas raced through the gap on a stormy night in April 1862, carrying an important message from Stonewall Jackson near Harrisonburg to General Ewell, on the other side of Culpeper. A short time later, Ewell brought his army of 8,000 across Swift Run Gap to a bivouac near Jackson's force just east of Elkton.

In his book, author Wayland says of the area today, "sound rather than silence prevails, but perchance in some quiet midnight hour a dreamer may sense a ghostly presence and hear a muffled hoofbeat upon a stony path." Wayland may have been more prophetic than he knew, for there have, in fact, been numerous reports by travelers, hikers, campers, and others of hearing unaccountable sounds during the dark night hours at Swift Run Gap. Some have sworn they have heard what sounded like the tromping marching of large groups of men, and the distinct echoes of horses' hooves, although nothing is seen in the blackness. It has been, of course, impossible to determine if such haunting sounds date to the 19th century or the 18th, or perhaps even earlier.

Wayland notes one specific incident where an apparition may have transcended the ages. He tells of the time when the

Confederates were entrenched in the area. A soldier allegedly found a gem-studded golden horseshoe. This was the gift that Alexander Spotswood had made special for his companions during their exploration and party in 1716. The soldier found the shoe on New Year's Eve, and, as Wayland described it, "As he pinned it on his breast a fearful bugle-blast smote his ear and an olden knight 'in scarlet clad, with spur and plume and hat,' appeared before him."

Whether such a manifestation actually occurred or not, its telling, plus the historic background of Swift Run Gap, was enough to inspire Shenandoah Valley poet Aldine Kieffer to write about the spirits at the gap. Following are a few lines from his work:

"Once by a ruined church they rode,
Round which a churchyard lay;
Strange specters stood among the graves
In judgment-like array.
Then, like the summer's noonday sun
That golden horseshoe shone,
And over mountain, tow'r and cliff
A flood of light was thrown;
And, ringing on the wintry tide,
Strange bugle-blasts rang wild and wide.
Old knights from graves of long ago
Now gathered near the spring,
And drank as spirits only may
A health to George the King;
And turning on the trooper cried,
'This is a merry New year's ride!'
But when Sir Fontaine raised his hand
He broke the magic spell,
And forth from heaven's blue starry vault
An awful meteor fell:
It smote the spring — then far and wide
Deep silence filled the midnight tide."

CHAPTER 19

Letters from the Author's Mailbox

(Author's note: After writing and publishing ten books on Virginia's ghosts, I now receive scores of letters (and calls) from citizens all across the commonwealth, telling me of their experiences and encounters with spirits. For example, in the fall of 1996, travel editor Stephen Harriman of the Virginian Pilot (Norfolk) wrote a major feature article on me and the ghosts of the plantations on historic Route 5 in Charles City County. At the end of the article he suggested that anyone with a haunting tale should call or write me. I got several interesting letters.

As a result, I here include a sampling of the mail.)

* * * * *

A SCARY SIGHTING AT BLANDY
(Front Royal)

From Stephen MacAvoy, teaching assistant at the University of Virginia:

ear Mr. Taylor: Reading your book brought to mind a Virginia ghost story I heard, and would like to relate to you. The events took place at the Blandy Experimental Farm on the grounds of the Orland E. White Arboretum near Front Royal. Blandy is currently owned by the University of Virginia, and is used as an ecological research facility.

It used to be the slave quarters for a plantation house (which is still there). In addition to the slave quarters there is a library, meeting rooms, laboratories, etc. The facility is 'U' shaped and one of the wings is the slave living quarters.

"A professor, who has an apartment in the building, reported that sometimes he will wake up to the sound of the bed creaking, and sees an indentation on the edge of the bed as if someone was sitting on it.

"Last fall I took my students up to Blandy for the weekend and encountered a post-doctoral student who lived at Blandy and had studied there for years. I asked him what he thought about the haunting. He just looked at us for a while, and then said, 'if you are one of those people who has to know the reason for every noise or strange sound, then this place will bother you.' Then he just walked away. At least one of my students kept their light on all night.

"But here is the main story about Blandy as I heard it. A few years ago a literary club held a retreat of sorts at Blandy. The group was staying in the 'dorms' where the actual slave quarters were located. After getting settled for the weekend they decided to go into town for dinner. One gentleman who was not feeling well decided to stay behind.

"After the group left, he was sitting on some steps opposite the dorms looking at the landscape when he saw two people coming over the fields towards Blandy. He saw a middle-aged black woman leading a young white child. They were dressed in 'colonial' clothes. He was a little surprised, but not excessively so, since Blandy sometimes hosts historical events.

"However, when he tried to get their attention they took no notice of him. They walked right by and didn't even look in his direction. They walked around the edge of the building where the dorms were located. The confused man hurriedly followed, but when he got around the corner there was no one in sight! He searched around but there was no evidence of anyone. Baffled, he hurried to his room to write his wife about the strange incident.

"When the dinner party returned, he was dead!

"The only way they knew what happened was from the letter on his desk."

* * * * *

THE CRAB PIRATE OF COBB'S MARINA
(Virginia Beach)

From Bob Ruegsegger, a newspaper reporter who lives in Virginia Beach:

I have to admit that I am what you might call a skeptic in regard to psychic phenomena. Still, years ago, probably 10 or 15, I wrote down a ghost story that I heard as a youngster while I was working at Cobb's Marina near Little Creek. I suspect I might have heard it from the owner of the marina, or maybe from one of the charter boat skippers. I'm really not certain. I've enclosed a copy of the story as I wrote it down.

"Men who spend much of their lives on the water are full of tales of ghosts, phantom boats, and strange apparitions. Take, for example, the phantom boat 'Anna B.' which is said to ply the waters of Little Creek Harbor near the mouth of the Chesapeake Bay on warm summer nights.

"Local residents have long reported sighting this Chesapeake Bay dead-rise silently traveling back and forth along the rock jetties near the entrance to the harbor. Regularly, the phantom dead-rise stops while her ghostly skipper examines the crab pots that usually line the channel there.

"The 'Anna B.', Virginia certification records reveal, was registered to William 'Bill' Shepherd. Shepherd was widely known in the vicinity of Little Creek as a 'crab pirate' who regularly and cleverly harvested the crabs from the pots of other crabbers under the cover of darkness. Although many attempts were made to catch Bill in the act, he avoided penalty for several years.

One particularly dark summer night, Bill's luck ran out, and he finally was punished for his years of crime. Bill, it seems, stuck his hand into a crab pot that imprisoned a small starving shark — probably placed there by an irate waterman who resented having his crabs stolen. With one vicious bite, the shark removed two of Bill's fingers.

"He was a marked man for the remainder of his life. The other crabbers never let Bill forget the incident. As a result of the 'accident,' he became known as 'Three Fingers.'

"Several years later, Bill drowned in a gale somewhere off Cape Henry. Presumably, he went down with the 'Anna B.'

"Local watermen claim that Bill still searches the crab pots along the Little Creek jetties, seeking, not crabs, but the fingers he lost that dark summer night."

* * * * *

AN ENCOUNTER AT THE OLDE TOWNE INN
(Manassas)

From David Rossel, Chantilly:

Dear Mr. Taylor: Since this is Halloween (1996), I thought I'd write you about an odd experience I had while spending the night in downtown Manassas. My friend, a resident of Manassas, told me about the Olde Towne Inn, in the heart of old town Manassas. (Originally covered in "The Ghosts of Virginia, Volume III.") Evidently, the motel and its adjacent tavern, date back to the Civil War. According to local history, during the war, the motel was a hospital. Needless to say, many Union and Confederate soldiers must have lost their lives in this hospital. The motel has a reputation of being haunted, and is usually booked every weekend because of this notoriety. My friend and I decided to get a room there (room 34 to be exact) and hope for a 'close encounter.' I will try to explain what happened that night.

"My friend and I pride ourselves on being extra-sensitive to the unknown world. Right before we clicked off the light, the barometric pressure changed and my friend claimed he felt eight presences surrounding our beds. I did not see anything, but I cannot deny the fact that the atmosphere around us felt different. After a few minutes, the room returned to its original, 'normal' state and we clicked off the light.

"My first occurrence happened about an hour later. I was barely asleep, when I felt a pulling sensation throughout my body. Again, the pressure and temperature in the room changed. It did not get colder, as I expected it would — it felt warmer. After a few seconds, the sensation stopped, and I wrote it off as my active imagination getting the best of me. However, the brief pulling sensation occurred two other times during the course of the night, with the pressure and temperature changing each time. I was half awake when I felt these sensations. I was not scared and, for the most part, got a good night's sleep.

"At six in the morning, I was literally shaken awake. The

pulling sensation was so strong that I thought I was being pulled off the bed! The sensation was accompanied with a humming sound, which sounded like a freight train going through my head. The sound was not in the room; it was IN my body! It lasted a minute. Immediately after the sensation passed, I called out to my friend, who was in the bed next to mine. I asked him if he had felt anything unusual.

"He described the feeling as a 'subway, passing through his body.' It was a strange feeling indeed, but it did not scare either of us. About an hour later, I awoke to another pulling sensation, but this one was not as strong. To prove I was awake, I focused on a point in the motel room and then tried to call out. The first word that came to mind was 'stop.' I could not vocalize this, or any word while experiencing this sensation. I could not move my hand. It was as if my entire body was being used as some sort of stepping stone. The warm feeling accompanied the sensation, and it literally felt as if someone (or something) was on top of me! This experience was the longest — it lasted about a minute and a half.

"I've read stories about people who have claimed to 'feel' ghosts, as opposed to seeing them. I did not see anything in that motel room. Throughout the night, when I awoke, I sat up in bed and looked around the room. I saw nothing. My friend saw nothing. However, we can't stop thinking about that night.

"Does this story sound like a case of a preconditioned, overactive imagination? I thought so initially. But if the motel was in fact a hospital during the Civil War, odds are that it is haunted!"

* * * * *

RETURN OF THE SOLDIER IN THE MUD

From Gary Norman, Chief Archaeologist, Kenmore Plantation & Gardens, Fredericksburg:

ear Mr. Taylor: I take the liberty of sending you the following memorandum which circulated today at Kenmore. While we have no official position on 'ghosts' at Kenmore, we find it fun to collect these stories, and visitors often ask about such things.

"Linda Westerman, one of our volunteers, ran across the following story in the Fredericksburg Ledger; September 23 1870:

'APPEARANCE OF A GHOST.' 'The people in the western part of town near Kenmore are very much excited about the appearance of what is supposed to be a ghost in that quarter last Sunday morning between 10 and 12 o'clock. It is said that about that time of the day, during the shower of rain, Mr. Mills saw a man crawling on his hands along by the fence dragging his feet after him, as though his legs were paralyzed. He spoke to two ladies standing in the door and asked, 'What does that mean?' Of course they could not tell, and Mr. Mills said that he would see and stepped out of the fence, which was but some ten or fifteen feet, by which time the supposed man had passed him some few feet. Mr. Mills got over the fence, and started after the man and asked where he was going.

" 'The man straightened up on his feet to full height — which was higher than that of a medium sized man — and said in a distinct tone: 'I am going down,' and vanished out of sight. The figure was dressed in the full uniform of a Federal soldier which was clean and apparently new, with the blue overcoat coming down to near the feet. Mr. Mills did not see the face of the man, but the two ladies did and say the face was bronze with hard features.

" 'The persons who say they saw this are of undoubted veracity, and although they do not believe in ghosts, they are unable to account for the sudden appearance and mysterious disappearance in broad daylight. It has created quite an excitement in that part of town.'

The Kenmore memo then continues: "The following is an excerpt from our Civil War walking tour which will be ready soon:

" 'At dusk on December 13, (1862) the 124th New York Volunteers advanced and took positions along 'garden terraces, hillocks and mounds' around Kenmore. That evening, the 122nd Pennsylvania Volunteers 'deployed as skirmishers . . . between the two canals, above the city, and upon the crest of the ridge upon which stands Mrs. Washington's monument, and two companies of the 124th New York were advanced in front of Kenmore mansion, supported by the 12th New Hampshire Volunteers . . .' They lay upon muddy ground in full sight of Confederate guns for 20 hours before being relieved. At 10:30 p.m., Battery A, 4th U.S. Artillery took position in a field 'upon the left' of Kenmore. On December 14, Confederates opened fire on it, firing fuse shell, solid shot, and spherical case, using rifle and smooth-bore guns.' Confederate artillery fire rained 'so thickly around and about (them) as though thrown broadcast . . . a head could not or dared not rise . . . The battery at Kenmore replied and, after returning 50 rounds, silenced the

Confederate guns.'

"What's the connection?" Norman continues in the memo. "I have recently found evidence to suggest that members of the 124th New York Volunteers, who lay on the muddy ground for so long in December 1862, were treated and died at Kenmore in May 1864, after the (Battle of the) Wilderness. From period photos we know that many were buried at the border of Kenmore with Judge Chew's property (in the middle of the block between Winchester and Prince Edward).

"I leave it to you to discover the similarities of a Federal soldier lying upon muddy ground in a battle, and what Mr. Mills saw during the rain shower that Sunday morning in 1870.

"Just something to think about."

* * * * *

THE LOCKET OF THE GOVERNOR'S GHOST

From Brenda Bradshaw Smith, Richmond:

I was looking into some Virginia ghost stories for my radio show. I called the Governor's office to check on a lady ghost that was reported in the 1890s by

The Governor's Mansion in Richmond

Governor Philip W. McKinney himself. (Covered in the "Ghosts of Richmond," 1985, and in "The Ghosts of Virginia, Volume I, 1993). He saw a young woman sitting in the window in a bedroom. After that, some capitol police reported some strange sightings and noises around the mansion. During Governor Andrew Montague's administration at the turn of the (20th) century, two guests of the Governor heard the famous noises of the lady ghost one night. Two other Governors have heard the ruffling sounds of her dress as she runs down the halls.

"I felt she was looking for something she had lost in the house. This was the reason for her energy to manifest itself. Using my intuitive abilities, I went into the guest bedroom and saw a picture on the wall that I knew was the lady ghost.

"In the picture, the lady was holding a locket. I knew that was why her energy stayed in the house. I asked the Governor's secretary for permission to look in the dresser in the room. She informed me that each new year, new paper is put in the drawers.

"I asked, 'May I pull back the paper?' She said, 'yes.' As I pulled back the paper, we saw a locket in the corner of the drawer! I had been led to the correct drawer. The locket was just like the one in the picture. I asked, 'Who is the woman in the picture?' The secretary went and got the book of records that would help us find the name of the woman in the picture. We found no record of the picture in the book. I gave the locket to the secretary who said she would give it to the Governor's wife.

"Many years have passed since I have thought about the ghost. I began to wonder if 'she' was happy I found her locket. I believe she wanted the locket. Now the question is, 'Who is she?'"

*****

THE SWINGING LANTERN

From Cathie Morris, Chesapeake:

ear Mr. Taylor: I don't know if this is the kind of story that you are looking for, but I have two for you.

"(1) My father passed away three years ago, January 2, from massive heart failure. Two days later, as I was still grieving, and still am, that evening I heard a sound at the foot of my bed, and there he was, smiling at me, as if to say it's okay. I'm fine and happy now. Sometimes I still feel him near. He did have a hard life.

"(2) My cousin and I were sleeping outside in her front yard, one time when I was 13. There used to be a house two doors down. It's been torn down for a while now, but the inside of the house was gutted. Not by fire, but from just being old.

"Anyway, on this night, there were no stars or moon and only one or two street lights, but not anywhere near this house. Around midnight we were talking about checking the house out, you know, for ghosts. All of a sudden we heard a loud noise and looked toward the house. Hanging from the inside of the house, in the top floor window, we saw a lantern swinging and a, well, what looked to be a rope hanging from the top part of the window. As 13-year-olds, no one believed us, but I was told that someone did die in that house in the late 1700s or early 1800s, and I do believe that I saw what I saw!"

* * * * *

THE REAPPEARANCE OF COUSIN CURTIS

From Barbara Creekmore, Virginia Beach:

y beloved cousin, Curtis, committed suicide on October 15, 1995. The night before he died I dreamed that my deceased father and I were driving towards my cousin's house. Daddy and I never made it.

My father was very close to Curtis and I had gone to daddy's grave previously and asked him to watch over him (Curtis) because I could not be there to take care of him. Now, I know that in some way daddy was trying to tell me to get to Curtis. The road we were on (in the dream) was the same road that I traveled the next night, the night my cousin shot himself.

"The following day I came home from work around 4:30 p.m. All at once there was a haze, and my cousin appeared coming into the den. He came in with his head down so I could not see his face. He was wearing his green plaid shirt and khaki pants with black loafers. He walked up the steps to the kitchen, but when I turned around to absorb this, he backed down the stairs and faded away.

"My cousin's family (at that time) had not told me of his death!

"Since that day, I have had many visits from Curtis. I see his black loafers out of the corner of my eye. My rocking chair will rock unattended. My lights do strange things. They are always being turned on with no explanation. Sometimes, while I am in the room, they become unplugged. My television set has changed channels on its own and has even turned itself off.

"The night my daughter told me that she was getting married, light bulbs blew out all over the house. Curtis did not care for my daughter's boyfriend. My car has automatic door locks. There are times that they go up and down very rapidly. One time, at his grave, as I approached my car, the locks immediately locked.

"When my cousin was in a depressed mood, he would call my house and not say anything, and very gently disconnect the call. He would tell me that he called just to hear my voice. To this day, I still receive that call. Today, I smile when a strange encounter occurs. I feel that it is quite comforting to walk with my cousin every day."

* * * * *

A VISION FROM THE PAST

From Danielle Cowles, College Park, Maryland:

I love your book, The Ghosts of Virginia (Volume I). When I read the book's first story, 'Caught in a Colonial Time Warp,' I had doubts about the credibility of the storytellers. That is, until I happened to inquire as to if Portobello, a historic home in St. Mary's County, Maryland, had any apparitions. The caretakers of the house go to the same church as I. One day at a social function, I casually asked if Portobello is haunted. I was not expecting the reaction I received. A strange and embarrassed look crept over the overseer's face. He was quiet for a moment and then began, 'You're not going to believe this, but.' It seems Mr. Goddard experienced something quite similar.

"According to him, he was outside mowing the lawn on a hot, breezy day this past summer (1996), when suddenly the air became perfectly still. Suddenly, a carriage driven by a black man and occupied by a woman dressed in emerald whirled around the corner. The carriage circled the graveyard before stopping in front of the house. The lady then got out and opened the front door. But before she went in, she turned back and looked directly at Mr. Goddard. Then the man, woman and buggy vanished as if it were never there! Reasonably sure that Mr. Goddard is not crazy or a liar, I am now convinced that 'Caught in a Colonial Time Warp' and the other accounts are true."

* * * * *

THE LITTLE 'SEE-THROUGH' GIRL
(Fort Monroe)

(Author's note: In "The Ghosts of Tidewater" (1990), and repeated in "The Ghosts of Virginia, Volume I," (1993), I included a chapter on the multiple ghosts at Fort Monroe. Here is an update, received from Mike Namorato in July 1996:)

My wife, Janice, and I were at Robert E. Lee's quarters at Fort Monroe on July 15 for a birthday party for a three-year-old girl. Later, I went down to the laundry room to look for a broom. I was alone. Suddenly, I felt the presence of someone else standing in the room. As I turned around, I could feel the hair on the back of my neck standing up. It was then that I saw a little girl, maybe about six years old. She had blonde hair and looked a lot like my wife. She was wearing a blue and white dress of another era. It looked sort of like an Amish-type dress.

"I could see right through her! I could see the line of the wall behind her. I heard the faint whisper of a giggle. She appeared to wave to me, and then she turned and *walked through the wall*!

"I got out of there as fast as I could. When I told the people upstairs what I had seen, they laughed at me. But when they saw how pale and white I was, and how serious I was, they stopped. It was then that Dennis Harrington, who lives there now, told me he had heard the sounds of children crying downstairs when he was upstairs, but he never went down to investigate. And he added that his three-year-old son told him that sometimes 'little kids' play with him in the house during the day, and tickle his feet in bed at night.

* * * * *

OLD HAUNTS IN ALEXANDRIA

From Ms. Corrinne M. Broadt:

I was born in Alexandria and so was my son. I am 72 years of age now and have many many memories of Alexandria in the 'old days.' I was born on Bashford Lane, at the foot of North Pitt Street. Miss Margaret J. Bashford was my godmother and we lived on her farm. My father cared for the farm animals and gardens. He delivered milk all over Alexandria. . . Your books prompted me to write this letter and may bring back memories to you." (The author lived in Alexandria as a child.)

* * * * *

THE SEAPORT INN ON KING STREET

During World War II, I worked at the Torpedo Station. After work a group of us used to go to 'Uncle Billy's Crabhouse,' where the Seaport Inn stands today. My cousin worked on this building when they decided to locate on this block. He said there were disturbing noises the entire time he was painting. He said it was very 'eerie.' Some of his tools were constantly 'misplaced.' There were some old papers found in the rafters of the building, found during the refurbishment. They pertained to the founding of Alexandria.

* * * * *

THE INT. ASSOCIATION OF THE CHIEFS OF POLICE BUILDING

This was once a spark plug factory and then I heard it was a cotton mill. I remember it being a vacant building until they refurbished it and made it into Belle Haven Apartments. The building is located at 515 North Washington Street — the same side as the Lee-Fendell House. Well this was another reason why I was frightened of this area. There was a figure with a fisherman's hat and coat, and I believe it has moved to the cupola. I remember it being on the top floor.

"Well, I heard on a ghost tour that the night watchman was murdered in that building, and so they came up with this figure so as to make the murderer think it was his victim watching him. They were always in hopes the criminal would return to the scene of the crime. On Halloween some kids broke in there and stole the figure and hung it from the bridge, but it was eventually returned. It attracted the attention of everyone crossing that bridge, because folks thought a man had committed suicide.

"But you know what? I was compelled to look up and gaze at that figure when I was walking on the other side of the street."

* * * * *

A TANGLE WITH A 'SPOOK' TREE

The following letter, with some paraphrasing from the author, is from Calvin Webb of Lauren Fork, Virginia:

Why I am so interested in the old tales and folklore I do not know. All I can think of is the reason youth leads us all to adventure and exploration of anything to do with the nature of the unknown.

"I always used to go bow hunting in the dark. On one of my trips out of the big woods, I stopped to visit with my aunt. She was in her early 70s then. She told me old tales about witches and the sort. I laughed at her foolishness, and she became stern with me. She said that if I believed in the Bible I would know there is a Devil and that he has helpers, too.

"The night was dark. Not a star or moon in the sky when I left her house. I was really tense and wound up. I was thinking about the tales I had heard and the pitch black night didn't help."

(At this point, Calvin thought he had an encounter with the supernatural. He said it felt like someone's giant arms had grabbed him, and something was banging him in the back of the head.)

"I kicked, bit and spit with all my might. I fought tooth and nail for what seemed like several minutes."

(Calvin thought he was literally fighting for his life. In reality, he had walked into a tree with low hanging branches, and had gotten all tangled up in the darkness. He was thrashing about with limbs and branches.)

"Finally, I realized what had happened. The next day I went back. There were needles and limbs everywhere. I tried to tromp back the roots, but everyone wondered what had happened to that old tree for years. I never told."

* * * * *

PHANTOM FOOTSTEPS IN THE DARK

From Thomas Drumheller, Craigsville, Virginia:

nclosed is a picture of the old Norfolk & Western railroad bridge (near Front Royal). It was said that many tramps lost their lives trying to cross this bridge, that people could hear footsteps walking on the ties, but no one ever saw anyone doing the walking. Quite strange isn't it?

In a full moon night this writer and three others were walking on this same railroad bridge, and about half way across we started to hear footsteps coming from behind us. When we turned to look backwards, no one could be seen, however, when we started to walk again, the same footsteps started up, too. Every time we'd stop, so would the invisible being, whoever or whatever it was.

"Mr. Eston C. Cook, who died recently, once told me that he was on the bridge one night and felt like someone was touching his back pants pocket. He thought that someone had sneaked up behind him and was trying to rob him. But he turned around and there was no one there.

"The bridge was near the Riverton Lime & Stone Company plant in the vicinity of the hamlet of Riverton. There were several quarries located in that area. Mr. Cook told me they had once found a skeleton in one of the quarries."

(Author's note: In doing some research on this area I learned that on September 22, 1864, two of Colonel John S. Mosby's men were hanged in the vicinity of the bridge by order of General George A. Custer. Five other Confederate soldiers were shot at Front Royal. Later Mosby retaliated by capturing and executing some of Custer's men. Thus, if there was a spirit haunting the bridge, there were several possible candidates with good cause.)

The Ghost Train at Lomax Crossing

(Nottoway County)

(Author's note: In past books in this series I have written about ghost-like lights that mysteriously appear and disappear on train tracks. Perhaps the best known phenomena occurs near West Point, Virginia, between Williamsburg and Richmond, at a remote site known as the Cohoke Crossing. A light appears far down the tracks to observers, gets progressively larger as it nears, and then, just before it passes, vaporizes. The legend behind it is that a Confederate troop train, loaded with wounded and exhausted soldiers, left Richmond sometime in 1862, bound for West Point where the men could rest and recuperate. It never arrived, and no one seems to know what happened to it. Hence the spectral light.

What is unusual in this case is the number of witnesses who have claimed to see this light over the years. There are literally hundreds, if not thousands. They all swear by it as a genuine manifestation.

Apparently, it continues to be sighted, for late in December 1996, I got the following letter from Bobby Corson of Ooltewah, Tennessee. He wrote of an experience he had encountered a short time earlier.)

y father decided that he wanted to take me to go see a thing he said would scare me to death . . . the West Point light. We arrived at the tracks, and I must say it was quite frightening, and no more than five minutes after we got there, the light began its journey down the track. I was kind of afraid at this point, and I can very easily recall my hand shaking as I reached down to get my binoculars. I brought them up to my eyes, and it seemed as though there was a silhouette in the middle of the light! We didn't make a move, and the light vanished 20 feet away."

There are other "light" encounters. There is one, for instance, in Suffolk near the Great Dismal Swamp. On an isolated stretch of track here, people have reported seeing a light "dance" down the track for a few seconds, as if someone were swinging a lantern, and then vanish. Here, the prevailing theory is that it is the spirit of a brakeman who was killed at this site in a horrible train accident decades ago. Some say he was decapitated and he returns to search for his head.

But certainly one of the most fascinating instances I have heard involves the sighting of an entire ghost train, engine and all. It was written about in 1985 by Kay Ragland Boyd, who lives near Crewe, and whose grandfather was a railroad man and often told her tales of the yards when she was a young girl. This particular account, published in the Crewe-Burkeville Journal, was told to her by the late W. L. Bass, W. T. Bradshaw and W. T. Vaughan as an unexplained and true incident that occurred in the 19th century. Here is Kay's write-up, reprinted with her gracious permission:)

The early spring night was cool with a thin crescent moon low on the horizon. Above the single track of the Southside Railway, a plume of black smoke showed darker than the unclouded, star-patterned sky. At intervals, a lonesome whistle of a steam engine cut through the stillness of Nottoway County.

"The westbound train, part passenger, part freight, thundered by the sleeping village of which the courthouse was the dominant building. In the after-midnight silence, the melody of the whistle indicated its passing Cherry Tree Crossing: another two long, two short blasts signaled the train's approach to Lomax Crossing. And then, a roar, a crash, an outpouring of steam, a flash of fire, and screams that tore the night to shreds.

"In the latter third of the 19th century, train accidents were frequently followed by the horror of fire which fed on wooden furnishings, equipment and oil lamps for passenger coach illumination. The engine and all five cars derailed, all but the last car crashing down a high embankment west of Lomax Crossing, known to this day as Rodgers' Bank. The town of Crewe was not yet in existence and how and when help arrived is not known.

"A number of passengers were seriously injured and the engineer and fireman killed in the accident. It was presumed that a 'hot journal box' was the cause of the train's derailing. Whatever the reason, however, a short time after repairs were effected and service resumed over that stretch of road, strange occurrences began in the vicinity of Rodgers' Bank and Lomax Crossing.

"A belated farmer and his wife, returning from Black's and White's (Blackstone), approached Lomax Crossing shortly after midnight. Both saw a train coming toward them from the direction of Nottoway Courthouse. Its approach was silent; no harmonious whistle of the locomotive rent the air although its headlight was visible and as they waited for the engine and five cars to pass, they saw lights gleaming in the two passenger coaches. After the last car had passed, the flickering red tail lights disappeared up the track to the west.

"The farmer's horse, usually a tractable, easily controlled animal, snorted with terror and shied violently. When finally quieted, the creature had to be led across the track by its owner.

"Not long thereafter another strange incident took place in the same locality. The engine crew of an eastbound freight saw what appeared to be the headlamp of a train coming at them from the opposite direction on the then single track line. As the fireman shouted 'Head on!', the engineer set his brakes, believing the proximity of the 'other train' would result in a collision momentarily. Both men were aware of a fleeting, penetrating chill, but no collision.

"On looking down the track they saw nothing. The rails, faintly visible ahead of their engine, were clear of all obstructions. As the train moved on toward its destination, the fireman said in an awed tone to the engineer, "I guess we've seen the ghost train we've been hearing about.' To which the engineer replied, 'I thought we were goners for sure. I hope we never see it again.' The fireman resigned from the company and the engineer requested and obtained a transfer.

"The owner of a sizeable plantation some three miles southwest of Lomax Crossing had spent the day with friends at Locust Grove. The gentleman had heard tales of the mysterious phantom train, but had laughed at 'some folks' imaginations running way with them. He was to be convinced that very night.

"As his buggy approached the track, he saw the headlight of a westbound train. He whipped up his horse and made for the crossing to pass over the track ahead of the train. One of the front wheels of the buggy caught in the rail in some manner, placing both himself and his horse in what he considered to be imminent danger.

"When his frantic efforts to free the wheel failed, with the headlight moving inexorably closer, he ran a safe distance, abandoning his horse and vehicle to their fate. The planter saw an engine and five cars reach Lomax Crossing, pass harmlessly *through* his stalled rig, and disappear up the track toward Rodgers' Bank. The horse, completely uninjured but wild with fright, bolted, freeing the buggy and going off at a mad pace toward home. The planter, shaken and thoroughly bewildered by the strange encounter with the spectral train, was obliged to walk the remaining distance to his residence. The story, told and re-told by his descendants, assumed the flavor of a legend.

"As the eye witness accounts of the ghost train escalated, a group of Nottoway County planters and businessmen decided to investigate the matter and to find some explanation. Lomax Crossing was being avoided even in daylight and the party of men formulated a plan. Three of them went to Cherry Tree Crossing (east) and several more to Eleven Oaks Crossing (west), while the remainder stationed themselves on both sides of the track at Lomax Crossing (located east of Crewe within sight of the Hillcrest Dairy Farm). This was done routinely for a week or more from 10 p.m. until 1 a.m., for the sightings had all been in that time frame.

"Their perseverance was rewarded at last. Those at Lomax (a total of seven responsible witnesses) saw the headlight to the east rapidly approaching their position. No sound of locomotive, no rumble of wheels over track accompanied the light. Some admitted to having been aware of the black smoke drifting upward, and all saw illuminated passengers coaches and the dim red lights of the last car as it vanished to the westward.

"When the entire group assembled to compare notes, the following facts became known: those stationed at Cherry Tree saw and heard nothing out of the ordinary — no train passed their check point. The men who had waited at Eleven Oaks told the same: no train had come from either direction. Yet the group at Lomax all saw the phantom engine and five cars.

"Shortly afterward, the Norfolk & Western Railway purchased

the line, made extensive repairs and improvements, and rail traffic increased until the spectral train lost its significance in the frequent passage of freight and passenger scheduled runs.

"Is it not possible that the mysterious silent steam engine with its nebulous five cars may yet pass Lomax Crossing in the night, unnoticed by the progress of modern rail travel? Does a ghostly plume of smoke occasionally hang low over the gleaming rails of steel and is it swept away as a four-unit diesel freight thunders down the track at high speed?

"Will anyone ever know?"

CHAPTER 21

The Mad Carpenter of Cocatamoth

"Henrico County"

he small headline in Richmond Enquirer on Sunday, September 27, 1874, said cryptically: "The Henrico Ghost: A Specter Carpenter Running His Saw." The brief article beneath it described an extraordinary mystery that has remained unsolved for well over 100 years.

It occurred at the old Cocatamoth estate, about two and a half miles "below" the city on the long-extinct Osborne turnpike. The house was an old fashioned two-story framed building which, in that day, commanded a beautiful view of the James River. It was formerly known as the Tatum residence, bore a "splendid reputation," and was the scene of "many a hospitable gathering."

All of that changed abruptly shortly after J. W. Southard, collector of Varina township, and a "gentleman of good standing," moved into the house with his family. Specifically, the date was Wednesday, September 23, 1874. On that night "commenced manifestations upon the premises which are beyond the ken of any man, and which, to say the least, are passing strange."

Southard, who slept on the ground floor, was awakened early that evening by a noise of what he described as "the drawing of lines on the under side of the floor of his chamber with some blunt instrument." This was followed by the unmistakable sounds of sawing and blows of a hammer and other noises "similar to those made in using various carpenters' tools."

Southard got up and investigated, but could find no source for the disturbance. The next night he heard the same sounds, but again could find nothing. In fact, as soon as he got out of bed, the noise stopped. He walked around the house and then stood outside in the dark for some time, but heard only the natural sounds of nightfall. Maddeningly, as soon as he returned to bed, the phantom carpenter began banging away again and continued until about two in the morning.

When the sawing and hammering began again on Friday, the third successive night, Southard decided he had had enough and was going to get to the bottom of things once and for all. By this time his wife, terrified, said she was leaving to visit relatives in the country until things cleared up.

Working like a man possessed, Southard tore up the floor boards of his chamber, but there was nothing there. He then loaded his double-barreled shotgun, took extra shells, grabbed a knife and a light. He went outside, placed the knife in his teeth, pirate-style, and crawled as far under the house as he could go. He then fired both barrels in the direction of where the noises seemed to be coming from.

Satisfied that he had done all he could, and that if the noises were being made by any mortal being, he had silenced the source for good, he retired to bed. No sooner had he turned down the lamp and pulled up his covers, when the hammering and sawing began anew and continued through the night.

Curiously, it was noted that Southard had two "vicious" dogs that slept under the house. Not once during all the activity did they stir, except when he blasted his shotgun.

Southard was described in the article as an "ex-Confederate soldier, and a man who is afraid of nothing, and not the person to make a statement of this character unless it was true." In fact, he offered to take anyone to his place "who doubted his experience with the ghost," and said he was determined to resolve the dilemma if possible.

There is no record of what happened after that — of whether he ever did find out the cause, or whether the incessant nocturnal work of a persistent spirit carpenter eventually drove him and his family from the house.

An Evil Presence
in Powhatan

(Powhatan County)

(Author's note: I don't know about you, but it would be scary enough for me just to work in a prison, especially one where all sorts of criminals, including murderers, are daily processed, classified, and transferred to other institutions. I mean, like they used to say on the old Shadow radio programs, "Who knows what evil lurks in the minds . . ."

That would be frightening enough, but at least you would know you were dealing with live human beings, regardless of what terrible acts they may have committed. You would be dealing with known entities. But what if, at that same institution, there was also an element of the unknown? What if there were all sorts of ghostly manifestations, too? What if locked doors mysteriously opened, and open doors were slammed shut by unseen hands? What if machines, showers, fountains and other things turned themselves on and off seemingly at will? What if dark shadows were glimpsed out of the corner of one's eye, and figures materialized and then vanished when one looked directly at them? What if whispers called your name in the dead of night and no one was there? What if one saw a pair of eyes glowing in the dark, or felt the overwhelming presence of an evil spirit in an otherwise empty room? And what if you knew you weren't crazy experiencing such inexplicable phenomena, because many of your fellow officers saw and felt the same things you did?

Such apparently is the case at the Powhatan Reception and Classification Center at State Farm, Virginia, about 25 miles or so west of Richmond in Powhatan County. A broad range of such ethereal manifestations was brought to my attention one evening in September 1996 by Sergeant Carl Tuten, a 15-year-veteran of the commonwealth's prison systems, who has been at the Powhatan facility since 1989.

He told me that there had been reports of ghostly activity even before he began work there. But things had been pretty quiet until October 13, 1995 — Friday the 13th. It was then that a young man was brought to the prison for processing. He allegedly had murdered his grandmother in what was, at the time, a highly publicized case. According to Carl, from that day, and continuing up to the present, "things started to happen." Whether or not the "things" are in some way tied to this particular prisoner is not known. It could be only coincidence. Nevertheless, for the past two years there have been a series of mysterious incidents which have occurred, whatever the cause. Carl Tuten, in fact, documented this activity. Whenever something happened, he took notes. He recorded the encounter and who experienced it. In a series of conversations, and from his notes, here is what Carl had to say:)

F irst, let me emphasize, that all I have personally witnessed is true. I have no reason to make such things up. I cannot explain a lot of the things that have taken place, yet I either saw or heard them myself, or others told me about them. Sometimes more than one person would tell me about a specific occurrence, unaware that others had experienced the exact same thing. I feel that there have been too many different witnesses for all this to be just coincidence. There is something more here."

What are these manifestations? Carl says they seemed to start right after the prisoner previously mentioned was admitted in October 1995.

** "I work the midnight shift, 12 a.m. to 8 a.m. When I came in to work on October 14th I went upstairs to the clerical department to run off some copies on the copying machine. The machine suddenly came on by itself. I checked it out. There was no way that that machine could have tripped itself.

"I then felt a heavy presence in the room, like there was someone or something else there. It's hard to explain, but it felt like there was an evil force. It was so powerful, my senses were running wild. A really eerie feeling came over me, all over my body, from head to toe. I had to get out of there.

"As I was walking by the treatment area, I heard a weird laugh. It didn't sound human. I looked around, but there was no one there.

** "The next day I had to go back to the clerical department to run some copies off, and when I closed the door, I again felt a powerful force in the room. It was invisible, but it was like someone was watching me. Why, I don't know. I searched all around, but I was alone. Yet it was the most powerful feeling I had ever had, and I believed it was evil.

"I was not the only one to sense this," Carl says. "Another officer told me that there was 'something wrong' in the records department. He said that on three successive nights, October 14th through the 16th, he had been in the room by himself and felt like someone was watching him. He said it also got very cold in the room. The feeling ended when he left the room, but he was visibly shaken.

** "That same week I asked a fellow officer to open the front door to the Treatment Room because a doctor was coming in. He did, but then the door closed by itself. There was no one there or nothing to cause it to close. There was no wind. It's like a tomb in that area. The officer said when it happened a 'bad feeling' came over him.

** "Another officer was in the clerical department running off copies. He was standing, reading a paper on the wall, when he said he felt something move up to his right side. Out of the corner of his eye he saw a man standing there. When he turned his head to look directly, there was nothing there!

** "A sergeant who has a skeptical nature told me he once saw a face looking at him from one of the empty offices in the treatment area. The doors have a small glass in them which you can look through. He also said he saw a dark shadow move across the treatment door on the inside. Another officer told me he had seen a shadow lurking inside the treatment area. He described it exactly as the sergeant had, although he didn't know the sergeant had seen it, too.

** "Two secretaries told me that they have felt 'something' in the clerical department. One said that she felt a sudden cold rush of air, as if the roof had opened up. Others have also told of feeling the coldness in this area.

** "A few days later I stopped and talked to one of the inmates. He told me that at about 2:30 in the morning he was awakened by a female voice calling his name. He thought it was the nurse bringing him some medication. He got up and went to the bars in front of his cell, but there was no one there. I asked him if he had heard voices before, and he said he had. He asked me not to tell, because he didn't want anyone to think he was crazy. They might send him to the psychiatric ward. I assured him I wouldn't tell. He then lit a cigarette and told me the past week had been 'hell;' that he had heard his name being called four or five times, always late at night, by a female voice, and every time he got up there wasn't anyone around.

** "One night an officer was at work in the main control area. He controlled the doors. The door to one gate had been out of order for several weeks. Yet somehow the light came on for that door to be opened. It hadn't been working. He got up and looked down the hallway. There was no one there. Who pushed the button for that light to come on? And how did it come on, since it wasn't working? ** "There have been other door 'incidents.' One evening, for no apparent reason, six doors in a control room opened by themselves. Now they have to be opened either electronically or by key. There is no way they can open by themselves.

** "One night a sergeant was getting some information in the records department when he heard water running. He saw that the water fountain was on, but no one was there. He went over and turned it off. Then it came on again by itself. I saw this myself.

** "An officer once witnessed a shower that came on by itself. How did this happen? Showers are regulated by depressing a button. You must keep pushing the button.

** "Another officer and I saw water running from a toilet sink one night. You could put your hand directly under the water and *not get wet*! It was as if something was holding a hand under the water.

** "There have been a couple of strange things involving inmates. Once, an officer said that during a thunder storm he saw what appeared to be 'fire balls' coming out of a cell. And one sergeant said he saw an inmate's eyes 'glowing orange' in the dark. He said there was an eerie glow all over the inmate's cell.

** "Once a computer printed out the words 'blood born' about 25 times although no one had pushed the print button.

** "The numbers 666 keep coming up in different ways. As one example, when we processed a prisoner his numbers added up to 6, he was put in cell C-3 (the third letter plus three equals 6), and 6 copies of his forms were run off. These numbers keep surfacing.

** "There are many other things. Doors open and shut with no reason; toilets flush without being touched; an adding machine keeps turning itself on; voices are heard in areas when no one is there; faces and forms appear and then disappear right before your eyes.

** "One of the most recent, and to me, one of the most telling events, was witnessed by me and two other sergeants. We were standing in a room when a potted plant started spinning by itself. We all saw it. Now, this plant is suspended from the ceiling and there was no air flow whatsoever in the room. It was perfectly still. All of a sudden the plant started spinning from side to side. Then it stopped. I said if that plant starts up spinning again, that's a sign. And just then it started spinning again! You explain that to me.

"Like I say, a lot of things are happening here. I don't know if they are related to that incident on Friday the 13th in October 1995 or not," Sergeant Tuten says. "All I can tell you is that it seemed like things started up then, and they are still going on. There are some very serious minded people here who have seen these things, not to mention myself. One sergeant, for instance, discounted everything until he saw that plant spinning. That made a believer out of him. Too many things have happened to too many people here for this not to be something supernaturally related.

"I know I cannot explain it. And I know how I've felt. There have been times up in that clerical department when I felt an evilness there. What causes it or why it's there, I don't know. But believe me, it's there!"

CHAPTER 23

Cases of Disappearing Families

The Vanishing Judge
(Near the Kentucky state line)

t was a magnificent plantation, located in the Cumberland Gap area. It was owned by a man and his wife. They had three daughters, a son and a small baby. Inexplicably, one day in 1858, the entire family vanished without a trace. Friends came to the house and found everything in place, furniture, clothes, food. Nothing had been touched, yet no word of the family surfaced.

As the mansion lay unoccupied, it lapsed into disrepair. As the war clouds were gathering, scavengers stripped the wooden outbuildings and fences for firewood. They did it in broad daylight, because no one would venture near the house after dark. The strange and inexplicable disappearance of the man, woman and five children quickly caused the spread of rumors that the plantation was indeed haunted.

A year later such rumors seemed to be confirmed. It was in June 1859 that two men approached the decaying mansion. They were Colonel J. C. McArdle, a lawyer, and Myron Veigh, a judge. Both were from Frankfort, Kentucky, and knew nothing of the dark secrets held within the walls of the house. It was purely by chance that they were riding by when they became caught in a fierce thunderstorm.

Curiously, they saw lights coming from the house and decided that it was their best opportunity to ride out the storm there. They hitched their horses in a nearby shed and then approached the mansion. They pounded on the front door, but there was no response. They tried the door but it wouldn't budge. They managed to force in a side door. Inside was darkness and an eerie silence. For a moment, in fact, McArdle thought he might have been struck deaf, for he could not hear the pounding of the rain outside, the howling of the wind, or the crackle of the thunder. He decided to go back outside, and turned a doorknob through which he thought he had entered. But in the darkness he instead opened an inner door leading to another room.

McArdle told what happened next years later in an interview published in the Frankfort Advocate in August 1876: "The apartment was suffused with a faint greenish light," he said, "the source of which I could not determine, though nothing was sharply defined. . . . The only objects within the blank stone walls of that room were *human corpses*! In number they were perhaps eight or ten — it may well be understood that I did not truly count them."

McArdle continued: "They were of different ages, or rather sizes, from infancy up, and of both sexes. All were prostrate on the floor, excepting one, apparently a young woman, who sat up, her back supported by an angle of the wall. A babe was clasped in the arms of another and older woman. A half-grown lad lay face downward across the legs of a full-bearded man. One or two were nearly naked, and the hand of a young girl held the fragment of a gown which she had torn open at the breast. The bodies were in various stages of decay, all greatly shrunken in face and figure. Some were little more than skeletons.

"While I stood stupefied with horror by this ghastly spectacle and still holding open the door, by some unaccountable perversity my attention was diverted from the shocking scene . . . Among other things, I observed the door that I was holding open was of heavy iron plates, riveted . . . I turned the knob and three strong bolts were retracted with the edge; released it, and they shot out. It was a spring lock. On the inside there was no knob, nor any kind of projection — a smooth surface of iron." At this point, Judge Veigh pushed McArdle aside and began to enter the room with the corpses. McArdle pleaded: "For God's sake, do not go in there. Let us leave this dreadful place at once!" The judge paid no heed and went in anyway, walking quickly to the center of the room where he kneeled beside one of the bodies.

"A strong disagreeable odor came through the doorway, completely overpowering me," McArdle said in the interview. "My senses reeled; I felt myself falling, and in clutching at the edge of the door for support, pushed it shut with a sharp click." He thus locked the judge in the room of death. Colonel McArdle must have then passed out from fright. How else would one explain the fact that he was found the next day lying unconscious in the road several miles from the mansion. For six weeks he lay in a state of nervous fever and constant delirium. Only then did he regain his senses.

Continuing his account in the newspaper, McArdle said: "No one believed a word of my story, and who can wonder? And who can imagine my grief when, arriving at my home in Frankfort two months later, I learned that Judge Veigh had never been heard of since that night?"

Apparently, friends of the judge searched the house thoroughly after McArdle had been found. But they failed to find any mysterious room, locked tight, as McArdle had described. "After all these years I am still confident that excavations which I have neither the legal right to undertake nor the wealth to make, would disclose the secret of the disappearance of my unhappy friend, and possibly of the former occupants and owner of the deserted and now destroyed house," McArdle said. (The house was burned to the ground in 1863.)

"I do not despair of yet bringing about such a search, and it is a source of deep grief to me that it has been delayed by the undeserved hostility and unwise incredulity of the family and friends of the late Judge Veigh," McArdle concluded.

The colonel died on December 13, 1879, going to his grave with the mystery still unsolved.

* * * * *

RETURN OF A MURDERED VICTIM?
(Richmond)

In the decades before the town of Manchester, south of the James River, became part of Richmond (1910), there was a long-standing legend surrounding an old house said to have been built before the Revolutionary War. It was described as a two-story brick mansion with beautiful paneling and a magnificent circular staircase. It is believed the house was built by a Mr. Wardlaw. It was a house of suspected tragedies and deep mysteries.

According to the legend, the house was suddenly deserted shortly after its construction was completed. No one seemed to know why those living there suddenly departed, or where they went. It stood empty for several years, and during this period a number of witnesses reported strange sights when they passed by. It began to garner a reputation as being haunted.

And then, sometime shortly before the turn of the 19th century, the house just as suddenly — and just as mysteriously — was reoccupied. But the new tenants seemed to generate more new questions than answers. It became apparent a couple had moved in with a small child, but they were rarely seen by their neighbors. Two servants did most of the shopping, and performed the chores. One evening three men from the town went up to the house and knocked on the door. In peering inside, they glimpsed the man and woman and the child. They asked if they could be of any assistance, but were abruptly told to leave.

Three years later the tenants vanished, again with no hint of where they went or why. Curiously, the house was still furnished, complete with a child's toys. The mansion and the grounds then fell into disrepair, and the reputation for its haunting grew.

One night, on a dare, a young man entered the house to spend the evening. Friends found him in a field outside the next morning, semi-conscious. He said he had been led out of the house by a beautiful female ghost.

There were other reports of supernatural phenomena. One young boy, riding by the house at dusk one day on his pony, swore he heard screams, and saw a white figure in the window, waving a skeleton!

The questions festered for more than a century. Why had two different families suddenly moved out of the house, without a trace? If there was a resident ghost, who was it, and why was it there? What dark secrets did the house contain?

A possible answer surfaced more than a century after the mansion had been built. It appeared in the form of a newspaper article in the Richmond Times Dispatch in August 1879. According to the news item, a "young and dashing" English officer of "high rank and wealthy personage," may have lived in the house. He apparently fell in love with a local beauty, but "she spurned him despite repeated attempts to win her." In 1787, he is said to have killed her on the spot in what the newspaper called "one of the most shocking murders known to the people of this vicinity." He then fled to England to escape prosecution.

* * * * *

WHAT HAPPENED AT THE HURT HOUSE?
(Lynchburg)

 he mystery has remained unsolved for the past 80 years.

Something bizarre must have happened at the Hurt family home in Lynchburg in the year 1918. The house had been built in 1884, and apparently, 32 years later, there must have been an argument of monumental proportions. The argument was about what color to paint the mansion. At least it is thought that was what it was about. Nobody really knows what happened inside its walls. Whatever it was, the house suddenly was vacant, and remained that way until 1948, when a contractor was hired to demolish the house.

When the crew arrived to begin the dismantling, they were astonished to find everything inside — *intact*! It was just as it must have been when the family left the house, never to return, in 1918. There were clothes of that era still hanging in closets, period furniture untouched, even dishes still on the table.

The contractor sold all of the furnishings except for one beautiful antique bed. This he gave to a family member, but when that person tried to sleep in it the first night, the bed reportedly shook so bad, it frightened the new owner. The next day he chopped it up for firewood.

CHAPTER 24

A Tragedy of
Gold and Greed

(Goochland County)

here is a splendid folklorian tale of greed, gold, mystery, brutal murder, and incessant hauntings worthy of Edgar Allan Poe himself, that has been passed down through generations of Goochland County natives for more than a century and a half. Like many such legends, the details have worn so thin with the passage of time that the actual names of the principals are as lost today as are the ill-gotten gains upon which the story revolves. The last accounting of this particular drama surfaced in the form of a letter to the editor of a Richmond newspaper more than 60 years ago. However, it is such an interesting — and plausible — narrative that it is worthy of retelling even if there is no way to authenticate the facts.

One gathers from the letter that the "old Waller gold mine" in Goochland County, "about 40 miles up the James River from Richmond," was reopened sometime in the early 1930s, after having been shut down and forgotten for three quarters of a century. This mine had been one of a number actively mined in the 1830s and 1840s. And, apparently, quite a horde of gold was harvested here, for the letter's author refers to Waller as being: "known the world over as the richest gold mine in America and in which was found some fabulously rich ore." So, obviously, this had to be some years before Mr. Sutter discovered the first huge nuggets in

California which led to the great gold rush of 1849.

Near the Waller mine there was a large wooden frame house which has been described as being two stories high with "gray, weather-beaten boards and gaping doors and windows (which) conspire to make it far from inviting." It was still standing in the 1930s, at least, and was said then to be haunted. Further description includes a yard "within the crumbled fence, grown with tangled shrubs and weeds (which) shows that for a long time there has been an absence of human life there. Even the big chimney . . . assumes a towering and suggestive look."

According to the legend, strange noises have been heard there, especially late at night. Among these are, "the despairing cry as of someone about to pass into the unknown." So scary and realistic were these sounds that the house became known as "a place where no one cares to go and where many hurry by."

It was here where several employees of Waller mine lived during its heyday. Some of them were a little bit less than honest, and secretly pocketed some of the gold. One man in particular had squirreled away a sizeable cache which he kept hidden in a secret spot near the house. One of his fellow roomers followed him one day and learned the location of the steadily-building treasure trove.

A few nights later the occupants of the house were awakened by a piercing scream from the room of the man who had stolen the gold. They rushed in and found him lying unconscious on the floor. His head had been bashed in by some kind of blunt instrument. He died without regaining consciousness. A following investigation failed to turn up the slightest clue as to who killed him or why, and the case remained unsolved for many years. Waller mine subsequently ran out of the mother lode and was boarded up with the employees scattering in all directions of the map.

The roomer who had followed the employee to his hiding place met with an accident of his own years later, and, on his death bed, attempted to atone for his sin by confessing that it was, indeed, he who had murdered the man. He told how he had crept into the room that night with the intention of killing him, and that when he stepped on a creaky board in the floor, the man had risen from his bed asking, "Who's there?" He had then crashed a lethal blow upon the man's head with a pole ax. When the man screamed as he fell, his assailant ran back to his room, hid the ax, then came out and joined the others seeking the source of the scream. He later buried the ax, and, in time, when things settled down, he dug up the hidden gold and left for the north.

But, he added, he had never enjoyed his sudden wealth. Rather, he gave a vivid account of how the dead man had relentlessly haunted him by day and by night; how he had suffered more than "a thousand deaths," and had never known a peaceful moment from the time he struck the fatal blow.

Even his last minute confession, however, did not seem to appease the spirit of his victim, for the strange noises in the old house, long vacant, continued to occur for decades afterward. Goochland County oldtimers say it was the restless ghost of the dead gold miner still searching vainly for his lost treasure.

CHAPTER 25

The House of Tombstones

(Petersburg)

(Author's note: What is it about strange old houses in Petersburg? In "The Ghosts of Virginia, Volume II," (1994), I wrote about the truly bizarre Trapezium House of the eccentric Charles O'Hara, at 244 North Market Street in the city. He had the house built with no right angles anywhere inside — in the belief that such a design would ward off "evil spirits." Hence the name Trapezium — a four sided figure with no two lines parallel. It was never fully determined whether O'Hara was successful in his quest.

Through more recent research, and a conversation with Richmond Times Dispatch staff writer Jon Pope, comes yet another unusual, to say the least, structure in Petersburg. It is known, simply as "The Tombstone House," and, understandably, it is now one of the stops on annual Halloween tours put on by the Tourism Department of the city.

The house is located at 1736 Young's Road, and, also understandably, it is vacant. It is made of 2,200 tombstones of the Civil War dead! No wonder Gwyn Headley, author of the book, "Architectural Follies in America: An Illustrated Guide to 130 of the Most Unusual Structures in America," called it "The Eeriest House in America." As she put it, "The eeriest house in America is not the Bates' mansion from Hitchcock's 'Psycho,' but a simple, unassuming little house standing in a quiet suburb of Petersburg, Virginia."

"It looks just like a normal old house with a front porch made of these stones," says Suzanne Savery, of the Tourism Department.

"Houses are built out of marble occasionally, but not very often. And houses built out of tombstones are probably very rare. I'm not aware of any others."

Pope, who wrote a feature article on the house for Halloween 1996, says the slabs used to build the house are "mostly the bottom portions of tombstones of Union soldiers buried at nearby Poplar Grove National Cemetery." Petersburg National Battlefield historian Chris Calkins says that from 1866 to 1869, the remains of 6,178 soldiers were moved to the cemetery from Petersburg and surrounding areas. Here they stood until 1934.

Then, the National Park Service, in a move to make maintenance easier, pulled the tombstones from the ground and cut off the bottoms. The upper portions, in most cases, were reset horizontally on the graves.

Along came an enterprising builder, a man named Oswald Young. He bought the stones for $45. Mixed in with the lower slabs, were the upper portions of some tombstones. Some still had inscriptions, such as one which reads, "3611, A. Harrison, U.S.C." Calkins said this stone probably belonged to a soldier from the U. S. Colored Troops who was killed at the famous Battle of the Crater on the Petersburg Battlefield. Other top stones were built into the house facing inward.

Calkins believes that only damaged stones were sold. He says the Park Service probably replaced these with new tombstones. "It's not like they got rid of anybody's grave or anything," he told Pope.

Oswald Young built his economic house in 1935, and according to his daughter, never thought much about it. That was, however, until a short time afterward when two ladies from some northern historical society descended upon him and accused him of the desecration of the graves of Federal soldiers. "I thought they were going to put me in jail, Young was quoted in an old newspaper article. Young's daughter, Ruth Vaughan, and his daughter-in-law, Thelma Young both lived in the house at one time, but neither seemed concerned with residing among the tombstones of forgotten Civil War soldiers.

One might well suspect that such a house might harbor some disturbed spirits of the men whose markers were taken from their resting places. But apparently this is not the case. When asked, Calkins said he knew of no ghostly manifestations at the Tombstone House. In his article, Pope quoted Sammy and Ima Jean Conkle, who have lived next door for more than 20 years. "I'm not afraid of it because it's made out of tombstones"' Mrs. Conkle said. "We ain't never seen no ghosts."

Strange indeed.

* * * * *

Speaking of tombstones, there is a most curious one in the old Tombstone Cemetery in the Hollins vicinity of Roanoke County. It was carved sometime in the early 1800s by Laurence Krone, the most noted of the early 19th century Valley German stone carvers, and was designed as memorial to a young boy who tragically died. His name was Robert Denton. Says the Virginia Landmarks Register: "The monument is in the form of a small coffin containing a folk image of the deceased child. It is decorated with Germanic folk motifs and is covered with a lengthy inscription in Latin, German and English. The head and upper torso were originally covered by a removable stone which has since disappeared." Mysterious.

CHAPTER 26

The True Story of the
Trueheart Ghost

(Richmond)

(Author's note: In "The Ghosts of Virginia, Volume I," (1993), I
included a chapter titled "The Skeleton with the Tortoise Shell
Comb." It is one of my favorites. When I give talks I generally
include it, and when I come to the twist ending, I often hear gasps
from the audience.

To refresh memories, it involved the apparitional appearance
of a small woman with a high, finely-carved tortoise shell comb in
the back of her hair. It was first told by Mrs. Elizabeth Terhune,
who, under the pen name of Marion Harland, became one of
Virginia's finest writers of the 19th century. In her autobiography,
"The Story of My Life," she wrote that the ghost appeared to her
when she was a child in her family home, then known as the
Hawes House on East Leigh Street in Richmond. She and others in
the house saw the apparitional figure on several occasions. No one
knew who the spirit lady was or why she materialized there.

Some years later, after the family had moved from the house,
workmen, digging in the front yard, found the skeletal remains of
a small woman, unconfined, with a tortoise shell comb behind her
skull! The theory was then advanced that this woman, whoever
she was, had been trying, in ghostly form, to let others know she
had not been properly buried. Once she was reinterred, the apparition was never seen again.

That, in a nutshell, was the legend. In my research for this volume, however, while browsing in the Daedalus book store (90,000

used books) on Fourth Street in Charlottesville during the 1997 Festival of the Book, at which I spoke, I pulled from the extensive Virginiana section there, a dusty volume, "Judith -A Chronicle of Old Virginia." It was published in 1883. I became absorbed with it when I saw the author's name — Marion Harland. I didn't even look at the price. I had to have it.

It was a compelling study of the "everyday" reminiscences of a young girl in 19th century Virginia complete with historical vignettes of infamous Richmond events such as the great 1811 theater fire, and the "Gabriel" slave insurrection. Then, when I reached chapter 11, I was thrilled to see that it related to something Mrs. Terhune called "The Trueheart Ghost." I read on with excited fascination. It turns out, "The Trueheart Ghost" is, in reality, another, more detailed, and more spellbinding version of "The Tortoise Shell Ghost." The setting is different. It occurs to a woman Mrs. Terhune refers to as "Aunt Betsey," and at another house; one then called "Selma," which once was located on the outskirts of Richmond. The principal characters are Aunt Betsey, who may, in fact, have been Mrs. Terhune, and a woman named "Madam Trueheart."

Whether the author is referring to her own encounters, as being those of Aunt Betsey's, or to her real Aunt Betsey, I don't know. Mrs. Terhume, however, vouches for the absolute authenticity of the experience. Whatever, I found it to be such a riveting classic of suspense, told in the author's rich style, and different enough from the rendition published in volume I of this series, that I include it here in excerpted form. The setting is sometime in the early to mid-19th century. There is a terrible winter storm howling, and Aunt Betsey is relating the Trueheart ghost story to a group of young people who have gathered for a holiday party. Amidst the flashes of lightning and the crackle of thunder, in the darkened, candle-lit parlor, she begins:)

adam Trueheart . . . was a widow when she married Colonel Trueheart. She was a cousin of my mother. . . Her features were fine and distinguished, and her carriage was a model of dignity and grace. . . As she grew older she was reserved and grave. After the death of her husband and the loss, one after another, of four children, she was rarely seen to smile. Colonel Trueheart was a jolly, loud-talking, loud-laughing, fox-hunting 'squire of the old English school.' His (first) wife had been dead a year when he paid a visit to Mrs. Bland's (Madam Trueheart) brother, in Amelia County, fell violently in love with her, and gave her no peace until she married him.

". . . His residence, Selma, about half a mile beyond the city of Richmond, was left to these two. It was a beautiful place, and had a large plantation attached to it. The Colonel lived like a lord — plenty of servants, blooded horses, a pack of hounds, a cellar of choice wines, and a houseful of company the year around. His table was celebrated as one of the best in the state.

"He got louder in talk and redder in the face; ate and drank more, and hunted harder every year, his wife all the time growing paler and quieter. It was said she got out of the habit of talking through spending so much time alone, for the Colonel was very little at home, except when his dining days and game and oyster suppers were on hand. . . Madam Trueheart gradually fell into a way of remaining behind at Selma . . . she was not in strong health, and had no relish for gay society.

". . . She read a great deal and wrote much, generally at night, sitting up very late at her secretary, writing for hours and hours. Her desk was full of manuscripts — so said those who had chanced to see it open during her lifetime. When she died it was empty. She had burned every page, even the letters she had received.

"The Colonel went first, ten years before her, and, as everybody had predicted, was carried off by apoplexy. . . The homestead was left to her during her lifetime. . . Five or six years after his death I went to Richmond to visit my friends, the Pleasantses. Madam Trueheart drove into town to see me as soon as she heard I was there and invited me to spend a week at Selma. The house was of brick and large, with a deep hall running throughout the entire depth. At the right of this as you entered was a great drawing-room, with windows at the front and side. Behind this was 'the chamber' where Madam sat by day and slept by night . . . On the other side of the hall was a sort of ante-room, a cross-passage, out of which the staircase ran up to the second floor. An arch, filled with a Venetian-blind door, separated this from the main hall, and another archway, just like it, divided the front hall from the back. Next to the ante-chamber was the dining room; back of it a smaller apartment, which I was to occupy. The library was in a wing, jutting out at the rear of my bedroom.

". . . It impressed me sadly that (first) evening to fancy how many nights she must have sat just there, with no company but the lamp and the fire. I wondered, as I had often heard others do, that she could be willing to lead such a solitary life.

"She had not told me to bring my maid, and one of hers had waited on me when I arrived that day. This woman was in my bedroom now. Madam dismissed her when she had seen that fire, water and towels were all right. I recalled then, as one of the peculiarities I had heard spoken of, that she never let a servant stay in the house overnight. An immense Newfoundland dog slept on the hearth-rug in the chamber, and in the day patrolled the premises. Madam may have been eccentric in some respects, but she was all goodness to me . . ."

(Two nights later, Betsey is about to retire to her room.)

" . . . My brain was not excited by talk or stimulant. I never felt better or brighter than when I lighted my candle to go to my room. Rosina, the servant who waited on me, had gone to bed early with a headache.

" 'I will see that all is in order in your chamber,' said Madam.

" 'Please don't stir,' I begged. 'I am surely sufficiently at home to look after myself a little,' and off I went.

"My wax candle gave an excellent light, and I carried it before me. In closing the door of Madam's bedroom I faced that of mine just across the passage. This was narrower than the square front hall, being not more than six feet wide, and shut off from that by Venetian blinds. These I had seen Madam bolt at the same time that I locked the back door at the other end of the passage . . . Just as I shut the chamber door behind me, a little woman started right out of the opposite door, glided slowly along the wall, her head bowed upon her hands — in this way — crouching as she went, and vanished at the green blinds.

"Who was that?' thought I, catching my breath. 'Probably one of the servants who had fallen asleep in my room, and slipped out of sight when she heard me coming. She moved like a cat.' Then, like a flash of lightning — 'How did she get through the blinds without unbolting them?' Lastly — 'She did not open my door — *only came out of it!*'

"We come of a brave race, and I had always prided myself upon being afraid of nothing. My father had trained us to hold ghost stories in profound contempt. I had never had a thrill of superstitious dread in my life; yet I staggered back into Madam's room, white as a shroud, set down the candle I was too weak to hold, and said: 'I have seen a ghost!'

"Madam was as pale as I — stood up, straight and rigid.

" 'Child! what do you say'

" 'If there is such a thing as a ghost, I have seen one!'

"Without a word she picked up my candle and walked into the hall. I heard her try blinds and back door, go into my room and examine the fastenings of my windows. When she came back she poured out a glass of wine and made me drink it, looking so set and stern that I was afraid she did not believe me.

" 'Indeed, ma'am,' I said, sick and trembling, and stammering on every word, 'I am sorry I startled you — very much ashamed to seem so foolish! But I did see something! Quite near to me — so close I could almost have touched it!'

" 'I do not doubt it, child. What was it?'

"A small woman, dressed in some sort of grayish-yellow gown. Her head was bent low, so that I could not see her face. She seemed to shrink away from me as she slipped along close to the wall. She disappeared at the blinds. But they did not open; nor my door, to let her out!'

"I began to shake again.

" 'Do not try to talk, my dear! You shall sleep with me tonight,' said Madam, soothingly. 'Tomorrow, if you wish it, you shall go back to town.'

"Not another syllable would she let me speak about the fright. She went to my room with me to get what I needed for that night and next morning, for which I was infinitely obliged to her. I could not forget that IT had come out of that chamber, and I dared not glance over my shoulder.

" . . . I told Madam (the next morning) that I preferred to remain a few days longer with her if she would allow it. What I had seen might have been an optical illusion — a trick of my brain, caused by too much reading and too little exercise. . . She was gratified and touched. . . She only stipulated that I should tell nobody.

" 'I should be extremely sorry were the house to get the reputation of being haunted,' she remarked. . . 'If this story were to get abroad it would lower the value of (the house) seriously. It would be hard to dispose of it at any price.'

"That night I stayed again in her chamber, resting well and seeing and hearing nothing unusual. The next evening, just before supper time, we were agreeably surprised by a visit from Captain Macon.

"At ten o'clock he arose to go, and I went with him to the parlor door. 'Why, the hall is all dark!' I exclaimed.

"It was usually lighted by three wax candles in a chandelier hanging from the ceiling. We supposed, in talking of it afterward, that they must have been blown out by a gust of wind from the back door when the servants left the house for the night. The door of the drawing-room had a way of swinging-to of itself, and as I passed the threshold it shut behind us. Our eyes were naturally drawn, in the absence of other light, to a window directly opposite. The shutters of this were open, and the moonbeams streamed in. I have described the sort of ante-chamber at the left of the front hall.

"Through the archway connecting the two we had a full view of the staircase. It was broad, and had two landings. On the lower was the moonlit window, opening down to the floor. Somebody was descending the stairs between the upper and lower landings. A small figure, all in white, a gown that trailed on the steps behind her, and over her head something like a long bridal veil.

"I caught Captain Macon's arm, too terrified to utter a word. It did not occur to him that there was anything supernatural in the appearance, but imagining that I meant him to be quiet, he stood perfectly still with me in the recess made by the closed parlor door. The Thing came down very slowly, step by step, making no noise as it moved; crossed the flood of moonlight, turned on the landing and glided down the four remaining steps, its back to the window, and, therefore, facing us. It was within ten feet of us when Madam Trueheart's voice was heard from the back hall.

" 'Did I hear you say that the lights are out, Betsey?' she called.

"The Creature — whatever It was — disappeared instantly! It did not run away or sink into the floor or rise into the air, but simply was *not*! The place where it had stood a second before was empty, and we had not moved our eyes from it.

". . .Why I neither fainted nor went into hysterics I do not know . . . Captain Macon complimented me on my nerve. Madam expressed her thankfulness that the shock had not been a serious injury to me. She was cool and collected through it all. At Captain Macon's earnest request, she let him take a light and examine every part of the house. Besides ourselves not a human being was in it.

" 'May I ask of you, as a great favor, to spend the night in this house?' she said to our guest.

"He bowed. 'I am honored by the invitation, Madam, and accept it with pleasure.'

"Madam did a singular thing (for her), yet it was the most sensible step she could have taken. She took us into her confidence.

" 'It was within six months after I came to Selma to live that I had the first intimation that all was not right with the house,' she said. 'Colonel Trueheart was not at home, and I had gone to bed rather early one night, leaving the fire burning as brightly as it does now. I was not drowsy, but the firelight was too strong to be comfortable to my eyes, and I shut them, lying quietly at ease among the pillows, my thoughts busy and far away. There was no sound except the crackling of the blaze, but suddenly I felt the pressure of two hands on the bed clothes covering my feet. They rested there for a moment, were lifted and laid upon my ankles, moving regularly upward until I felt them lie more heavily on my chest.

" 'I was sure that a robber had found his way into the house and wanted to convince himself that I was really asleep before beginning to plunder. My one hope of life was to remain perfectly still, to breathe easily, and keep my eyes shut. This I did, the sense of hearing made more acute by intense excitement, but my reason singularly steady. When the hands reached my chest Something looked close into my face. There was no breath or audible movement, but I felt the gaze. Then the pressure was removed — the Presence was gone! I lay still until I counted deliberately 50, to assure myself that I was in full possession of my senses, and sat up. The fire showed every object distinctly. I was alone in the chamber. I arose, looked under the bed and in the wardrobe, but found nobody. The windows and shutters were bolted fast, the door was locked. Yet, so strong was my persuasion that the visitation was not a trick of the imagination that I sat up for the rest of the night, keeping fire and candle burning.

" 'When Colonel Trueheart returned I told him what had happened. He laughed heartily, and 'hoped the like might occur when he was at home.' Three months later I felt the same pressure in the same order of movement. It was on a warm night in spring, and through the lighter coverings I fancied I could discern that the hands were small, the fingers slight, like those of a child or a little woman. I tried to call the Colonel, but could not speak until the Presence had stooped, as before, to look into my face and departed.

" 'Colonel Trueheart awoke at my voice, was greatly amazed at what I told him, and insisted upon making just such a tour of the house as you have just instituted, Captain Macon. This over, he tried to convince me that I had been dreaming, or that the sensation was caused by some obstruction of circulation. I did not argue the point, but when, some weeks afterward, I had a similar experience, asked him seriously if he had ever heard that anyone else was disturbed in this way. He hesitated, tried to put me off, and finally owned that his first wife had declared to him privately her belief that the house was haunted. That she had complained of hearing unaccountable noises at night; that Things passed and touched her in the halls after dark; and once in the daytime, when she was sitting alone in her room, Something had plucked her by the elbow with such force as almost to pull her from her chair.

" 'If sickly women and superstitious Negroes are to be believed, half the country houses in Virginia are haunted,' he said.

" 'He cautioned me to say nothing on the subject, else 'there would be no such thing as keeping a servant on the premises, and the house would not sell for the worth of the bricks should it ever come into the market.'

(Madam Trueheart continues.) " 'Two years went by without further disturbance. Then it came in a different form. One night, as I was locking the back door, holding a candle in my left hand, I heard a slight sound, like a sigh or long breath, and, looking up, saw a woman moving past and away from me, just as Betsey has described. She was dressed in a misty yellow-gray or grayish-yellow gown, as Betsey saw her, but with a white handkerchief or cap on her head. I had time to notice that she was small of stature, and that she glided along noiselessly. At the closed Venetian blinds she vanished.

" '. . . Again, for months, nothing unusual occurred. Then the pressure of the hands became frequent. From that time up to the night preceding Colonel Trueheart's death scarcely a fortnight elapsed without my feeling them. Always beginning at my feet — always ending at my chest; always that long *felt* gaze into my face, then It was gone! Sometimes I strained my eyes in the darkness to catch some outline or shadow; again and again I opened them abruptly in the firelight or moonlight to surprise whatever it might be into revealing Itself. I never beheld face or shape or any visible token of living thing.

" '. . . On the night before he died he had retired in his usual health, and I sat up late writing. My desk stood at one side of the fireplace, my back being toward that window. About twelve o'clock I was startled by a rustling behind me, and turned quickly, but saw nothing. Something swept right by me, with a sound like the waving of silk drapery, and passed toward the bed. I followed It, looked under the valance, behind the curtains — all through the room, but found nobody. I said aloud, to reassure myself, 'It must have been the wind!' and returned to my desk.

"'In perhaps 15 minutes I heard the same sound going by me, as before, toward the bed. In just half an hour more by my watch, which I had laid on the desk, It came again. Carlo (the dog), then hardly more than a puppy, howled and ran behind the chair.

"' . . . Colonel Trueheart arose next morning to all appearances perfectly well. At nine o'clock he had an apoplectic stroke. At twelve he died.

"'. . . But once in five years have I had any reason to believe that the uneasy spirit — if spirit it was — still walked the premises. One night, in the second year of my widowhood, as I was coming down stairs, soon after supper, with a light in my hand, I heard the sweeping of a gown, the tap of high heels behind me. On the lower landing I stopped, wheeled short around, held up my light, and looked back. The steps had been close on my track, but the staircase was empty and now silent.

"'I had flattered myself that there would never be a return of ghostly sights or sounds after four years of exemption. Least of all did I dream that one not connected with the family would be visited by such apparitions should they come.' (With this, Madam Trueheart concluded her story. Aunt Betsey continues.)

"Captain Macon privately instituted inquiries, at a later period, regarding the past history of the house, but without striking any trail that promised to unravel the mystery. It had been built by a Trueheart, and the estate had descended in the direct line to the Colonel. We pledged our word voluntarily to Madam never to speak of what we had seen while the truth could affect the value of the property, or cast imputation upon the character of those who had owned it. We kept silent until Madam had been 15 years in her grave. Then Captain Macon rode over one day to show me a paragraph in a Richmond newspaper. I can repeat it word for word:

"'The march of improvement westward has condemned to demolition, among other fine old mansions, Selma, the ancestral home of the Truehearts. . . In order to effect an equitable division of the estate, the residence and contiguous plantation were sold. The extensive grounds have been cut up into building lots, and the mansion — a noble one in its day, although sadly neglected of late years — standing directly in the line of extension of _____ Street, has been bought by the city to be pulled down and carted away.

"'In grading the sidewalk of the proposed thoroughfare, it was necessary to dig down six feet below the present level, laying bare the foundations of the building. At the depth of four feet from the surface, directly under the windows, and distant scarcely three feet from the drawing room, the workmen disinterred the skeleton of a woman of diminutive stature, which had evidently lain there for years.

" 'There were no signs of a coffin or coffin plate. A high tortoise-shell comb, richly wrought, was found by the head. The oldest inhabitant of our city has no recollection of any interment near this spot, nor would decent burial have been made so close to the surface. The whole affair is wrapped in mystery.'

"How the storm roars," (Aunt Betsey said to her audience of young people.) "Heaven have mercy upon the homeless souls wandering between sky and earth tonight! Papa told me that the secret is a secret still, the tragedy unexplained.

". . . I know nothing beyond what you have heard. But — women who die natural deaths and have Christian burials do not wear expensive combs, such as belonging to party-dresses, when they are shrouded for the grave. Nor are they thrust into the ground unconfined!"

To this, author Marion Harland, a.k.a, Mrs. Mary Elizabeth Terhune, added this strange footnote to the chapter: "The author deems it well to state that she vouches personally for the authenticity . . . in every particular, of the story related.

"She offers no explanation, nor is she herself a believer in 'spiritualistic' phenomena, or in the vulgar hypothesis of apparitions from the world of shades. The history of the Trueheart Ghost is, from first to last, one of *facts*, supported by testimony that cannot be impugned. She has not been able to withstand the temptation to put these upon record as a curious study of the supernatural — or the unaccountable."

CHAPTER 27

A Haunting Game of Hide and Seek

(King William County)

I t is almost hidden in time; all but lost from the mad rush of modern civilization that daily charges through Virginia's cities and suburban areas. It is a lone and lonely beacon reflecting on a resplendent past when grace, grandeur and chivalry reigned in the commonwealth of 200 or so years ago.

This is state road 600, which runs northwest of the hamlet of Aylett in King William County, roughly halfway between Ashland and Tappahannock. It is an historic corridor that connects a number of the magnificent plantation homes of yore. The names ring out as reminders of an era all but swallowed by a high-tech, super-highway, electronic, televised society. Yet as one meanders down this country lane, passing by these 18th century monoliths, there comes a glimpse, however brief, into the storied heritage of our ancestors. Here, for example, one finds Elsing Green, Cownes, Burlington, and The Meadow — each with a thousand stories to tell.

"All of these old homes are supposed to have their ghosts, aren't they?" asks Bette Gwathmey, wife of retired surgeon Owen Gwathmey, who grew up in the area. And, indeed, it seems they may well have. Take Elsing Green, which the Virginia Landmarks Register describes as "One of the most impressive of the Tidewater plantations . . . marked by a prodigious U-shaped house that ranks

Burlington

among the purest expressions of colonial Virginia's formal architectural idiom." Here, the land stretches along the Pamunkey
River, and was owned in the 17th century by Colonel William
Dandridge. The property was purchased in 1753 by Carter Braxton,
a signer of the Declaration of Independence, who, the Register
says, "probably built the main house." The mansion burned in the
early 1800s, "but its brick walls, regarded as a superb example of
Virginia's colonial masonry, survived unmarred." Hence, it was
rebuilt within these walls and developed into a model farm.

Bette Gwathmey recalls the time she and Owen were invited to
Elsing Green and she abruptly asked her hosts if there was a ghost
in the house. "It was strange," Bette says. "I had a vision of a beautiful young woman with raven-dark hair standing over a bed
upstairs. She was wearing a red dress." The owner then told her
that, yes, such an apparition had been sighted, but she had red
hair, not dark hair. "Maybe I got the hair mixed up with the red
dress," Bette offers.

At another house on route 600, Cownes, Bette was visiting one
day when she, and others, clearly heard the loud clomping of
heavy boots upstairs walking across the floor and then descending

the stairs. It frightened the guests, but when they went to see who it was, no one was there. There was a legend that the spirit of an old sea captain continued to reside there long after his death. "A friend of mine, Olive Lewis, now deceased, told me she saw a lady in an old-fashioned hoop skirt on the stairs at Cownes once," Bette says. "We never found out who that might have been."

At the Meadow, which dates to the early 1800s, Bette's daughter has heard doors opening and slamming shut, and dresser drawers opening and closing when no one was in the house.

But perhaps the most interesting legend is centered at Burlington — a house with a curious and controversial history. It has been in the Gwathmey family since the third quarter of the 18th century. It was built on Indian land. This was once the domain of the Mattaponi Indians, and evidence of their prehistoric occupation has been found at the site. The most important artifact discovered, according to the Virginia Landmarks Register, is a rare log canoe. It is now the property of the Valentine Museum in Richmond.

The main portion of the house, in Classical Revival style, was built in 1842 for William Gwathmey, grandson of Owen Gwathmey II, who settled in King William County as early as 1767. The land descended through five generations of the Gwathmey family. For most of the 20th century, the house was owned by John Ryland Gwathmey, who, in his later years, childless, turned into somewhat of an eccentric.

The present Owen Gwathmey, who lives "next door" to Burlington, assumed for years that he would inherit Burlington from his great uncle. But in the last five of his 94 years on earth, John Gwathmey rewrote his will 17 times. In a rather bizarre twist, Owen says John "got mad at him because he came down here once with a girl who wore blue jeans. John allegedly said that the madam of the house should dress better than that. He then wrote Owen out of the will, and, instead, gave the house, at his death in 1982, to the Virginia Historic Preservation Foundation.

John's tombstone, in the family graveyard, reads, "A friend to all . . . A succourer of many." Ironically, the foundation did not have the money needed to successively restore the house, and, recently, it was purchased by Owen's son, who is now in the process of renovating it.

Whether or not the ghostly "gray lady" of Burlington will remain through the repairs until the former splendor is restored, is not known. This lady haunted the house earlier in the century when John lived there with his old maid sisters. "He told me about it ever since I was a child," says Owen. He said the lady appeared to him, and to his sisters, on innumerable occasions over the years.

"It was always the same. He said he would be sitting at the dining room table, eating, and the woman would appear in the doorway. She was always dressed in gray. My uncle would get up from the table, but when he got to the doorway, he would see her disappear into the library. He would follow her, but when he got to the library, he would catch a glimpse of her going up the stairs. He would go up after her. He would last see her entering the attic. But when he reached the attic, she would be gone — vanished."

Owen said they never really knew who the lady was. "My uncle believed that it was a woman who either had died or been killed in the house long ago. He said John's father, who died in the 1920s, had told John he had seen the apparition, too. Anyway, she always led him to the attic. Maybe that's where she died."

Is she still there? Will she reappear once the work on the house is completed? Only time will tell.

CHAPTER 28

The Merry Spirits of Michie Tavern

s there a party still going on in the wee hours of the night at historic Michie Tavern on the outskirts of Charlottesville? There are some, including psychic experts and off-the-street tourists alike, who have sworn they have heard the raucous sounds of unbridled gaiety in and around the third floor ballroom of the tavern. And there is no denying that this room was the scene of many wing-dinging bashes during the days of our forefathers, more than 200 years ago.

But there seems to be a split in the opinion of the official hostesses at the site. Some today say such tales are likely figments of over-active imaginations which have been embellished in the telling and retelling over the years. They contend the party ended centuries ago and there are no ghostly revelers in the old tavern today. Some of their fellow workers disagree strongly. "I'm sure there's a ghost here," said one recently. "I personally haven't seen it, and it's always in the ballroom." "Is there a ghost on the third floor," another hostess repeated the question asked her. "Oh, yes. I haven't experienced it, but enough people have told me about it, so there must be something to it. They say they hear the noises of a party going on, things like that."

One lady even offered that there might be two spirits in the tavern area — one in the ballroom and quite another in the old general store and grist mill down the hill from the tavern proper. A subsequent inquiry to a cashier-hostess there drew a positive response. "Yes, there definitely is something here. 'He' opens cupboard doors at times, and we hear him walking around upstairs when all the tourists have gone for the day. We think he just wants to let us know 'he's' around."

So there remains some debate as to whether or not supernatural manifestations occur at Michie. Perhaps the spectral merrymaking may be heard only by the psychically sensitive which could well account for the difference in opinions. Either way, however, Michie (pronounced Mickey) Tavern is a splendid and colorful edifice that was, for eons, a favored stopover in stage coach days, and currently carries on that tradition of hospitality. At an adjacent, 200-year-old slave house called "The Ordinary," present-day visitors can be treated to typical dishes of the colonial period, including Southern fried chicken, blackeyed peas, stewed tomatoes, cole slaw, potato salad, green bean salad, tavern beets, homemade biscuits, cornbread and homemade apple cobbler. Local Virginia wines are available to, "slake one's thirst."

The building itself was opened as a tavern in 1784 after Scotsman John Michie had purchased the land in 1746 from Patrick Henry's father. It was opened, the senior Michie said, to accommodate the many travelers seeking food and shelter at his home. Its original location was on Old Buck Mountain Road in the Earlysville area, about 17 miles from Charlottesville. Just what statesmen-celebrities frequented the place is a matter of conjecture. Actually, confusion might be a better word.

According to the accounts of many writers, including some area brochures, the tavern was the one-time haunt of such giants of history as Jefferson, Madison, Monroe and Andrew Jackson. But in his fine history, "Albemarle: Jefferson's County," author John Hammond Moore indicates the only notable former guest cited by the Charlottesville Progress was "Lafayette, who, it was said once was put up there by Jefferson so he could enjoy a few days of hunting." Whatever, in 1927, the inn was dismantled piece by piece and moved to its present location, near the city, on Route 53, close to both Monticello and Ash Lawn.

While it may be questionable as to who frequented Michie in the late 18th and early 19th centuries, it is nevertheless generally agreed that it has been beautifully restored and maintained in the traditions of that colorful era. The tavern contains a large and fine collection of pre-revolutionary furniture and artifacts, including many of those from the original Michie owners. William Michie's rifle, for instance, hangs over the mantel in the Keeping Hall.

Michie Tavern near Charlottesville

It also is interesting to peruse a copy of the old tavern rules which were dispensed with stern authority in the 18th century. One specified, for example, that no more than five men could sleep in a bed at night. When one tours the tavern and sees the size of the beds, which are smaller than current double beds, one wonders how five people could even cram into such tight space, much less sleep. Boots in bed were forbidden, thankfully. The price was right. Lodging was cheaper than the evening meal; four pence a night for bed and six pence for supper. There was some discrimination, though. Organ grinders were relegated to sleep in the washhouse, and no razor grinders or tinkers were taken in!

The tavern has three floors and a large number of rooms. One of the most interesting — and the one many people say is haunted —is the ballroom on the third floor. It has a long-held reputation of harboring a cluster of ghosts. But they are friendly, high-spirited ones. It is in the ballroom that psychics and others psychically sensitive have said that they have heard the sounds of partying, and felt the presence of a group of men and women thoroughly enjoying themselves. They have heard and sensed this, but no one has seen any of the people participating in the fun making. The most common manifestations reported have included the distant sound of laughter, of gay music, and the tinkling of glasses.

Others have said and written that they felt some sort of confrontation, a kind of embarrassment, took place here. It also has been written that the waltz, introduced from Europe, was danced here in the ballroom for the first time in America. Tying in with this, there is a legend that during the first waltz, a Charlottesville belle, a young girl, danced with a dashing Frenchman and he had held her closely. This had never been seen before, and caused considerable social shock waves through the town's gentry. It has been speculated that this was the alleged source of embarrassment that has been sensed there. As for the partying, well, there were many gala occasions in the ballroom two centuries ago.

Perhaps some of the participants enjoyed themselves so much, they decided to linger on and share their happiness with visitors from other eras. Whether one can "tune in" on such festivities today probably is doubtful, but then again, Michie is now, as it has been since 1784, a hospitable retreat from which the dust of the road can be pleasantly washed away.

CHAPTER 29

The Sad Secret at Dulwitch Manor

(Amherst County)

(Author's note: Gary Duden of Virginia Beach (who talks about his four past lives in another section of this book) and his wife, Peggy, spent a night some time ago in a beautiful Victorian bed and breakfast called Dulwitch Manor in Amherst County, north of Lynchburg. That evening Gary was in bed in an upstairs bedroom, lying in the dark, when he sensed someone walking around the foot of the bed. He assumed it was Peggy. He asked what she was doing, and then, to his complete surprise, heard Peggy answer from the bathroom. He turned on the lights. There was no one else in the room.

The next morning he told the inn's owners, Bob and Judy Reilly, about what happened. They smiled. It was not the first time such phenomena had been reported at the 85 year old mansion. Dulwitch Manor was built in 1912 by Herman Page, who also built the well-known Page House in Norfolk. He was a real estate tycoon and built in Amherst County because he believed it would become a major railroad center. When that didn't happen he left the area and his son moved in.

Located just east of highway 29, the main artery between Charlottesville and Lynchburg, and right off route 60, the house is "at the end of a winding country lane and set on a hill of five secluded acres," It features Flemish bond brickwork and fluted columns. The area abounds with natural beauty and is surrounded by the Washington and Jefferson National Forests.

"Our bedchambers are reminiscent of an English country home

with canopied brass or beautiful antique beds," says Judy. Some rooms have their own fireplaces or window sets. The Scarborough room includes a whirlpool/tub. Also included is a, full scrumptious country breakfast with inn-baked muffins, and specially prepared entrees, accompanied by country sausage or bacon.

Being a native of Lynchburg — my grandparents moved to the area in the late 1800s and settled in Amherst County — I was especially interested in possible ghost activity at Dulwitch Manor. I talked to Judy Reilly. She and her husband have run the inn for the past eight years, having moved south from New Jersey.)

I don't know if I believe in such things or not," she says. "I know my husband doesn't, and I have to say nothing out of the ordinary has happened to either one of us here. But some of our guests seemed to have experienced strange things. I will say that when we first moved in, a friend of ours said she got a very chilly feeling when we went up to the third floor. And there's something else I can't quite explain. I took a photo of the house once for a brochure. When I got the pictures back there was someone sitting on the porch waving. I know there was no one on that porch when I took the photo."

There may, in fact, be two separate spirits residing here. "Not

Dulwitch Manor

long ago," Judy continues, "we had a man and his wife come into the dining room one day. The man asked me who the lady in the red dress was. I didn't see any lady in a red dress. He said it was an older lady, with perfectly coiffed hair. He said she walked around the side of the dining room and then disappeared. His wife said she hadn't seen the woman, and I know we didn't have any guest in the house at the time that fit his description.

"Another time we had a family staying here. In the third floor bedroom one night, the father said he saw a young man enter the room. He was wearing white shorts and mumbling something. He also vanished. We thought it may have been another guest who could have been sleep walking. We didn't think any more about it.

"Then, later, another guest reported a similar incident. A lady from Ohio said she was in bed one night, in the third floor bedroom, when she, too, saw a young man in white shorts. She said he was leaning over the bed, 'fanning' her. She said she knew it wasn't her husband, because he was in bed next to her."

The lady in the red dress remains a mystery, but there may be a clue as to the identity of the young man in the white shorts. He may have been the grandson of the manor's builder. It is believed that he was a cadet at the Virginia Military Institute who lived there sometime in the 1940s. He apparently was a physical fitness enthusiast who had rigged up some exercise and weight lifting equipment with barbells, pulleys and cables.

According to local tradition he was found dead one day, strangled in the cables. There were some in the county who believed foul play was involved, but that was never proved. The bedroom on the third floor was his room.

"We really don't know what happened back then," Judy Reilly says. "But if it is his ghost, it seems to be a benevolent one."

Civil War Spirits
Continue to Roam

(Various sites)

(Author's note: Civil War spirits just won't seem to die! In 1995 I wrote a book on ghosts of the War Between the States, and in "The Ghosts of Virginia, Volume III," published a year later, I added some additional accounts. And still there are more! In the Civil War book, I quoted from an article written by a gracious lady named Kay Ragland Boyd. Kay lives in Manakin Sabot, Virginia, which is near Crewe, which is a few miles southeast of Farmville.

She is a columnist for the weekly Crewe-Burkeville Journal. During the first or second week of April each year, Kay has written a number of Civil War-related articles to coincide with the anniversary of Robert E. Lee's last march from Petersburg to Appomattox, which went through the Crewe area. Here, for example, is Saylor's Creek, scene of one of the last great battles.

Kay called me one evening in January 1997, and told me about other ghosts she has written about. "It goes back to when I was a child," she said. "My grandfather was a railroad engineer, and he could tell railroad stories by the hour. I was fascinated by the accounts and I started taking notes. I wrote on scraps of paper, anything. I've been writing about the tales I've heard ever since." In fact, Kay and her son have had their own spectral encounter — near the site of Gaines' Mill. There is, she says, a ghost there named Amos Fremont, from Texas, who was with General Hood's brigade. She believes he is still there, and still trying to get home to the Lone Star State.

Following are some incidents Kay wrote about in 1983, along with historical notations by me.)

* * * * *

THE ANGEL OF MARYE'S HEIGHTS

here is a ridge behind Fredericksburg known as Marye's Heights. At its base was a breast-high stone wall, which marked the path of the famous sunken road. It was here, in December 1862, that one of the most fierce battles of the Civil War was fought. It was here that Union General Ambrose Burnside led a massive army of 120,000 to attack Robert E. Lee's forces. But first, Burnside's men had to cross the Rappahannock River. As Federal engineers tried to set up a system of pontoon bridges, they were picked off, one by one, by a brigade of Mississippi sharpshooters. Infuriated, Burnside ordered his artillery to fire on the beleaguered city. One hundred cannon bombarded Fredericksburg at point-blank range. Houses and buildings were blown apart, heavily damaged or collapsed under the relentless onslaught.

Meanwhile, Lee had a force of 78,000 Confederate infantrymen and 300 cannon. He set them up strategically at Marye's Heights,

protected by the stone wall. The morning of Saturday, December 13, 1862, dawned cold and foggy. It was late morning before the fog lifted enough for Burnside to order an attack. Alarmed at the huge mass of manpower, Confederate General James Longstreet asked his artillery officer if he could stem a frontal attack. He reportedly told the general that once he opened fire down into the huge, unobstructed plain which lay before him, that "not even a chicken could live" under such a barrage from the cannon.

And so it was. All during that fateful day Burnside ordered wave after wave of Union troops to storm the Rebel position. The artillery cut gaping holes in the ranks. As historian Bruce Catton put it, "In the end the battle was decided by the infantry." One Union soldier later wrote that the Confederate gunners, visibly busy around their pieces, looked "like fiends who stirred infernal fires." Sheltered by the stone wall, the Southern infantrymen literally mowed down the charging Yankees, time after time. Bullets flew in sheets of fire and flame, and the plain became littered with the dead, dying and wounded. So intense was the shelling that the entire battlefield at times became totally clouded in huge billows of smoke.

Amidst all this noise emerged another, and perhaps more fearful sound — the Rebel Yell. Cannon: "Across the open plain, shaken by the blast of many guns, there rose the high unearthly keen of the Rebel Yell — that hellish yell." Wrote a Federal surgeon: "I have never, since I was born, heard so fearful a noise as a Rebel Yell. It is nothing like a hurrah, but rather a regular wildcat screech." Added a veteran from the Sixth Wisconsin: "There is nothing like it this side of the infernal region, and the peculiar corkscrew sensation that it sends down your backbone under these circumstances can never be told. You have to feel it, and if you say you did not feel it and heard the yell, you have never been there!" Of the yell, Stonewall Jackson called it, "The sweetest music I ever heard."

The fighting continued all afternoon and right up until the curtain of darkness fell. It was a devastating defeat for the North. Union casualties were 12,600 killed, wounded and missing. It was a massacre, reminiscent of the Confederate debacle at Malvern Hill, and the ill-fated charge of Pickett at Gettysburg. Southern casualties were 5,300.

That night there was an incredible act of personal heroism. A young Confederate sergeant from South Carolina, Richard Kirkland, could not sleep. He heard the moans and cries of dying and wounded men only a few yards away from his position behind the stone wall.

An article in the March 1908 issue of "The Confederate Veteran" magazine describes what happened next: " . . . The plain was covered with the enemy's dead and wounded. The weather was very cold, and the dying men were crying piteously for water. Kirkland was touched by their cries, and, going to General Kershaw, said in a spirit of seeming insubordination: 'General, I can't stand this!'

" 'You can't stand what, Kirkland?'

" 'Those poor fellows out there are our enemies, it is true; but they are wounded and dying, and they are helpless! I have come to ask leave to carry water to them.'

"General Kershaw, looking with unspeakable admiration upon the boy, said: 'Why, Kirkland, don't you see the danger? If you were to place your cap on your ramrod and elevate it above the wall behind which our line is formed, it would be riddled with bullets instantly. But what you propose is so noble and indicates so magnificently what a glorious soldier you are that I cannot say no. Go, my dear boy, perform your mission, and may God shield and preserve you.'

"General Kershaw said that he watched the brave fellow as he went about his self-imposed task: how he collected all the canteens he could and crawled to a well nearby and filled them, and then crawled back to the wall and leaped over; how he was greeted by almost a volley from the sharpshooters; how he went about under fire among the wounded; how he adjusted one poor fellow's wounded arm or leg and arranged another's knapsack under his head, so that he could rest more comfortably; how the wounded over the field, discovering that he was an angel of mercy, sat up and beckoned to and called him; and how the enemy, observing and realizing what he was doing, ceased firing in admiration of the boy's noble conduct, and Richard Kirkland completed his self-imposed task and returned unhurt! Does history furnish a finer type of heroism or self-denial?

". . . Kirkland faced the sharpshooters and almost certain death to relieve the distress of his enemies. And we may rest assured that on that cold December night one Confederate soldier, though chilled and hungry and covered only by his blanket, sank to rest with his heart warmed by the thought of a humane act bravely performed.

"After Chancellorsville and Gettysburg, through both of which he had passed unscathed, poor Kirkland was killed at

Chickamauga where the monument marks the spot rendered glorious by Kershaw's Brigade. Kirkland fought to the last gasp, saying: 'Tell pa goodby. I did my duty. I died at my post.'

"His body was recovered and buried with his kindred on White Oak Creek in Kershaw County, South Carolina, in a most sequestered, unfrequented, and inaccessible spot." (Even so, it was said that when they brought his body home, "you couldn't hitch a horse within a quarter mile of his house, there was such a crowd.")

Richard Kirkland had become a legend.

He has forever since been known at the "Angel of Mayre's Heights."

Here is what Kay Ragland Boyd wrote about this historic site: "At Mayre's Heights, Fredericksburg, the story arose around a bizarre incident that reportedly occurred on the anniversary of the battle for many years. Indeed, it may still be taking place there.

"Out of a white mist a phantom horseman emerges, vague and shadowy, but becoming ever clearer as he rides the length of the Confederate front. His gray dress uniform and slouch hat indicate an officer. He carries a sword upraised. There is no sound; no audible hoofbeats from his ghostly steed. He slowly rides deeper into the twilight gloom and vanishes.

"Who is he? No one knows."

* * * * *

THE STILLNESS BROKEN

t Manassas," Boyd wrote, "the stillness of the far-reaching battleground is broken at irregular intervals by the distant sound of heavy artillery — the low, sullen rumble of cannon fire, and the staccato crackling of musketry. The battle sounds seem to advance and retreat until all is silent again. The South was victorious twice at Bull Run, and even now the phantom Rebel men stand guard over their hard-won, bloody ground."

*****

MOURNFUL CRIES AT THE WILDERNESS

Grant had not expected Robert E. Lee to fight at the Wilderness, but the battle took place amid forest, underbrush and scrub growth, which caught fire from the exploding shells of both armies. Cavalry was immobilized, caissons and guns could not be repositioned. Many wounded, unable to escape the raging, relentless fire in the forest, perished where they fell. Commanding officers, blinded by smoke, did not know the length of their own lines. Friend and foe alike were indistinguishable in the acrid flaming forest.

"In the years that immediately followed the Battle of the Wilderness, strange stories arose among the residents of the adjoining areas. No phantom guns were heard, but instead anguished cries for help, moans and screams that caused the grim ground to be studiously avoided. At times a lurid glow lighted the skies, red, flickering, smoky, ascending and spreading as if the forest were afire. On a number of occasions, farmers, positive that there was fire in the Wilderness, would ride out to investigate, but always the burned-over area was dark and silent on their arrival. A choking odor of burning wood pervaded the ground, and the unmistakable smell of gun powder was borne on the breeze.

"Hunters told tales of finding human skulls, bones, skeletons among the new growth and pitifully inadequate graves. The Wilderness was neither a Confederate nor Federal victory. The two armies fought to exhaustion where violets and arbutus bloomed and partially grown spring foliage showed until the heat of battle turned the once-serene Virginia countryside into a funeral pyre for thousands of blue and gray, thereby adding a new dimension to the horror of the haunted ground . . ."

* * * * *

THE DISAPPEARING CONFEDERATE FLAG

Much has been written about the Confederate flag, which was so much revered by Southerners. For example, here is what a Rebel prisoner, Henry Benson of North Carolina, wrote while in a northern prison: "The colors drop, are seized again — again drop and are again lifted, no

man in reach daring to pass them by on the ground — colors not bright and whole and clean as when they came first from the white embroidering fingers, but as clutched in the storm of battle with grimy, bloody hands, and torn into shreds by shot and shell. Oh, how it thrilled the heart of a soldier to catch sight of his red battle-flag, upheld on its white staff of pine, its tatters snapping in the wind! — that red rag, crossed with blue, with white stars sprinkling the cross within, tied to a slim, barked pine sapling with leather thongs cut from a soldier's shoe!"

It is, in fact, difficult to over-estimate the meaning of the flag to Southerners. Consider: When Union Colonel Elmer Ellsworth of the Eleventh New York Regiment entered Alexandria on May 24, 1861, he spotted a Confederate flag on the roof of the Marshall House tavern. Incensed at the sight, he dashed to the roof of the building and took it down. As he came back down the stairs, he was shot and killed by tavern owner James Jackson, thus becoming the first casualty of the Civil War. Consider, too: A Confederate flag was prominently displayed outside the Martinsburg, Virginia, home of the famous female Southern spy, Belle Boyd. When a rowdy bunch of Union troops talked of taking the flag down, Belle killed the leader of the group with a hunting rifle, thus scattering the Yankees and leaving the flag intact.

Kay Boyd writes of another most curious incident involving the flag. This occurred during the first week of April 1865, as Lee pulled out of Petersburg and began his retreat to Appomattox.

"The guns fell silent, the lines were evacuated, the campfires extinguished. The Southern Cross no longer waved its tattered banner over the Confederate lines: Lee's armies were moving toward the west and Grant was in hot pursuit.

"But back at one abandoned Southern outpost, near Petersburg, the flag of Johnny Reb still flew derisively, defiantly, though the enemy now held the city. The Federal holding forces hauled it down. An officer seized it as a trophy. The following morning, as April's dawn broke over the silent Confederate side, the Southern Cross had been run up the sapling that served as a staff. The Union officer in charge looked in his gear for the tattered banner he prized, only to find it where he had placed it. He was astonished at the strange incident and sent a scouting party, expecting to find a Confederate who was still holding out against the enemy. They found Confederates — all dead — and no flag!

"In the few remaining days until Appomattox, the battered, shot-torn flag of the dying Confederacy remained aloft. If the Yankees approached it, it vanished into thin air, and yet some phantom hand hoisted the Southern emblem in its now familiar place by dawn.

"On April 9, 1865, the Union officer looked for the faded banner and to his surprise, saw it moving slowly down the staff. Fascinated, he watched until it seemed to dissolve into the early mist of daybreak.

"A mounted courier thundered up later in the day with a message. 'General Lee has surrendered at Appomattox Courthouse this date.'

"No one ever saw the conquered banner again. It would appear that the lonely ghost of an unknown Johnny Reb knew about the surrender first . . . "

*****

THE SERGEANT WHO SAW HIS OWN DEATH

here is a fairly well documented event in the annals of supernatural phenomena, one that has been widely written about, known as the Sergeant Adams case. It occurred in 1862. Adams was a sergeant major in the Union army who had been severely wounded in battle. He had been taken to a private house, and, there, doctors realized he was dying and there was nothing they could do for him. They sent for his father, who arrived one afternoon.

That evening, at about 11 p.m., Sergeant Adams "to all appearance," died. An attending physician, a Dr. Ormsby, led the lad's father, who had been standing by the bed, to a chair in the room. He then went back to close Adams' eyes.

Dr. Ormsby was then quoted as saying, "As I reached the bedside the supposed dead man looked suddenly up in my face and said, 'Doctor, what day is it?' I told him the day of the month, and he answered, 'That is the day I died'."

The father then approached the bedside, and Sergeant Adams told him that his brother, who also was a Union soldier, had fought in a battle, but wasn't hurt. He also said, "I've seen mother and the children and they are well." Then, for the next five minutes or so, Adams, speaking in a clear voice, gave explicit directions regarding his funeral. He next turned to Dr. Ormsby and asked again what day it was, and the doctor repeated the date.

Sergeant Adams then said, once more, "That is the day I died." . . . And he was dead!

It was later learned that everything he had said about his family was true. His brother was uninjured and everyone was fine.

* * * * *

CIVIL WAR SPIRIT SIMILARITIES?

(Author's note: In "Civil War Ghosts of Virginia," (1995), I printed a remarkable photograph of a possible apparitional figure taken in a building on the Manassas battlefield known as "The Stone House." It had served as a makeshift hospital during the Civil War. The photographer, park service administrative officer Jane Becker, had taken the picture when no one else was in the house. She had her camera and film checked. Everything was in working order, but no one could explain what it was that appeared on the print, or why.

In September 1996, I received a letter from Lou Ann Sadowski of Pittsburgh, Pennsylvania. She wrote: "Enclosed please find a picture taken by me on September 17, 1996, at the Hollywood Cemetery in Richmond, Virginia. The time was around 4:30 p.m. I took several pictures of the cemetery and they all turned out perfect. This picture was supposed to show the large granite pyramid (the Confederate Memorial). I saw nothing out of the ordinary. When I saw this picture I didn't think much about it. It wasn't until two days later, when I started reading your book that I came across the picture on page 52 (Jane Becker's photo). I noticed the similarity and decided to send it. I would like to know what your opinion is."

I, too, was struck by the similarities of the apparitional appearing figures. Herewith are the two photos.

Administrative officer Jane Becker of the Manassas National Battlefield Park was shooting photos of period furniture in the Stone House at the park, which was used as a hospital during the Civil War. Many young men died here before their time. No one else was in the house at the time the photo was taken. When the apparitional figure appeared on this print, she had her film and camera checked by Eastman Kodak in Rochester, New York. There was nothing wrong with it. A friend of hers at the FBI laboratory in Washington also checked. He said the figure appeared to be human like, but couldn't explain what it was.

Lou Ann Sadowski of Pittsburgh, Pennsylvania, took this photo at Hollywood Cemetery in Richmond on September 17, 1996. She was taking a shot of the large granite Confederate memorial, which is virtually obliterated by this wispy, cloud-like figure. Notice the similarity of the "entity" with the Stone House one.

WHERE ARE THE GHOSTS?

(Author's note: Sometimes I wonder about ghosts. Sometimes it seems like they haunt the most unlikely sites, and, conversely, at places where one would strongly suspect the spirits to show themselves, they are mysteriously absent. For example, at the October 1996 Garlic Festival in Amherst County (go if you like garlic!), I was told to inquire about possible spectral activity at Chimborazo. I had to confess I had never heard of it. Turns out it was one of the largest, if not the largest hospital used during the Civil War. It was located in the 3400 block of East Broad Street in Richmond. I learned it was named for a mountain range in the Andes — why, I don't know. According to Civil War guidebooks, it was made up of 150 unpainted frame buildings, 30 feet wide and 150 feet long, covering approximately 40 acres. In addition, at times, as many as 150 Sibley tents complemented the wooden buildings.

I was told to call Mike Andrus, a National Park Service historian in the Richmond area. Mike was very gracious. He told me that more than 75,000 Confederate soldiers were treated at Chimborazo during the Civil War, and he estimated that from 10 to 20 percent of them died there and were buried at Oakwood Cemetery. He said he didn't know why, but not much had been written about the hospital. "There are a few accounts in the old Richmond newspapers of the day, but relatively little has been covered by historians," he says. One would expect such a site of trauma and tragedy might be fertile spawning grounds for returning spirits, but such apparently is not the case. Mike says he knows of no ghosts legends at Chimborazo.

I then asked him about Castle Thunder. This was a three-story building, similar in design to the infamous Libby Prison, located on the north side of Cary Street between 18th and 19th streets in Richmond. It had once been a barrel factory, and was confiscated by the Confederacy during the war and used as a prison for persons who: had committed serious crimes; were spies; or were deserters. This, too, might have been a seedbed for vengeful spirits, because it was a notorious den for the dregs of human society. It was full of cutthroats, and assaults and murders inside its walls were commonplace.

But such is not the case. Mike says there are no reports of ghostly activity there either.

Curious.)

CHAPTER 31

The Civil War Couple Still Searching for Each Other

(Catlett)

s it possible for a man and a woman, who were lovers in real life 135 or so years ago, to return as ghosts to the house in which they professed their love — and not be aware of each other's ethereal presence? One could possibly come to such a conclusion after hearing about the psychic manifestations which have taken place at an old two-story frame house known as Longwood. It lies near Catlett off route 28, a few miles southeast of Warrenton, and southwest of Manassas.

According to Margaret DuPont Lee, who wrote about this phenomenon in her 1930 classic, "Virginia Ghosts," one of the spirits here was allegedly Kate Hooe, who lived at Longwood in the middle years of the 19th century. She fell in love with a young man from the area, but their romance was interrupted by the Civil War. It is not specified as to his fate, although it is assumed that he was killed in battle. Kate, who pined for him in life, apparently "came back" afterwards to wait for him. She reappeared in the evenings by entering the parlor, sitting in a rocking chair by the fire, and reading a book. Whenever any mortal entered the room, she disappeared.

Her apparition in this form was sighted by several members of the household in the years after she died. For instance, one evening the then-current mistress of Longwood went into the parlor and lay down on the couch to rest before dinner. She fell asleep.

Sometime later, Carrie, the maid, entered the room, and saw a woman sitting in the rocker with her face in her hands, appearing to be "in deep grief." Not wanting to disturb her, the maid left. When she closed the door, she awakened the mistress, who then arose and asked the maid why she had not awakened her. When Carrie stammered that she had seen her in the rocking chair, the mistress was astounded. She told Carrie she had not been in the chair, she had been asleep on the sofa. Carrie replied: "Well, then, I've seen Miss Kate's ghost!"

A week later, the mistress went upstairs to bed. As she walked down the corridor she saw "a man" come out of one room, go down the corridor, and enter another room. She at first thought it to be her husband, but when she entered the bedroom, her husband was already in bed, reading! She and her husband then took a lamp and searched the room the man had entered. They found nothing. Then they realized that this was the anniversary date of Kate Hooe's death. They and others had seen the apparition of a Confederate soldier on other anniversaries of the date. He was always seen going into the one room at the end of the hall. It came in time to be known as the haunted room, and no one would spend the night in it.

At some point the Hooe family then living in the house had a party, and invited a number of guests. A severe thunderstorm hit the area that evening, causing several guests to spend the night at Longwood. The then-current Mrs. Hooe said that because of the crowding, someone would have to sleep in the haunted chamber. The guests drew straws to see who it would be, and Howison Hooe, a cousin, lost.

Fearing the playing of a practical joke more than the appearance of a ghost, Howison locked the room door and put the key under his pillow. This way, he felt safe that none of the others could sneak in during the night and attempt to scare him. At 2:30 in the morning, he was awakened by the sound of the locked door opening. He looked up and saw a man dressed in a Confederate uniform and wearing cavalry boots, enter. The man walked over to the window, sat down, and began to pull off his boots.

Curiously, young Mr. Hooe was not frightened. He believed one of his friends had somehow managed to get in the locked room, dressed as a soldier, and was playing a trick on him. So he sprang from the bed and grabbed hold of the man's collar. As Mrs. Lee stated, "His hand clutched only the air! The man had vanished." Hooe was so weak from the terrifying experience, that he barely managed to get to the door, opened it, and then collapsed on the hall floor.

When others found him, they revived him with a glass of whiskey, and he told them what had happened. He then moved into another room and crawled into bed with two other guests. There was no way he could be enticed back into the haunted chamber.

Mrs. Lee added a footnote to this episode: "This weakness of which Mr. Hooe spoke, and his subsequent fall, were not due to fear, but to the fact that he had touched the ghost. This is a condition well known to students of psychic phenomena. Mortals have been known to faint, unaware they had walked into an apparition!"

It was not known whether or not Kate Hooe and her Confederate soldier lover ever reunited, in ghostly form, in the house. They were never seen together, always separately. Perhaps they did, in the haunted chamber — and that is the reason manifestations took place in that room. Maybe they wanted to be alone, to consummate their love.

CHAPTER 3 2

Psychic Curiosities of the Civil War

(Author's note: I bought an old book at a Civil War show in Richmond in 1996. It was titled, "Anecdotes and Incidents of the War of the Rebellion," published in 1867, and written by Frazar Kirkland. It was a fascinating read. Herewith are a few passages from the hundreds included in the book. Some have ghostly overtones, while others were just plain interesting. I have edited the excerpts slightly for clarity.)

* * * * *

A PRESENTIMENT OF DEATH
(Manassas)

Colonel Cameron seemed to have a presentiment of his death. In a conversation with him at his tent, on the evening prior to the battle, he said that he had accepted the command of the gallant Highlanders because he admired them, and inasmuch as he had only a short time to live, he might as well devote it to his country. He asked a correspondent whether he was going to the battlefield. Receiving an affirmative answer, he said: 'Good bye, God bless you. We may meet again, but I am afraid not in this world.

"Some sixteen hours afterwards the gallant Colonel was shot from his horse and killed."

* * * * *

ENTOMBMENT OF A LIVING MAN
(Petersburg)

As the Civil War clouds gathered, emotions ran high. A classic example involved a Petersburg merchant named John A. Ford. Apparently, he made such a disparaging remark about the cause of the South that his life was suddenly in danger. "He was soon after waited on by an excited crowd of people who demanded to know if he had used this language. He replied in the affirmative, whereupon a cry was raised of 'shoot him! hang him! kill him!,' and demonstrations were made to carry out the demand of the excited mob.

"Meantime, however, it had become quite dark, of which some friends of Mr. Ford took advantage in dragging him out into an open store, through which he was urged into an alleyway in the rear, while the crowd in the street who had lost sight of him, were clamorously in search. A friend accompanied him rapidly through the alley, and conducted him to the only place of safety which probably could have concealed him — a tomb in his family burial ground!

"Taking the key from the vault hastily from his pocket, he opened it, urged Mr. Ford in among the coffins, locked the door upon him, and quickly disappeared. That night and the following day every place and by-place in the town was ransacked in the eager search of the mob for the victim who had so terribly and so narrowly escaped their clutches. They finally concluded that he had been spirited away, and relaxed their vigilance. Meantime, Mr. Ford remained undisturbed, with darkness and the dead. There were several bodies deposited there — far less feared, however, by him than the living.

"At three o'clock the following Monday morning, the train was to leave for Richmond. At an earlier hour, Mr. Ford's protector and friend came to deliver his friend from the charnel house, where, for two nights and a day, he had fasted with the dead. He was faint and weak from exhaustion, but the emergency lent him strength. Mr. Ford wended his way cautiously and alone to the depot . . . and when the train rolled out of the station on its way north, Mr. Ford sat on one of the car seats." He eventually made his way to Washington and safety.

* * * * *

A DOUBLE TRAGEDY
(Alexandria)

lady had resided with an only daughter for many years in Alexandria. In the course of time, a mutual friend introduced a young gentleman of his acquaintance from Richmond, to the family. The young people soon became quite intimate in their social relations, and, very naturally, fell in love. The parents on both sides consenting, the parties were betrothed, and the marriage day fixed for the fourth of July (1861).

"In the meantime, however, the Virginians were called upon to decide on which side they would arrange themselves in the great political and military conflict then spreading its dark wings over the land. The ladies declared themselves heartily on the side of the (federal) government, but the gentleman joined the forces of the state.

"Such was the rapid and widening progress of events, that no opportunity was afforded for any interchange of sentiments between the young folks, or anything settled as to their future movements. Matters thus remained till the fourth of July, when, exactly within an hour of the time originally fixed for the marriage, intelligence was received at the residence of the ladies that the young man had been shot by a sentry two days before, while attempting to desert and join his bride.

"His betrothed did not shed a tear at this sudden and overwhelming information; but, standing erect, smiled, and then remarked to her mother, 'I am going to desert, too,' fell to the floor, while the blood bubbled from her lips, and she was soon in the embrace of death!"

* * * * *

A PREMONITION CAUSES PAIN
(Western Virginia)

rs. John Eastwick, the wife of a respectable farmer, was the mother of seven children, all boys. In the early part of the war, two of these enlisted (in the Confederacy). One of them, the eldest, Ezra, died of exposure in camp, and his brother, Thomas, soon after suffered an amputation of the right leg from injuries received in a cavalry skirmish. These casualties operated upon Mrs. Eastwick's mind to such a degree that she lost all fortitude and a presence of mind, and sat during whole days weeping and full of forebodings.

"Among her premonitions was a curious one, namely, that her third son, Stark, would also die in battle. As the war advanced and conscription began, Mrs. Eastwick's fear on this point grew intense. . . She endeavored to persuade her son to leave the country and make a voyage to sea. He endeavored to pacify her and left home for a time. On his return, finding her in the same melancholy frame of mind, he threatened, in jest, that if she made further reference to the matter, he would enlist voluntarily.

"Mrs. Eastwick, doubtless laboring under some hallucination, or uncontrollable operation of her mind, seems now to have resolved upon the sad act of mutilating her son in such a manner as to prevent his being accepted for military service.

"She deliberately pressed a burning coal upon his eyes while he slept on a lounge, and the optic nerves were thus destroyed with but a momentary pang of pain to poor Stark. He became entirely blind.

"It may well be supposed that this unfortunate issue from her fears did not contribute to the mother's peace of mind. On the contrary, insanity took hold upon her, her sane moments being marked by melancholy regret at her frenzied act."

* * * * *

THE DEVIL IN THE STEAMER
(Site unknown)

good story is told about a soldier, who, in dodging away from a patrol, hid himself in a restaurant, by jumping into a large box used for steaming oysters. The lid closed with a spring lock, and the disappointed patrol went on his way baffled.

"In a little while the colored man attending the apparatus turned on a full head of steam in order to prepare a mess (of oysters) for some customers. The soldier began to grow uncomfortably warm, and soon kicked and yelled lustily for liberation, until the frightened Negro ran away shouting that 'de debbil was in de steamer.' Other employees gathered around, hearing the noise, and released the perspiring soldier, who bounded with the speed of a machine whose motive power is steam."

* * * * *

A DARK PROPHECY FULFILLED
(Site unknown)

resentiments on the battlefield often prove prophetic. Here is an instance: While Colonel Osterhaus was gallantly attacking the center of the enemy, a sergeant requested the captain of his company to send his wife's portrait, which he had taken from his bosom, to her address with his dying declaration that he thought of her in his last moments.

" 'What is that for?' asked the captain; 'you are not wounded are you?' 'No,' answered the sergeant, 'but I know I shall be killed today. I have been in battles before, but I never felt as I do now. A moment ago I became convinced my time had come, but, how, I cannot tell. Will you gratify my request? Remember, I speak to you as a dying man.'

" 'Certainly, my brave fellow; but you will live to a good old age with your wife. Do not grow melancholy over a fancy or a dream!'

" 'You will see,' was the response.

"And so the treasured picture changed hands, and the sergeant stepped forward to the front of the column, and was soon beyond recognition.

"At the campfire that evening the officers after a while made enquiry for the sergeant. He was not present. He had been killed three hours before by a grapeshot from one of the enemy's batteries!"

* * * * *

AN APPARITION AT DEATH
(Fredericksburg)

Sergeant Charles H. Stevenson, of Henrietta, N. Y., was one of the killed at the Battle of Fredericksburg. A strange incident connected with his death is stated to have transpired. . . On the day of that battle his wife was out in the yard, when suddenly she was made aware of a presence behind her, and turning, she felt a warm breath on her cheek, and saw her husband, who, however, almost immediately vanished.

"As she turned she cried out, 'Oh! Charlie, is that you?' and returned to the house where she at once told some friends that she had seen her husband, and that she knew she would never see him alive again. As near as could be ascertained, the event occurred just at the time of day when her husband was killed."

* * * * *

A DYING BOY'S VISION
(Site unknown)

In one of the large hospitals for the sick of the Union army, surrounded by the wounded and dying, lay a mere boy. One glance at the fever-flush of his fair cheek, the unnatural brilliancy of the beautiful blue eyes, together with the painfully restless movement that tossed the bright curls from his heated forehead, told with mournful certainty the tale that his hours were numbered.

"Yet only a fellow soldier sat beside him. No fond mother's or sister's hand bathed that fevered brow; and tender tones whispering words of love and comfort were wanting by the bedside of the dying lad. 'Poor boy,' said the physician. 'I wonder where his mother is. But she could never get here in time. Ah, well, it's fretting so much has done it.'

" 'It's not the fretting, it's the vow," answered the boy. "Since I cannot see my mother in the body, I mean to see her in the spirit, and before night.'

" 'Delirious,' said the doctor. The boy then turned to his soldier companion. 'Will you hear me tell it, James?' he asked. 'It would make the time seem shorter to speak out what is in my head.'

James listened.

"'Well, then, I'll begin at the time when father, mother, Jessie, and I all lived in that sweet wee home among the mountains. We had not much, to be sure, but enough to keep ourselves and somewhat to spare for our poorer neighbors. Jessie (his sister) was a very fine bonnie lass, older than myself by some years, and it wasn't long till she was promised to the minister of the place. A nice young man was he, and all the country round was glad when it was known.

"'It came Jessie's birthday just three months before the wedding day. She was very sad, and kept saying how happy she had been at home, and how no other spot could ever be to her what it had been; and then, in the middle of the dancing and fun, she up and threw her arms round my mother's neck, and vowed that always, on that evening, so long as my mother was alive, she would come -- whether in the body or in the spirit, she would never fail. Twas a wild word for her to speak, and many of the neighbors shook their heads as they heard, and the talk went round the town that Jessie Graeme had bound herself by such a strange vow.

"'I must be short; it is near the time. Jessie was married, and our hearts were just as glad as children; til one day word came that Jessie and her husband were drowned. In crossing a little lake to visit some sick folk, the boat must have overturned, for it was found floating; but we never saw them again.

"'Oh! twas a bitter time. My mother fretted much; for though she knowed it true, she could not think of our bonnie lassie lying dead and cold in her husband's arms on the stones at the bottom of the lake. My father fretted, too. He would not think that she was dead, but kept saying she would soon be back to gladden our hearts once more; but she never came; and we three, with sickening hearts, waited for her birthday; we knew right well that, dead or alive, her promise would be kept.

"'The night came, and we sat with open door and curtain drawn from the window (for when they come in the spirit, it's only through the window they can look.) We three by the bright fire sat waiting for the first sound of her footstep. I heard it first, as with the water dripping from her clothes, she came swiftly up the walk, and, putting aside the rosebush, looked in -- only for a moment; then she was gone; but by that we knew she was dead.

"'It seemed to comfort my mother, so that, when I left soon after to come here, I made the same vow, that so long as my mother lived, whether in the body or in the spirit, I would, on the same night, stand by Jessie's side.

"'Does no one see?' the lad continued. 'Don't you hear the water dripping from her dress? My mother, with her long gray hair! See, she is putting the roses away. How cold and clammy her hand is! It is dark.'

"With these words, the boy fell back lifeless on the bed. In awestruck silence his eyes were closed, and the cheeks of the bravest paled at the thought that the spirit they had so loved and revered for unfailing tenderness and true courage might be, at that moment, standing by the sister it had so dearly loved, looking through the casement on the home and parents of their childhood, while the beautiful frame it had inhabited lay motionless before them."

THE DOG WHO GUARDED A GRAVE
(Site Unknown)

remarkable incident is related of the manner in which Mrs. Pfieff, the wife of Lieutenant Louis Pfieff, who was killed in battle, was enabled to find her husband's body. No person, when she arrived on the field, could inform her where her husband's body was buried; and after searching among the thousands of graves for half a day, she was about to abandon the pursuit.

"Suddenly, she saw a large dog coming toward her, which she recognized as one that had left with her husband. The dog seemed delighted to find her, and led her to a distant part of the field, where he stopped before a single grave. She caused it to be opened, and found the body of her husband. It appeared, by the statements of the soldiers, that the dog was by the side of the lieutenant when he fell, and remained with him till he was buried. He then took his station by the grave, and there he had remained for 12 days, until relieved by the arrival of his mistress, only leaving his post long enough each day to procure food in order to sustain himself in his faithful service."

* * * * *

HE CARVED HIS OWN HEAD BOARD
(Petersburg)

singular incident is related of Sergeant Major Polley of the Tenth Massachusetts regiment. A day or two before that regiment left for home, while lying in the trenches before Petersburg, he carved with his knife upon a wooden head board, similar to those placed at soldiers' graves, the words, 'Serg. Maj. George F. Polley, 10th Mass. Vols., killed June ___, 1864,' remarking to the colonel, 'I guess I'll leave the day blank.'

"The next day he was instantly killed by a shell which struck him in the breast, tearing his body to pieces. Colonel Parsons, who was standing near by, narrowly escaped. He was buried on the field, and the same head board that he had lettered was placed over his grave."

* * * * *

A REFLECTION OF DEATH
(Washington, D.C.)

When Mr. Lincoln received the news of his first election, he went home to tell Mrs. Lincoln about it. She was upstairs in the bedroom, and there he went, throwing himself down on a lounge, in a careless manner. 'Opposite where I lay,' the president said, 'was a bureau, with a swinging glass upon it,' and here in relating the matter to a friend, he got up and placed the furniture so as to illustrate the position . . . 'And in looking in that glass, I saw myself reflected, nearly at full length, but my face, I noticed, had two separate and distinct images, the tip of the nose of one being about three inches from the tip of the other.

" 'I was a little bothered,' Lincoln continued, 'perhaps startled, and got up and looked in the glass, but the illusion vanished. On lying down again, I saw it a second time — plainer, if possible, than before; and then I noticed that one of the faces was a little paler, say five shades, than the other. I got up and the thing melted away, and I went off, and, in the excitement of the hour, forgot all about it — nearly, but not quite, for the thing would once in a while come up, and give me a little pang, as though something uncomfortable had happened.

" 'A few days after, I tried the experiment again, when (with a laugh) sure enough, the thing came back again; but I never succeeded in bringing the ghost back after that, though I once tried very industriously to show it to my wife, who was worried about it somewhat. She thought it was 'a sign' that I was to be elected to a second term of office, and that the paleness of one of the faces was an omen that I should not see life through the last term.'

"The President, with his usual good sense, saw nothing in all this but an optical illusion; though the flavor of superstition which hangs about every man's composition made him wish that he had never seen it. But there are people who will now believe that this odd coincidence was 'a warning'."

CHAPTER 33

Incredible Incidents in Roanoke

(Roanoke)

(Author's note: Following are two intriguing incidents in the history of Roanoke. While neither is ghostly related, there are some strange psychic overtones, which make the accounts, I believe, worthy of inclusion here.)

THE RIOT OF 1893

On September 21, 1893, Mrs. Sallie Bishop of Botetourt came to Roanoke to sell fruit and vegetables at the city market. She was approached by a Negro named Thomas Smith. He said a Miss Hicks, who lived nearby, wanted 60 cents worth of wild grapes for preserving if Mrs. Bishop would deliver them to her house. He told her he would show her the way. She followed him several blocks, through an alleyway and into a building. There, he slammed the door shut and demanded her money. Horrified, Mrs. Bishop gave him her pocketbook. She had two dollars in it. Then she pleaded for her life. Smith, however, drew a straight razor and attacked her. She managed to knock the razor away, but he beat her with a bat and choked her senseless. Leaving her for dead, he ran toward Woodland Park.

About half an hour later, Mrs. Bishop regained consciousness, and, caked in her own blood, staggered her way out of the building, and reached help. As she was telling what had happened, two men several blocks away saw Smith running away and decided to chase him. Ironically, one of these men was W. P. Blount, Mrs. Bishop's cousin. As they did, others rode up on horseback to tell of Smith's attack. They caught him minutes later near the old Wood Novelty Works.

A detective brought Smith back to town and took him to a saloon where Mrs. Bishop was having her wounds dressed. Though she could hardly see — she had lost the sight of one eye in the struggle — she identified him as her assailant — by his hat! By now a crowd of enraged citizens had gathered, yelling for blood. The detective dodged the crowd by telling them that Mrs. Bishop had not identified the Negro. He then sped Smith on horseback to the city jail.

When the mob, now estimated at about 1,500 people, learned the truth they went to the jail and demanded Smith's release to them. The Roanoke Light Infantry and the Jeff Davis Rifles of Salem were alerted to stand by. Soldiers marched to the front of the jail and stood guard. By now, word had reached Mrs. Bishop's friends and neighbors in Botetourt, and they headed straight for Roanoke.

At eight p.m., the angry mob made a mad rush at the front of the jail but the attack was repulsed when soldiers drew their bayonets. A few minutes later, hundreds of men forced their way into the west side of the building and stormed toward Smith's cell. Suddenly, a shot rang out. Then another. Then all hell broke loose. It was later estimated that more than 150 shots were fired It was never learned who had fired first, but in the aftermath nine prominent citizens were dead and dozens of others wounded, some critically. In the furious crossfire, hundreds of others hastily retreated to safety.

In time, the mob reassembled. They stormed to the mayor's house to demand Smith's release to them. When he was found not to be home, they searched the town. The vigilantes then raided some hardware stores and commandeered rifles, pistols and cartridges. Judge John Woods and J. Allen Watts, a leading citizen, attempted to reason with the crowd but they were shouted down. As this was being done, Smith was spirited from the jail by two police officers and taken through an alley to the banks of the Roanoke River in an attempt to elude the pursuers.

The mob then charged the jail a third time, and were successful, only to find no prisoner behind bars. The men then fanned out throughout the area in a desperate search for Smith. At about three a.m., the officers who had taken Smith thought that things had quieted down enough to bring him back to the jail. But on the way they were ambushed by about 15 men hiding in a vacant lot and armed with guns. The police were forced to give up Smith. The men then dragged their prisoner to a hickory tree, put a noose about his neck, and hanged him.

They left him dangling, and during the next day, thousands came to view the corpse. These morbid spectators stripped Smith of his clothes and fought for "souvenir" pieces of the rope. The crowd stayed in the streets surrounding the tree all night long. Then someone got the idea to take down the body, haul it to the mayor's house, and bury it in his front yard. (They were mad at the mayor because they believed, mistakenly, that he had ordered the first shot when the jail had been stormed.) Reverend W. C. Campbell, however, talked them out of the impromptu burial, but that did not satisfy the sadistic bent of the crowd. They next hauled Smith's corpse in a cart to the edge of the river, and placed it atop a pile of firewood. They soaked everything in coal oil, and then lit it, cremating the body. This ritual drew hundreds more.

To help restore order, 150 "reputable citizens" were sworn in as special deputies, but they were not needed. The number of those dead and wounded, and the atrocious conduct of the mob before, during, and after the lynching, had shocked and sobered the city. Several men were indicted for the shootings at the jail and a few were sentenced to prison.

There was, as Roanoke writer Raymond Barnes noted in his book on the history of the city, a curious footnote to the tragedy. The tree from which Smith was hung, died soon after. As Barnes noted, "Immediately the superstitious credited the lynching and the 'foul deed' as arousing the fury of Providence to destroy the instrument of vengeance."

* * * * *

THE DAY EVERYONE RACED FROM TOWN

On July 4, 1901, a second, most singular event occurred in Roanoke. It began a month earlier when an itinerant Negro evangelist came to town. He was described as being tall, angular and having unusually long eye lashes, presenting a "most formidable appearance. He called himself a prophet, and apparently many believed him, for when he preached, great crowds gathered.

He said he received "warnings" of impending tragedies from "an inner voice." To back this up, he told listeners that he had predicted the Johnstown Flood, and all that had heeded his advice were saved from drowning. He then delivered a bombshell. He said that his "inner voice" urged him to tell the people of Roanoke that their city would be destroyed by fire at four p.m. on July 4th, and that "by a living flame all who remained here would perish miserably!"

Then a strange thing happened. People believed him! Word of the coming calamity spread throughout the town, and among both blacks and whites. To enhance the fears of the superstitious, a terrible heat wave hit Roanoke, and a man dropped dead on the city streets from heat prostration on July 2nd. By the next day, people began leaving the town, taking bundles of food and clothing with them. one man said he was headed to the hills, and when asked why, according to author Barnes, he replied, "Ain't you hear dat Sodom and Gomorrah is on the way to Roanoke? Yessir, that town is going up in fire!"

On the morning of the Fourth of July, it was reported that the roads leading out of the city were clogged with heavy outbound traffic. Many rented rigs and transfer wagons and packed up their entire families to "escape." Barnes said many white citizens crammed Vinton-Salem street cars, they said, not out of fear of the predicted holocaust, but "just in case."

At about four p.m. — the hour that doom had been predicted, thunder skies opened up and a deluge drenched Roanoke.

The so-called prophet's "inner voice" had failed, and there were a lot of embarrassed people who then reentered the town. The itinerant preacher, meanwhile, had gone on to Boone's Mill and Rocky Mount to warn the citizens there of yet another "disaster."

Murder at the Mortician's Mansion

(Roanoke)

(Author's note: I love this job. I travel all over the common-wealth. I learn so much about Virginia's history — the richest in America. I get personalized tours of some of the most beautiful and charming old mansions in the nation. And I meet some of the most fascinating people.

One such person is Carol Shepherd, a native of Roanoke who now lives in the Richmond area. Carol is a psychic. Psychics run in her family. Her great-grandfather, for example, was a shaman (a priest who uses magic for the purpose of curing the sick, divining the hidden, and controlling events.) When she was young, her father told her that she had inherited psychic abilities. He told her that she would sense things which others didn't. She does.

She sees auras — luminous radiations which surround people. She has sensed warnings. Once, she got a strong sensation that her cousin would be seriously injured or killed near water. When she learned, soon afterwards, that he was going to Virginia Beach, she begged his mother to not let him go. He went anyway. At the beach a storm blew up. As her cousin and two other boys were walking off the beach, lightning struck them. The two boys were killed. The bolt blew off the soles of her cousin's feet and he was in a coma for some time, but he survived.

Some years ago, Carol had a near-death experience. Suffering

from a severe brain fever, she envisioned herself leaving her body and being escorted across a marble bridge. Across the water she saw her friends and relatives who had passed on. Just before reaching the other side she was told they were not ready for her yet, she still had work to do on earth. She was returned.

Carol has worked for years as a rescue volunteer. She, and many others at the East Hanover Rescue Squad in Mechanicsville experienced a number of psychic events in their building. Inexplicable noises were heard; blue lights flashed through the place at times, and, once, for the fleeting few seconds, the face of a black man crying was seen in a window. They later learned the building had been constructed over an old Negro cemetery.

The most chilling experience Carol encountered occurred at an old house in Roanoke when she was just a young girl, perhaps seven or eight years old. She was not the only one who was a witness. Others, both children and adults, also attest to the weird events which eventually led to the discovery of a dark tragedy. This is how she remembers it:)

I t was a big house. It was in the 1100 block of Patterson Avenue in the southwest section of the city. There were three stories. It had turrets and gables and a big wrap-around porch. I think it dated to the 1880s. There was a vacant lot next to it. It was a white house. There was a big rock wall around it. I guess you could say it was a spooky house, but we played around it all the time in the daytime and never really thought about it. What I remember best was a playhouse that had been built for the children there. Of course, they weren't there when I was growing up. They had been gone for years. It must have been about 1950 or so when I remember playing there. But I'll never forget that playhouse. It had three rooms, and we loved it. There was a carriage house in back of the place. I think it was used as a garage. We got in there one day and found a treasure trove in some old trunks. We found some old clothes, button up shoes and things like that.

"I didn't know much about the house then. We had heard that it was a mortician's house, and that a family had once lived there — a man, his wife, and four children. But that had been a long time ago. We used to play around the place all the time. We played baseball, and rode our bikes around it.

"Looking back on it, I guess there were some very strange things happening, but as kids, we didn't think much about it at the time. It had been vacant a long time. Every once in a while some people would move in, but they always moved right back out within a few days or weeks. No one stayed in the house very long. The last renter was a lawyer, but he moved out quick, too. It was such a pretty house, it wasn't hard to get people to move in, but it sure was hard to keep them there.

"In retrospect, I guess we should have been scared about some of the things that went on, but we were too young to realize how frightening it was. I mean when the house had been vacant for some time, we would see things in it. At night sometimes you could see blue lights flashing inside. It had once been a funeral home. The man must have used the first floor for his funeral parlor and the basement for his work in preparing the deceased for burial. The basement had a dirt floor. The family lived on the upper floor.

"Some of the things we saw scared us and some things didn't. For example, my sister reminded me that we saw what appeared to be a body on a gurney with a sheet over it. She says the sheet moved up and down, like someone was breathing underneath it. We would see the windows in the attic open and shut, but we didn't think about the fact that no one was in the house. If we had, I guess we would have been scared. One thing that did frighten us was that we occasionally would see what looked like a cat with red shining eyes inside the house.

"And then there was the woman. We would see a woman in the house. Sometimes she would be standing at a window upstairs, watching us play. It never really dawned on us at the time that there was no one in the house. She would always be dressed in a long flowing white gown, kind of like a nightgown. The gown was yoked at the top and had long sleeves. She had beautiful blonde hair. She would just look down at us and smile. Sometimes, if you looked through the windows, you could see her on the stairs. Back then, we had no idea of who she was or why she was there. She was pretty, and I would say she was in her mid-thirties.

"Sometimes I would babysit for the people who lived next door, and we would see lights going on and off in the house at night. This was strange because the electricity had been cut off. You could hear doors slamming, and people yelling inside. We heard screams a few times.

"I didn't learn till later the story about the people who had once lived there. Like I said, it was a mortician, his wife, and four children. Years ago, the woman and the children disappeared. The man said they had gone to visit relatives, but they never returned. Then about two years later he disappeared.

"I would hear my parents and other adults talk about this. They would talk about the people who later moved in and moved right out again. They said things happened there. Apparently there were a lot of dark rumors floating around the neighborhood about the house.

"Well, when we told my father about seeing the lady in the house — and he knew there shouldn't be anybody there — it aroused his curiosity. So one day he and a man named Peck went over to the house. It had been abandoned for some time. The doors were locked, but they forced open a door and went inside through the back of the house. My father went up what he said was a very narrow staircase to the second floor. And then he saw her. He saw the woman in the white gown. She was looking out the window. He said she turned and smiled at him, and then dematerialized right in front of him. He got out of there.

"He later said he didn't understand her appearance at all, because there was about a two or three inch layer of dust throughout the house — yet there were no footprints anywhere! I think he was pretty shaken by the experience, because he next went to the sheriff, who was a friend of his, and told him that they had better explore the place. He told the sheriff to bring a long rod to poke around.

"They found five bodies in the basement, buried under the dirt floor. They suspect it was the wife and children of the mortician. They also found a number of graves in the yard surrounding the house.

"All I remember was that we were told we couldn't play near the house anymore. Later, they tore the house down, and I understand the city wouldn't let anybody build anything there. I know I recently visited Roanoke and drove out to the site, and all that was there was that old rock wall. Everything else was gone. As far as I know, they never did find out where the mortician went. He was never heard from again.

"One puzzle was solved, however — the cat with the glowing red eyes. It turned out to be a ceramic cat. It had ruby red eyes. I guess the reflection of light made them seem to shine. They found some old caskets in the basement, and a gurney with a sheet over it, like the one we had seen.

"But the mystery of the woman who stood in the window and watched us play has never been solved. Who was she? Was she the mortician's wife who came back searching for her children? And what unspeakable horror of so many years ago could she describe?

"I guess we'll never know."

A 'Closure' at the Alms House

(Roanoke)

(Author's note: Just before Halloween 1995, I received a letter from Deborah Carvelli of Roanoke. She wrote, "I teach parapsychology at Virginia Western Community College . . . My class meets on Tuesday and Thursday. During this time, my class picks up leads from the area, and we visit houses that want to tell a story." It would be nearly 16 months before I followed up and called Deborah. I called after talking to Louise Loveland, formerly with the Roanoke Historical Museum. Louise had been instrumental in developing a Halloween week tour of suspected haunted sites in the area. One of the sites now annually visited is Virginia Western Community College. Deborah, it turns out, not only helped Louise set up this tour, but she has often taken students to a particular building at the college, the Fine Arts Building, to study psychic phenomena there. This is what they had to report.)

The building itself is old. At one time it was used as an "Alms House." This was a place for the city's old, poor, and disabled. There were reports that it was poorly run and that the residents there were mistreated. One investigator said the house was not kept clean, was "filled with unsavory odors," and those living there were too afraid to complain. Up the hill in back of the building was what was once known as the "Pest House." This was where the contagious sick, mostly those wracked with dreaded smallpox, were sent. Oldtimers say that when the Alms House was filled, people were sent up to the Pest House, whether they were diseased or not.

The Alms House, in short, was a residence of misery. Many died there in uncomfortable and certainly unhappy circumstances. Some of the deaths may have been hastened by ill treatment and neglect. Perhaps for this reason, the building has long held the reputation of being haunted.

"There was a lot of human suffering here," Deborah says. "A lot of tragedy. There is a lot of residual stuff still here. It's trapped energy. In fact, this whole land around here is strong in spiritual energy. Whenever I took my students to this building they would pick right up on it. They felt the energy. It was like there was a strong presence. Some of the students would even be overwhelmed by it. Some would cry. They could sense the sadness."

Specific manifestations aside from the feelings of a presence, included lights that would be turned on at night when no one was there; unexplained noises at all hours of the evening; and occasional glimpses of shadowy figures lurking about, again, when no one was supposed to be on the premises. Such sensations have been experienced not only by Deborah's students on their visits, but by people who work in the Fine Arts Building.

Louise Loveland adds that one of the most singular ghostly manifestations occurred just outside the building, where a huge old oak tree, since removed, once stood. "When we went out to set up the site for our haunting tour, we talked to the security policemen there," she says. "They had some stories to tell. One officer said that he had an encounter that made his hair stand on its end. He said one night he and another policeman were making their rounds of the college, and when they pulled into a road-driveway, they saw a man standing there. It was at night and everyone had gone for the day, so there shouldn't have been anyone there. They said there was something 'odd' about the man. They wondered why he was there, so they stopped and asked if they could help him.

"He didn't speak," Louise continues. "He just laughed and gestured to the big tree with his hand. They asked him again, and he repeated the gesture. His attitude seemed strange. They thought he might be drunk. One officer got a very uneasy feeling, and suggested to the other to let the man go, but the other officer told him to wait a minute. This officer then reached out to grab the man — *and his hand went right through him*! Then the figure disappeared

The Fine Arts Building at Virginia Western Community College in Roanoke, formerly an Alms House.

before their eyes.

"Then the next day, something strange happened. The two officers went back to the tree. One of them had a theory that the answer to the puzzling apparition they had both seen had something to do with the tree. So one policeman grabbed a shovel and started to dig around the base of the tree. He stuck his foot on the top of the shovel head and shoved it down into the earth. But then it stuck. He couldn't get the shovel out of the ground. Both men tried, but no matter how hard they strained, the shovel wouldn't budge. They finally tied a rope to the shovel and attached it to the back of their vehicle, and had to pull it out that way. After that, they didn't bother with the tree anymore."

Early in February 1997, Deborah took a class of her students to the building. "I have always believed that timing is so important," she says. "They were just about to do some major renovations there. They were going to convert the area inside into offices, so the students and I wanted to try and alleviate any spirits still trapped there. We did an energy circle. That's where we all sit in a circle, hold hands, and try to send positive feelings and universal love inside.

"It must have worked, because we all got a feeling of a total transition. We all visualized something was happening. It was like there was a great release. We were, in effect, saying to the spirits that it was okay to move on, and there was a definite feeling that flight was opening up. We all felt that we had been heard, and understood, and that a heavy presence had been lifted. It felt wonderful."

Both Deborah and Louise say there are still many haunted areas in Roanoke. Following is a sampling of other places included on the annual Halloween tours:

** At the Blackhorse Tavern, Louise says on her first visit, "it felt like the breath was being sucked out of you." Past tenants and caretakers have told of hearing "tavern-like noises" and people clomping up and down the stairways late at night. "There is a great deal of activity in the oldest section of the building," Louise says. Maybe that's the reason no one seems to stay in the house very long. "Many people have moved in there and moved right out within a few days or weeks," she adds.

** At the Tazewell Avenue Cemetery, an old woman has been seen sitting on a wall surrounding a family burial plot. The legend is that she died during a flu epidemic in the early 1900s. Her husband and children survived her. When they died they were buried in this plot. The woman's wraith is seen there at times, crying, because she wasn't ready to leave her family so unexpectedly. On the night of the 1996 ghost tour, Louise says the attendants got an unscheduled thrill. "While we were there, in the midst of our talk, a solid white cat appeared out of nowhere and leaped up on the very headstone we were facing," she says. "There were quite a few audible gasps."

** At Hollins College, Deborah, who is psychic, says you can feel a strong presence. "It is especially powerful around the music department. It's like someone there is trying to pull you in from the outside. They want to share their music with you."

** On Yellow Mountain Road there used to be an old log cabin. The tradition is that a young girl accidentally burned the cabin to the ground long years ago, and lost her family. "Some people have told us," Louise says, "that the girl can still be seen there, wandering about and crying. She's stuck there, grieving."

** On Read Mountain there is a story that has been passed down, generation to generation, of an old hermit who lived in a cave. He was a tinker. A century or so ago he fixed people's pots and pans and other metal things. But he was rarely seen. He would only come down off the mountain every few months for supplies.

"When we investigated this, we were told that people today still see his apparition walking down the mountain," Louise says. A few years ago someone found some evidence of what may have been his old haunt. It may have once been his workplace. There were old pieces of tin scattered around.

** At the Patrick Henry Hotel on Jefferson Street in downtown Roanoke, employees may tell you they have a resident ghost, but they won't say which room she's in. One woman staying at the hotel said when she entered her room one night she saw a staircase extending from a wall where there was not supposed to be a staircase. She said it extended right across to the bed where she was lying, and a female figure walked down the stairs and out the door. She reported the unnerving vision, and a security officer checked the room but found nothing. The guest was told there had once been a staircase there in years past when the hotel then was an apartment complex! It still didn't explain what happened, or how the figure departed. Each door is deadbolt locked from the inside. Apparently, the apparitional lady is neither scary or harmful, however. For the word has leaked out to airline attendants who fly in and out of the city. Whenever they have a layover in Roanoke and they are at the hotel, they always request this particular room.

And so, if you aren't busy come next Halloween, and are in the area, it might be fun to hop on the bus and learn more about these and other haunting stops in and around Roanoke. But if you happen to stop at Virginia Western Community College and the hair on the back of your neck doesn't stand up, don't be disappointed. Be pleased. Deborah, Louise and the students may have convinced the spirits there, once sad and tragic figures, to move on to more pleasant surroundings.

CHAPTER   3 6

Another Woman in Black?

(Tazewell County)

(Author's note: In "The Ghosts of Virginia, Volume I," (1993), I wrote a chapter about a mysterious "Woman in Black," who appeared late at night and then disappeared on the streets of Roanoke in 1902. The Roanoke Times wrote at the time: "Her name was on every lip; strong men trembled when her name was spoke; children cried and clung to their mothers' dresses; terror reigned supreme." The Times reported that the woman had been sighted in Bristol only a short time before. Her appearances were always the same. She would just seem to materialize out of nowhere to accompany men walking alone late at night. She would follow them to the front door of their homes and then vanish. "It was as if she had arisen out of the earth," one frightened pedestrian said.

Here is how the Roanoke Times chronicled one encounter: "The most recent instance is that of a prominent merchant of the city, who on the night after payday, having been detained at his store until after midnight, was making his way home, buried in mental abstractions, when at his side the woman in black suddenly appeared, calling him by his name. The woman was only a couple of feet behind him, and he naturally increased his pace; faster and faster he walked, but in spite of his efforts, the woman gained on him until, with the greatest of ease and without any apparent effort, she kept along side of him. 'Where do you turn off?' she asked him. He replied in a hoarse voice, 'Twelfth Avenue.' Ere he was aware, she had her hand upon his shoulder. He tried to shake it off, but without success. 'You are not the first married man I have seen to his home this night,' she spoke in a low and musical voice.

"Reaching the front gate, he made certain she would then leave him; but into the yard she went. This was a little more than he bargained for. It was bad enough to be brought home by a tall and handsome woman with dancing eyes; but to march up to the front door with her — well, he knew his wife was accustomed to wait for him when he was detained, and he did not dare to go to the trouble of making an explanation to her; besides, such explanations are not always satisfactory. The merchant admits that he was a nervy man, but that in spite of his efforts, he could not help being at least a little frightened. 'Twas the suddenness of the thing,' is the way he expressed it. But as he reached the door, he looked around. She was gone. Where she had gone, and how, he didn't know. But he didn't tarry on the doorstep either."

The woman appeared to a number of men over a period of months and then was not heard from again. Later, there were reports of her appearance in Bluefield. It was speculated that perhaps she had been a wife herself once who had found her husband unfaithful, and thereafter she returned to make sure potentially wayward mates did not succumb to temptations of the night.

In researching for this volume, I found yet another reference to the "Woman in Black." Louise Leslie wrote about such an episode in her book on the history of Tazewell County.)

he phantom woman made appearances in Tazewell in 1905, three years after the Roanoke encounters. One overcast Saturday night that year, two well-known businessmen were walking down Pine Street. They crossed in front of what was called "The Hearse House." A hearse drawn by two horses used to be garaged in the building. As they passed, they noticed that the doors to Hearse House were wide open. Out stepped a woman wearing a long black dress and a black bonnet. The men then ran home as fast as their feet would carry them. The woman was seen on at least two other occasions in dark alleys. Unlike in Roanoke, in Tazewell she did not speak. She was described as being "as silent as the grave."

If her mission was, as some suspect, to straighten out wavering husbands, she unquestionably was successful in Tazewell. Prior to her arrival many married men had a habit of tarrying a bit in town on weekend nights. But once word got around that they may be accompanied on their way home by a strange and scary woman, they either went home early or walked in pairs. As in Roanoke and Bluefield, she was seen for a short time only. It appeared that once her point had been made, she would move on to a new location.

* * * * *

THE MYSTERY 'WOMAN' WHO WAS NO LADY
(Southwest Virginia)

(Author's note: The Woman in Black was not the only mysterious personage to appear periodically in Southwestern Virginia. Earlier this century there were numerous reports of a strange woman who was sighted in Bristol and other towns. Although "she" was not ghostly, her habits and movements stirred considerable fear wherever she showed up. She slept in barns and begged for food. No one knew who she was, or why she was there.

At one point she showed up in a rural area on horseback leading a pack of five dogs. She had two pistols buckled about her waist. Those who dared speak to her thought she was insane. Some even believed she was a witch, and it was said that when she rode through a settlement many people left their houses in fear. One woman was reported to have "become dumb with fright."

Actually, the woman wasn't a woman at all. It was a man dressed in women's clothes. His name was Colby and he was a Pinkerton detective tracking a man wanted for murder in Texas. He found the man somewhere across the Virginia line, sprang from his horse, threw off his feminine garments and leveled a pistol at the fugitive's head. The wanted man was so shocked he fainted.)

Virginia's Ghost
Poet Laureate

(Roanoke)

(Author's note: A change of pace! I gave a lecture sponsored by
the Roanoke Historical Society in October 1996. After the talk, a
gentleman named Richard Raymond approached me and handed
me a typed manuscript, saying only "read this when you can and
let me know what you think." It was four months later, after I had
started writing this book, that I opened the manuscript and began
reading. I was absorbed. It was titled "Unwelcome Visitors," and it
was a complete collection of original ghost poems, written over a
period of 45 years. Richard had given me his card. It says "Poetry
Performer Par Excellence."

While the poems are fictional in nature, they are, in some
instances, based on actual events, as will be noted. I consider them
a part of our folklorian heritage. Richard's foreword is prefaced by
this line from Shakespeare's Hamlet:

". . . The graves are tenantless, and the sheeted dead Did
squeak and gibber in the Roman streets."

In the foreward, Richard writes: "Nearly every civilized, liter-
ate person has at some time, in the course of reading for entertainment, encountered a tale of the supernatural, and despite all
pretenses to sophistication, read it through to the end, giving a
most satisfactory shudder when finished. In this, the reader does
precisely what the storyteller intended, to produce that shiver of
outward disbelief and inward credence. The reader need not be
ashamed for this — agitation of nerves and creeping of flesh is the

desired effect of ghostly tales reaching back to the dawn of humankind, and he would be a dull ass indeed who does not secretly admit that he loves it."

The first selection I chose concerns a common ghostly theme — that of the appearance and disappearance of a phantom hitchhiker. While Richard chose New Jersey as the setting, it could as well have been a rural road in Virginia, as such legends have been told and retold here and in other southern states.)

MARY CATHERINE

"These are dark hills — not high, but steep,
    Full of strange tales and stranger dreams —
Ravines are rocky, forests deep,
    Laced with swift-flowing, icy streams,
Threaded with narrow, winding roads,
    Sprinkled with pious faith and fear
In mountain folk, of mountain codes,
    Silent, suspicious and austere.
One night — it happened long ago —
    A young man drove from town to town
Through the din shades of Ramapo,
    Losing his way as dark came down.
Hoping to find his road — in vain —
    He blundered blindly through the night,
Until he saw, in mist and rain,
    A figure moving, something white.
Afoot, alone, slender and frail,
    A girl — sixteen, as he might guess —
Hurried along the roadside trail,
    Wearing a pretty party dress.
Approaching in his headlights' beam,
    She seemed ethereal and faint,
Blue eyes and auburn hair agleam,
    The picture of an Irish saint.
He stopped, some twenty yards away,
    Opened the window and hollared,
'Say, miss, I'm mighty lost today,
    Can you direct me to the road?'
'Oh, sir, it's miles away,' said she,
    'But I'd be glad to be your guide,
For I'm as weary as can be,

And grateful for the chance to ride.'
A moment as she clambered in,
    Then down the gravel lane they rolled —
She had no coat, her dress was thin,
    She shivered in the damp and cold.
'And what's your name, my fearless maid?
    How are you called by friends and kin?'
'Footsore, not fearless, I'm afraid —
    My name is Mary Catherine.'
'Now, miss,' the young man said, 'explain
    How on this lonely road I chance
To meet you, walking through the rain?'
    'Why, I've been to my high school dance!
It's held each year, near Christmas Eve,
    A pleasure I had never known —
I asked my mother for her leave,
    Having no date, I went alone.
We live so far from any town,
(And seldom have the cash to spare),
I've never owned a party gown,
    My mother made this one I wear.
My sweater kept me — mostly — warm,
(I guess I need a raincoat, though).
It's not much in a thunderstorm,
    And now it's coming on to snow.'
He turned the heater on, full blast,
    And wrapped his coat up to her chin.
'I think I'm coming warm at last,'
    Said weary Mary Catherine.
'You're a brave girl,' the young man said,
    'To walk so far without a light.
What could be in your mother's head
    To let you go on such a night?'
She laughed, and shook her lustrous curls,
    'These woods are friends, not things to fear —
The hills look after mountain girls,
    But strangers might just — disappear.
My friends were nearly out of gas,
    And could not bring me all the way —
I walk as far to Sunday mass,
    No more than seven miles, I'd say.
My home is just around this bend,

I'll stop here.' Timid as a fawn,
She murmured, 'Thanks, you've been a friend,'
Opened the car door, and was gone.
Around the curve his headlights showed
A modest house, white-painted frame,
And close beside the narrow road
A mailbox, with a single name.
He found his road, and spent the night
At a convenient tourist inn,
Beguiled until the morning light,
With dreams of Mary Catherine.
At breakfast-time he told his tale,
Asked who the elfin girl might be.
The waitress looked a trifle pale —
'Describe her. . . yes, yes, it was she,
So often seen, this time of year,
Young Mary Catherine Mahone —
Her mother lives not far from here,
A poor widow, all alone.'
Intrigued by this small mystery,
The man backtracked his evening way,
Hoping at least to find and see
His passenger by light of day.
Finding the house, he parked his car,
Walked up and rang the quaint doorbell,
Thinking that, as he'd come this far,
He'd just inquire if she were well.
A woman answered, bent with care,
With sorrows of some eighty years,
A lace cap on her snowy hair,
And eyes that brimmed with sudden tears.
He bowed and smiled, and gave his name,
She sighed with age and weariness,
"These forty years it's been the same —
You've seen my daughter, then, I guess?
Ah, pretty Mary Catherine!
That night she took a fatal chill —
The party gown you saw her in
Is buried with her, on that hill.
You're welcome, sir, to go and see
All that remains to me alone:
A lovely, precious memory,

A carven name upon a stone.'
Slowly, with numbness in his throat,
    He climbed the little hill, and found
His neatly-folded overcoat
    Lying upon the grassy mound."

* * * * *

(The second poem was inspired by a real-life walk Richard
took alone one night at the site of a famous Civil War battlefield.)

THE GRAY COMPANION

"I dreamt (that is, I *think* I dreamt) this scene:
    A moonlit hill, serene
    Beneath a summer sky,
Bathed in the balmy airs of young July,
Strolling the streets of Gettysburg was I,
    Alone, and musing deep,
While in our snug motel my family lay asleep.
I walked along an avenue of trees,
    Past silent batteries,
    Their cold bronze muzzles still
Trained on the crest of Cemetery Hill,
(I am a gunner — these were laid with skill),
    Then, from the moon-flecked shade
A figure moved, a man on midnight promenade.
He halted, as if waiting just for me.
    'Good evening, sir,' said he,
    With grave and courteous smile,
'The night is fair, I thought I'd walk awhile —
Would you walk with me? (only half a mile,
    I do assure you, sir!)
I could not sleep, such nights set my old blood astir.'
A strong, courageous, eldern man he seemed,
    (Remember now, I *dreamed*)
    Not tall, but soldier-straight,
In him I sensed a horseman's steady gait;
His suit well-cut, yet strangely out of date,
    And in the full moonlight
His neat-trimmed hair and beard shone richly, silver-white.
'Gladly,' I answered, captured by his eyes,

211

Calm, sympathetic, wise,
　　Yet filled with stern command.
Onward we ambled, artfully unplanned;
He gestured at the guns on either hand,
　　　　Smiling, as if to say,
'They're playthings, now, but these were mighty in their day.'
So wandered we a little way, and stood
　　　Close by the edge of wood
　　　Where Pickett's valient men
Set out to break Meade's line — scarce three in ten
Who went so brave, came stumbling back again.
　　　My gray companion sighed,
'So many old men erred, so many young men died.
That was . . . that *must have been* a stirring sight —
　　　　A mile from left to right,
　　　　Bright battle-flags ahead!
Unwavering, into that sheet of lead
They charged for victory, and won instead
　　　Their dark, undying fame —
A century from hence, men will know Pickett's name.
Afterward,' he went on, 'the rain poured down
　　　On battlefield and town,
　　　On Lee's long wagon-train,
Seventeen miles of misery and pain —
The wounded might have wished to join the slain.
　　　But that was long ago.
Now, of that day, alas, there's little left to show.'
His own regret seemed more than he could bear,
　　　'Look yonder, I declare!
　　　Where gallant Kemper fell,
Where Armistead defied the fires of hell,
They're putting up a luxury motel!
　　　Sir, this is hallowed land —
Was it for *this* they fought, a frozen custard stand?'
His worn voice broke, I could not well reply.
　　　He gave a heartfelt sigh,
　　　'Your pardon, sir, I fear
You think me mad — I may not hold you here.
Would you accept a modest souvenir?
　　　This button from my sleeve?'
He bowed and raised his hat — I never saw him leave.
At breakfast I retold it, (my wife smiled

As at an earnest child).
   'I tell you, it was *he*,
Confederate General Robert Edward Lee!'
My children crowed with incredulity.
   A dream? I cannot tell . . .
Yet . . . graven on this button is the letter 'L'."

* * * * *

(The third poem by Richard Raymond is based on a trip he took some years ago to the southernmost regions of Virginia.)

FAITHFUL JANE: THE LEGEND OF NEW RIVER
(Tune: "Naomi Wise")

"Now come all you good people, and listen to my song,
   About a brave young girl who saved a train,
She lived along New River, the year was 'twenty-nine,
   And everybody called her Faithful Jane.
Young Joe, he was her sweetheart, a railroad engineer,
   (Her daddy was a railroad man, as well),
Just south of old Pulaski, when rolling past her home,
   He'd wave his hand and ring the engine's bell.
For in that little white house, close by the railroad bridge,
   He promised they'd be married in the spring,
So all that lonely winter she sewed her bridal dress,
   And folks all knew that wedding bells would ring.
The trestle at Hiwassee was long and very old,
   It rocked and groaned with every passing train,
Its piers were weak and battered by every April flood,
   And every tree washed down by winter rain.
One night, she heard the whistle far up the valley line,
   When she was trying on her wedding gown,
Just then there came a rumble, a tumble and a crash,
   Her mother cried, 'O Lord! the bridge is down!'
Jane never stopped a second, she headed out the door,
   A moment's pause, she knew, would be too late,
She took her daddy's lantern, its bullseye shining red,
   And ran off down the tracks to flag the freight.
Across the bridge she scampered, through water washing high,
   She swung the old red lantern high and wide,
Joe saw her for a moment, right in the headlight's beam,

And cried, 'Oh, Jane, you'll never be my bride!'
The whistle screamed a warning, he threw on all the air,
    As sand and sparks went flying down the steels,
But when he'd stopped the engine, one foot before the end,
    Above the raging water hung its wheels.
They never found her body, New River keeps its own,
    But on the steel cowcatcher, gleaming white,
A strip of tattered satin, beside a broken lamp,
    Was witness to the lives she'd saved that night.
They cleared away the wreckage, another bridge was built,
    But Joe, he never drove another train,
They took him up to Staunton, he died within the year,
    For shock and grief had driven him insane.
The rails along the valley are gone, these many years,
    But on the line where engines used to go,
A stone to tell her story is standing by the bridge,
    A marble marker, shining white as snow.
But on some winter evenings, the neighbor folks declare,
    When that old river's swollen high with rain,
You'll see a young girl running, a lantern in her hand,
    And know you've seen the shade of Faithful Jane!"

* * * * *

(Richard added a footnote to this poem. He wrote, "The old ballard 'Naomi Wise' is one of the songs my father used to play and sing to us when we were children. And at Hiwassee, five miles south of Pulaski, Virginia, there really is an iron bridge (built in 1930) across the New River. There's a little white house, too, but the old rail line is now a hiking and biking trail. And *is* there a white stone, a story and a ghost? Well . . .")

CHAPTER 3 8

Buried Alive – For Real!

(Covington)

(Author's note: In Volume III of this series on Virginia Ghosts, I wrote a chapter entitled "On Being Buried Alive." I quoted Edgar Allan Poe, who wrote extensively on this subject, and had a profound personal fear of being interred before his time. Hence this quote from his works: . . . "No event is so terribly well adapted to inspire the supremeness of bodily and of mental distress, as is burial before death."

In May 1997 I did a book signing at the Mountain Book Company in Covington. Horton Bierne, the able editor of that town's "Virginian Review," dropped in to say hello. He handed me a copy of a special edition he published May 2, 1997. He turned to page 76 and showed me an article he had written titled, "Was 19-Year-Old Mother Buried Alive at Cedar Hill?" "You may find this interesting," he said, and if you want to use it in your next book, feel free to do so." In the article, Horton quoted from a Works Progress Administration report written in 1937 by Mary S. Venable. I did find the write-up interesting. Here is what happened.)

Martha Jordan was a member of one of Alleghany County's most prominent families in the 1840s. The Jordans, according to Horton, were "the iron barons of the Alleghany Highlands" from the 1820s until after the Civil War. Iron production was the first major industry in this area. Martha was the young wife of Hezekiah Jordan. He had a wharf across the road from his house where iron was loaded onto flat boats which were shipped down the Jackson River to the James

and on to Lynchburg and Richmond.

On November 9, 1847, Martha, then just 19 years old, gave birth to a baby daughter, Lucy Ira Jordan. The infant died just nine weeks later. Apparently, Martha could not fathom the grief, for she died, or at least it was thought she died, a month later, on February 28, 1848. As Horton wrote, "One can only speculate that she had some type of apoplexy (seizure) and was in a coma for some time . . ."

It is further conjectured that she may have suffered from one of several possible neurological problems, such as postpartum psychosis, which can occur in mothers following the birth of a child when the mother "loses touch with reality." This, according to Dr. Charles F. Ballou, III, of the area, could have caused a state of catatonia, temporary loss of consciousness. and breathing so faint as to be virtually undetectable. This could have caused attending physicians or family members to assume Martha had died. Horton: "In the mid 1800s bodies were not embalmed and burial was carried out as soon as possible because there were no facilities for preservation. The body would begin to decompose as soon as death occurred."

Here, WPA writer Mary Venable picks up the account: "Hezekiah's wife (Martha) was buried in Cedar Hill Cemetery (in Covington)." Her grave was marked with a tall double stone which was inscribed "Mother and Babe," across the top. It is believed she was buried beside her infant daughter.

Mary Venable: "After 40 years had passed the daughter of Ira Frank (Jordan) had the Jordan square moved to a new part of the cemetery, and new caskets provided for the bodies. The undertaker found that Martha Jordan had turned over on her face and her hand was up at her head. This is the only known occasion of anyone in this county being buried alive. The undertaker called witnesses to observe the position of the bones, so of that there is no doubt."

Thus if one hears the scratching of fingernails against the lid of a wooden coffin, or muffled screams emanating from beneath the earth in Cedar Hill Cemetery, there certainly would be just cause. But no such sounds have been reported. If, as it appears, Martha did regain consciousness six feet under ground, the horror of her situation would not have lasted long, for her oxygen supply would have been strictly limited. Perhaps it was too macabre a scene for even a ghost to reenact.

The Man Who Outdrank The Devil

(Alleghany County)

(Author's note: Over the past 15 years of writing about Virginia's ghosts I have included chapters on some of the commonwealth's most colorful and charismatic characters. They have included: Mad Ann Bailey, the Indian fighter, and Mad Lucy Ludwell who "rode" in stationary coaches; the gentle giant Phil Nunn of Lexington, and the legendary strongman, Peter Francisco; the sinister black sisters of Christiansburg; Doc Taylor, the fabled "Red Fox" of the Cumberlands; Colonel George Hancock of Elliston, the man who was buried standing up; and, elsewhere in this volume, the notorious Ab Redmond, the "meanest man in Virginia."

Here's another name to add to the list — Colonel John Crow of Alleghany County. He was one of the most famous, or infamous — depending upon how you looked at it — inn keepers of the 19th century, and was a drinker of epic proportions. Whether or not his spirit survived his mortal time on earth is questionable, although a poem was written about his ghost at his death.)

Crow began operating his tavern even before Alleghany County was formed in 1822, and his reputation spread far and wide. He was known for setting a delectable table, and for plying his guests with mint juleps that packed a wallop and for a mysterious libation called the "frozen imperial." Overnight guests could sleep alone in their bed for 8½ cents, or they could share it with fellow travelers for just 5½ cents, but no more than five could pile into one bed. A warm meal was 12⅔ cents and a cold dinner 2 cents less. Many stopped off at Crow's Tavern on their way to or from such renowned spas as White Sulphur Springs or Old Sweet. Some of them were famous, such as Daniel Webster, Henry Clay, John C. Calhoun, and Martin Van Buren, the eighth president of the United States. All came to drink, eat and argue politics with the feisty proprietor. None, however, could outdrink him or top his outlandish anecdotes. In fact, he was given a title he cherished — "the biggest liar that ever walked on two legs."

Still, some of his bizarre escapades were true. He had, for example, a pet bear named Bruin, which he often rode bareback around the grounds, to the delight of his customers. Captain Page McCarty, a Richmond editor, wrote about a celebrated incident involving the bear. It is recorded in the book, "Historical Sketches of the Alleghany Highlands," written by Gay Arritt, and edited by Horton Bierne. One day a number of his friends were drinking mint juleps at the tavern with Crow. The men then prepared to ride horseback to Covington, a distance of 17 miles, to attend a county court session.

Crow, well fortified with liquid courage, bet the gentlemen he could ride Bruin through the mountains and beat them all to town. The bet was accepted. Crow never made it to Covington. He got halfway down the mountain when Bruin, sighting a young female bear in the wild, bolted, hurling Crow to the ground. When he was found bathing his bleeding face in a stream, the colonel snorted: "It's a damn fool that tried to ride horseback on a bear. But what I mind about it most is the darned ingratitude of that onery varmint."

Crow died in 1861, and Captain Page penned a poem in his honor. It was said to be carved on a huge sycamore tree on the bank of Dunlap Creek in front of the tavern a year after the colonel departed.

"Old Crow is dead, that good old soul,
Who used to brew our wassail bowl.
His cheek was red and his nose was blue,
But his hand was strong and his heart was true.
He drank all day and he drank all night.
At last he drank old Satan tight,

For when the devil caught his ghost,
Crow never ceased to call his toast.
Till the devil thought he had caught a Monk,
And staggered back into hell dead drunk,
And Crow skipped aloft like a shooting star,
And asked Saint Peter to show him the bar."

The Specter At The Sawmill

(Blue Ridge Mountains)

(Author's note: The following episode was mentioned in a book written more than half a century ago. It involves a traditional ghost tale that was prevalent in the Blue Ridge Mountain area of Southwest Virginia; one that had been passed down, generation to generation, for years. The actual dates of the events and the precise location are not recorded, although the time was probably somewhere in the mid-19th century. The main participant was a mountain man named Dave Kinder.)

he old sawmill had been rumored to be haunted for a number of years. No one had ever seen anything, but several area residents told of hearing a strange noise as they rode by the mill at night. They described this noise as that of someone "shivering."

The legend began some years earlier when a stranger to the region was seen walking, carrying a "heavy sack" over his shoulder. It was hinted that he might be toting a sack of gold. He stopped to spend the night in an old sawmill, and from this point there is more conjecture that fact. No one ever saw the man or his sack again, and it was "bruited around" (said) that someone had killed him in the mill and thrown his body into the cold mill stream that flowed beside the mill.

For years, people told of hearing the "blood-churning" sound of someone shivering as they rode past the mill in the dark.

Dave Kinder had heard the stories. One night, fortified with a good supply of corn liquor, he announced he wasn't 'fraid of any ghost, and he set out for the mill to see for himself.

Alone in the dark mill, he suddenly heard the sound. He later said it was the "awfullest" sound he had ever heard. His hair stood straight up, as did his chin whiskers. He had taken a lantern and some matches, but he froze; he was too scared to light them. He questioned why he had done such a dumb thing as to come to the mill at night by himself.

Then he heard another sound. It was like something was rattling all around his feet. Finally, he stopped shaking long enough to light the lantern. Next, he heard footsteps. Someone, or something, was walking straight toward him. Dave raised his eyes and looked. He was petrified. He was staring at what appeared to be the corpse of a man, dripping wet!

He said the eyes were "great sunken stares, and the flesh was rotting away." The man's mouth was open, and Dave saw rotten teeth about to fall out, and blue-purplish gums. Dave later said it looked like someone who had been in the stream a long time, and then got up and walked out of it.

Dave stammered, "In the name of the Father and Son and the Holy Ghost, who are you?"

The specter didn't reply, but instead motioned Dave to follow him. It walked through the mill and into the brush in back of the building. There, it pointed to a spot on the ground. Dave jammed a honeysuckle stick in the ground at that point, and then ran home as fast as his wobbly legs would carry him.

He told his wife about the eerie experience, but instead of her being frightened, her eyes seemed to glow. She remembered the legend, and felt the ghost had been trying to tell Dave where his gold had been hidden. "You've just found yourself a fortune," she exhorted.

The next morning Dave and his wife walked back to the mill. They found the spot where Dave had placed the honeysuckle stick, and began digging feverishly. But as they dug, the ground all around them began trembling so fiercely, they became frightened and ran back home.

For years after that Dave said every time he rode by the mill, "something" seemed to try to pull him off his horse. He would then spur his horse and race away. He told friends he would like to have the gold, "but not that bad."

CHAPTER 41

Spooky Times Remembered

(Southwest Virginia)

(Author's note: In Volume III of the Ghosts of Virginia, I was delighted to include a chapter called "The Hauntings in Crouse Hollow." This was taken from material sent to me by Ruby Haynes of Natural Wells, Virginia, near Covington. She had written down, in a spiral notebook, ghostly legends passed down by family and friends that dated back a century and more. Obviously, some had been embellished through the years, nevertheless, I found them priceless.

So it was with equal delight that I received a package, in January 1997, from a young man named Dewey Plaster of Idaho Falls, Idaho. He had called earlier and asked if I would like to see a write-up on his ghost encounters. He, and members of his family, had lived in and around Pulaski, Tazewell, and Wytheville. Having a keen interest in the unexplained, Dewey had recorded strange occurrences which had happened to him, his relatives, and his friends, mostly during his childhood. Following are some excerpts, in the Crouse Hollow tradition, from his remembrances:)

THE ATTIC

y grandmother on my mother's side lived in Wytheville before she died. Originally from

Pulaski, she spent a lot of her time at the Witten homestead in Tazewell. There, she was taken care of by a former slave who stayed on after the Civil War. Her family had been in the area since the mid-1700s. Her house in Wytheville was near the Rock House where part of a battle during the Civil War was fought.

"Grandmaw used to tell me about a ghost that lived upstairs in her attic. The first time I had the impression that there was a ghost up in the attic was the feeling I got of being watched up there. Now being a little kid, that can be quite scary. I always got this feeling of someone standing behind me. When you would stand at the top of the attic stairs you had to get away from there. Sometimes it was real hard walking back down the steps. You had to run!"

* * * * *

THE SQUEAKY FOOT STOOL

any years later, when I was in high school, I got a rude awakening one night in my grandmother's house. My brother and I were sleeping in the living room. He was on the couch's hideaway bed and I was on the floor. Sometime during the night I awoke to a noise, and an eerie feeling. I thought I heard a squeak. rolled over to go back to sleep, then I heard the squeak again. My senses were alerted. It sounded like something being moved on the floor. I heard it a few more times intermittently. It would go squeak and pause a few minutes.

"I did not want to open my eyes at this point just in case I saw something I did not want to see. And I did not want 'it' to know I was awake. There was the noise again, and it was coming from the living room — next to me! I had to find out what was causing the noise, so I opened my eyes and looked. Several feet away was a foot stool. It moved! The squeak came from it. I thought I was seeing things, but it moved again. It moved several inches. Then it began sliding slowly towards me! In one step I was up and ran into the bedroom where my mother was sleeping. I told my mother, 'move over, I'm getting in your bed.' I didn't care. I was not staying in the living room."

* * * * *

A HEADLESS 'NON-GHOST'

In one bedroom my grandmother had a headless dress mannequin in the closet. I did not know about it until I opened the closet door one day. When I saw a headless woman, out the bedroom door, down the hall, through the kitchen and out the back door I went. . . A spooky house with a kid who is already spooked and has an overactive imagination has a way of bringing to life your worst fears.

* * * * *

THE CAT WITH TEN LIVES

A few times when going out the back door, I would see grandmother's cat (which had died). Once or twice it would let me get near it but I never could pet him. Just as soon as he went out the back door, he would be gone. I would be right on his heels when he would turn a corner and disappear. When he would duck down the steps that go down the stairwell to the outside basement door it was the same thing. I would look and he would be gone. I was right behind him and there was no way he could jump out. We loved that cat. I guess he just could not leave us.

* * * * *

STRANGE LIGHTS IN THE NIGHT

The one story my grandmother told was about the strange lights in the fields near the home in Pulaski. Since people were so spread out back then, you'd have to cross fields to get anywhere. People would report being followed by strange lights in the fields. At night my grandmother said she could look out over the fields and see weird lights. People would describe the lights as being round, or that they looked like light bulbs. Sometimes they would look like crosses. They said that when you got to a certain fence the lights would stop following you and disappear. There was some Civil War action in the area, and there used to be a forge — Graham's Forge. The lights may have been caused by the ghosts of soldiers or from those who worked at the forge. You could rule out head lights, because it was early in the century and cars were not very common.

* * * * *

THE 'HOLLER'

hen I was eight years old my family moved from Roanoke to a farm seven miles south of Buchanan. It was on a dirt road and was out in the sticks. We had few neighbors. Now for the holler. It has a dark history. There were several murders there.

"The road here is right off route 11, and is state route 642, recently named Old Hollow Road. Up the road there is a house that is on the site of an old homestead from the 1700s. It has two stories with a full attic, white siding and white columns. The Bakers lived there, and their son, Ted, and I were friends. He used to tell me things that happened there.

"He said one time that a woman who lived in his house in the 1800s died on the side porch. She went out the door one evening and saw a figure hanging in the tree next to the house. She screamed and died on the spot. I asked the lady of the house about the story and she confirmed that someone was lynched in a tree that once stood at that spot.

"Ted also said that you can hear screams coming from their red barn at night. Years later his mom said that a young lady was murdered behind the barn at some old stables, and the family living there packed up and left real fast and went west. One day Ted and his sister, Sarah, said they heard their mom scream. They ran to the red barn and asked their mom what was wrong. She asked why and they said they heard her scream. Their mom said that she hadn't.

"Another time, Ted said he got up one night to go to the bathroom. It was dark as he went down the hall. In the dark against the light coming from his sister's bedroom, he saw a dark figure; that of a little girl. He thought it was his sister, who was eight. He called her name several times. She turned and ran down the steps. For some reason he decided to look in his sister's room. She was there asleep. Who did he encounter in the hallway?

"The next summer we were in his room looking out he window through his binoculars. We saw something. Up on a hill we saw something white sticking up through the tall weeds and brush. So we decided to have a look. He, my brother, and I rode our bikes up the road to the bottom of the hill. We climbed up through stickers and burrs.

"We saw the white thing. It was a headstone! There was a little cemetery there on top of the hill that was long forgotten. There were three family names there, apparently of those who used to live in or at my friend's house. The dates went back ranging from the late 1700s to the early 1800s. And there was the grave of a little eight year old girl!"

(Author's note: Dewey says he plans to keep collecting ghost legends from Southwest Virginia and someday publish them. I hope he does.)

* * * * *

THE LADY WHO THOUGHT SHE WAS DEAD!

Dewey Plaster later sent me a letter and included a humorous incident involving a lady named Gloria Carter of Buchanan, Virginia. Seems Gloria was involved in a serious car wreck some time ago, and lost consciousness. When she awoke she was staring into the face of the local undertaker. For a moment or so, Gloria wasn't sure whether she had survived the wreck or not.

Turns out the mortician was a member of the rescue squad who responded when the accident call came in.

CHAPTER 42

The Haunting Disaster At Rye Cove School

(Scott County)

cott County, at the southwest bottom of the commonwealth, was formed in 1814, and named for General Winfield Scott. The face of the county is mountainous and uneven, and iron, coal, marble, limestone and freestone were staples of its past history. There also is a physical wonder here, about 12 miles west of Estilville. It is called the Natural Tunnel.

An article in the February 1832 issue of the American Journal of Geology, described this tunnel as a "remarkable and truly sublime object. . . The entrance to the natural tunnel, on the upper side of the ridge, is imposing and picturesque in a high degree; but on the lower side, the grandeur of the scene is greatly heightened by the superior magnitude of the cliffs, which exceed in loftiness, and which rise perpendicularly — and in some instances in an impending manner — more than 300 feet; and by which the entrance on this side is almost environed, as it were, by an amphitheater of rude and frightful precipices."

It is also in Scott County, on May 2, 1929, that one of the worst natural disasters in the history of Virginia occurred. It was a tragedy with supernatural overtones. Perhaps a psychic premonition of what was to come occurred about a month earlier. It was at that time that a seventh grade teacher named Effie Flanery at the Rye Cove Consolidated School, had a prophetic dream. The school then was a two-story frame building of seven rooms, serving 250 students from the surrounding area. She dreamed of teaching in a "new and entirely different building, and all about were evidences of a newly constructed building."

A month later, on the morning of May 2, a second omen of imminent danger occurred to Miss Flanery. It was recorded by Margaret DuPont Lee in her book, "Virginia Ghosts," published a year later. The teacher wrote Mrs. Lee: "About 10 o'clock in the morning I was teaching a review class in the sixth grade mathematics and was solving a problem on the board for their observation. Suddenly, something like a nicely finished mahogany table appeared at my right side, and a flash of something like lightning came down the wall and across the table and split it in two along an irregular line. I can't say if it were a voice or thought which came to me in these words, 'Rye Cove is not a safe place to be.'"

Miss Flanery was so astonished and frightened by this phenomenon that she thought seriously about going to the principal and asking him to dismiss all the students immediately. But for some inexplicable reason — perhaps she thought the principal would think her crazy — she did not act. And thus, the eerie premonition went unheeded.

Three and a half hours later, at about 1:30 p.m., an unbelievably powerful tornado struck about half a mile down the valley from the school. It destroyed several buildings in a path which led straight to the school house. It hit with such sudden and fearful force that there was no time to seek shelter. In seconds the unearthly vacuum created by the huge funnel blew out windows and snapped timbers like matchsticks. The entire building was ripped asunder, strewing the wreckage over a distance of several hundred yards. The entire school was torn from its foundations, lifted into the air as if by a giant hand, and then slammed back down to earth.

The air was filled with shards of glass, spears of shattered wood, and the bodies of horrified children. It was a terrifying scene. A six foot wooden plank was driven through one girl's body; another student was nearly decapitated by the hurtling glass. Scores of others were buried under heaps of fallen debris, their pitiful cries buried under the prodigious sounds of the roaring storm.

It was all over in seconds. When rescuers arrived, it looked like a Civil War battlefield. Twelve children and one teacher were dead. More than 50 others had to be hospitalized. And many more pulled themselves from the wreckage, battered, bruised and bloodied.

Everywhere, there were muffled cries, moans, and screams.

A memorial plaque was erected at the site honoring those who perished in that awesome moment of tragedy. The date was forever frozen in the memories of everyone in the county.

And those memories seem to have been perpetuated on each anniversary of the debacle. For it was said — and it has been passed down ever since — that every May 2nd, no matter what the weather is, calm or stormy, an ethereal wind of mighty proportions is heard gushing through the valley where the school once stood. . . and the anguished cries of the petrified little children are still heard . . .

Miss Flanery's dream came true. A new school was built.

CHAPTER 43

The Vengenful Return Of Virginia's 'Meanest Man'

(Charlotte County)

(Author's note: In past volumes in this series, I have written about many of Virginia's most charismatic, eccentric, and/or enigmatic characters.

And here is another to add to this intriguing and fascinating list: Ab (for Abner) Redmond. He was called, at one time or another — sinister, evil, wicked, diabolical, and Machiavellian. He was also a man "plagued by troubles," and was constantly brought before the law for charges ranging from debt evasion to trespass, assault and battery, and numerous murders. The story of Ab Redmond and his alleged ghost is perhaps best told by beginning at the end.)

On November 2, 1893, the Richmond Dispatch ran the following article: "DRAKE'S BRANCH, VA., (between Farmville and South Boston). Notorious Ab Redmond, the worst man that ever lived in Charlotte County, came to his death last night at the hands of a mob. He was arrested yesterday at daybreak by an officer and a dozen assistants, which was one of the few times he was ever captured without trouble. He mistook the officer for a friend.

"A few days ago he was after a Negro to kill him and caught the wrong one by mistake, but did not let him go without having beaten him nearly to death. He was taken before a justice of the peace, but for want of evidence was acquitted. Later, after threatening a number of the best citizens in the vilest manner, he acknowledged that he was the man who served the Negro so shamefully and only waited an opportunity to kill the right one.

"The prisoner was taken to Dupres . . . and after a day spent in looking up witnesses, he waived the trial by the justice and was sent on to jail. It being night, Constable Crutcher was ordered to take the prisoner to his house, which was on the way to the court house, under the guard of three men. They arrived safely at Crutcher's house without any sign of disturbance.

"About 11 o'clock, two of the guards were asleep and one on duty, when all at once the door was broken in with a crash and all hands were covered with guns and pistols. Without a word, the prisoner was taken out. It was a thoroughly organized crowd, every one knew his place, and in less than a minute everything was as quiet as before the mob came.

"One of the guards when asked the number replied: 'Don't know; they came into the light like men coming up out of the ground and disappeared in like manner.' This morning the body was found by a Negro on Crutcher's place swinging from a tree, white with frost. A coroner's inquest was held and the verdict was, 'Redmond came to his death by the hands of a mob of unknown men.'"

The newspaper report continued: "His life was full of deeds of the blackest hue, with but few good ones to counteract the bad. The community was in a state of terror while he lived. Every one feared his fiendish ways, and no one knew when he would become his (Ab's) victim. Punishment seemed to have no effect on him. He would come back from prison as soon as his stripes were off and would return to his fiendish ways.

"No one felt safe around him. If a cow or a horse crossed his place he would often shoot it down. Redmond was a man of means, and his whole fortune was spent in paying lawyers. This man's bad career began when he was but a boy. Some hot words passed between him and his old father. Shortly afterwards, the old man was walking along with his gun on his shoulder, when he was suddenly shot dead by Ab from behind the corner of a fence. With the aid of the ablest lawyers this was proven to be in self-defense.

"Later, a Negro was missing, and after a short time his body was ploughed up. This was proven to be the work of Redmond, and with the aid of the ablest lawyers in the state, he got off with a few years in prison. Then came the burning of the house of one of

233

our best citizens. Redmond confessed to the burning, but through technicalities proved that it was his own house. Shortly after this, the same man had a number of his barns burned.

"Later, a neighbor had a few words with Redmond, and in a day or two, four of his horses were poisoned. An old Negro was cut almost to death by Redmond, and for this crime he got two years in prison. When he came back he professed religion, joined the church, and pretended to lead a new life, but no sooner were his disabilities removed, than he went back to his old ways. He had a way of putting his neighbor's hogs into his fields and killing them, along with his own, and every one was too much afraid of him to attempt to regain them.

"These are but a few of his many crimes. This morning, while but few think his last deed justified death, all agree it is a good thing to be clear of such a character. Many of the old citizens say that now they can live in peace, a thing not known to them for years. While all good citizens deplore the horrible deed, yet all admit that it is a happy riddance."

Just who was Ab Redmond and how did he come to gain the evil reputation of being the meanest man in the county? Some answers can be found in an article published in a 1994 issue of "The Southsider. Local History and Genealogy of Southside Virginia." It was written by Carlton Monroe Dickerson, and titled, "Is the Ghost of Ab Redmond Still in Charlotte County?"

According to Dickerson's research, Ab was born in the county in 1841, the youngest of five children by Robert and Clarissa Redmond. It appeared that from an early age, Ab was despised and physically abused by his father. A couple of specific incidents paint a sadistic picture. Dickerson tells of a time when Ab was a teenager. He went to see his sweetheart, a girl named Emma, who was also his cousin. When he returned home his father met him with some switches, and told him to strip or "he would blow his brains out." Ab's mother stepped in and asked that she be allowed to whip her son because when Robert did it, he scarred the boy's back. Dickerson said Robert took "great delight" in relating the story to his neighbors, and even gave a demonstration of "the dance, kneeling down as Ab did when being punished."

Wesley Foster, Ab's brother-in-law, said that once, in 1858, Robert beat Ab so badly that blood came from his nose and ears. The beating had resulted because Ab had stopped ploughing to help some boys kill a mink. On another occasion, when Ab was suffering from a serious groin injury, it was suggested that he be sent to a local doctor. His brother, Bob, then replied "he had a damned sight rather pay ten dollars for a coffin to bury him than pay two dollars for a doctor."

Dickerson noted that whenever Robert Redmond became angry with Ab, which apparently was often, he would run him off the plantation, "threatening him with a gun." During these times, neighbors would take Ab in and feed him.

It was against this background of mutual hatred that things came to a head on November 5, 1859. Ab had pursued his romance with his cousin, a fact which seemed to set his father into a vengeful fit. The feud had been building for some time. Several days before Ab killed his father, Robert had ordered his son out of the house, and was heard to say he would put a ball through Ab's head. During that week, Robert carried his rifle wherever he went.

Exactly what happened when Ab and his father met on that fateful day in November 1859 remains a mystery. What is known is that Ab shot Robert Redmond in the right arm and right side, and he died a week later. Ab then hastily married his cousin, Emma. Ab was then apprehended and tried, in March 1860, for the murder of his father. During the trial, the jury had to be dismissed because Ab

Gravel Hill, home of Ab Redmond

had broken out of jail. He was recaptured, and on April 3, 1861, was convicted of murder in the second degree and sentenced to 15 years in prison.

Ab again escaped, this time on April 3, 1865, the day Richmond fell to Union forces toward the end of the Civil War. Sixteen months later he was caught once more and returned to the penitentiary. It was then that Ab's relatives and neighbors sent a petition to the governor requesting a pardon. Governor F. H. Pierpont said that this case had caused him a great deal of anxiety. He wrote: "This case is a terrible commentary on the bringing up of children without the fear of God; and without moral restraint. The child has been taught no law but that of violence and brute force." The pardon was granted on April 30, 1867.

But the bad seeds had by then been sewn. Although he was less than five feet six inches in height, Ab Redmond struck terror in the hearts of the citizens of Charlotte County. For example, less than a year after being granted his freedom, Ab was hauled back into court along with his brother-in-law, for a brutal beating of a man named John Quigley. The charge stated that the two had caused John ". . . great bodily harm, by striking . . . violent blows in and about the head and face and on the body, with their fists, and with sticks and stones then and there held in the hands . . . and by pulling and tearing off and destroying the clothes . . . of great value . . . $100."

Over the next two decades, in fact, the reign of terror caused both by Ab, and by his older brother, Bob, continued virtually unabated. As Dickerson pointed out, "Doubtless, one could call the Redmond brothers rebels." The fear in the county was widespread, and for every instance in which charges were brought against Ab, there were undoubtedly many more occurrences of thievery, assault, mayhem, and murder which went unrecorded due to the ever-present threat of retribution. Rarely, if ever, had the reign of a bully exerted such terror for such an extended period of time in a Virginia community.

But Ab Redmond did not get away with everything. He was convicted of the May 23, 1886, stabbing of a man and sentenced to two years in the penitentiary. It was only during the brief periods of such incarcerations that the people of Charlotte County got any relief.

And then came the day of reckoning. Ab was arrested on October 26, 1893. It was then that he made threats upon his neighbors and swore that he would find, and kill, "the right Negro." The citizens had had enough of fear. They banded together and on

Halloween night, 1893, dragged Ab from his captors, and lynched him.

The Charlotte (County) Gazette filed the following report: "The lynching of A.W.C. (Ab) Redmond on the night of the 31st, a few miles from this place (Drakes Branch), created quite a sensation here. While he was conceded a bad character, yet the deed was not warranted, and is universally condemned by good citizens of the county. Many characterize it as a most brutal and outrageous piece of outlawry, which cast a slur on the fair name of Charlotte County and the state."

There were some strange twists following the lynching. Although an investigation was supposedly held, the results were, as Dickerson wrote, "sealed, misplaced, or simply destroyed." He added that "the possibility of corruption and complicity reaching into the high levels of county law enforcement was whispered." Not one member of the lynch mob was ever indicted.

But did Ab Redmond, much feared in life, also come back to haunt his murderers from the beyond? There is some belief that he did. Based on comments from a woman who apparently knew some of Ab's abductors, they were taunted by the dead man. Dickerson wrote: "Ab Redmond's life was ended on the outskirts of Drakes Branch where he was lynched, at a place still known as 'Ab Redmond's Gulch.'

"It was said that Ab Redmond haunted the mob that murdered him. There are accounts of men committing suicide, going insane, and screaming on their death beds, 'Get Ab Redmond off my back'!"

(Author's postscript: In a telephone conversation with Carlton Dickerson, the author of the article on Ab Redmond in the Southsider historical publication, I learned that the Redmond house in Charlotte County, near Randolph, Virginia, is still standing. It is about a fifth of a mile north of state road 606, and three miles from the intersection of highway 360. Dickerson said that his great grandfather had married Ab Redmond's sister, and this has sparked his interest in researching and writing about this bizarre episode in the commonwealth's history.

To satisfy my curiosity, I asked Dickerson how it was that a man who was less than five feet six inches tall could create such a reign of terror, and he laughed, and said he must have been a little like a bantam rooster. "I can tell you this," Dickerson added, "it was a fascinating case, and even though it ended more than 100 years ago, people in the county still talk about it.")

CHAPTER 44

Who Haunts The Wilderness Road Museum?

(Newbern, Pulaski County)

I t was known as the Wilderness Road.
But to most of the courageous pioneers who traveled over it 250 years ago it was more than that. It was a highway of hope; a passage to paradise; a dirt road of dreams; a link to a new life.

And during the second half of the 18th century and well into the 19th, thousands of farmers, tradesmen, craftsmen, merchants, Indian traders, soldiers, missionaries, and others streamed along this treacherous turnpike which stretched from Philadelphia and Baltimore down through the Shenandoah Valley, on south via the Cumberland Gap into Tennessee, Kentucky and points west.

Down they came past what is now Winchester, Harrisonburg, Staunton, Lexington, Salem, Christiansburg, Pulaski, Wytheville, and Abingdon. Some then went south to Tennessee. Others went west to "Kaintuck," while some stopped along the way to settle in southwest Virginia.

Down they came, in Conestoga wagons, in buggies and coaches, on horseback or muleback, in just about any conveyance imaginable. They were loaded down with all their worldly possessions. Often, cattle, horses, sheep and pigs dragged along behind their creaky vehicles.

Down they came seeking a new start in the new world; fresh land and opportunity; religious freedom; a life of adventure. Few had any idea of how difficult the journey would be; hundreds of

The Wilderness Road Museum

miles over rutty, muddy roads; savage attacks by marauding Indians; inflated prices for food and lodging if such could be found at all.

Little wonder America became such a strong nation. If one could survive hardships such as these just to scratch out a living, one could well persevere over just about anything, including foreign armies. Such hard-earned independence would never be yielded without a fight to the death.

Of those who stopped along the way to settle in the valleys, mountains and foothills of the commonwealth, historian Henry Howe, in 1845, wrote, "Much of Western Virginia is yet a new country, and thinly settled; and in some of the more remote and inaccessible counties, the manner of living and the habits of the people are quite primitive." Of the pioneer, Howe said, "He leads a manly life, and breathes the pure air of the hills with the contented spirit of a free man."

As the migration continued, early entrepreneurs saw opportunity knocking. One such man was Adam Hance. He had gotten off the Wilderness Road at a site which is now Newbern, between Christiansburg to the north, and Wytheville to the south. There was, in the early 1800s, no other sizeable settlement between these two towns — a distance of about 60 miles. Hance envisioned Newbern would make a good stopover point along the trail for thirsty, hungry and exhausted travelers. He also thought the area was ideally suited for a community to be developed.

And so, in March 1810, at a location high and airy, and as Howe wrote, "giving a fine view of the neighboring valleys and mountains," Hance laid out 28 lots fronting the Wilderness Road. Decades ahead of his time as a developer, Hance specified that each lot purchaser must build "a hewed log house at least one and a half stories high, with a shingle roof, brick or stone chimney, and two glass windows with 12 lights each." The town of Newbern was born.

Hance's son, Henry, built the first house. Adam Hance then put up his house a lot away, and the two became connected by a covered "dog trot," which later was enclosed, creating one building 100 feet long. The Hances operated a post office and a tavern out of their residence, and it remained in the family's possession until the 1970s.

It was acquired, in 1980, by the New River Historical Society, and since has become the Wilderness Road Regional Museum, dedicated to "preserve the Appalachian culture." It is operated by society members from Floyd, Giles, Montgomery and Pulaski Counties and the town of Radford.

The museum houses period furniture, tools, papers, records and documents and other historical items pertaining to the colorful days when the Wilderness Road was as crowded as Interstate highway 81 is today.

There also may be a resident ghost.

Or maybe not. It depends upon who you talk to.

Some say the spirit or spirits reported to surface occasionally are nothing more than figments of over-active imaginations. Virginia Alexander, who was brought up in the house in the 1800s, said the haunted legend dates back to pre-Civil War days. She told of one non- ghostly incident that may have added to the tradition. It happened just after the War Between the States. She and a servant girl were upstairs cleaning in a bedroom when they suddenly heard a strange noise coming from the roof of the building. They both looked up, but saw nothing. The servant, believing the "hant" was after her, became hysterical and collapsed. Mrs. Alexander, however, discovered that mortal men were up on the roof working. This was little consolation to the servant girl, who remained convinced the place was bedeviled.

Local historian Ed Moorer, a man with a puckish sense of humor, told of another "scary" occasion at the museum. He said a young boy visiting the museum claimed he envisioned a large man with flaming red hair, dressed in "old-fashioned" clothing. The boy, Ed said, became terribly frightened when he saw "a stream of

blood" running down the man's face. Then the apparition dematerialized before the lad's eyes.

"Well, I guess you could say I have helped the museum's
haunting legend along," Ed told the author. "Actually, I made that
incident up." But Ed added that others are convinced there is a
genuine ghost in the building. A number of visitors have reported
hearing unaccountable sounds while touring the premises. The
noises seem to originate in the upstairs section when no one is
there. Rustling sounds have been heard in the attic, but no human
cause for them is ever found. Tourists have also told of walking
into, and out of, chilling cold spots in the upstairs rooms.

Sarah Zimmerman, who has served as curator of the museum,
is convinced there is an otherworldly presence. "The ghost is alive
and well," she has said. But she believes it is not a harmful presence, rather a mischievous one. She cites a number of manifestations she has experienced: the rustling sounds in the attic; the
feeling of someone being there when no one is; and the opening of
closed heavy file cabinet drawers by unseen hands. Sarah says this
has happened on several occasions and she has no logical explanation for it.

A volunteer museum worker also reported that once when he
was upstairs in a bedroom, he saw what looked like an impression
of someone lying on the freshly made bed.

If there is a ghost, who might it be? One possibility is the spirit
of a card player who was killed in an argument that ensued over a
game of chance in the 1830s when the building served as a tavern.
Locals offer the conjecture that the ghost may be that of a former
slave who was hanged across the street for stealing grain from a
barn to feed his family. He may be seeking retribution for being
dealt a punishment which far exceeded the crime.

Discounting the "near misses," and the fictionalized versions,
there do appear to be witnesses to enough unexplained phenomena to presume the Wilderness Road Museum does contain an
authentic ghost. Whether one encounters it or not, the building that
Adam Hance and his son erected in the early 1800s is nevertheless
well worth a visit for its historical significance alone.

And maybe its best to heed the lines of a poem Ed Moorer
wrote, one stanza of which reads:
"Now, I won't say there's a ghost in the house here
You see, I'm really not sure
And to tell you the truth, love
Perhaps I don't want to know."

CHAPTER 45

More From The James Taylor Adams Collection

(Southwest Virginia)

(Author's note: In volumes II and III of this series on Virginia ghosts, I included selections from what is known as the James Taylor Adams collection. During the Great Depression, the Works Progress Administration funded a program whereby writers were sent out into the mountains, valleys and hollows of the common-wealth to collect oral histories on Virginia folklore. One of the most prolific chroniclers was a man named James Taylor Adams. Among his papers are more than 200 ghost legends, sworn to have been passed along as true by the contributors. Taylor and others con-ducted the interviews. These are what I consider to be heirlooms of the state's heritage. Herewith is another sampling from that price-less collection. It is reprinted here through the permission and courtesy of Clinch Valley College and the Blue Ridge Institute.)

ames Taylor Adams was born in 1892 and was a native of Letcher County, Kentucky, although he spent most of his life in southwestern Virginia. He worked for 25 years as a coal miner in Wise County. Later he edited a quarterly magazine, "The Cumberland Empire," which included sketches, short stories, poems and songs descriptive of the mountain area where he lived. He also published a book in 1941 — "Death in the Dark: A Collection of Factual Ballads of American Mine Disasters, with Historical Notes." Adams conducted several hundred, possibly thousands, of interviews both during and after the writers' project in Virginia. He is said to have had a special interest in preserving various types of southern Appalachian folklore. He relished his work. Adams died in 1954, but his legacy lives on.)

* * * * *

THE TELL-TALE TEETHMARKS

The following account was told by James Taylor Adams himself in 1940. He said he had heard it as a child from his mother.

"Years ago the old log cabins didn't have any locks on their doors like they have today. They had a hole honed through the door and through the door facing, and they ran a chain through there and put a padlock on it, and they also had a hole in the door where the cat could go in and out at night.

"This one woman kept having this dream. She would dream of a night that she would hear the chains a'rattling on the door there, and every time it rattled, there would be a big black cat jump up on her head and get on her chest and it would just almost smother her to death. She said she couldn't hardly breathe with the cat on there — was like a dead weight. And this happened just night after night.

"She finally told someone about it, some of the neighbors, and the neighbors that she told said, 'You know this old lady that lives down the road here by herself, she is a witch, says she got mad at you about something, and this is her. She turned herself into a cat . . . The next time she does that, you get her by the foot and bite her, and that will stop her.'

"So the next night this woman went to bed and said just before she went to sleep, she heard the chains rattle on the door, and here come the cat and jumped right up on the bed and on her. It was so heavy she felt like it was going to mash her plumb through the bed, and said she couldn't hardly breathe. Said she grabbed the cat by its front paw and stuck its foot in her mouth and bit it real hard, and said the cat screamed out and squalled and jerked its foot back and took off out through the door. And she heard the chain rattle as it went out the door.

"And the next day some of the folks walked by the house where the old lady (witch) lived down there and she had her hand all bandaged up, and she died just a short time after that. But she wore that bandage on her hand as long as she lived. After she died some of them took the bandage off.

"There were teethmarks on her arm."

* * * * *

GHOSTLY HANDPRINTS

The interviewer, Emory Hamilton of Wise, Virginia, wrote: "The informant of this tale (not identified) told me her grandmother heard this preacher tell this story in one of his sermons while great tears slowly rolled down his cheeks, and that he also showed his coat with the hand-prints seared on each lapel. The interview: "In the mountains a woman died and after her death the house became so haunted no one could live there. At evening time a woman could be seen there and a thumping or beating noise heard. People became afraid to pass by the house. Some who were nervy enough to venture in during the day swore that human handprints were burned on the door facings and could not be rubbed off. Whittlers said they had tried to cut them out and that they were as deep as they could whittle.

"There was a certain preacher some miles away who said if his circuit carried him by the house that he intended to find out what was going on. One day he happened to be passing by late in the evening. He tethered his horse, dismounted, and went up to the door. He heard the beating noise as soon as his horse was tied, and when he went to the door, he saw the woman who had died standing with her hands on one of the door facings where the prints were seared in the wood.

"He asked her in the name of the Trinity what she was doing and what she wanted. She said, 'I am beating up me some pepper to make a tea.' (This was before ground pepper was known, when it came in berries and had to be beat at home.) 'I am staying here to tell someone why I died. I wanted some pepper tea which would have cured me, but they would not give it to me. I have, too, a

244

secret to tell you that I do not want told. You are the only one since I've been coming here who would speak to me.

"'I must touch you so that people will believe what I have told you is so, when you tell it.' So, coming over, she took hold of each coat lapel and when she turned loose her finger and handprints were scorched on the cloth. 'Now I go to Heaven and will be seen here no more,' she said. All at once beautiful music started playing and the woman started slowly to ascend upward. He watched her as she went until she looked no larger than a goose feather, and finally disappeared in the blue distance."

* * * * *

THE FRIGHTENED FIDDLER

Interview by Emory Hamilton of Mrs. Polly Johnson, Wise, Virginia, September 23, 1940: "I heard Elliott Mullins tell one. They called him 'Turtle Neck.' I was just a child — small, when I heard him tell it, but I was old enough to remember it. He was a fiddler.

"He'd been to a frolic one night, way back when I's a baby. He was an awful good fiddler and fiddled a lot for frolics and plays and such. He started home about midnight. He had to cross a creek near a grave. No, not a graveyard, just a single grave, some man had been buried there. I didn't know who. He turned off here, crossed a fence and went to a foot log that he had to cross to get to his daddy's. He had to step nearly on the grave to get by. Just a little pathway there.

"He got right 'fenenst' (atop) the grave and a big light flashed up around him. It was just like a rim of a wheel. it didn't look like fire . . . more like moonlight. The rim was around him. He said inside the rim was a man. He got down so he could see and looked sorta up. He could see the man but where his eyes was *just holes*! Places there for them, but it was just holes. The man in the rim of fire said to him, 'Why don't you go back and play the fiddle?' He finally got out of the rim and started on. Instead of going across the foot log, he went right through the creek. When he got home he just fell in the door. Aunt Tilda said he was scared to death when he got there."

* * * * *

A WIFE RETURNS IN SPIRIT FORM

Interview by Emory Hamilton of Mrs. Goldie Hamilton, Esserville, Virginia, January 24, 1940: "Once there was a girl married a man who had been married before she was married to him. He took her to his home and one day while he was away she was standing on the hearth by the fire. All at once there was a woman came and stood by her on the hearth. She said, 'I was your husband's first wife and he killed me and buried me under this hearth.

" 'I want you to bury my bones and then I won't bother you anymore!' It was night and the last wife said, 'I have no light. I can't go out and bury your bones because it's dark.' The (spectral) wife said, 'I'll give you a light,' and she held out the prettiest candle the other wife had ever seen. It was so bright she could see everywhere. She took the candle and raised the hearth stones, and there saw a pile of human bones. She got a sack, scooped up the bones, and buried them. She never saw the other wife's ghost anymore."

* * * * *

THE SPIRIT SINGING SPIRITUALS

Interview by James Hylton, of Mrs. Emily Thompson, Big Stone Gap, Virginia, March 24, 1941: "Old George Pease, who for 20 years was an old Negro man who came from the eastern part of the state and who worked around the old Lodge Hall below my house, was an odd old man who claimed to have power to (re)move warts and talk with the 'spirits,' as he called it. He died in a little shack there 12 years ago, but the old Lodge Hall is still there and you can go and see for yourself what I am telling you if the notion strikes you.

"Well, anyway, the old fellow . . . took care of the hall, sweeping and the like. He would sing and chant old Negro songs and walk around all hours of the night, and now when the night is still, you can hear a funny noise like somebody trying to sing some kind of old darky songs and you can hear a shuffling sound like somebody walking in shoes that might be loose on their feet or dragging.

"Girls and young boys dodge the place at night and many is

the time when I have gone out front and walked by the place with some of them when they was scared to go by themselves. You can hear a sound too like somebody sweeping and it sounds like trying to sweep slow like and with long strokes with a broom or something.

"... When the colored Lodge meets and comes to order, they get their business over and are gone before late in the night, and you can bet that they leave the place all at once and they won't come to clean the floors or clean the windows unless there are at least two or three of them. I heard them all piling out of there one night and went to my gate and asked them what was wrong, and one big fellow told me they heard too many noises that night, and they thought they heard old George Pease singing one of his old songs like he used to sing while living there. You could tell from the looks in their eyes that they must have really seen or heard something out of the ordinary."

(Author's note: During the interview by Hylton, Mrs. Thompson, then aged 66, filled in some of the details about George Pease. She said he had been born in slavery in 1829 a few miles east of Richmond, and was 100 years old when he died. She added that he "seemed to possess powers that would cure moles, warts and corns. He said that he could talk to the spirits and the warts or whatever it was would leave and I know in several of the cases I know about he did (remove the blemishes)."

Mrs. Thompson said that old George had learned one of his songs from his mother, who sang it to him in tears shortly before she died in pre-civil War days when they were slaves. It was George's favorite, and it went like this:

"Dar's a great day a-comin,

When da Lawd'll call us home,

An' de chains'll all be breakin,

An' He'll turn us loose to roam.

Up in he'ben dar's no slavery

An' de chains Ire made ob gold,

All de swords Ire blades of silvery

An' de wars're noble an' bold."

* * * * *

THE CAT THAT WOULDN'T STAY DEAD!

("... The corpse, already greatly decayed and clotted with gore, stood erect before the eyes of the spectators. Upon its head, with red extended mouth and solitary eye of fire, sat the hideous beast whose craft had seduced me into murder, and whose informing voice had consigned me to the hangman. I had walled the monster up within the tomb!" Edgar Allan Poe - "The Black Cat")

Interview by James Hylton of Mrs. Mary Harrison, 56, who "lives on the road between Wise and Coeburn, Virginia," March 27, 1942: "Lennie, my daughter, killed a cat we had here several years ago and an old man we knew passed the gate and saw her kill it with a stick. It was a mean cat and we had to get rid of it someway.

"He said, 'Don't you know a cat has got nine lives and you can't kill that cat?' Anyway, Lennie buried it in the back of the yard after digging a hole about a foot or so deep. It had been in the habit of going in the corner in back of the cook stove and laying down

during the early evening. We figured we were through with it. Anyway, that night after we'd eaten our supper and I reached back in the corner for a broom to go about sweeping the floor, there was that old cat, alive as ever. It had dug out of the shallow grave and come on back into the kitchen as ever before!"

* * * * *

THE CURSE OF THE CARBINE

Interview by James Taylor Adams of Finley Adams, Big Laurel, Virginia, May 7, 1941: "You've heard of John Dick Adams, old uncle Jess Adams' boy . . . He was a dangerous man. When the Civil War broke out he got up a company and was a captain. Some sort of home guards. They raided around. He owned a fine carbine gun. One time he was at grandpa's and told him if he was to be killed that he wanted him to see that his carbine was buried with him. He was on the rebel side.

"One day his company got into a fight, somewhere on the Kentucky River I think it was. John Dick he got shot through one arm. After awhile he was shot through one leg. He couldn't walk or use but one arm, but he kept shootin' his carbine rifle. At last they shot him through the other arm. He was helpless then. They charged up on him and he said, 'Well, men, I've always said I'd never surrender, but I'm helpless now and will have to beg for my life.' One of Bates' I think it was, said, 'I'll give you your life,' and just up and shot him through the heart. Then he took his gun.

"Well, they say that that fellow never rested after that. He would holler out all times of the night, 'Take John Dick Adams away from here. He's come to kill me.' He even got so that he would see John Dick in his cup of coffee when he set down to the table to eat. He heard about the request that John Dick had made about his gun being buried with him, and he sent word to grandpa to come and get it.

"Grandpa went and got the gun, but it had been several months and he didn't bury the gun with John Dick then, of course. But him getting the gun didn't do any good. That feller just kept seeing John Dick wherever he went. He didn't live long. Got so he couldn't eat. Said John Dick Adams was in every bite he tried to swallow. So he just dwindled away. Died in about a year after he killed John Dick."

THE DOCTOR'S PATIENT RETURNS

Interview by James Taylor Adams of James Kilgore, Esserville, Virginia, June 2, 1941: "Fifty-seven years ago, I guess it's been. When the flux was raging in this country. My uncle, Dr. Jerry Wells, was going everywhere doctoring for the flux. One of his patients was William Kennedy's wife. Kennedy lived somewhere in the valley. She died. About the same time, Uncle Jerry's boy, Taze Wells, a school teacher, took it and died, too. I've heard Uncle Jerry tell this and I've heard other people tell it. Said that his wife was worrying a sight about their boy. Afraid he was lost.

"So one night Uncle Jerry was a coming home way long in the night from seeing some one who was sick. He got right close to where William Kennedy lived and was laying down some draw bars to take his horse through, when he heard something behind him. He turned around and there stood Will Kennedy's wife just as plain as he'd ever seen her in his life.

"She said, 'I just wanted to tell you that you need not worry about Taze. He's saved, and all the people who have died around here are saved. So do not worry about Taze or any of us. We are all happy and better off.'

"Well, Uncle Jerry went on home and his wife seen there was something wrong with him by his actions. She asked him what was the matter and he told her he couldn't tell her then. He didn't want the children to hear it. The next morning he told her while she was getting breakfast . . . He told how Mrs. Kennedy had said to him that night, 'You read in the Bible that the Lord is a spirit. You can't touch me.'

"He said he reached out his hand to see if he could feel anything and there was nothing there! She then disappeared."

* * * * *

GHOST LIGHT ON THE MOUNTAIN

Interview by James Taylor Adams of Thomas Countiss, teacher at the Hurricane School, Wise, Virginia, February 24, 1942: "I have heard my father, Schuyler Countiss, tell that when he was a young man . . . that a man disappeared in the neighborhood and was never heard from again. Then one night they saw a light shining far up on the side of the mountain. They didn't pay much attention to it that time, but the next night they saw it again. This set them to wondering. They got to watching for it, and every night they could see it, right in the same place.

"At last, several of the neighbors got together one evening and waited until the light appeared and they started to it. They climbed up the mountain for a mile or more and when they were right close up to the light they saw it suddenly go out. They were afraid it was moonshiners or some other lawless characters, and that they might be fired upon, so they searched about, but using caution.

"At last, they discovered a small cave right about where the light seemed to go out. They made a light and went in, and found the skeleton of a man. They never knew who it was, but it was thought to be the skeleton of the man who had disappeared from the neighborhood. Most people believed the light was put there to guide people to the skeleton."

* * * * *

THE GHOST WITH THE GRAY BEARD

Interview by James Taylor Adams of Mrs. Nancy Emily Collins, Glamorgan, Virginia, August 14, 1941: "Seems like there's two sorts of things to be seed by people. I believe you will be showed things that's going to happen, and then there's just regular haunted houses and places. These places are haunted by the spirits of the dead, I reckon. Mostly nothing follows seeing one of them.

"Now you can take that place were we lived on the mountain. The old Purkey place it was called before we went there. Old man Bill Purkey lived and died there. Everybody said it was haunted. Oh, I don't know how many had said they'd seed Bill Purkey there and heard something like barrels rolling in the loft and on the floor.

Emmett Gibson said he wouldn't stay a night there for a million dollars. But we wasn't afraid. Hadn't never done nothing to Bill Purkey for him to want to harm us.

"We moved there about 35, 36 years ago. Hadn't been there but a week or so and me and the children was a-laying there when we heard something just like somebody rattling a bridle in the other room. It just kepon and on, and I got up and stirred up the fire and got one of the children up and we went in there. Not a thing in the world was to be seed. We come back and it started in again. Kept it up nearly all night. We never found out what it was.

"Been living there a year or two. A passel of men was prospecting for coal, and we took them to board. Didn't have much house room. So we put up five beds in one room. I had to have a hired girl to help me do the work. She had to sleep in the room where all them men slept. They was all young boys like. Course I wouldn't put her in there by herself. So I slept in there with her. It was Samantha Perry. She'd tell you just what I'm telling you.

"The bed sat right by a window. Window hadn't any curtains or blinds. Moon was shining bright as day. I was laying there and had drapped off to sleep. Something waked me up a-groaning and taking on the awfulest noise I ever heard in my life. Went like somebody dying. I sort of raised up on one elbow and looked, and right at the foot of our bed, sort of humped over, was an old gray-bearded man. I could see his face and his beard. Come way down on his breast. He was moving right up the side of the bed toward the head.

"I jerked the kiver up over my head and nudged Samantha and asked her if she was asleep. She said no. I told her what I'd seed. And she looked and seed it, too. Then it just seemed to vanish away, and the taking-on hushed, too. I laid there and couldn't go to sleep. I'll tell you I was feeling quare. Then all at once it started in again. Just taking on like somebody dying. It was a man, too.

"Then here it come again, just creeping right up the side of our bed. I kivered up my head again and after awhile it hushed and I never heard it anymore. But I didn't go to sleep anymore than night. My first thought was that it was Bill Purkey, but I looked good, and it didn't look a-tall like Bill Purkey looked. Stranger to me. I never seed him before. Awful old looking man. Great long beard."

* * * * *

THE HAUNTED HORSE SHOES

Interview by James Hylton of Willard Froeman at Wise, Virginia, October 7, 1941: "I've heard my mother tell about her knowing about Seltzer's Rock many times. The tale they tell coincides with the many tales told about this rock. There are people who still believe in this 'hant' stuff you know, and in the hills they believe in it very strongly.

"They were coming in to vote from Guest's Station, or what is now Maytown, Virginia, along in May (passing by Seltzer's Rock). Uncle Dan Ramey run into town and said he'd heard some noise there and wanted somebody to go back with him to the spot where he'd heard it. . . Finally he got some men to go back there and there was a man's hat and pipe. Later they found a (dead) horse, and it belong to Seltzer (who had died.)

"Well, the horse had new shoes on it, and in them days good shoes for horses were scarce and cost a lot, and some of the men suggested it was no use to let them to waste on a dead horse, so they started to taking them from the dead horse's feet. Then, the men heard a walking around like somebody calling to them saying something about hearing them take off his horse's shoes and to stop. They all believed Uncle Dan then and got to looking around more, and then found Dan Ramey's hant, as he called it.

"It was Seltzer dead, and after that they said you could hear him walking down the old path there, and grumbling about the fellows taking off the shoes from his dead horse. I have talked to some of the people in Stone Mountain and they all say the same thing, even the very best of nice and educated folks. They say to this day you can hear a rustling noise on the path leading to the rock, and it really sounds like somebody walking down in the leaves, and some say you can hear a noise of somebody mumbling something about a horse. The folks in the mountain there swear it is the spirit of Seltzer coming back to worry them over taking his horse's shoes from his dead horse.

"Later, a man by the name of Johnson put on the horse's shoes from the dead horse, and when he was late coming in, he could hear some kind of a clinking sound in the shoes, and thinking them loose, and it might be harmful to his horse, he'd got down off his mount and looked at his horse's shoes, but found nothing wrong. But when it came to his mind about Seltzer, he made a hasty movement in getting them off, and giving them away.

"Later, the fellow he gave them to had the same experience and did the same thing. For as many as six men, these shoes seemed to give the same trouble, and somebody later threw them into a creek down near Tacoma, Virginia, and some boys fishing there later said they heard a funny sound there and when they described it, it sounded as did the tales the men had told about their horses and their shoes, too."

* * * * *

RETURN OF THE WRETCHED RECLUSE

Interview by James Hylton of Mrs. J. W. Thompson, Big Stone Gap, Virginia, January 29, 1942: "It was back about 1923, when John Payne, an old fellow who was awful tall — about six and a half feet — here in Big Stone, took his own life. He lived not far from here with his little boy of about 12 years old. They lived in a big house on a little knoll . . . Something happened to the little boy and he died. (John Payne) sold strawberries, apples, etc., to make a living along with a pasture field he rented out. Nobody knew where he came from or much about his people. It seemed that he'd come out of a clear sky.

"After this boy died, he became a man to himself. I remember people talking about it and they all said that he would not even go to the store for anything he needed, hardly. Nobody hardly ever saw him, and people got so they dodged his place. The children in the neighborhood dreaded the place and walked around it when they had to pass by. Once in a while when he could be seen in his field at work, which was seldom, he would have an old shotgun slung over his shoulder with a rope or strap, working away.

"If anyone got near him he walked away from them and never spoke. Not so long after this little boy died, the big old house burned down to the ground. At the time of the fire, there was no way to save it. Many people feared that the old fellow was burned up in the place, or the house, but when officers went there to investigate, they found nothing. They assumed that he and his old dog had gotten out all right and were just keeping to themselves as they usually did. . . Some people at times would say that they had seen him and his dog, but others would deny it and say that they never would believe it.

"This place was near a place where most of the people in this community went to pick salad greens, and lots of times when they would start there they would meet somebody coming back and when asked if they had gotten their baskets full, they'd say, "No, I heard something up there and I was not caring to go any closer, and come away. I heard somebody say something up there and thought I heard a dog moving around trying to growl or bark or something.' Well, it happened that way many times.

"Then, in 1923 . . . somebody was passing there and they heard a gunshot, very loud, and it seemed to shake the old barn nearby . . . The next morning some people went over there to see what it was. They had all dreaded the place anyway, and most of them took guns with them. So many people had still dreaded the thought of old man Payne. They found him where he'd shot himself with the old shotgun. The queerest part though was how he had done it. He had lain there in the old barn upstairs or in the loft until he had starved almost to death. The bones of his dog were near him, and it must have been dead for a month or so before this happened. He had tied his old shotgun up on a rafter and to the trigger a long stout cord. Over the rafter he brought the cord and had it tied to the big toe of his right foot which protruded through an old wornout shoe. He had waited until he was almost dead from starvation to do it, but he had at least been able and strong enough to pull the rusty trigger of his gun.

"Ever since this happened, people are more so afraid of the place. The field there is a good place to pick greens and lots of people go there now and pick them when they are growing in season. Some come back with tales of hearing somebody yell for you to get out of their field just like old man Payne did in his lifetime. The doors (of the barn) creak and the place has a queer air about it all the time. Many are the tales that have come from there even to this day about these noises. some say they can hear the old dog yelp as it did when he'd be working in the field years ago.

"Anyway, he'd saved all his money in a five pound salt sack and it was found near him when he shot himself, and they used the money for funeral expenses. Yet he would not even go to the store for anything he needed to eat and he and the dog both had done without things they needed to eat. The barn stands today and the place is there for you to go and see yourself."

* * * * *

A FASCINATING 'J.T.A.' FOOTNOTE
(Tazewell County)

James Taylor Adams was a prodigious interviewer/writer and chronicler of Southwest Virginia folklore. He was practicing his craft long before the Works Progress Administration writers' program was begun, and long after it had been disbanded. In 1935, for example, years before the WPA project, Adams wrote about an intriguing phenomenon which occurred in the small town of Cedar Bluff, roughly halfway between Pulaski and Norton and just off highway 19/460.

During an overnight stay there in a boarding house a 78-year old woman named Mrs. Norman began telling Adams about her extraordinary granddaughter, Nannie Ruth Lowe, who had died two years earlier at the age of seven. Mrs. Norman said that Nannie Ruth, from the time of her birth, demonstrated the incredible intelligence that is only associated with gifted geniuses.

At the age of nine months, Nannie Ruth got out of her bed one night, walked across the room and began talking to her mother about "events of the day" in perfect English. Her mother was stunned, for the child had neither spoken, or walked a step before that. When she was one year old, Nannie Ruth could read the Bible, or "any other book," and knew the alphabet. Such unbelievable feats drew widespread attention in the rural community, and Adams wrote that people came from miles around to hear the infant read.

By the time Nannie Ruth was three years old, she led the singing at revival meetings, and directed prayers in public. Mrs. Norman said that although her granddaughter never went to

Crown and Cross of Feathers

school or had any formal education, she could "write in a perfect hand," and knew more about spelling, math and the Bible than anyone around.

Then one day in 1933, when she was seven, she went to her mother and said that her "mission has been brief, but it is finished and I must go home to the Father." Two weeks later, on December 9th, she was suddenly stricken seriously ill, and died the next day. More than 2,000 people, from all over the area, attended her funeral.

Shortly after this an event most strange and inexplicable occurred, according to Adams. On January 11, 1934, a month after Nannie Ruth had died, her mother emptied the feathers from the child's pillow. In the center of the feather mass she found a "perfect crown and cross," molded together from the feathers. Nannie's mother, and Mrs. Norman carefully put the items in a shoe box. A few days later, when they went to the box to show the crown and cross to a neighbor, they were astonished to find that it had out-grown the box! They put it in a larger box, and it "outgrew" that as well.

When word of this got out, thousands came to view the phe-nomenon. Adams himself went to the house of Nannie's mother to see for himself. He found that 500 people had been there the Sunday before he arrived. He described the objects as appearing to be a "network of fine silky threadlike substance running all through the mass of feathers." He added that Nannie's mother picked up the crown and cross in his presence and it "didn't come apart."

Louise Leslie, who recorded the incident in her fine book on the history of Tazewell County, in 1982, reported that neither Adams or anyone else could explain what they had observed. Adams was quoted as saying, "I have with my own eyes seen this thing . . . I know it is there."

CHAPTER 46

A Plethora Of Pittsylvania Phantasms
(Pittsylvania County)

(Author's note: "Our county," Mollie Holmes kept telling me, "is the largest one in the state — and the friendliest." Mollie is a charming young lady who keeps trying to interest me in writing about the ghosts in her area, which lies at the extreme southern part of the state. The county includes Danville. When a permanent courthouse was to be built, in the early 1800s, there was a great dispute over just where it should be. Consequently, when it was finally decided, they called the site Competition — a name which stuck until 1874, when the county seat was rechristened Chatham in honor of William Pitt, Earl of Chatham, for whom the county had been named in 1767. This event caused Henry St. George Tucker, clerk of the House of Delegates at the time, to pen: "Immortal Pitt! How great thy fame, When Competition yields to Chatham's name." Anyway, Mollie said to come on down for a visit, and we would look for the haunts in Pittsylvania.)

CEDAR HILL

he ghost or ghosts in Mollie Holmes' 1762 house, known as Cedar Hill, have been fairly inactive over the past year or two and she wishes they would step up and make their presences known. One of them, Mollie believes, is the spirit of a little girl, maybe about six years old. "I'd

258

love to see her," Mollie declares. "I know she's friendly."

Mollie's house, about eight miles from Chatham, features a long, curving, old-fashioned staircase, a large parlor and entrance foyer, and three bedrooms upstairs. The Holmes have added a dining room and enlarged and improved the kitchen area and the bathrooms. Mollie says the house was a stage coach stop in the old days. The stage would ford the Banister River and come up the hill, and people would get out and stretch their legs and eat.

Says Mollie, "We've had at least two encounters with the little girl ghost in the house. One time my daughter felt a terribly cold sensation in the room where 'she' appears. It was a little peculiar because I didn't feel a thing. On the other occasion, my daughter's best friend was staying overnight. She has beautiful red hair. In the middle of the night she was awakened by the sensation of someone or something *stroking her hair* in the bed. She assumed it was our cat rubbing up against her. She sat up in bed and turned on the light. There was no cat. There was no one in the room. She was so frightened, she got up and put on her coat and went down into the parlor and sat up all night!"

Mollie says that some of the unusual activity at Cedar Hill occurred before she moved into the house, and was passed along to her by previous occupants. It is this information that has led her

Cedar Hill

to believe there is more than one spirit in the house. She explains: "Back a hundred years or so ago, they used to do the cooking outside on the porch on a wood stove. They also did some of the canning outside because of the heat in the summer, long before air conditioning. The story we got is that, for some reason, a ghost lady didn't like the outside cooking, and she would make her displeasure known by moving the stove on occasion. It was a very heavy old stove. It would take several strong men to move it. But it was said that the ghost would move it several inches at a time."

Mollie was also told about a music loving spirit. "The house was empty for about 50 years before we moved in," she says. "But many people said that during this time they would hear piano music coming from inside the house when they passed by. Of course, there was no one there, or at least no one was supposed to be there. But those who heard the piano playing said they were too scared to go up and investigate. Several people have told us they used to hear the piano music."

Mollie doesn't know who the piano player and the stove mover might have been. She does, however, have a clue as to the young girl ghost. "There is," she says, "a six-year-old girl buried in the little cemetery on the grounds. We don't know how she died, but we have a feeling it is her who stroked my daughter's friend's hair."

* * * * *

MOUNTAIN VIEW

Steve Law is a friend of Mollie's who lives not far away in a house called Mountain View. This is listed in the Virginia Landmarks Register as having been built between 1840 and 1842 — a time when there was an era of agricultural prosperity in this area of the commonwealth. According to the Register, the house's double parlors "are noteworthy for their plaster-work ceilings, glazed cupboards, and Greek Revival mantels. The place has remnants of an extensive formal garden and landscaped park, features found at many of the region's estates."

Steve says that old houses contract and cool off at night, thus making creaking and groaning noises. This may explain some of the strange activity which occurs here, but not all. "Oh, we haven't seen anything fly across the room, but there are things which are not easily explained," Steve adds.

Perhaps the most prominent phenomenon is that of the sound of tires, or coach wheels, on the gravel driveway in front of the house. Steve and others in the family have had this sensation a number of times over the years, but whenever they look outside there is nothing; no apparent cause for the sounds. This has led him to believe that whoever it is that may have formerly lived at Mountain View may have been socially active.

The other manifestation centers on the doors in the house. "We hear doors slamming when there is no one there to slam them," Steve says. "Now maybe some of this can be explained by natural causes, such as the wind. "But one of the doors weighed over 300 pounds. It would take more than the wind to open and slam that door!"

* * * * *

THE LEGEND OF SOOKIE SHORT

ill Guerrant today is a lawyer in Tampa, Florida. He grew up in Pittsylvania County, however, near a community no longer on the maps known as Slatesville, next to the Halifax County border. He called one day and asked if the author had heard about a ghost in that county known as Sookie Short. (The author hadn't). Bill said that she was "well known" in the area about a century or so ago, and that his father and his grandmother had told him about her when he was a young boy.

Sookie was a black lady who apparently had some strange habits, because in her day she was suspected by her neighbors of being a witch. She apparently was much feared. When any misfortune struck, it was always blamed on Sookie. People would say she had put a hex on them.

According to the legend, Sookie's fire went out one night in the dead of a severe winter, and she went out to get some hot coals from some of her neighbors to restart a fire in her fireplace. She went from door to door, but when people saw who it was they slammed and locked their doors, such was the superstition-inspired terror she fostered.

Frustrated, she walked back toward her cabin, and along the

way sat on an old stump. They found her there the next morning, frozen to death. "She's been a 'hant' in that area ever since," says Bill. For years after that, many people reported seeing her ghost allegedly riding a horse through their pastures late at night.

But the strangest manifestations seemed to occur in the vicinity of the old stump upon which she rested and died. It was commonly reported that whenever a wagon or buggy passed by that stump, the horses would get spooked and rear up, although nothing was ever seen. And ladies' hoop skirts would fly up, even when there was no wind.

"It's a story that has been passed along in that part of Virginia for generations," says Bill. "I'm keeping up the tradition. I've told my children about it."

CHAPTER 47

The Gentle Ghost Of Eldon

(Chatham)

(Author's note: You just never know where the next ghostly chapter is going to come from. I got a call one day from Molly Jenkins, a staff writer for the Lynchburg News Advance. I had sent her a review copy of "The Ghosts of Virginia, Volume III." She was interested in the chapter on Ottie Cline Powell, the little boy who wandered off into the Amherst County mountains a century ago and froze to death. Hikers, hunters and others have sensed strong psychic activity at the site where his body had been found.

"You won't believe this," Molly said, "but my son had a frightening experience on that mountain. He was camped out there and during the night he heard a loud 'report.' He never saw anything, but he didn't understand what had made the noise. The next morning he found out he was right next to Ottie Cline Powell's memorial marker. It sent quite a chill through him."

Molly then told me that I should contact Bob and Joy Lemm who run a country inn and restaurant in Chatham, in Pittsylvania County. "I understand they have a ghost there. A young girl even wrote a poem about it." Subsequent research resulted in the following chapter.)

The inn run by the Lemms is called Eldon. The 13-room mansion was built in 1835 for James Murray Whittle, a noted Virginia lawyer of his day who named the house for a British jurist he admired. It was then a 500 acre plantation. In 1902 Claude Swanson, then governor of the

Eldon in Chatham, Virginia

commonwealth, bought Eldon and lived there until he died in 1939. The original icehouse, smokehouse and stable are still in existence. The Lemms purchased it in 1991, and today one can dine and spend the night there in antebellum elegance.

"We have four guest bedrooms upstairs and one downstairs," says Joy. The old billiard or entertainment room has been converted into a sitting room. There also is a parlor, a library, a dining room, and an enclosed kitchen. Joy's son, Joel Wesley, a graduate of the prestigious Culinary Institute of America, is the head chef who features "Southern things with a flair." Here, Wednesdays through Saturdays, one can dine on pork medallions with ginger, grilled quail stuffed with fruit dressing, an award-winning beef cassoulet, or pita rarebit.

The Lemms searched for five years to find the perfect inn from which they could offer the hospitality of a bygone era. They fell in love with Eldon the minute they saw it. "We were captivated by the scenic beauty, the difference in terrain," Joy says. "We especially loved the history, the cultural opportunities. But even more than that, Virginia provided a more gentle lifestyle. I was looking for a place not only to have a business but to have a home. Chatham was a haven. The historical and architectural significance of the structure, with its marvelous columns, was a bonus."

Eldon also had its resident ghost. The legend of its haunting goes back for generations. "Many of the local citizens knew about it and wouldn't come near the house when they were children," Joy says. In fact, Isabel Starbuck, who lived in the house as a child wrote two poems dedicated to the spirit:

"To the Eldon Ghost"

"O gentle ghost, I like you most, when I can only hear you;
The shutter creak, you do not speak, but yet I know I am
near you.
I am not clever, and I would never attempt to exorcise you;
If I should do it I'm sure I'd rue it, and it would quite
surprise you.
You are not frightful, but quite delightful while you remain
unseen;
In fact, I'd truly say that you are the nicest ghost that's
been."

"Eldon"

"Broad-roofed and welcoming it stands,
Like a kind host, with outstretched hands,
To greet all those who enter in,
Comrade or stranger, friend or kin.
Sometimes within it, and around,
The happy children's voices sound,
Sometimes o'er those who lie asleep
It seems a midnight watch to keep.
It offers balm for bitter grief,
For troubled minds a sweet relief.
And if as some, half jesting, say
Within these rooms and hallways stray
Sad visitants from days long past,
May they too here find peace at last."

It manifests in a number of ways. "We've had guests who know nothing of the history of the house tell us we have a ghost here. Sometimes it appears in the form of cold spots in the dining room. Guests have told us they suddenly felt a distinct chill, and then it passes."

Other guests have reported seeing an apparition in an upstairs bedroom. "One lady was reading in bed one night while her husband slept," Joy continues. "She said an apparition appeared at the foot of her bed. Instead of being frightened, she just looked up and said 'go away, I'm reading.' The figure disappeared.

"There have been times when I am alone in the house and I hear someone calling out my name, 'Joy, Joy.' I turn around, but there is never anyone there. The phenomenon seems to come and go sporadically. It will go on for awhile and then there is no activity for a period of time. I understand that previous owners once tried to have the house exorcised by a psychic. I guess it didn't work."

Who is the spirit? Joy believes it dates back to Civil War days. "We know that James Murray Whittle was a strong Confederate sympathizer. His brother was a colonel in the Southern army. It is said that Whittle took in wounded and exhausted Confederate soldiers to recuperate here.

"We have heard that a young man who had been badly wounded in the leg was brought here during the war, but by the time medical help arrived, his leg had to be amputated. Later that night he died in the house. Most people around here think it is his spirit which has remained.

"All I know is that, whoever it is, he is a gentle ghost," says Joy. "I'm glad of that. He is welcome to stay as long as he likes."

A Sampling Of Spectral Vignettes

THE GHOST WHO DISLIKED COUNTRY MUSIC
(Occoquan)

(Author's note: While signing books at a craft show in Occoquan, that quaint (and haunted) little village 20 miles or so south of Alexandria, in the fall of 1996, a woman told me the following:)

few months ago, I bought an antique trunk at a shop, and the lady who sold it to me said she thought that was something 'eerie' about it. She couldn't quite explain what. She just said she had a weird feeling about the trunk.

"Well, once I got it home, some strange things began to happen. There have been times when I have seen streaks of lines of light emanating from the trunk. They are white lines and they just seem to shoot out of it. I don't know what the cause is, but I would love to learn the history of it, like who owned it and where.

"One thing is, if there is a ghost associated with the trunk, it must be one from another era. I can tell you this, and it's the gospel truth! Whenever I play any kind of country music on my tape player, the ghost, or something, turns the volume down. But when I play any old music, like say a minuet, the volume gets turned way up!

* * * * *

GHOST HOUNDS OF THE CHICKAHOMINY
(Near Richmond)

For some years now, there have been recurring reports of strange lights flickering in the woods on the banks of the Chickahominy River near the Mechanicsville Turnpike. A number of people who have seen them say they look like small campfires. Yet those daring enough to venture toward them and learn their source, find nothing. The lights seem to disappear as they approach them.

One man, some time ago, stopped his car and walked through the woods adjacent to highway 301, tracking the lights. He was armed only with a flashlight. He said when he neared the site where the lights seemed to come from, he heard the howling of a pack of dogs. Wild dogs have long been known to roam this area — dogs that some people say are more like wolves in appearance. They are known to have killed chickens and pigs in this region. Understandably, the man picked up a big stick and back-tracked quickly to his car.

There is, possibly, an historic explanation for the howling dogs and the flickering lights. In May 1864, a unit of Union soldiers, under the command of Colonel Charles Chandler, commander of the 57th Massachusetts Infantry, lost its way in the woods shortly after the North Anna campaign. On June 1, 1864, some of the stragglers set up a bivouac on the banks of the Chickahominy east of Old Stage Road.

That night they were attacked by a band of wild dogs. Two of the men were killed. Is it their spirits who sit by a campfire at night, sticks in their hands, to ward off the ravaging mongrels?

* * * * *

WHO LEFT THE TRACKS IN THE POWDER?
(Portsmouth)

The original Portsmouth Naval Hospital, built in 1830, has long had the reputation of being haunted by the ghost of a Civil War soldier. According to a time-honored tradition, the unfortunate young man was sent to the hospital in 1864 for treatment of a severe leg wound. There, he fell in love with a beautiful nurse. She, however, did not share his feelings, and married a naval officer. Whether or not this affected the soldier's fate is unknown, but his condition worsened. His leg turned gangrenous and had to be amputated. But it was too late. The poison spread through his body, and he died several days later.

Over the past century and a quarter plus, a large number of people — nurses, technicians, patients, and visitors — at the hospital have reported seeing the apparition of the soldier sadly roaming the lonely corridors at night. Others have heard mysterious footsteps when no one was there.

Thirty years ago, two hospital corpsmen, fascinated by the tale, devised a plan to "catch" the ghost. They sprinkled talcum powder over the floor of a room where the footsteps had most often been heard. They then "stood guard" over the two doors with access to the room.

Several hours later, at about three a.m., the corpsmen stiffened. In the darkness, they heard sounds as if something was being dragged across an adjacent room. They heard cupboard doors being opened and shut. Then they heard footsteps approaching the door to the haunted room.

They immediately turned on all the lights, flooding the room. There was no one there.

They looked down at the powder they had spread. There were footprints, but only of the *right foot*! The Civil War soldier's left leg had been the one amputated!

* * * * *

A PHANTOM BREATH ON THE NECK
(Highland County)

dozen or so years ago, Gladys Ryder Griffith, who in her youth lived on a farm at Dixon's Hill, near the town of Mustoe, close to the West Virginia border, west of Staunton and north of Clifton Forge, told about a haunting experience she had had as a young girl.

She was then, in the early part of the 20th century, living with the Frank Kelly family on the farm, and she said members of the Kelly family had long talked about "spirits" in the area. Kelly children told of hearing the sound of a crying baby at times when they went to fetch water at the old spring above the house. They said they would hear the sound until they would get down the hill, some distance away. Mrs. Griffith said the story would make her shiver each time she heard it.

There were other strange and unaccountable noises heard between the farm house and the school. Old timers told about the time some young people were walking home one night when they approached a rail fence. As they were climbing over the fence, a "thing" got tangled in one boy's hair, frightening him so bad, he fainted on the spot and had to be carried home. He never would cross that fence again. There were also periodic reports of the sighting of "balls of fire" in that area.

Mrs. Griffith's curiosity was piqued. She wanted to encounter the "thing" herself. So one Sunday evening, after attending church, she talked her boy friend and a nine-year-old girl into walking up the hill, by the fence, where the hauntings seemed to occur. She remembered her father had once told her that if she ever heard anything strange or scary, she should say, "In the name of the Father and the Son and the Holy Spirit, what do you want?"

When they reached the fence, Mrs. Griffith said she needed to rest a minute. They had walked so fast, she had a pain in her side. As she sat on the fence, with the little girl on one side and her boy friend on the other, her arm linked through his, she said she suddenly heard "this awful noise coming up from a sinkhole below. It kept coming up by the fence and getting closer."

The boy said he thought it was a sheep under a tree, but this didn't seem to calm the girls. Mrs. Griffith said then that "something like a strong wind" brushed her off the fence. She was afraid, but forgot to say the words her father had told her about. The "thing" then climbed the fence and jumped down behind their backs. Although the moon was bright that night, they didn't see anything.

Whatever it was, it seemed to follow them down a path, "blowing down their necks." Mrs. Griffith said she became so weak and frightened she could hardly walk. She added that the sensation continued until they reached the farm house. "When people would talk about this afterwards, I would know it was true," she said. "This is so true that I, Gladys Ryder Griffith, will make oath on a stack of Bibles!"

* * * * *

A LONG TERM PREMONITION

(Author's Note: At a talk I gave to an elder hostel group in Williamsburg in December 1996, a lady came up afterwards and told me the following:)

I had a friend who, when he was a young man several years ago, went to the beach with his girl friend. Although the surf was pretty rough that day, he went in swimming anyway. There was a strong riptide and before he knew it he had been carried out far from the shore. He was nearly exhausted, and felt he couldn't make it back to land. He sank under the water a couple of times.

"Then, he said, as he was swept up on the crest of a big wave, he saw a vision on the shore. He saw his girl friend and two young girls with her. Something in him said, 'you've got to make it back. They need you!' Tired as he was, and strong as the currents were, he somehow found the energy to swim in to safety.

"He eventually married the girl. And they had two daughters!"

* * * * *

THE GHOST WHO BECAME A CORPSE
(Petersburg)

In his fine book, "Home to the Cockade City, the Partial Biography of a Southern Town," published more than 50 years ago, author M. Clifford Harrison tells of a most unusual murder case that occurred in Petersburg, probably some time late in the 19th century, or early in the 20th. It had been told to him by his grandfather.

It seems, at that time, there was a shoemaker who somehow had gained a reputation among the townspeople as being totally fearless. It was said that he had never been scared in his life. Apparently, some young men, with mischievous intentions, decided to put the cobbler's courage to an ultimate test.

He was told that a certain house was haunted, and that a person had recently died there, but because of the threat of ghosts, no one would "sit up with the dead." It was the custom then for someone to sit up all night in the parlor where the recent departed lay in a coffin. The shoemaker accepted the challenge. He would sit up with the dead by himself.

He took some of the tools of his trade with him so he could repair some shoes during the nocturnal vigil. As Harrison wrote: "An open coffin stood in the middle of a bleak room. Outside, the wind wailed. Eerie creaks and groans sounded through the lonesome building. The shoemaker unceremoniously drew up a chair and went to work."

At about midnight, a strange thing happened. Silently, the corpse began to rise "until it was sitting up in the coffin." Instead of being frightened out of his wits, the shoemaker looked at the scary phenomenon, and commanded, "Lie down!" The "body" laid down. An hour or so later, the same thing occurred. The body rose. This time, the cobbler shouted, "Lie down and stay down, and I'm not going to tell you so again." The order was again obeyed.

At about two a.m., the body arose a third time. The shoemaker, without a word, took his hammer and cracked the skull of the corpse's head! As Harrison concluded, "This time the practical joker in the coffin, whose friends had powdered him up to make him look cadaverous, was a corpse sure enough."

* * * * *

NEVER SHOOT A GHOST!
(Southwest Virginia)

ow the mountain people of Southwest Virginia love a story! The following account is said to have actually occurred a few years after the end of the Civil War, although it is impossible to verify the date or the facts. It is one of those time-honored tales that has been passed down, family to family, through the years. And while, in a sense, it is not funny, it is nevertheless a priceless bit of backwoods humor.

The incident involved a man called "Grandpappy Sparks." He was known throughout the region as a coon hunter. There was nothing he loved better. One night at about midnight, he woke up from a sound sleep, feeling "kinda quare." A beam of moonlight shone down through a hole in the roof, and illuminated the room. Grandpappy looked down, and then rubbed his eyes in disbelief. At the foot of his bed he saw "somethin' white and quare, goin' back and forth."

He always had his trusty rifle by his side, even when he slept. He grabbed it, aimed it toward the foot of the bed, and yelled out, "Speak, if yo're human." There was only silence. Grandpappy repeated the warning, "Speak, if yo're human!" When again there was no answer, he aimed his shotgun and fired.

He blew off all five of his toes!

* * * * *

AN INDIAN CHIEF'S HEREAFTER
(Near Richmond)

That Indians in Virginia three or four hundred years ago believed in the existence of ghosts and evil spirits, is evidenced in a passage from the classic book, "The Virginia Plutarch," by Philip Alexander Bruce, published in 1929. Of the great chief, Powhatan, Bruce wrote:

"Powhatan was governed by all the religious convictions of his people. His worship, like theirs, assumed the logical form of propitiation of those evil spirits which manifested themselves in nature through the agency of fire, lightning, thunder, storm, famine, and epidemic. Annually, with the company of his wives and bodyguard, he took part in certain violent ceremonies which were thought to be necessary for their protection against the furtive designs of the principal devil. In the temple of Orapaks there was an image of this devil, which was most hideous in feature, but adorned in body with beautiful chains of beads and pearls and copper.

"Powhatan expected to be translated after death to a heaven where his associates would be limited to priests and werowances. In this aristocratic company he would remain forever, his body anointed with oil, painted with puccoon, and ornamented with gay feathers and strings of pearls and beads. His only occupation there would be to dance and sing. This paradise was supposed to lie beyond the mountains in the West. Entrance to its precincts could never be obtained by subjects at large. These, when consigned to their graves, had no other destiny but to rot like carrion. Their plebeian spirits had been extinguished so soon as the breath had left their frames."

* * * * *

THE OPOSSUM THAT CAUSED A PANIC
(Paris, Virginia)

If it was just a sheer coincidence, you could have fooled everyone who witnessed it. It was said to have occurred long years ago in the small town of Paris, southeast of Berryville. There was an old gentleman there who had told friends and neighbors that when he departed from this earth he would return in the form of an opossum. This, of course, usually brought chuckles.

Some time later he died during a summer. As was the custom then, he was laid out peacefully on his bed, and relatives and acquaintances came over for the ritual of sitting up with the dead. The food and the conversation were virtually depleted around midnight, when the silence was broken by a loud scratching noise. Everyone in the room looked up. There, near an open window, sat what was described as a "big, fat opossum" sitting on the headboard of the old man's bed! The guests departed abruptly.

* * * * *

THE BODY SNATCHERS
(Harrisonburg)

 The following was extracted from the reminiscences of Maria Graham Carr. It is believed to have been written about 1820.

"There were two men hanged in Harrisonburg. Ben Hopkins was hung on top of the hill where Sherdins' vineyard was afterward located. Sprouce, who killed his wife in Fluvanna County, was brought to Harrisonburg, tried, condemned, and hung in the woods back of Mr. Rutherford's house (east of town.) I saw the procession pass on its way to the gallows; Sprouce, with several preachers, among them Mr. Smith, who sat beside him on the coffin, talking to him.

"As it was raining, Mr. Smith took off his overcoat and put it around Sprouce's shoulders, talking to him and trying to make him understand his condition; but Sprouce took no heed, but was looking at the crowd. His wagon was surrounded by 50 mounted soldiers, well armed. Then came hundreds of men and women whipping up their horses, trying to get as near as they could to the wagon. I could not bear to look at it, only for a few moments.

"The medical students came from Staunton, with a covered carry-all, determined to have Sprouce's body. As soon as the hanging was over they buried the body right under the gallows. The Harrisonburg students wanted the body and were determined to have it if they had to fight for it. The Staunton students took up the body as soon as the people were gone, and hid it in some brush wood. The Harrisonburg students, after having searched for some time, found the body, put it across a horse, and went four or five miles around on the west side of the town and hid the body in Mr. Gibbon's tan house.

"Afterwards, the body was taken to the log house where I went to school, where it was then skinned and (the skin) tanned. The Presbyterian prayer meeting was held every Wednesday evening in this log house, and we did not know that Sprouce's body was above us."

* * * * *

A SPECTRAL REUNION AT THE GHOST HOLE
(Irvington)

(Author's note: In 1993, while I was doing research on historic Christ Church in Lancaster County, near Irvington, (see "The Ghosts of Virginia, Volume II," 1994), I noticed a couple of intriguing signs along one of the by-roads. They said, "Ghost Hole." I wanted to stop and ask some locals what that meant, but time was short and I had to drive on to the church.

I forgot about the signs. Four years later, in doing research for this volume, in the College of William and Mary Library, I came across a book titled, "Irvington, An Album of Its First Generation." It was written by C. Jackson Simmons in commemoration of the 100th anniversary of "A Unique Virginia Village, 1891-1991." In thumbing through the pages I came across a reference to the Ghost Hole.

I called Mr. Simmons and asked him about it. He is a lawyer by profession, with an office in White Stone, and a historian by avocation. His ancestors first came to the Northern Neck area in 1663, and his family has lived in Irvington for more than 100 years.

"Years ago what was known as the Ghost Hole was a large

pond," he says. "There was a glebe across the road from it. People coming from Irvington to Christ Church by foot would have to cross the pond over a log that spanned it, or they would have to ford the water.

The legend was that a rector's daughter fell in love with a young man, but the rector held him in disfavor and would not allow them to see each other. When the young man died, the daughter pined, and after her death, there were reports that their spirits, in the form of spectral figures, would rise in the evening."

In his book, Mr. Simmons phrased it this way: "Here the specters of those star-crossed lovers, whose trysting place this was, arose in the miasma that hung over the Hole at dusk."

"I can remember," he adds, "that when I was a child, workers in the area would have to be let off early enough in the late afternoon so they wouldn't have to walk past the Ghost Hole at dark. The workers then were a superstitious lot, and they were convinced that the place was haunted."

* * * * *

Mr. Simmons also told me about a rather humorous anecdote connected with Christ Church. It seems one evening a gentleman and his companion entered the church when no one else was supposed to be in it. Unbeknownst to the man, however, there was a woman in the building, and her last name was Angel. After the man had been inside for awhile and his eyes grew accustomed to the dim lighting, he saw the other woman, dressed in white. It startled him, and when his companion said, "Oh, that's just Sister Angel," he took the meaning literally and promptly bolted out of the church.)

* * * * *

A *REAL* SKELETON IN THE CLOSET!
(The Eastern Shore)

ccomack County, on the Eastern Shore of Virginia, was formed from Northampton County in 1672. The name descends from the Accawmacke Indian tribe which once inhabited the region. If one has the time to dig into the colorful history here, he or she can be amply rewarded with all sorts of extraordinary historical vignettes.

The town of Accomac still contains a number of houses surviving from the mid-18th century. One of these is known as the Seymour House, and it is reported to be haunted. The property on which this house stands was sold, on April 13, 1791, to Fenwick Fisher, "doctor of phisick," for 21 pounds and 14 shillings. The house itself has been described as a fine example of the indigenous Eastern Shore architectural style — "big house, little house, colonnade and kitchen" — all linked together.

According to L. Floyd Nock, III, in his 1976 book, "Drummondtown — A One Horse Town," there was a belief that a Mrs. Seymour, then owner, had hidden a fortune in money somewhere beneath the cellar. During the Civil War, Union soldiers dug up every section of the basement floor, but found nothing.

The ghostly traditions are these:

— A century or so ago, an elderly aunt became gravely ill while visiting the Seymour House. From nowhere, a big black dog appeared. Someone shot the dog as it was climbing the stairs from the first floor to the second. Perhaps the dog was menacing, or possibly the shooter considered the appearance of such a dog an omen of impending death. He may have been right because the dog disappeared without a trace, and the aunt died within the week.

— The second legend is called "The Irate Visitor." He apparently appeared to a lady who visited the house often. She stormed down to the breakfast table one morning and bruskly announced she would never spend another night there. When asked why, she replied that she had heard the sounds of "a man breathing heavily in her bedroom." She interpreted the sound as coming from a deceased resident.

— And, finally, there is the "Crying Infant," tradition. The cries of a newborn baby are heard late on blustery nights. The most popular version of the suspected cause is that a child, long years ago, was conceived illegitimately and was smothered to death soon after birth. This was the result of a clandestine union between the mother, a member of the family living in the house at the time, or a member of the household staff — and the father, who was living across the street at West View.

In his book, Nock says the body or skeleton of the infant was found in a closet, or under the eaves on the third floor of the house. The discovery caused a feud between the two families, and those at West View bricked over all the windows in the end of their house facing the Seymour House.

Current residents say they still hear a "moaning, crying noise" on windy, stormy nights.

* * * * *

THE GHOST WHO ADOPTED A PET
(Suffolk)

Can ghosts have pets? Apparently, according to Melanie French of Suffolk. Melanie lives in a house built in the 1920s located in the downtown area. "I've always been open to the spirit world," she says. Consequently, when she first encountered an apparitional youth in the house, she wasn't afraid. She did have some prior warning of what to expect before she moved in. Her stepdaughter had told her there was a "being from another world" residing in the house.

"I moved in in January 1994," Melanie says. "The first indication I had of a presence was one day shortly after getting settled I was alone, listening to a radio station. Suddenly, the station on the radio changed. I wasn't near it." This was to happen a number of times.

Then one day, while upstairs in her youngest son's bedroom, she was drawn to glance toward the closet. It is a large closet that goes back into the eaves. She suspects it may have been a child's playroom long years ago. "I looked up and saw the darkened outline of a young boy. I wasn't afraid, but it startled me for a minute. I said, 'welcome. This is your house, too'."

Over the next several months, Melanie was to see this apparition often. "It's not an everyday thing," she says. "Sometimes he will appear two or three times in a few days, and then I might not see him for several weeks. I never know." Melanie says the wraith conveyed to her that his name was Timmy. "I said, 'Timothy?' and he let me know it wasn't Timothy, it was Timmy." He appears sometimes as a "dark shroud" to her, but she also has seen him up close. "He has the most angelic face I have ever seen," she claims. "He was — is — a beautiful child."

She had not done any extensive research into the background of the house to determine if a young boy died a tragic death there in the past, but she has the strong feeling that Timmy did die in a fire. "Either he died in the house, or when his family moved here from somewhere else, he followed them," she says. "I get that feeling." She adds that he appears to be about 12 or 13 years old.

A few months after moving into the house, the French family acquired a kitten named Tippy. "We all loved him," she says, "he was our baby, but he died in January 1995 when he was only seven months old. He died of feline leukemia." Since then, Melanie's son has seen the apparitional boy holding the kitten in his arms. "He's adopted him," Melanie says. "I personally haven't seen Timmy holding the kitten, but my son has."

"I feel very close to Timmy. Each time I see him, I try to communicate with him. I try to let him know it's okay to be here with us. I know he is not going to harm me in any way. I feel comfortable with him, and I think he feels the same way. I don't want him to leave. I think if we were ever to move, he would go with us. He would move on a spiritual plane. He's become like a son to me. I love him."

* * * * *

A GUARDIAN SPIRIT?
(Various sites)

Did a guardian spirit watch over the Father of Our Country during the tumultuous days of the French and Indian Wars in the 1750s when a young George

Washington had close brushes with death dozens of times? One has cause to wonder, considering a couple of written accounts of the times.

One example was recorded in the booklet, "Virginia's Revolutionary Legends," collected and interpreted by Robert F. Nelson and published in 1974. He in turn quotes W. T. R. Saffell of Alexandria, who wrote it in his memoirs in 1864. According to the account, an Indian chief named Sachem asked to meet with Washington in 1770. At the conference, Sachem arose to speak.

"I am a chief and ruler of many tribes," he said. "My influence extends to the waters of the great lakes and to the far blue mountains. I have traveled a long and weary path that I might see the young warrior of the great battle. (Washington).

"It was on the day when the white man's blood mixed with the streams of the forest that I first beheld this chief. I called to my young men and said 'Behold the tall and daring warrior. He is not of the red coat tribe; he hath an Indian's wisdom and his warriors fight as we do — himself is alone exposed. Quick, let your aim be certain and he dies.'

"Our rifles were leveled, rifles which, but for him, knew not how to miss. Twas in vain, a power mightier far than we, shielded him from harm. He cannot die in battle. I am old and soon shall be gathered to the great council fire of my fathers. But ere I go there is something bids me speak in the voice of prophesy.

"The great spirit protects this man and guides his destinies. He will become the chief of nations, and a people yet unborn will hail him as the founder of a mighty empire. I have spoken."

The second account that Washington may have been afforded some sort of special protection came from himself in the form of a letter to his brother in the mid-1750s. Apparently, there had been a report that Washington had been killed. He addressed this point in the letter. "As I have heard since my arrival at this place (Fort Cumberland) a circumstantial account of my death and dying speech, I take this early opportunity of contradicting the first and assuring you that I have not as yet composed the latter.

"By the all powerful dispensations of providence, I have been protected beyond human probability and expectation, for I had four bullets through my coat and two horses shot under me, yet escaped unhurt, although death was leveling my companions on every side of me."

History has many strange twists.

* * * * *

AUNT PRATT STRIKES AGAIN!

Readers of past volumes in this continuing series on Virginia ghosts may recall the saga of "Aunt Pratt's" portrait at historic Shirley Plantation on Route 5 in Charles City County, the ancestral home of the Carter family for nine generations. The background, quickly, is this: her portrait hung prominently in a downstairs room for ages. Once, some Carter family members decided to remove the painting and relegate it to the attic. That night and for some time afterward, strange noises were heard in the attic. It sounded like furniture being moved around and a woman crying. Investigations found nothing. Finally, it was decided to bring back Aunt Pratt to her proper place. Once this was done the noises in the attic ceased.

Some years later the portrait was loaned to the Virginia travel office for an exhibition on psychic phenomena in New York City. Aunt Pratt apparently didn't like that. Workmen found her off the

Aunt Pratt

wall one morning, and, in their words, "headed toward the exit." For security reasons, they locked the painting in a closet at night. The sounds of a woman sobbing were heard through the door, yet no one was inside. And one morning, the portrait had somehow escaped the closet and was again halfway to the exit. Once the exhibition was over and Aunt Pratt returned to Shirley, the manifestations stopped.

In the past year however, another incident occurred, giving rise to the speculation that Aunt Pratt's spirit may still be active. A male tourist was standing beneath the portrait one day as Aunt Pratt's story was being told. He turned his back and scoffed, calling the legend a lot of baloney. According to eye witnesses, just as he said this the doors of an armoire beneath the portrait suddenly sprang open and struck him smartly on his backside.

The man hastily left the premises.

Historical interpreters said they could not recall ever seeing the armoire doors open by themselves.

CHAPTER 49

The Haunting Hostess at the King's Arms Tavern

(Williamsburg)

(Author's note: I shouldn't be by this time, yet I continue to be amazed at how and where I collect material for this series of books on Virginia ghosts. Sometimes it happens when I am least expecting it. For example, I got a call one night in April 1997 from a tour and convention booking agency. They asked me if I would conduct a ghost tour of Colonial Williamsburg. There is a nightly ghost tour, but this was to be a one-time special event. I thought it might be fun so I agreed. We walked up and down historic Duke of Gloucester Street and talked about the alleged haunts on the campus of the College of William and Mary, at the Peyton Randolph House, the George Wythe House, the Ludwell-Paradise House, and so forth. We wound up at the King's Arms Tavern, one of several such dining establishments in the colonial area.

While bidding my adieus in the entrance area at the tavern, a young man saw me holding a copy of my book, "The Ghosts of Williamsburg," (1983), and, after one of the tour executives introduced us, he announced that "we have a ghost here at the King's Arms!" He then proceeded to tell me about it. Now I have to say that I have lived in Williamsburg for the past 24 years and I thought I had covered just about every haunt that ever existed here. I have even eaten a number of times at the King's Arms. And yet, here was a fresh account, right under my nose, that I had not heard of before. You just never know.)

o get a literal flavor of the foods of Colonial Williamsburg — typical of some of the foods served more than 200 years ago to such notables as George Washington and General Thomas Nelson of Yorktown, one might opt to dine at the King's Arms Tavern. It is considered one of the most "genteel" of the 18th century restaurants in Williamsburg. Featured on the menu are such old Virginia staples as peanut soup, country ham, Southern-style fried chicken, game pie and Sally Lunn bread. There is also an oyster-stuffed filet mignon, Cavalier's lamb, and apple cheddar muffins. Desserts include pecan pie, meringue shell and "Grand Trifle" — a sherry-soaked sponge cake with vanilla custard and dark cherries. It is said to have been a British favorite since the 17th century.

On February 6, 1772, an enterprising young woman named Jane Vobe ran the following advertisement in the Williamsburg Gazette: "I have just opened TAVERN opposite to the Raleigh (Tavern) at the sign of the KING'S ARMS. . . and shall be much obliged to the Gentlemen who favour me with their company." She apparently was successful from the start. During the Revolutionary War Mrs. Vobe supplied food and drink to American troops, and it is said that Baron von Steuben ran up a bill of nearly 300 Spanish dollars for lodging, meals and beverages. It is not specified whether or not he paid such a bill. For years, the tavern served as a popular local gathering place where customers met to discuss business, politics, news and gossip. Artifacts found on the site and sketches of the building, drawn on late 18th century insurance policies, assisted in the authentic reconstruction of the King's Arms. Today, there are 11 separate dining rooms with seating for up to 250 people.

Whether or not one encounters a haunting experience there, however, is chancy. The ghost appears only infrequently, and mostly to Colonial Williamsburg employees and not guest diners. One might suspect the female phantom who has been reported there to be Jane Vobe herself. But this ghost apparently is one of much more recent vintage. Some believe it, in fact, may be the return of a former manager of the tavern — a woman named Irma.

"She lived here years ago," says current assistant manager Jeffrey Pilley. "In those days they didn't serve in the upstairs rooms and these were used as her apartment. We had a lead hostess here named Betty. She was here for 40 years. Well, the story, as I got it, was that Betty would come in on Saturday mornings, go up to

Irma's apartment, and the two of them would read the newspapers together.

"One Saturday morning Betty came in, but she said she couldn't go upstairs to the apartment that day. She didn't know specifically why, but she steadfastly refused. So an assistant manager went upstairs. He got no answer to repeated knocks on the door. Then he stooped down to look through the keyhole. Irma was lying on the floor. She had died."

Jeffrey says that since then there have been a number of unusual things that happen at the tavern. Trays fall off stands when no one is around. Candles are extinguished by unseen hands or breath even though they are protected by glass globes. Menus sometimes topple out of wall stands.

Jeffrey has had his own encounters. "I've never seen her," he says, "but there are some things that happen." Once when he was closing up and standing outside with a night host, he looked up and saw that a window upstairs was wide open. "I went up about half past eleven to close it," Jeffrey says, "but when I got there it was not only closed but locked as well. I thought the host had done it, but he said he hadn't. There was no one else in the place.

At other times, when alone in the King's Arms, Jeffrey has felt a peculiar chill. "I have felt the hair on the back of my neck stand up. One night in particular, I had this chill in every room I went in, upstairs and down, as I was closing up. When I got to the front

door I turned around and said, 'Irma, leave me alone!' Just as I did the chill was suddenly gone and I felt a warm feeling wash over me. It was kind of eerie."

Others have told Jeffrey they have seen Irma, or at least the apparition of a woman. One hostess said she was upstairs in the women's rest room washing her hands. She heard the door open and when she looked in the mirror there was a lady standing behind her. She reached for a towel and turned around. There was no one there and the door had not been reopened.

On another occasion a hostess and a pantry worker both saw the appearance of a woman dressed in colonial costume. They said she had long flowing gray hair. At first they thought she was a balladeer, there to entertain the guests. But then, to their astonishment, the woman walked through a door. Jeffrey asked them what they meant. They told him the woman didn't open the door and pass through — she walked *through* the closed door! Still another hostess told of feeling a gentle shove in her back when she was at the top of the stairs one night. She skidded down the stairs but was unhurt.

Then one night a year or so ago, Jeffrey was standing on the porch at about nine o'clock when a woman, walking up the street, stopped in front of him and told him he had "interesting energy." She said she was a psychic from California. She asked him if she might go in the tavern to look around. There still were about 150 diners inside.

"She told me that 'George is here'," Jeffrey recalls. "Then she said no, he's not here, but he used to run this place." Jeffrey had not known any previous manager named George. "We went upstairs and as we started to walk into what is called the 'Gallery Room,' she stopped. It was like she had walked into a wall. She said, 'she's right here.' I said, 'who's here?' And she said it was a woman. She said she didn't see the woman, but she saw an aura around her. I didn't see it. Then the psychic told me that the woman was very happy and that she liked me. She said that I was good for the tavern. The psychic said the woman's name either started with an 'M,' or had an 'M' in it. At that time I hadn't known about Irma. The next day I asked Betty, the long-time hostess, had we had a previous manager who had an 'M' in her name and Betty then told me about Irma."

Jeffrey continues: "I later did some research, and found out that there had been three past assistant managers named George.

"Another thing the psychic had told me was that Irma would

be there to help me if I ever needed help in the tavern. Some months later we had a group of 34 in one party and they all wanted to be seated in one room. We had a room upstairs that would hold 24, so I told them we could put 24 there and 10 in an adjoining room, but they refused. They insisted on all being together. Somehow, and I can't explain how to this day, I got all 34 in that one room, and they had a great time. We had never done that before and all the other workers thought I was crazy to try it. There wasn't room for 34, but I got them in and they were fine. Then I thought about what the psychic had told me — that Irma would help me. Maybe she did that night. I have to say Irma, or whoever she is, has been good to me. I say good night to her every night when I leave."

* * * * *

There is an interesting footnote to the ghost at the King's Arms Tavern. It was related to the author by the Reverend Dick Carter, a Virginia historical scholar who once worked at Colonial Williamsburg and now lives in Wakefield. He said that in the 1700s, when the colonial capitol was located in Williamsburg, there used to be a lady who sold muffins at a spot between the King's Arms and Shields Tavern on Duke of Gloucester Street. She sold them to the gentlemen legislators as they made their way to the capitol building.

"You know," Dick says, "every time I walk by that spot, I swear I can smell the sweet scent of fresh muffins!"

CHAPTER 50

The Gray Lady of Sherwood Forest

(Charles City County)

(Author's note: In the first book I wrote on Virginia haunts, "The Ghosts of Williamsburg and Nearby Environs," (1983), I included a chapter on historic Sherwood Forest, on Route 5, about 20 miles or so west of Williamsburg. It was the home of John Tyler, 10th President of the United States. Here is a reprint of that chapter, along with a more recent postscript.)

O ne of the most impressive of the plantation houses fronting the James River along the historic corridor in Charles City County which connects Williamsburg with Richmond via Route 5, is Sherwood Forest. Standing on a magnificent 1,600 acre estate in the midst of a towering grove of oaks, this rambling, 300-foot-long mansion, built of framed timbers, boasts the unusual distinction of having been owned by two United States Presidents — William Henry Harrison, and his successor in the White House, John Tyler. It has remained in the Tyler family now for nearly 150 years.

Aside from its architectural attractiveness and historic eminence, Sherwood Forest and its grounds apparently are a primary source for the occurrence of strong psychic phenomena. Through the centuries a number of strange things have happened here ranging from a premonition of death that came true, to mystery voices in the night, to the bizarre slaying of a young Civil War soldier.

Most prominent of all, however, is the continued occupancy — for perhaps a century and a half or longer — of the mysterious "Gray Lady," a persistent spirit who walks through certain parts of the house and often rocks in an invisible rocking chair in the wee hours of the morning.

First called the Creek Plantation, the house was built around 1730 at a point on the James River opposite Brandon Marsh. Later, it was owned by Thomas Brown and the property was known as "Tom Brown's Quarter." He, in turn, sold it to a Dr. Rickman, who was surgeon general of the Revolutionary Army. William Henry Harrison inherited it some time after this.

It was President Tyler who named it Sherwood Forest shortly after he bought the house in 1842. He thought the name appropriate since he had been "outlawed" from his Whig party, and also because of the "new green wood" surroundings. Tyler made extensive alterations and renovations to it.

The main part of the house is two and a half stories high, with various passages and wings at different heights. It has been described as a "picturesque old clapboard mansion," and features many dormer windows, several chimneys and numerous entrances. Inside, there is a seemingly endless array of rooms, including a private ballroom 68 feet in length. It is said to be the longest house in America of its kind.

Sherwood Forest has been a working plantation for more than 250 years. When Tyler bought it there were 60 to 70 slaves on the estate. His second wife, the vivacious, beautiful, and much younger New York socialite, Julia Gardiner, furnished the interior in a lavish style, importing French mirrors, new rugs and a massive chandelier. The Tylers entertained frequently, and the President, in fact, served his specialty, mint juleps, to visiting heads of state on the plantation's piazza. Formal dinners were served on heirloom porcelain and china, and coffee in private collection demitasse cups to guests seated in petit point chairs.

Today, Sherwood Forest is owned by Harrison Tyler, a grandson of the President, and his wife, Payne. They have made a considerable effort to preserve the historical integrity of the house and grounds, including the reacquisition of many of President Tyler's original artifacts. It is today open to the public, and for special fee, Payne Tyler will host group dinners in the presidential dining room, using family silver, porcelain and china.

Whether or not current visitors will experience psychic phenomena during a visit is questionable, although a number of people have through the years. One was Julia Gardiner Tyler herself. When the Civil War broke out in 1861, John Tyler then was in his early seventies. He had worked hard in vain to maintain peace, but once the hostilities began, he sided with his native South and was elected to the Provisional Confederate Congress.

In January 1862, Tyler rode to Richmond, 35 miles away, to attend a conference. Julia and their baby daughter, Pearl, were to join him a week later. Before that could happen, however, Julia had a nightmare in which she envisioned her husband dying in a large bed with a headboard of "a great carved eagle with outstretched wings." She was so upset at the vividness of her dream she went at once to Richmond by carriage. However, he was found perfectly healthy and scoffed at his wife's disturbing vision.

Two days later he suffered an attack at the Exchange Hotel and died in a bed that in detail matched precisely the one Julia had seen in her dream!

As the War between the States progressed, Union troops marched through Charles City County, and for a while General McClellan encamped at Sherwood Forest. He and Tyler had been friends, and McClellan had guards posted around the house to protect it. General Burnside also quartered his men in the "40 acre field" between the house and the James River.

Later, the hated General Benjamin Butler arrived. Many called him a cruel man, and he often left destruction in his wake. Julia Tyler, fearful of what Butler might do to her family and the estate, took five children and escaped to Wilmington, North Carolina. There, courageously, she ran the Union blockade and traveled north to New York. One Tyler niece and one maid were left at Sherwood Forest.

At this point, the exact details get a little hazy, but there is a legend of a Union soldier — it is not known if he came with Butler or before him — who stood by a kitchen door and tried to set fire to the great house. He was killed before he could succeed, but again, the exact circumstances are in question. One version has it that he was shot in the neck or head by his commanding officer. Another contends that he was struck in the neck or head by someone wielding an ax.

Whatever, more than a century later, Payne Tyler had a woman psychic out to Sherwood Forest, and when the psychic walked up to the kitchen door she froze. She told Payne she felt a definite "coldness" at that spot. "A death has occurred here," she said. "It was a young man and he died with a piece of metal in his head or neck." Payne says the psychic had no way of knowing about the Civil War incident.

As an interesting footnote, General Butler did, in fact, try to burn the house as he left the area. He burned books from Tyler's library, furniture and the wheat fields, and he put lime in the wells. A bale of hay was stacked in the front hall under a table that had been used in the White House and set ablaze as he and his troops rode off. But fate saved the house.

A Union gunboat captain positioned in the James River only a half a mile away saw the smoke. Realizing the historical value of the mansion, he steamed to shore and had his crew put out the fire. He was helped by the maid, who had managed to get some of the hay out of the front hall before a great deal of damage was done.

As to the "mystery voices" at Sherwood, Payne Tyler says they are only heard at night, and usually in the summer when the windows are open. "The first time I heard them, I thought it was late night guests," she recalls. "But I looked outside and saw no one." Payne says the voices are always very low and difficult to make out, although once she distinctly heard the voice of a young boy, "about 16 or 17 years old," calling "John."

"Of course, the President's name was John," she says, "but I doubt this was who the voice was referring to. Perhaps it was one of his sons, who also was named John. I do know that others have clearly heard the voices, too, although no one has ever found any explanation for them. We had a gentleman named Anderson occupying an area of the servants' quarter once. One morning he came to me with a funny expression on his face and asked me if I minded if he asked me a very peculiar question. He wanted to know if I ever heard strange voices in the night. He had also heard them."

But all of these assorted incidents are merely preludes to the real spirit of Sherwood Forest — the "Gray Lady."

Precisely how long this lively ghost has inhabited the house is not known, nor is the exact reason why she is there. But it is probably safe to say she has been active since possibly late in the 18th century, long before President John Tyler moved in, because many residents over the years have experienced her presence, and all in the same fashion.

"I wish I could authenticate her origins," says Payne, "but I can't. I can tell you this. She is definitely in the house. I know, because I have personally had encounters with her, as have my husband who was a non-believer in such things, and others."

Sherwood Forest in Charles City County

What Payne has pieced together is that the Gray Lady is called that because she apparently wore gray. This leads to the assumption that she was in the service of the family that owned the house when she lived there, because servants then wore gray when cleaning at Sherwood Forest.

"It is thought that she was a governess, who had charge of a small child at one time here," Payne says. "She would take the child from a first floor bedroom (which is now known, appropriately, as the Gray Room) and walk her up through the hidden staircase to a second floor nursery. There, she would rock the child on her lap in a rocking chair."

Unfortunately, the child was ill and died soon after. This presents a speculative motive for the Gray Lady's ghost to remain in the house. It could have been that the Gray Lady was not nearby when the child passed away, or she might have perceived that had she been more attentive the tragedy would not have occurred. No one knows for sure.

What is known is that ever since, the sounds of the Gray Lady have been heard in the house — always in the same forms. Her footsteps are heard going up or down the hidden stairway, and the sound of her rocking is heard in the second floor nursery, and in the Gray Room.

"Many people have heard it, and I am one of them," Payne

unashamedly admits. "The sounds are very distinct and clear. They are footsteps, not creaks or groans of the house. There is an absolute distinction. I have heard the steps or the rocking three separate times since I have been in the house — twice within the first two weeks and once a few months later. Sometimes it sounded like, when she was descending the stairs, she was dragging something. I have no idea what that might have been."

Payne says each time she heard the sounds it was in the early hours of the morning. "What was so peculiar was that I always sleep with two guard dogs who bark at the slightest sound, but for some reason neither one of them stirred at all." When asked if she went to investigate the source, she replied, "are you serious? I was scared out of my wits. It frightened me so. You have no idea of the fear such a thing can evoke. I actually ran a fever."

At first, her husband scoffed at the idea of a ghost. Harrison Tyler is a chemical engineer and a practical man. "He was not a believer in this sort of thing," Payne says. But then it happened to him. "She walked through his bedroom one night," Payne relates. "Harrison turned as white as a sheet and nearly fainted. He even lost his breakfast," she says.

On another occasion, a 16-year-old girl was staying at the house as a guest. She screamed — Payne says "I never heard such a shriek" — and came running in to say she had just heard a woman walk through her room.

Then there was an incident with a gardener. Payne was working in the yard and asked him to hand her a trowel. It lay only a few feet away, but the man refused to go directly to it. Instead, he walked all the way around the 300-foot-long house. When Payne scolded him for taking so long, he stammered something about not wanting to walk past a door that he said was being opened and closed by some invisible person. The gardener then abruptly left the Tyler's employ, still mumbling, almost incoherently, about "ghosts."

After her third experience with the Gray Lady, Payne had had enough. "I know this sounds ridiculous," she says, "but I sat down and had a talk with her. I felt it was something I had to do." What Payne did — and what other people have done in similar circumstances — was tell the ghost that Sherwood Forest had been in the Tyler family since the 1840s, and descendants had every right to move in and claim the house as their own. If the ghost had designs on the house of her own, that was fine, too, as long as they could peacefully co-exist. "I said, maybe you feel I am an intruder and that this is your domain, but that's not the case and I'm not moving out. We're just going to have to learn to get along together," Payne said.

The frank discussion must have had a positive effect, because Payne has not heard from the Gray Lady since, except for one incredible incident. "That was when a cousin of Harrison's was over for a visit," Payne says, "and I told her about the little talk I had with the spirit. She laughed, and chided me, saying she thought I had more intelligence than that. She just kept laughing. Then the most amazing thing happened. The room we were in, the Gray Room, began vibrating wildly, and there were loud bangs, like shutters slamming against the house. It was an eerie feeling. It so unnerved the woman that she quickly left the house. As soon as she was gone, the vibrations and the noises stopped. She didn't come back for another visit for three or four years."

Intrigued by all that had happened, Payne Tyler, sometime later, was visited by two psychic experts, separately, to go through the house and give her their impressions. One said she saw a "tiny woman in an off-color dress with an apron and black shoes," at the top of the stairs on the second floor. It was decidedly not an apparition, but a real woman. The woman disappeared as the psychic climbed up the stairs.

Interestingly, the other psychic reported experiencing the same phenomena. She said she saw a tiny woman at the top of the stairs "in a neutral dress with an overlay down the front (an apron?) and black shoes." Payne believes they both saw the same woman. This psychic, however, followed the woman into a bedroom and observed her sorting clothes in front of a wardrobe. She described it explicitly as an Empire wardrobe, dark brown, with a wide flange at the center, a large brass strip, and having the design of dolphins at each foot.

"When she told me this I was stunned," says Payne. "Julia Tyler was enamored with dolphins and this was the exact description of a piece of furniture that had been in the house, but had been removed two years earlier. It had never been mentioned in any literature about the house and it had never been photographed. The psychic had no way of knowing it had ever been there, much less what it looked like down to the precise detail."

Postscript: When the author researched the chapter above, 15 years ago, tour guides did not mention the Gray Lady to groups which visited the house. Today, however, ghosts have become fashionable as tourist attractions. In fact, they are a "hot" item. So today, when one tours Sherwood, the legend of the Gray Lady is included during walk throughs of the house. In fact, each Halloween week, Sherwood Forest, along with neighboring plantations Evelynton, Edgewood and Shirley, put together a special haunting tour of these magnificent homes along Route 5.

It was thus in October 1996, that the author was asked to revisit Sherwood Forest, to sign books for their gift shop, and to participate in an interview with Stephen Harriman, travel editor for the Virginian-Pilot, Norfolk's daily newspaper. Also participating would be Kay Tyler, Payne and Harrison Tyler's daughter-in-law.

Kay had long been a skeptic when it came to recountings of the Gray Lady's exploits. But, as she told Harriman, subsequent events had changed her opinion. "My husband, William, and I were staying here, and we went out to visit our cousin Alice," Kay said. "We had been talking about the Gray Lady. I had expressed my doubts. Alice said, 'Kay, trust me on this.' When we came back (to Sherwood) every light in the house was on. We had not left them on! And all the fireplace pokers had been knocked over. I'm sure no human being had been in here, because all the dogs were in the house."

Another time, Kay related, "We had gone to bed upstairs. It must have been 2 or 3 o'clock in the morning, something like that, when I woke up and there was this feeling in the room and a sort of whiteness all around. And we both distinctly heard footsteps."

Kay continued: "There was a woman here at Christmas-time, helping to serve tea. When she got ready to leave late in the afternoon, she looked out the window and saw a woman at the edge of the woods dressed in the long garb of ages ago. She called me and said, 'Kay, you're not going to believe this' . . ."

But as Harriman wrote, "Kay *does* believe now!"

Kay Tyler, Harriman and the author met for the interview in the house. Of this, Harriman said, "If ever a ghost would want to make itself known, I figured it would be to Taylor. He knows of more ghosts, knows more ghost stories, than probably anybody in Virginia. He's become Virginia's most prolific 'ghost writer' . . ." and then Harriman added, "We inspected the staircase and we sat listening in the Gray Room. We heard nothing. It could have been the Gray Lady's day off."

(Second postscript — author's note: Some months ago I

received a letter from Mrs. Lori DiMaria of the Bronx, New York. She wrote of two strange experiences she had — one in the Bronx, and one at Sherwood Forest. Here is what she said: "One day, on our way home, we took a wrong turn, and started to head toward the South Bronx . . . As we were driving toward the old Bronx County Courthouse, which was completed in 1934, and unfortunately is closed and boarded up — though architecturally still beautiful — I suddenly had the strongest feeling of deja-vu . . . My eyes started to tear terribly, and I actually could not breathe one breath of air.

"All of a sudden, I literally 'saw' a scene that must have been from the 1930s: large black cars, men strolling down the street in long overcoats, wearing fedora hats. The area was no longer sad and neglected with burned-out tenement buildings . . . it looked as though it must have looked back then; buildings still beautiful, streets clean of all debris, the courthouse with shining glass windows in place of those boards!! Jamie (her husband) almost pulled over, I looked so pale. Though for the rest of that day I had the 'creeps,' I would not have wanted to have missed that for anything.

(However,) "The reason I am writing is to tell you of an experience my husband and I had while visiting Sherwood Forest (in November 1995). . . As we entered the Gray Room, I was overcome by a very strong 'presence.' This happened before our guide even mentioned the name of this room or the ghost. . . Whatever, there was an antique wooden chair in the corner of this room, painted black with a small flower pattern adorning it, that I could literally not take my eyes off of, and I had much trouble breathing. Whenever I tried to focus on something else in the room, I felt my eyes pulled back to this black chair like a magnet, and my eyes would start to tear! I must say it was a creepy feeling. When we were outside, Jamie said to me, 'Did you feel that chill? It was colder in there than in the rest of the house, or even out here'.")

(Postscript number three — author's note: In a book, "Old Williamsburg and Her Neighbors," by William Oliver Stevens, published 60 years ago, I found this:)
"For a good many years (after the Civil War) Sherwood Forest was tenantless, but once on a hunting trip, another John Tyler, a grandson of the President, entered the deserted house, made a fire on the hearth, and sat down before it. As the twilight of the long winter afternoon deepened, suddenly in a dark corner, an ancient

music box started up and gaily played through its entire repertoire.

"This apparently had escaped destruction in 1862. Perhaps some bluecoated soldier had wound it up then, but it had indignantly refused to play for him. Then when its master, another John Tyler, entered the door, it was so happy that it played every tinkling note it possessed. At least, let us believe that is the true explanation."

Where the Spirits Live On!

(Chesapeake)

In the midst of modern day suburbia, with its manicured lawns, double garages, and street after street of pleasant but boring white and pastel dwellings, the old house stood alone on East Point Drive at the water's edge in the Western Branch section of Chesapeake, Virginia. It was one of a kind, a relic of three centuries past. The original four-room section of what was known as the Bruce-Speers House, had been built in 1690 on a land grant given by King Charles I of England to his cousins. The site was on an old Indian burial ground. The property had once been an 1,800-acre plantation run by slaves.

George Speers, an historical interpreter in Portsmouth's Olde Towne historical district, and his mother, Ethel Oast Speers, moved into the ancient dwelling in 1981, after George's grandparents had died.

"This house was put together with pegs, there were no nails'" George says. "There was horsehair in the plaster, which was unbelievably thick. When they made additions to the house, they said the nails broke off because the wood had become so petrified. When we moved in, there were 10 rooms altogether. Six had been added on to the four dating to 1690."

George and his mother soon found out that the old house also was haunted, possibly with multiple spirits. "I never believed in ghosts until I moved here," George says. "But I believe in them now."

After moving in, George notes, he and his mother would hear strange sounds coming from an upstairs bedroom. They always seemed to start about midnight. Upon investigating, George found the cause. It was an old wicker rocking chair. It would rock on its own with no visible person in it.

As unnerving as this phenomenon was, it paled in comparison to what was heard next by the Speers. As the chair rocked, George and Ethel would hear someone, or something, singing Brahm's Lullaby. "Well, it is not a comforting voice," he says. "In fact, it's awful. It sounds like a dog chasing a cat through an off-key piano. It's enough to wake the dead."

After some discussions, George decided to take action. Whenever he heard the chair rocking, he would go up to the bedroom and turn the chair over. This seemed to work — for awhile. And then one night two guests from Delaware were visiting, and staying in the strange bedroom. The chair started rocking. The couple remembered what George had told them. They turned the chair over, and went back to bed.

Sometime later that night, both the man and the woman were rudely shoved out of their bed, one on each side. When they turned on the lights, there was no one there.

After doing some research on family history, George came to believe the ghost in that room may have been Louisa Bruce King, his great grandfather's sister. She apparently was a headstrong, colorful, and resourceful woman who had lived in the house during the Civil War years.

One day in 1863, a Union army officer, searching for a runaway prisoner, rode into the house on his horse. (George says the hoof marks were still visible when he lived there.) As the Yankee, still mounted, reached the dining room, Louisa blew a hole in his chest with a shotgun. Then she killed the horse. Realizing that she could be hanged for such an offense, she buried the officer's body beneath the floor boards of the house, and gave the horse to her slaves for food.

"I don't blame her for what she did," Ethel says. "If that officer had been a gentleman, he would have properly asked her for permission to enter the house." George agrees. The Speers still have the man's sword, which George believes had a blood stain encrusted on it. Curious, too, is the spot of blood on the floor where the soldier fell. George says they tried for years to wash it out, but it kept reappearing.

This is one reason George believes the officer may also have returned to the house in spirit form. "Many times our windows, which are somewhat hard to raise and lower, will suddenly slam so hard it breaks out the window panes," he says. "Sometimes you can see the window braces floating in the air as the windows come banging down. I think it's that Yankee trying to get out."

There may have been a third presence involved. There was a large portrait of George's great-great grandmother, Elizabeth Everhart Speers, hanging in the living room. Whenever anyone was in the living room, George says Elizabeth's eyes followed them with a "hypnotic glare." "I've had people move from one chair to another and she's still looking right at you," George says. "People have been really spooked by her picture. She always knows what's going on in that room. She was a very interesting woman. During the Civil War, she had one son fighting for the Confederacy and one for the Union."

Apparently, one or more of the ghosts took a keen interest in renovation work being done there. In 1981, for example, George and his father had several workmen in the house to reconstruct the kitchen. They left to run an errand, and when they came back the workmen were all out in the front yard, "trembling and as white as sheets." Says George, "My father told them to go back to their work. One of them said, 'We ain't going back in there, never!' They said that while there were in there working, the kitchen doors and all the cabinet doors started slamming open and shut. My father said it was the wind, but they didn't believe it."

George and his mother also tell of finding wall paintings and family portraits "askew, upside down, or moved from one spot on the wall to another."

In 1993, one of the ghosts materialized. George says it was a very chilling experience. A newspaper reporter and a photographer had come to do an article on the hauntings. The photographer asked to go up to the bedroom to take some pictures of the rocking chair. "He asked me to rock the chair," George recalls. "It was then that we both saw a woman appear. You could see right through her." George believes it was Louisa King. "She was hopping mad. If her eyes had been daggers, we both would have been dead," George says. The apparition disappeared within seconds, but he will never forget it. She was really upset.

Two years later, George and Ethel sold the house to a real estate developer. It was then that a most curious thing happened. A mysterious fire, of unexplained origin, burned down the old barn and slave quarters on the property. The developer had told the

Speers that he planned to fix up the house for himself, but soon after he bulldozed the house to the ground.

"I think something must have happened to him in that house," George says. "Something made him tear it down."

When George and Ethel moved into a modern townhouse, they took the old rocker and the portrait of his great-great grandmother with them, but he says their spirits didn't move.

"I think they're still there, in the area where the house was," he adds. "One of our former neighbors told us that right after we moved, the toilets in her house began flushing all hours of the night on their own."

The developer subdivided the land to build houses. Realizing that some of them likely will be built on the old Indian burial grounds, and that the spirits in the Bruce-Speers house may still be around, George muses that whoever buys a lot there "will have some interesting tales to tell!"

A Vision of Evil

(Virginia Beach)

t was said by many that there "never was an evil bone in Arthur Ward's body."

Ward has been described as a devout man whose life centered on his family and his church. A retired supervisor for the Norfolk and Western Railway, he was a founding member, in 1959, of the Westwood Hill Baptist Church in Virginia Beach.

Ken Riedel, a friend and church colleague, once said of Ward: "He was a devoted family man. There has never been a disrespectful thing said about this man. When his wife would come home from school, he'd be waiting at the door with a cup of coffee for her. They would sit on the sun porch together, drink their coffee and watch the birds, and just talk. That was Arthur Ward."

Ward died of natural causes in April 1979. Because he was so revered, the Sunday School class he had taught for many years, raised money to build a garden memorial to him adjacent to the church. A large cross was erected on a brick wall. A rose bush was planted beneath it, and in time grew up around the cross. Azaleas, crape myrtles and a dogwood tree were added. Old cobblestones were used to line brick pathways and planters. A stone was placed there with a plaque dedicated to "the loving memory of our teacher and friend, Arthur S. Ward." The garden, said one church member, was a peaceful place where people could find a moment for quiet meditation.

Seventeen years later, in late April 1996, several members of the congregation, along with the pastor, took sledge hammers, shovels, and other tools to the garden site, and — incredibly, in a frenzied few minutes — totally destroyed Ward's resting place. They tore down and burned the large wooden cross and the rose bush that had grown through it. They dug up and smashed the cobblestones, broke up benches, unearthed bricks, and set fire to the plants, the dogwood tree and everything else that grew on the small plot of land. The plaque dedicated to Ward was smashed to pieces. Then they sprinkled the ground with holy water.

When church members found out about the desecration, they

The "Garden of Evil"

were shocked beyond belief. Why?, they asked.

One of the lay members who helped destroy the garden said, "We knew beyond a shadow of a doubt that we had to do what we had to do. . . the Lord said, 'Destroy it all'." Although the reason for the bizarre action has never been made crystal clear, even to this day, apparently one or more members of the descecrators had nightmarish visions of evil welling up from the ground of the garden.

They believed, for example, that the cross on the garden wall with roses wrapped through it, and the placement of the paving stones were symbols, "rooted in the occult." The church pastor, the Reverend Jess Jackson (not to be confused with Jesse Jackson), said he and his followers "remained steadfast" in the belief that the garden had a "powerful hold" on the church, and had to be destroyed.

In the weeks that followed, rumors and fear spread throughout the congregation, and there were continuing whispers of "a lingering evil." According to a newspaper article, Sunday School children believed unaccountable "bones and bodies" were buried in the garden.

One reporter, Dave Addis of the Landmark News Service, asked: "Can evil forces invade wood and stones and flowers? Was there evil in the rose cross at Westwood Hill Baptist Church, or in the garden, or in the actions of the people who felt its force?" Reverend Jackson said a "pivotal issue was the presence of the rose cross in the garden." At a meeting of the congregation, he said, "For many of you that may not mean a thing. But if you're familiar with satanic ritual, with those types of things, there is a strange symbolic message in the rose cross, an occultic symbol."

Richard D. Marks, an ordained Baptist minister and doctor of philosophy who has studied cults, satanic ritual and demonology, said he did not doubt the power of evil, but he approaches claims of demonic possession and visions of evil with caution. He believed the men who tore up the garden were driven by a "vision." "We recognize evil exists, we recognize Satan, that they are out there," Marks added, but he seemed unsure about the possibility of evil inhabiting inanimate objects. "It's just something we ordinarily would not deal with."

CHAPTER 5 3

More Than She Bargained For

(Various sites)

(Author's note: Is it possible for television reporters to get so caught up in a story they are doing that they actually become a part of it? Such may have been the case with Karen Jones, a weather anchor-person for WVEC TV, channel 13, in Norfolk, when, on a feature assignment in the fall of 1995, she visited a number of Virginia mansions for a segment on haunted houses. She selected the sites from my series of books on the subject. In investigating the houses, she may have gotten more than she bargained for.

I met Karen a year and a half later at a book signing event. She had just published her first novel. She told me that when she went to film the show she encountered a number of scary incidents herself. At Belle Grove Plantation, near Middletown, for example, Karen said the haunting legend there was frightening enough, without a couple of strange occurrences she experienced there.)

t this antebellum plantation, the mistress, Hetty Cooley, was allegedly beaten to death during Civil War days by an irate slave gone mad. (See "The Ghosts of Virginia, Volume I.") Within a few years, household members began seeing "a white figure standing by the stone fireplace in the basement, gliding along the flag path to the smokehouse where the beating took place. It was believed to be the apparition of Hetty seeking vengeance.

"A couple of strange things happened to me in that house," Karen recalls. "First, as we were getting ready to shoot a scene, I was combing my hair with Hetty's hairbrush. Suddenly, there was a cold spot all around me. I couldn't explain it, but when I poked my hand out, the air around me was frigid. It seemed to envelop me. The second thing involved one of my gloves. I had a pair of gray leather gloves. As we were packing up to leave, I discovered one of the gloves was missing. We looked everywhere. We retraced all the steps we had taken. Nothing. We packed up the truck, and I decided to go back in for one last search. And there, in the middle of the dining room floor, was the missing glove. We had looked all over that room before, and I know it wasn't there then. It was as if someone had taken it, and then put it back later." I asked Karen if maybe Hetty's ghost might have wanted to try it on. She raised her eyebrows at the thought.

Another house the TV crew filmed was Scotchtown, near Ashland, north of Richmond. (Also in Volume I.) Here, multiple supernatural phenomena are said to exist. This was once the home of Patrick Henry. His first wife, Sarah, went mad and for years was

Karen Jones

re-strained in a dungeon-like cellar room. Among other things, visitors have: heard a woman screaming from somewhere downstairs when they are walking on the first floor above; the eyes of a woman in a portrait follow those who walk past the picture; and a cradle seems to move about on its own when no one is in the house.

When Karen was at Scotchtown she heard a woman moaning and then screaming. She thought someone was trying to play a trick on her, a practical joke. "We were in the room where the cradle is, she says, "and I yelled turn that tape off. I thought someone had put on a tape. But they told me there was no tape. I'm telling you that was the absolutely creepiest place I was ever in."

A third choice for the filming was a stately old mansion called Auburn on the North River in Mathews County, near Gloucester. ("The Ghosts of Tidewater.") It was built in 1804 and was once owned by the late John Lennon. In the middle of the 19th century, one of the daughters of then-owner Henry Tabb, on her wedding day, tripped on her gown on the stairway, fell, and died of a broken neck. Ever since, her beaded slippers, part of her wedding ensemble, have been passed down from owner to owner at Auburn in a curious tradition.

Many people have told of hearing strange sounds in the house which they have connected with the unfortunate bride. Peggy Licht, a former caretaker at the house, says she has heard footsteps on the stairs when no one else was at home, but they sounded to her like the heavy steps of a man — perhaps the returning groom, searching for his lost love. Others have heard doors mysteriously slamming, and have felt cold spots outside beneath a tree where the young couple used to meet.

Karen Jones says she was told that when the bride fell, she was carried to what was then her father's bedroom. It is now a den. Karen says the owner of the house at the time of the TV filming was Steve Phimister, a retired Navy captain. He invited her back to the house several times. "I have been in that den and I have heard the bride falling down the stairs, more than once," Karen notes. "I also understand that the bride played the piano. I have heard piano music in that house, and I asked Steve if he were playing a tape. He said no. There is no piano in that house, nor has there been for a number of years.

"Others have heard the same thing I have, a loud noise on the stairway, like someone is falling down. But each time we went to see what caused the noise, there was nothing there. It is a spooky place. I even tried once to talk to the spirit, if that is what it is and tried to tell her to move on. But as far as I know the sounds are still going on."

(There is, however, a happy ending to this encounter. Karen and Steve fell in love and became engaged.)

The 'Non-Ghosts' of Thoroughgood House

(Virginia Beach)

(Author's note: In 1989 I went with my cousin, Jane Ward of Norfolk, to investigate ghostly reports I had heard about one of Virginia's most famous, and one of America's oldest, buildings — the Adam Thoroughgood House in Virginia Beach. Subsequently, after interviewing a number of persons, and researching old records, I wrote an account of this in the book, "The Ghosts of Tidewater," published in 1990. More recently, while reviewing old documents for this book, I came across a little-known episode that may offer one possible explanation for why this house allegedly is haunted, and who one of the haunters conceivably could be. Following then, is a reprinting of the original chapter with a post-script covering a most mysterious death which occurred at the site in the year 1647.)

he question is, really, is the Adam Thorough-good House haunted?

"Definitely not!" says Alice Tripp, an historical interpreter who has worked at the house for the past several years.

"It was haunted even before it was opened to the public,

The Adam Thoroughgood House in Virginia Beach

declares Mrs. Martha Lindemann Bradley, the first curator at the house.

"Oh, you might hear a creak or a strange noise from time to time, after all it is a very old house and you should suspect that. But I have not experienced anything out of the ordinary in my years here," adds Nancy Baker, another current historical interpreter.

"I can tell you for a fact there is a ghost there, because I personally experienced its presence once and it scared the life out of me," states Cindy Tatum, who once worked a summer at the house while she was attending college.

And so the argument continues. Present-day hostesses, to the lady, contend there is nothing to the legend, while others, who worked there or visited it as recently as the 1970s swear by their testimony that there are, or were, some spectral phenomena associated with the house.

What no one disagrees with is that Adam Thoroughgood, and his house, are both interesting in their own rights. Captain Adam arrived in the Virginia Colony in 1621 as an indentured servant. He worked hard and did well. By 1626, he had purchased 150 acres of land on the Southampton River.

For his recruitment of 105 new settlers, in 1635, he was

awarded 5,350 acres of land along the western shore of the Lynnhaven River. That Thoroughgood was a prominent citizen is also agreed. He was named one of the original eight commissioners of Elizabeth City County, the shire from which New Norfolk and eventually Princess Anne were formed. He also was a burgess, and a member of the governor's council.

There are, however, differing accounts as to actually when the house — said to be the oldest brick house in America — was constructed. Some authors have estimated he built it as early as 1636, three years before he died. But according to the fact sheet visitors are given today, the house was probably built by one of the Thoroughgood descendants about 1680.

It is a one and a half story structure made of brick and oyster shell mortar, with huge chimneys at each end. In an inventory made by Adam's grandson, Argoll Thoroughgood, the house is listed as having hall, parlor, parlor chamber, kitchen, porch chamber, passage and milk house "in ye sellar". In restoration processes, sections of the walls were left exposed inside so visitors may see the mortar and the mortised and pegged rafters. Second story windows are in gable ends only, on both sides of the chimneys. A formal garden with oyster shell walkways separates the house from the Lynnhaven River.

It was sometime after the last major restoration, in 1957, that the ghostly manifestations began to surface.

Charles Thomas Cayce, grandson of the great psychic, Edgar Cayce, and now head of the Association for Research and Enlightenment in Virginia Beach, says the A.R.E. has received calls at times about "strange experiences" at the Thoroughgood House, particularly in an upstairs bedroom. "They were curious, but didn't necessarily want to publicize it," he notes.

He adds that his father, Hugh Lynn Cayce, and a physician friend of his once went to the house to look into some of the reported happenings. "A lady there told them of seeing things fly off of shelves, of little glass objects falling to the floor, and of furniture being moved around when no one was in the house," Cayce says.

Mrs. Bradley says old timers in the area told her of seeing a woman standing in the window with a lighted candle before the house was opened to the public. After it opened, she and other tour guides experienced all sorts of unexplained activities.

As she showed the house to a party including the wife of the ambassador of Denmark, Mrs. Bradley is quoted as saying, "All of us saw a candlestick actually move." She adds that children in particular reported the sighting of a small man in a brown suit. A lawyer visiting from Texas also claimed to have seen an oddly dressed little man. "Children became very restless in the house," Mrs. Bradley adds.

And there was other apparent poltergeist-type movement. Windows mysteriously opened and closed when no one was standing nearby. Tapes recorded in the house turned out blank. Once, in front of about 30 tourists, four glass domes protecting Christmas candles suddenly levitated and crashed to the floor. Such actions brought in newspaper reporters, some of whom said they experienced "things".

The person possibly most affected by all this was Mrs. Tatum. She worked at the house, giving tours, in 1972, when she was 17.

Cindy says there are a lot of stories about the place which are not told during tours. One is that it may well have been the first house of ill repute in the United States. "After all," she says, it is on Pleasure House Road." She also tells of the resident who shot himself in the head halfway up the stairwell sometime in the 1700s. "We never talked about that to visitors, but it may be his ghost which came back," Cindy adds. "Actually, there was more than one violent death in the house. A psychic came through one day and said she sensed an unhappy trapped spirit."

Cindy says that when she worked there, the curator told her they had a few spiritual readings and table tappings in the evenings, and at times the table would rock violently. On another occasion during that eventful summer, she recalls coming in one morning and the hostesses found all the upstairs furniture pushed up against the walls, as if someone had cleared the room for a dance. "There were some heavy pieces of furniture, too. We couldn't even move them." Cindy also tells of inexplicable cold drafts on one side of the kitchen during the July heat, and of rush lamps which would "singe up" without being lit.

But the occurrence that convinced her beyond doubt that there was a presence in the house took place just before closing late one afternoon as she took a group of about 15 visitors to the master bedroom upstairs. "I was standing inside the doorway with my back to the room, talking to the group," she remembers, as distinctly as if it happened yesterday. "All of a sudden several of the women started screaming, and then they began running down the stairs. I turned around and you could see the bed being depressed, as if someone were sitting or lying down on it. This is the truth.

There was a definite indentation at least a foot deep!

"I began screaming, too. We all ran outside and we closed the house for the day. A couple of the women later said they saw a vision of a small man on the bed. I didn't see that, but I did see the impression being made. I became hysterical. It really upset me. I'll never forget it as long as I live. My father, who is a minister, didn't want me to go back to the house. He said you don't mess with demons!"

Ornamental owl at the Adam Thoroughgood House, said to ward off evil spirits.

Postscript: The following is excerpted, and edited, from a write-up titled "Foul Play at Thoroughgood," published by the Norfolk County Historical Society of Chesapeake.

"One day in June 1647, the 'dead and stiffe' body of Mr. Peregrine Bland was found lying in the Widow Gookin's barnyard at Lynhaven." The widow Gookin, it was noted, operated an inn at that time, and was known as a woman of "considerable means." Curiously, her first husband had been Colonel Adam Thoroughgood.

Mr. Bland's demise was described as his "soe strange and sodayne death," and it prompted an immediate investigation. Testimony revealed that Bland had joined his cousin, Robert Eyres, and Dr. Edward Hall ("the chirurgeon") at the house of widow Gookin on June 10. According to the article, they stayed there overnight, intending to leave for the Eastern Branch after breakfast next morning, but their trip was never made.

Captain Francis Yardley declared that Bland "broke his fast at the table in company with me . . . and others . . . drinking moderately a Dramm, and a cupp of Sark . . ." The Bland party lingered for sometime after eating, passing their time in pleasant conversation with the other guests.

Suddenly, Bland "became most anxious to leave," and charged out of the house, ahead of his bewildered companions. Captain Yardley went with him as far as the gate, where, concerned about the man's condition, he "requested him to go in again till the heat of the day was over . . . but he preferred to sit down at the gate." In a few minutes, Yardley said, "he rose suddenly again and went on the way, whereupon I returned in to call Mr. Eyres, who went forthwith after him . . . some three hours after, Mr. Windham and Mr. Eyres brought me in the sad tydings of his death in the Barne Forte. I went out to see him, and found him lying on his right side, his arm under his head, dead and stiffe."

At the inquiry, Eyres and Dr. Hall confirmed Yardley's statements. They added that while they remained behind for a few moments, they then hastened to overtake Bland, but could not find him. Later, they began to search for him, and found him "lying asleep in the widow's barnyard." They tried to rouse Bland and persuade him either to proceed on the way or to return into the house to rest. "But he would do neither." They did manage to get him to move into the shade of a small shed to rest, and then they returned to the house. Sometime later Eyres went out again to see how his cousin was. He found him awake and tried again to get him up. Bland, however, replied, "Good cousin, let me alone a little, and I will go by and by." It was about half an hour after this that Captain Windham . . . "found him dead."

Dr. Hall's testimony was that he went out to check on Bland shortly after Eyres had gone out. He said he saw both of them "lying feet to feet (asleep)," and "hearing him (Bland) talk as though he were in a dream," left.

Records of the Lower Norfolk County Court contain the report of the coroner's inquest into Peregrine Bland's peculiar death. It was stated that "we duely viewed the corpse and the place where it was found dead, and made diligent inquiry concerning all circumstances and passages, which passed immediately before his death as well upon oath as otherwise . . . (We) do declare and testify to the best of our knowledge and judgments that neither any act of his own nor anything done to him the said Mr. Peregrine Bland by any other, hath been the cause or occasion of his so strange and sodayne death; but rather do conclude that he died a natural death having finished the course which God had appointed him in this life, and that he was not sensible of death when it came upon him, but determined his life in his sleep.

"And we are the rather induced to this opinion because that as he was seen sleeping so he was found dead with his eyes and mouth closed and his arms and other parts of his body lying after the same manner as they were when he was sleeping."

But apparently there were some who questioned the findings. What, in fact, had caused Bland's death? Had he died of natural causes as he slept, or had he been murdered? And if someone had killed him, who? And why? Such questions, of course, will never be answered on earth. Yet it could lead to speculation that Peregrine Bland may be one of the ghosts who periodically haunts the Adam Thoroughgood House, seeking to clarify the enigma of his demise.

It is a mystery that has endured for 350 years.

CHAPTER 55

The Four Past Lives of Gary Duden

(Virginia Beach)

"Through the travail of ages,

    Midst the pomp and toil of war,

Have I fought and strove and perished

    Countless times upon this star.

So as through a glass, and darkly

    The age-long strife I see

Where I fought in many guises,

    Many names — but always me.

So forever in the future,

    Shall I battle as of yore,

Dying to be born a fighter,

    But to die again, once more."

General George S. Patton
(A great believer in reincarnation)

(Author's note: I meet some of the most interesting people in this business of tracking down Virginia's ghosts. I spoke to the Hampton Roads Civil War Roundtable at the Virginia Beach Library in March 1997. After the talk a man and his daughter came up to get a book signed. The man said his name was Gary Duden, that he was psychically gifted in the areas of medical diagnoses, healing touch and counselling, and that some strange things had happened to him. Then, as he was leaving, he mentioned that he knew of the previous four lives he had led prior to his current one. In one of them he had been a Confederate cavalry officer during the Civil War. Bing! My antennas shot up. "I'd like to talk to you about that," I managed, barely able to conceal my interest. "Sure," he said. "Give me a call anytime."

I did a little research. The theory of reincarnation, of course, has been around for a long, long time. Like the existence of ghosts, it is a subject that has been debated for centuries. In recent years, however, it has gained widespread popularity through the use of a technique called hypnotherapy. Simply stated, a hypnotist, psychic, or whoever, hypnotically induces people to regress backwards in their lives, eventually past their point of birth to earlier lives they may have led.

Such a process has become increasingly popular. In fact, a year or two ago, author Barbara Lane wrote a book called "Echoes from the Battlefield," in which she interviewed a dozen or so Civil War reenactors. Each of them, she found, under hypnotherapy, recalled lifetimes during that war. Ten said they were soldiers, which the author said may explain their intense interest in reenactment.

I called Gary and had a long interview with him. I was impressed by several things. One, essential to me, was his sincerity. I am convinced that he deeply believes what happened to him *really* happened to him. Gary is an intelligent, articulate man who served in the U.S. Navy, all over the world, for 22 years, and presently is a technical writer and consultant. His experience was very vivid and real. What further impressed me was the fact that since his regressive experience, he has encountered real-life happenings — call them coincidences if you want — that directly support the possibility that he had lived before. To me, there were too many incidents to be ruled coincidental. Judge for yourself.

Here is Gary's story as related to me:)

Gary Duden

irst, let me say that I am a psychic. I don't know if that means anything in regard to my regression into past lives or not. I mean things I can't explain just happen to me at times. I have seen the apparitions of deceased family members, and have had angels and other entities visit me. I get strong feelings sometimes. Like one time when I was in the Navy, I was sent to San Antonio, Texas. I went to visit the Alamo, where, as you know, all the Americans were put to death. I went into the chapel where the famous last stand took place. When I entered, I got such a profound feeling of dread, hopelessness and despair, that I could not stay there. I had to get out. I had never felt anything like that before. It washed over me in waves. I could literally sense the end was coming for those heroic men and that nothing could be done about it.

"I got the same sort of sensation years later while visiting the Civil War battlefield at Fredericksburg. I stepped into an area about 25 yards short of the stone wall there, behind which Confederate soldiers killed and wounded thousands of charging Union men. I got chilled to the bone. Every nerve in my body tingled. Even if I hadn't known the history of that battle, I would have known that something terribly tragic had occurred here. The tragedy still lingers.

"As far as precognition goes, I have had some dreams which not only were scary, but turned out to be true. A few years ago, for example, I dreamed about a terrible earthquake in a Latin American climate. I saw buildings collapse and people crushed to death. It was horrible. It was so vivid I told my wife about it. Well, a week later the great Mexico City earthquake hit, killing hundreds of people. I had visions of the space shuttle blowing up a few days before the Challenger tragedy. I had told my wife before the Challenger was launched that it was going to blow up during the launch.

"To get back to the reincarnation, in 1990, I went with several others, to a well-known hypnotherapist in Virginia Beach to participate in hypnotic regression. I went with a couple of very close personal friends. We went into the session kind of skeptical. The woman hypnotherapist told us we would experience four past lives during the session. People have different beliefs on this subject, and although my personal feeling is that the soul goes through many lifetimes during its progression, I nevertheless was skeptical on going in.

"She hypnotically relaxed us. We were all laying on the floor on blankets and pillows. As we eased into a state of peacefulness, she began to lead us backwards through our present lives. I was moved back to the time when I was six years old. What struck me about this, was that I began to remember things about my youth that I had long forgotten. I'm sure it was all there somewhere in my subconscious all the time, but things I had forgotten just seemed to pop into my head.

"Then she regressed us back to an earlier time, to our birth, and even before we were born. There was nothing visible. Everything seemed to be smoky white. Next, she told us to go back to the life previous to the present one. She said to remember what we saw, heard and felt, so that we could write it down when the session was over.

"Suddenly, I was greeted by the loud report of several muskets. It was so loud and so real, I tensed up. I let out a gasp and jumped. It disturbed those around me. I was in the middle of a battle. Then there was like a flashback. I had a vision that I was a Confederate officer in the cavalry in Virginia in 1863. I had black hair, parted down the middle, and a huge, walrus mustache. Somehow I knew my first name was John, but I couldn't distinguish my last name. I want to say I was with the 32nd Virginia cavalry but that was a bit hazy.

"I seemed to be at home, and I was leaving. I was on a horse and I was departing. My wife was standing beside the horse. She had blonde hair pulled back in a bun. She was wearing a calico dress with a white apron. My two young children were with her. They each had black hair. They were just standing there looking at me.

"The scene shifted back to the battle. Bullets were flying to everywhere. Suddenly, I was hit by a shot. I fell off my horse and hit the ground. I injured my lower back in the fall. I lingered for six days and then died. I'm not sure if I died from the wound, from infection, or pneumonia.

"Some curious things have happened to me since. For one, I have long suffered from lower back pains. Is that related to a past life? I don't know. One day, a few years ago, I was driving on the Oceana Naval Air Station. It was a nice summer day and I had the windows down. There is a horse club there, and there were a lot of people riding horses on the side of the road. I could hear the hooves, and I could smell the horse sweat. I heard the clinking and clanking of accoutrements and the creak of leather harnesses and tack. The most unusual feeling came over me. I couldn't explain it.

"Another thing I remember was that I was watching a documentary movie on the Civil War on television. They were showing a lot of those old black and white still photographs. I left the room for a minute and when I came back I was stunned.

"The picture on the screen was me! I mean it was exactly the face I had seen in my regression! There was the black hair parted in the middle, and the walrus mustache. It was me! I got that feeling again. Every nerve in my body tingled. The photo was of an officer in the Confederate cavalry and I just caught the name John. Now I had looked through scores of Civil War books, looking for such a person and never found one. Here it was right on the television screen. Was that a coincidence?

"Back to the regression. Next, I found myself further back in time. I saw the date 1754. I was in France. And *I was a woman*! A lot of people don't know that a person can be either a man or a woman in a past life. It can influence your present characteristics, however, or your psychological feelings. If a man has effeminate characteristics, it may be because he was a woman in the previous life.

"I saw myself as being very attractive. I had been married to a wealthy French nobleman who had been killed in a battle. I had inherited his estate. I was in a grand house with fine furniture and portraits. The servants had powdered wigs and wore satin britches down to the knee, with tight stockings and waistcoats. There were candlelit chandeliers and there were gay parties. This time I died in old age. I was in a canopied bed with servants, staff and physicians standing all around me.

"Now this is going to sound wild. Sometime later, after the regression session, I went to a psychic fair. There was a very talented young artist there named Kathy. I had given her a psychic reading once. She began sketching. She worked for about 15 minutes and then she said, 'Gary, you may not sense what I am feeling, but I sense some strong feminine presence about you in your aura." She mentioned the name Arabella. She then showed me what she had been sketching. Again, I was dumbfounded. It was the face of a beautiful woman. It was my face in my second regression — the face of the French woman! The eyes, the long lovely hair, everything was just as I had envisioned! She even got the name right and I had never shared my regression experiences with her.

"In the third lifetime I experienced during the session, I was in the British Navy. I saw the year 1650. I was a cannoneer. It was a small ship by today's standards. I saw that we were caught in a terrible storm. The ship went down and I was cast into the angry seas. Somehow I made it ashore on some wood debris to what I think was the coast of Ireland. I climbed up a steep cliff. I was tired, worn and haggard. I came upon some rolling farmland. It was rocky and there were stone fences. I saw a small sod hut. There was a woman there. She was poor and a widow. She took me in. The navy thought I had died in the sea, and I didn't want to go back, so I married the woman and we had one child.

"Here again, this may sound crazy. But my close friend Robert, who went to the regression with me, well, his face was superimposed over that of the widow's! I feel he had been reincarnated as a woman! I have to tell you how we met. I had just moved back to Norfolk and didn't know anyone. I was out riding a bike with my wife and children one day when I saw this couple sitting on the steps in front of a house. I don't know why, but I was strongly drawn to them. I told my wife I had to go over and meet them. I just walked up and said, 'Hi, my name is Gary and I believe I'm supposed to know you.' We became the best of friends.

"Let me add here, too, that having been a sailor in my third past life certainly coincides with my career in the navy.

"Now, to the final regression. This time it was a great deal earlier. Each of the three past lifetimes had been separated by about 100 years. This time I was a lot further back. I was a soldier, either Greek or Roman. Again, the parallel to my career in the military. I rose up through the ranks as a commander of 1,000 men. I was victorious and earned a lot of fame. I saw myself in a short leather skirt with a breast plate. There was a scene where I was being lauded. They were placing a laurel wreath on my head.

"Then there was a flash forward, to a time when I had retired. I had white hair and a long beard, and I was sitting on some circular marble benches. All the men around me were old. We were wearing togas with red and gold trim. I sensed what I would describe as an epitome of wisdom. We were discussing trade agreements. I believed I was in the senate.

"In the final scene, I found myself still older, and in a picturesque country villa. It reminded me of Tuscany in Italy. The center court of the house was opened to the skies. It was hot. There were olive trees all around, and I was surrounded with vineyards. A man servant brought me a large wooden bowl full of grapes, and we discussed what type of wine we would make.

"Here's another coincidence, if you will. I love fine wine. Is that a carryover from my past life? Another thing. Several years ago I met a woman who was married to a co-worker of mine. She was from Quebec. Her mother was a full-blooded Huron Indian. I later learned that this woman had psychic abilities. She could see auras and sometimes sensed different parts of past lives in these auras. I met her at a Christmas party, and the first words she said to me were, 'You were a Greek in one of your past lives!' I had just met her, and she came right out and said that. I had been told that one can carry traits from past lifetimes.

"So that was it. Those were the four past lives I experienced. And it seems like in each one, things have happened to me which seem, more or less, to add credence to the belief that I really did live those lives. Being a Civil War officer might explain my deep interest in being a reenactor, and the strong sensation I get around horses. And then there was the photo likeness on the television screen. I reenact with the 47th Virginia infantry regiment and so, once again, I wear the gray. When I was participating in my first reenactment at Cedar Creek I had a feeling as if I belonged there, and it was good to be back in the ranks again. As I stood there amongst my company, surrounded by the regiment and brigade, my heart was racing. I felt light headed and nervous. The sun glistened off 1,500 bayonets. It was like it was the real thing to me, the real Civil War. In fact, as I watched the approach of over 1,000 Union soldiers to within 200 yards of our position, I became angry at our officers for allowing us to be put into that predicament. We would now have to advance uphill under fire and were already in range of the Federal troops. Then I snapped back to the reality that this was 1996, and it was a reenactment, not a real battle.

"As to my being the French woman in the 1700s, how do you explain the drawing my friend the artist did — depicting the woman's face exactly as I had seen it?

"The sailor in the 17th century — is that why I was drawn to service in the navy? Is that why I felt a special bond with my friend, Bob, whose face was superimposed over that of the woman I married? And the ancient warrior who loved his wines. Have I inherited his passion? And so many lives in the military. It all fits. Could all these things be coincidences? I wonder.

"I have heard about others in regression speaking in foreign languages they had no knowledge of. Did they draw these from past life experiences? Others have found old tombstones bearing names they envisioned in their regressions. How do these things happen, and why? It suggests to me that there is something to this. I can only speak for myself. I know what I experienced was not a dream. It was real. I was there. It was me."

CHAPTER 56

The Uplifting Spirit of Selma

(Norfolk)

he ghost is supposed to be a young girl, possibly in her early teens. It is believed she lived in the house in the mid-1800s. She is said to have died a traumatic death at a tender age, but no one knows the exact nature of her tragic demise. She is called Selma, but this may just be a nickname for her haunting spirit. She may not be there anymore. A couple had the house exorcised a few years ago and the manifestations stopped.

It is known as the Llewellyn House and it is located in the heart of the fashionable Ghent district of Norfolk. It was built circa 1812, and in its original form was small by today's standards. In the 19th century it was surrounded by hundreds of acres of rich farmland.

In the late 1930s a young girl used to visit her grandmother in an apartment adjacent to Llewellyn. Her name was Phyllis Brown. "I can remember one time I pulled up some hollyhocks that were growing through the back fence to the Llewellyn property," says Phyllis Brown Snow today. "My grandmother scolded me."

Forty years later, Phyllis bought the property — for the princely sum of one dollar. By then, the late 1970s, time had passed the house by. Urban sprawl had all but swallowed it up. It had not been lived in for years, except as a hangout for area winos, and it was in sad disrepair. The city of Norfolk then owned it and was reluctant to tear it down because of its historical value. They sought someone who would lovingly restore it. Phyllis wrote a moving letter to those in charge and the house was hers.

She had it moved across the street, and then began some serious renovation. She reversed the original floor plan, installed a modern kitchen, stripped wood, refinished floors and replastered walls. She added a section in the rear. An interior designer by profession, Phyllis did much of the work herself. "I can't tell you the number of hours I put into it," she says. "I used to work late into the night using my car headlights to see by.

"From the beginning, I had a good feeling, good vibrations about the house. I can't really put it into words. But it was like there was a benevolent presence there, like I was being welcomed in some way. I intuitively felt encouraged and welcomed. It was like I was being accepted for what I was doing. Every time I would get depressed or discouraged about something that went wrong, it was like a spirit was there telling me that everything would be all right, to keep going."

About six months into the endeavor, Phyllis experienced a sighting. "I saw her," she says. "I really did. She was standing in the upstairs hallway. It was a young girl. She looked to be a teenager. She had on a blue dress with a full skirt. It appeared to be of Civil War vintage. It was a beautiful shade of light blue. I couldn't make out any distinct features of her face, but it definitely was a girl. She had a slight build. She was standing just outside what once was the old sewing room, or the nursery." The vision lasted for about 35 or 40 seconds, and then it dematerialized.

Phyllis never felt frightened. She suspected this was the encouraging presence she had felt from the beginning of the restoration. She began calling the spirit Selma. "I somehow felt this had been Selma's home once," Phyllis says. "She must have been happy here and that's why she stayed behind."

Phyllis saw the figure once more, just before she married Mr. Snow in 1979. "She was in the same place in the upstairs hallway, and she had on the same dress. But this time she moved quickly down the stairs, and when I got to the top of the stairs she was gone. I had the feeling that maybe she was shy because of my husband-to-be. I tried to talk to her many times. I asked her if she wanted to tell me something, but she never answered."

Another who has experienced a possible ethereal presence at the Llewellyn House is Dr. Joe Dilustro, a Norfolk neuro-surgeon. He and his wife, Sharon, lived there about eight years ago. "We had heard a couple of things about the place from previous residents," Dr. Dilustro says. "There was a couple named Delucci who lived here before us. Mr. Delucci told me that he once gave an anniversary card to his wife. It was one of those cards that when you open, it plays a tune. He said they were upstairs in bed one night when they heard the tune playing downstairs. They didn't understand this because they had folded the card up earlier. So they went downstairs and there was the card standing up. The folded it up again and went back to bed. Then they heard the tune again. They checked again, and the card was open again. There was no way that card could unfold itself and stand up."

The Deluccis also told Dr. Dilustro about another incident involving their daughter. When they had moved into the house, their daughter was attending William and Mary College in Williamsburg. She had not been in the house. The night before Thanksgiving one year the daughter decided to come home the next day for a visit. Inexplicably, the Deluccis found their daughter's framed picture, which had been standing up, lying face down.

Dr. Dilustro had his own personal encounter at Llewellyn. "This is going to sound crazy," he says, "but let me assure you, it really happened. I am not an alcoholic and I did not imagine it. I will never forget it. It sticks vividly in my mind to this day. My

Llewellyn House

wife and I were in bed one night when we both heard a loud thump. The best way I can describe it is it sounded like someone had dropped a big book, like a dictionary, on the floor.

"I got out of bed to investigate. When I got to the stairway I heard the exact sound repeated. It was just above my right ear. I looked up and there was a blue cloud of light hovering right above me beneath the ceiling. I reached up with my left hand, and as I did, the mass of light seemed to dart down the hallway toward the front door. The further it got from me the faster it moved. Then it went *through* the front door!

"Sharon and I went through the house calling out the name Selma, but we found nothing. I opened the front door, and as I did, we both noticed that a lamp hanging on a little chain was rocking back and forth. This was strange, because there wasn't even a hint of a breeze. Not even a leaf was stirring. What caused that? I don't have any idea what that blue light was, but I did feel incredibly excited and exhilarated. There definitely *was* something there!"

Phyllis says the blue color the doctor saw coincided with the blue dress she saw Selma wearing. After the Dilustro's left, Carl and Donna Woods moved in. They have told Phyllis they have never seen Selma, but some strange things have happened during their stay at Llewellyn House. Donna, for example, had an old wicker sewing basket and a blue bracelet sewn into the weaving. At times, for periods up to several days, the basket would be mysteriously missing, and then, suddenly, it would reappear. The Woods would sometimes hear noises in the house, especially when they were in the dining room, but they never found a rational cause for them. And sometimes books would tumble out of bookcases by themselves.

Still, the Woods, like Phyllis, did not feel threatened. However, when Donna told her sister about the happenings, she said she would not come to visit unless they had the house exorcised. And so, an exorcism was performed. And Selma has not been heard from since.

"I guess I'm kind of disappointed," Phyllis says. "I liked having her around. I'm an only child and she was almost like a sister to me. It was her house, too. But then on the other hand maybe she has gone on to where she should be. I just hope she's happy wherever she is."

A Lilac Presence at the 'Mace House'

(Norfolk)

eople had been telling us that we had a ghost in our house before we even moved in," says Dr. Lucy Herman of 50 Prospect Street in the Freemason Harbor District, overlooking the Elizabeth River in Norfolk. She and her husband moved into the house in 1977, after spending more than a year restoring the house, which dates to 1845. It is a large place with five floors, and includes an English basement and a ventilator room that is not unlike a widow's walk. It is also known, by some, as "The Mace House."

"That's because during the Civil War Colonel Lamb, the mayor then, lived here," Dr. Herman says. "His father is said to have buried the Norfolk Mace on the second floor under the hearth to keep it from falling into Yankee hands. I know that when we were restoring the house, it was obvious that someone had been digging in that area."

The mace, it should be noted, was a gift to the city from Governor Robert Dinwiddie. In the minutes of the borough for April 1, 1754, it is stated that: "At a common council held this 1st day of April, 1754, the Honorable Robert Dinwiddie, Esq., His Majesty's Lieutenant Governor and Commander-in-Chief, this day presented to the Borough of Norfolk a very handsome silver mace, which was thankfully received.

"Resolved, That the humble thanks of this Borough be made to the Honorable Robert Dinwiddie . . . for his valuable present, assuring his honour that the same was received as a token of his great regard and affection for the said Borough."

'Mace' House

The mace is of pure silver and weighs about six and a half pounds. It has nine sections and is 41 inches in length. The head has three sections, the staff six, bearing the hallmark "F.W." and a lion rampant. According to a history of Norfolk, the staff, "elaborately ornamented with leaves and scrolls, measures 28 inches, and is of irregular size. The bowl, or head of the mace, is cylindrical . . . the top is slightly rounded, and on it, under the open crown work, are the Royal Arms of Great Britain in the reign of George II, the letters G and R and the usual mottoes between the lion and unicorn. The emblems of England, Scotland, Ireland and France are engraved in a separate panel . . . The rose of England and thistle of Scotland growing from the same stem, the fleur de lis of France and harp of Ireland, and a crown over each panel are significant embellishments."

The mace was a symbol of authority, and was passed to each new mayor during installation ceremonies, a gesture carried over from ancient British custom. It is believed to have been carried before the mayor on entering court and in all public processions. It is also believed that mayor Paul Loyall buried the mace at Kempsville during the early stages of the Revolutionary War before the British destroyed the city in 1776.

In the book, "Through the years in Norfolk," it also states that the mace has "survived wars, pestilence, conflagration, carelessness and neglect. It is the only civic mace in America." Apparently, this neglect occurred in the latter half of the 19th century, after the Civil War. It is known that in the 1890s, then Chief of Police C. J. Iredell, "discovered the mace in a state of disrepair, lying in a heap of letters and old records at the police station."

It has since that time regained its status, and is today used on occasions of state celebrations and patriotic observances. It is, says a historian, "the one relic redolent of our colonial era, of the Revolution, the War Between the States, and the present years of growth and prosperity." It can be seen today at Norfolk's Chrysler Museum.

Getting back to the hauntings, Dr. Herman says that shortly after she and her husband had moved into the house, on a particularly hot day in August 1977, they heard the doorbell ring on the second floor. "We have two Scotty dogs, and when we opened the door," she recalls, "the dogs acted very peculiarly and backed off. But there was no one there. I said 'you must be the ghost, so come on in and I'll tell you what we're going to do with the house.' I will say I felt very strange in that room. It was like there was a presence there. One dog hid and the other jumped in my lap. Anyway, we told the ghost it could live here with us, and then it felt as if the presence, or whatever it was, departed."

Over the years a number of odd incidents have taken place in the house.

** "I was working with one of my students a couple of years later," Dr. Herman says. "We were still a little unsettled, still renovating. One of my students came in with a little plastic flute he wanted to show me. I had one, too, and we showed each other how to play 'Twinkle, Twinkle, Little Star' on them. Then we laid the flutes down and started to work. The next thing you knew, we heard someone else trying to play the tune. Well, there wasn't anyone else there! I didn't see anyone, but the boy said he did and he drew a picture of the entity he saw.

** "We had a German girl staying with us one summer," Dr. Herman continues. "She was up on the third floor, and when I entered her room there was an overpowering odor. I said, 'what are you pouring all over yourself? What are you using that smells like that? Go easy on the perfume.' It was a strong lilac smell. She said she hadn't used anything. Neither one of us had. Lilac is definitely 19th century, so I believe the ghost is a female."

** Dr. Herman asked Mr. Lamb's sister, a former tenant, about the ghost. "She was then 90, and she said that her grandmother, during the Civil War, told her that Colonel Lamb had married a girl from Rhode Island, and apparently she had a ghost in Rhode Island. So she thought she might have brought the ghost to Virginia with her. Others have heard the sound of high heels on the stairs in the house, and have smelled the scent of lilac.

** There are a lot of unexplained sounds in the house according to Dr. Herman. And also strange incidents. She said once a roofer was taking off part of the main roof and he told her that "somebody was pushing up the nails from below." There was no one below.

** One day two ladies came over to clean in the house. One rushed up to Dr. Herman and told there was a ghost in the house. Something was opening up the cabinets on the third floor while she was cleaning. She said that part of the house was "full of ghosts." She abruptly quit. She said she couldn't go back into that room with all the ghosts in there.

"After the maid quit," Dr. Herman says, "I sat on the top step of the third floor and I had a heart-to-heart talk with the spirit. I told it I was cross. I said you can stay here, but unless you are willing to pitch in and help clean, don't scare away any other maids!"

After that, Dr. Herman adds, "things quieted down."

CHAPTER 58

Tall Tales at Timberneck

(Gloucester County)

(Author's note: In the past I have written about a number of the historic old houses in Gloucester County, including Rosewell, White Marsh, Church Hill, Auburn, Midlothian, and Enfield, not to mention Abingdon Church. One I had missed was Timberneck, which lies on a broad peninsula bordered by creeks flowing into the York River. The Virginia Landmarks Register doesn't say when the house was built, although it "was a Mann family homestead in the 17th and 18th centuries. The property was purchased about 1793 by John Catlett from John Page of Rosewell." The Register describes the present house as "a rambling post-Revolutionary farmhouse . . . With its rural setting, early smokehouse, rare 19th century picket fence, old trees, and commanding view of the York, Timberneck is a substantially undisturbed Tidewater plantation . . ."

I ran across the fact that Timberneck may be haunted in an old Gloucester tabloid newspaper-magazine, "Glo-Quips," published 30 years ago. In the paper was the reprint of a manuscript written by Sallie Nelson Robins in December 1912, and titled "Ghosts of Old Virginia." She gave a vivid description of how superstition and hauntings were viewed in the late 19th and early 20th centuries in the commonwealth. Following are excerpts from her article:)

Some are born to see ghosts come into this strange world by way of a tester bed in a big room in rambling country houses. There is a house (Timberneck) which faces the bold York River, in Gloucester County, and the lawn is bounded on one side by Werocomoco Bay — on which (we maintain) once stood old Powhatan's wigwam in which Pocahontas rescued John Smith. The first tomb in the graveyard bears the date 1685, and in this old house ghosts have been seen.

"Virginia children of long ago heard much of ghosts from their mammies, and perhaps this life-long superstition — planted in the subsoil of the soul by a beloved mammy — is one of those earliest impressions which are most lasting. On the other hand, some of the most earnest thinkers of today believe in spiritual significance, and claim that when our spirits are sufficiently tuned, we shall, even in this mortal body, penetrate the great unseen.

"My colored mammy initiated me into many mysteries. Seriously, she informed me: 'Friday night's dream on Saturday told, comes to pass however so old. . .'

"One Friday my mother left me for the night, the very first time I had been so long bereft of her presence. She was coming back on Saturday. Friday night I dreamed that my grandfather came in his 'sulky' in the early morning to tell me that my mother was so sick she could not return that day." (Unwittingly, Sallie Robins told her mammy of the dream and was immediately admonished for telling of a Friday night dream on Saturday morning.)

"The dream came too true, my mother was very ill and stayed away a long time, and superstition gained a strong foothold in my young faith.

"My first ghost was a queer one — rather might it be called the embodiment of vicious materiality. When I was a little girl and holding tight my mammy's hand, I was going through the great drawing room about dusk.

"'There it is — before God!' my mammy said as we scurried along over the rose-strewn carpet. 'The beast! The beast! — eyes behind and eyes before!'

"Crouched by the window was a creature of abnormal size and shape, and very terrible. Its coat was yellowish and shaggy, and from its great head gleamed two glaring eyes which glittered over the darkness of the big room. The beast kept still, but my hair arose and my feet turned to lead. I can see it plainly now, and there is no explanation, try I ever so hard to find it.

"One night as we played in our fire-lit nursery, there was a sound overhead. We looked at the 'oracle' (the mammy), and she answered: 'Poor old miss — she are rockin' her child.'

"We got very close together. 'Where, mammy?'

"'Up there.' She pointed to the garret. 'Twas your grandpa's ma. She left her little baby one cold winter night, and she went to Marse Jeems Dabney's pa's, to a party. The child had the croup, and he was dade when she come back. He was sick before she went. She moaned, and she pined, and she died. The rocking (began). Cy (her husband) has seen her, and we all can see her now if we go up to the garret.'

"'Bip! bip! bip!' went the old wooden cradle, but not one of us seemed to wish to go up to see it.

"'Bip! bip! bip!' At first I would draw cover over my head and lie sleepless. Afterwards I got bold enough to peep through the cat hole in the garret door if the sun was shining, and once I crept up by myself and looked at the funny little cradle.

"'Let's burn it up, mammy,' I ventured to suggest after a night of violent rocking.

"'No — no,' she answered. 'Tis old miss' repentance. She got to come and rock before she gets good and settled up yonder. She left her child — you see.'

"As we lay tucked up in our bed, mammy would rock also and croon . . . and the wind would howl over the chimney tops, and the screech owl would cry from the weeping willow limbs, and the little wooden cradle would go 'bip — bip — bip'.

* * * * *

A SURE SIGN OF DEATH

hen I was about eight years old my mother and I, on a lonely spring evening, walked to the front gate. As we stood gazing upon the last tints of the sunset, Aunt Sally Johnson, a fine old Negress, came along the road driving home her cows. She stopped to greet us, her cows browsing the sweet grass along the road bed. The sun was cold down, and shrilly upon the stillness fell the crow of a lusty cock.

"'Um — um,' said Aunt Sally, 'rooster crow after sundown shore sign of death.' We watched her striding along in her skimp frock until she got out of sight.

"The next day company came for dinner. Aunt Sally was the neighborhood 'cake maker,' and my mother sent me over the fields to her house to get her to make her a 'butter-sponge.' I trotted along in the dreamy sunshine, pulling the flowers that bloomed in my way. When I got to Aunt Sally's, her husband, Uncle Chilles, was seated in the square little yard made hard and bare by the constant picking of the restless hens. He was leaning on his hickory stick and looked very grave. 'Where's Aunt Sally,' I asked cheerily.

"Uncle Chilles raised his stick solemnly and pointed to the house door. Off I ran and stopped suddenly just within the threshold. Upon the wide four-poster was a rigid form covered with a snowy sheet. I heard again the cock's shrilly cry after sunset, and Aunt Sally's words — but 'how, how' was my terrified query, 'how did the rooster know?'

"A few years later I was watching a beautiful young aunt as she tried on a soft, filmy gown. Suddenly she fairly tore it off, crying: 'Ah me! ah me!' and put her auburn head into her mother's lap, weeping as if her heart would break.

"It was not long before she lay very, very still in the same soft white gown — she must have caught the far notes of God's call as she tried it on."

(Another ghost of Timberneck was) "a tall old woman in grave clothes with a white 'kerchief tied under her chin. She could not be explained, and her appearance had no apparent significance. When there was gay company in the drawing room, the old woman would appear outside the window. One of the company would see her and exclaim: 'There she is!' then a hush would fall upon the crowd.

"Of summer afternoons when the family sat upon the porch she would stand within the drawing room and wistfully look out. I never saw her, and I am sorry — but those I trusted did.

" . . . Places must possess age before they can claim the privilege of a ghost. They must have the dust of years in the garret, and old things about before the disembodied will honor them . . . They haunt mellow places, and flit about wainscotted rooms and dart up broad stairways over which a century or more has rolled. . . There must be time enough for history, ere mystery will prevail."

CHAPTER 59

The Reincarnation of a Ghost?

(Gloucester County)

(Author's note: The following is excerpted from an article written more than 100 years ago by the noted Virginia author, Thomas Nelson Page. It concerns an old house somewhere in Gloucester County, although the exact location is not specified. The date also is missing, but it can be assumed with some certainty that the events described occurred in the second half of the 19th century (since the piece was published in Harper's Magazine in 1893.) Further, it is couched in the first person by a young lady, who tells of incidents involving her great grandmother. It is not known if this lady was a relative, friend, or acquaintance of Page. Nevertheless, it is a riveting story with unusual twists, in the manner of Page's masterpiece fictional ghost tale, "No Haid Pawn." It is, however, thought that this writing may have been based on actual events. When the article was reprinted in a Gloucester newspaper in the 1960s, an effort was made, in vain, to determine what house was involved and where was its location.)

I was not a particle superstitious in my early days, but I had a singular experience once. . . You know my people all came from Gloucester County, and the old family place is there. It was too expensive to keep up after the (Civil) war, the house being one of the large old-fashioned colonial brick mansions, and my father having no taste for country life . . . So he removed first to a city in Virginia, and then to New York. He never would sell the place, but at every sacrifice kept it just as it was, with the old furniture and all in it . . . getting a neighbor to look after it, as well as to take care of Uncle Benny, the old butler, who still lived.

"He always talked of going back there, telling us stories of it in his childhood, when the large grounds were kept up, and the house was constantly full of visitors. I got thus an accurate idea of the house, except that I always pictured it as being of immense size, and I knew every room and crevice in it as well as if I had been brought up there, instead of never having seen it since I left it at three years old. I knew as well as if I had lived there the old garret where the trunks and chests used to stand; the wide stairway, with the landings and turned balusters; the big hall, with its settle around the large fireplace; and the drawing rooms, with the straight-backed chairs and the long mirrors coming down to the floor, and the old family portraits on the walls, from one of which the faded lady with the brown ringlets and the black dress used to come down on summer evenings and rock in the big rosewood rocking chair, so that every one could hear her all over the house.

"She was the daughter of my father's great grandfather, and having lost her husband soon after her marriage, came home to live with her father. When he died, which was not long afterwards, she lived with her little boy all alone in the house, and used to spend hours by herself in the drawing room, sitting in the rocking chair, weeping or looking vacantly before her.

" . . . Finally she was induced to leave; but one day when the old butler went into the parlor she was sitting in her rocking chair as usual, only paler than ever. She did not seem to know him, and asked who he was, and then sent him to look for her carriage, saying she was going away. There was no carriage in sight, nor had any been seen to drive up, and when he went back she was dead in her chair.

"My father always said I looked like her.

"My father died suddenly, you know, without ever having fulfilled his wish to go back there to end his days. I was seized immediately with an irresistible desire to see the place, and I wrote to his old friend and neighbor that I should come down on a particular day to see it. . . The impulse was so strong that I could not wait till the day I had appointed; so I packed up and set out at once. I thus arrived at the wharf two or three days before I was expected, and there was no one to meet me. The man who kept the little store there, however, learning where I was going, kindly agreed to send

Timberneck

me over to my destination, and called a boy to hitch up a horse to a
buggy.

"... The hitching up of the horse took some time so the man
invited me to dinner at his house. There I was received by a moth-
erly woman... I asked them if they had ever been to the old place.
The man said he had, and that it had been a fine place once. The
woman gave a little half-nervous laugh. 'I ain't ever been there and
I don't want to go,' she said. I asked her why. 'Too many ghosts
there,' she laughed, as if half ashamed of her superstition. 'They
say that old lady can be seen there any time in broad daylight, and
that old Negro too; and they'd be sure to be there now the place
has been shut up so long.' I said that I was not afraid of ghosts.

"In a short time I was on the way in a little rickety, high-
pitched buggy, with my host's son, Tommy, a sleepy-looking,
shock-headed boy of 14 as my driver... He had never been to our
old place, and would not care to go by himself, though he would
not admit that he was afraid to do so.

"... Presently he pointed to a road almost grown up. 'That's
your place,' he said. Suddenly an irresistible impulse seized me,
and I asked him if he would mind going in there with me. He said
no, though he was evidently surprised and a little startled; and as
we drove along the old road, washed into gullies and grown up in
weeds, he intimated that we should probably see the lady in black

and her old Negro.

" . . . The grounds were really quite extensive, or had been, for the fence around the house and yard had once enclosed several acres. It was now all broken down, and many of the trees were gone, so that the old house, standing up stark in the hot sunlight, looked gaunt and bare. . . 'That's the graveyard,' he said, pointing to a group of tombstones, some still standing, and others lying about, off to one side under a clump of trees which I knew had once been in the garden.

" . . . The place did not appear very terrifying, and as I wished to be left to wander about quite alone, I told my companion that he could drive back down the road a few hundred yards and wait for me. He seemed to be relieved, for he had hardly taken his eyes from the old door since we drove up, as if he momentarily expected the ghostly lady and her sable butler to walk out on us . . . I sprang out, and he rattled off across the grass and was soon out of sight.

". . . I stood and gazed at the house with a strange feeling. It filled me with emotion; I was fascinated by it. Here was where my father was born, and had lived; and where I was born, the last of my branch of the family. The silence and softness of the warm summer afternoon settled down about me, and I walked about on the short grass under the trees almost as if I were in a trance.

" . . . I observed that several of the window shutters were open — blown back, I judged, in some wind. I went up the steps and walked to the front door; but it was fastened. I put my eye close to the windows beside the door and peeped in. . . I went around and tried a door at the side, and found it either unlocked or so shrunken that the bolt did not catch, and I could push it open. This let me into a narrow passageway which I knew led into the hall; so, leaving the door slightly ajar, I went in.

"The place was oppressively close . . . I went to the door of the drawing room or parlor on the right. I found the door unlocked, and entered. The room was large and high-pitched, and filled with old- fashioned stiff black furniture. A half-dozen old portraits, more or less faded, hung on the walls in frames dim with age and neglect.

" . . . Among the pictures, the most striking one was that of a lady in deep black which hung over the old mantel-piece. I knew at once that she was my ghostly great-grandmother; but I was struck by two things. She was not half as old as I had always imagined her to be; indeed, hardly more than a girl, and even in the dim light

I could see *the resemblance to myself.* This picture fascinated me. Whichever way I turned, those large melancholy eyes followed me until I forgot everything else and could look only at them.

" . . . As I sat there a strange feeling came over me. To think that I, sitting alone in that old house, was the last survivor of my family. Suddenly I felt a singular nearness of the woman in the frame before me. Of all who had lived there only two could come back. At least she could come back to me, if only in the imagination. She too had suffered; she too had sat right there in her loneliness, where I sat now in my loneliness. If I might but die there in that chair, as she had died, and be at rest.

"How long I sat there I do not know, but I seemed in a little while to *have changed places with the woman in the chair. She was in the rocking chair and I was in that by the wall.*

"I became gradually conscious of a presence. I opened my eyes, and they fell on the long mirror to my right. In it I saw through the open door — an old Negro man he seemed, though the shadow of the door on his face prevented me seeing him plainly. He wore a curious- looking old beaver hat, and had a very serious expression on his face. His hand was on the knob, and he pushed the door silently wider open as if to enter.

"At sight of me he stopped short, with a startled look on his face, and the next moment took off his hat and bowed low. 'Your servant, Mistis,' he said, in a low voice. I was afraid to move. Was he a burglar or what? I tried to speak, but my throat and tongue were dry, and though I made a motion with my lips, there was no sound. I did not dare to take my eyes from the mirror. Presently, with an effort, I said, without moving, 'What do you want?' 'I am your butler, ma'am,' he said, with another low bow, his voice sounding very far away. 'Do you live here?' 'Yes, ma'am; dat is, I did live here,' he said, with some hesitation.

" . . . I turned quickly towards the door; but the door was shut. For the first time my nerves seemed shaken. What was he? After a moment's hesitation I roused myself and came out into the hall. It was empty. I made my way out by the same door by which I had entered. . . In the sunlight my courage revived, and I went over to the old graveyard. . . Of course, the one tomb which interested me more than all the others was that of my great grandmother. It lay behind the bushes . . . She had died at the age of 22, just my age then. . . I found my driver almost in a fit over my long absence. He was sure that I had been caught by a ghost. I did not tell him what I had seen.

"On my arrival my host (the neighbor) received me with great cordiality . . . Old Uncle Benny was even more delighted to see me. He appeared almost startled at my looks.

" 'Lord, Master! You is like old mistis,' he exclaimed. 'Am I! Like my grandmother!' 'No ma'am; like your pa's grandma — like that on what hangs on de wall an' walk all 'bout there, and come down and set in her big chair in de parlor.'

" 'But you never saw her?' I said. 'Ain't I? Yes,'m! I is, too. Done see her and talk to her too. You know my grandaddy he wuz de butler there in her time, just like I wuz in you' pa's time, and they say I is just like him; maybe dat's de reason she is so friendly to me. I done see her right in broad daylight; I see her settin' in her big chair, and I see her when she come out and took her carriage to drive back to the graveyard. You know she was so proud she have her carriage even to drive her from the graveyard to the house, and you is just like her.'

"I said, 'Yes, that my father always said I was like her'."

CHAPTER 60

Where the Spirits Are All in the Family

(Urbanna)

rbanna is a scenic, postcard-picturesque, sleepy little town on the Rappahannock River about 40 miles or so north of Williamsburg. It is a friendly place where most everyone knows everyone else, and for 363 days each year it is so quiet and peaceful one can almost hear the grass grow. But, oh, on those other two days — the first weekend in November — pandemonium reigns! Tiny Urbanna is besieged by tens of thousands of tourists who pour in from all over the commonwealth, for this is the site of Virginia's annual Oyster Festival. Here, one can become sated on raw, steamed, baked or fried oysters, or done just about any other way you like them, and enjoy the annual town parade which includes every fire engine from 100 miles around.

Actually, Urbanna is an historic little village which features a number of homes dating to the 18th century. There are stories here dating back to the Civil and Revolutionary Wars when local plantations were bombarded and ransacked. One of the more famous houses in the area — Hewitt — was covered in volume II of "The Ghost of Virginia," and was noted as one of the most haunted homes in the state.

(Author's note: In May 1997 I learned of another house of spirits while giving a ghost talk to students at nearby Middlesex County High School in Saluda. There, I met a vivacious young woman named Beth Stewart, who told me what went on at her family mansion on the waterfront in Urbanna.)

Burton House was built in 1850 on a hill overlooking the river (or rivah as they say it there), and during the Civil War citizens stood watch here looking for invasions by Yankee ships. Members of the Burton family have lived in this house ever since. It began with two rooms, according to Betty Burton, Beth's mother, and today it has 14 rooms.

"My great grandfather bought it and he and my grandfather owned all the property around here on Watling Street," Betty says. "In the late 1800s, and for some years, they ran a boarding house and many people would come in by ship. So I guess you could say a lot of things have happened here over the years. People have been born here and people have died here."

There also is, say Beth, Betty, and others, a continuing swirl of psychic encounters at Burton House. They both believe the active spirits may well be former family members. "We know they are gentle and not harmful," Beth says. "And sometimes they lend a helping hand." How? Beth remembers a time when her three-year-old daughter, Hannah, was uncovered in bed. "She doesn't like covers, and she always kicks them off. One night I went into her room and the covers were all very neatly tucked in all around Hannah. When mother came over a little later I thanked her for it.

Burton House

She looked at me kind of queer-like and said she hadn't been near Hannah's room. No one else was in the house."

One of the resident ghosts could be Beth's grandfather. Her grandmother, Olga Burton, is 92, and says she has seen her late husband in apparitional form. Others have seen him, too. Roz, a nurse who cares for Hannah, told of seeing an old man sitting at a table under a tree in the backyard. It was one of grandfather's favorite resting places. Visitors also have reported seeing an elderly man sitting there. He seems to vanish before their eyes.

Beth and Betty say they hear so many footsteps and so many doors slamming when no one else is in the house that they don't even pay attention to this phenomenon anymore. "I suppose if someone else was in the house alone and heard what we hear all the time it might frighten them," Beth says. "But I hardly notice it." Still, she admits there is one room upstairs, in the oldest part of the house which gives her "the heebies." "I get chills every time I go in there, but I can't explain why. It always feels like someone is watching me. Maybe something tragic happened there years ago."

Beth says that one of the spirits, perhaps her grandfather, is a real gentleman. "There is a door to a room upstairs that is tilted and hard to open. Sometimes when I approach it, it opens by itself, as if by unseen hands. I just say 'thank you'."

"There always seems like there's a presence here," adds Betty. "When I'm alone, I never feel like I'm alone." Another who has experienced things is Morgan, Beth's four-year-old daughter. She sometimes asked her mother 'who is that little boy?' She apparently has seen the apparition of a boy in the house, a sight also witnessed by another nurse who has spent the night there. Sometimes family members also hear a baby crying. There is no baby in the house.

Not all of the manifestations are pleasant. Beth says that she has been hit in the face by "a loaf of bread that flies across the kitchen" on more than one occasion. "I don't know why that happens," she muses. Once, Morgan came running in to her to say she heard something crash in the hall. When Beth ran out she saw that a gallon jug of bottled water had broken and smashed on the the floor. "There was no way that jug could have fallen by itself," Beth declares. "Someone would have had to lift it up over a rack and then let it drop. My husband and I had been having a knock-down dragout argument at the time. Maybe the ghost didn't like that and this was its way of showing its disapproval.

"I must be obsessed with the house," Beth adds. "Every time

I'm away from it, I have vivid dreams about it. When I lived in Richmond, for instance, I had recurring dreams in which I saw myself floating around at Burton House with the spirits here. The longer I was away the more frequently I dreamed. It was like when I was not here I was still connected to the place. I really do believe whatever or whoever is here, they are part of the family, and they're looking out for us in their own way. This may sound strange, but somehow I find that a comforting feeling."

CHAPTER 61

The 'Ordeal of Touch'

(Eastern Shore)

Superstition was strong in Colonial Virginia, even before the famous witch trials occurred in Salem, Massachusetts, and the infamous case of Grace Sherwood, a suspected witch, in Virginia. Such superstition was brought over to the New World with the settlers; ancient beliefs in the bizarre handed down family to family for centuries in Europe.

One of the weirdest of these old rituals was known as the "Ordeal of Touch." For some reason it was believed by some that if a murderer touched, or came into the presence of the body of his or her victim, the wounds which had been inflicted upon the victim would "bleed afresh." This archaic custom can be traced to 17th century England and Scotland, where it was widely prevalent even among the educated people.

Michael Drayton, an English poet of that era, penned:

"If the vile actors of the heinous deed

Near the dead body happily be brought,

Oft has been prov'd the breathless corpse will bleed."

Even William Shakespeare was drawn into the tradition. He wrote the following in Act I, Scene II, of Richard III, where Lady Anne, in the presence of the body of the dead king, is made to accuse Gloster in this passage:

"O gentlemen, see, see, dead Henry's wounds

Open their congeal'd mouths and bleed afresh!

Blush, blush, thou lump of foul deformity,
For't is thy presence that exhales this blood

From cold and empty veins, where no blood dwells."

There are at least two recorded instances of actual cases where the Ordeal of Touch occurred in the commonwealth. They have been documented in: "The Virginia Magazine of History and Biography," the book "Ye Kingdom of Accawmacke," by Jennings Cropper Wise, a member of the Virginia Historical Society; and in the book, "Drummondtown — A One Horse Town," by L. Floyd Nock, III.

One such example is in the records of Northampton County. It states, "On December 14, 1656, Captain William Whittington issued a warrant for a Jury of Inquest over the body of Paul Rynners," suspected to have been murdered by William Custis. The jury reported: "We have viewed the body of Paul Rynnuse, late of this county deceased & have caused Wm. Custis to touch the face and stroke the body of said Paul Rynnuse which he willingly did. But no sign did appear unto us of question in the law." Custis was thus freed.

The second incident involved the alleged murder of an infant, born of Mary Andrews in Accomack. Mary was the unmarried daughter of Sarah Carter and the stepdaughter of Paul Carter. Both Paul and Sarah were accused of the crime and brought to trial. The following is from Accomack court records:

"Att a Court held and continued for Accomack County, March 18, 1679. The Confession of Paul Carter taken the First day of March, 1679.

"Question. What doe yu know concerning a child born of Mary the daughter of Sarah, the wife of the said Paul?

"Answere. That he doth know that the said Mary had a man child born of her body and that the said Sarah assisted at the birth of the said child, & that he certainly knoweth not whether it were born alive or not & that they did endeavor to preserve the life thereof and that it lay betwixt his wife and her daughter all night and that ye next morning he saw it dead & he and his wife carefully buried the said child but that his wife carefully washing and dressed it."

The body of the baby was exhumed so that it could be

346

"stroaked" by the accused couple. A jury consisting of 12 women was enpaneled. Paul Carter was found guilty of the crime, because while he was "stroaking" the child — "black and sotted places" on its body grew "fresh and red."

It is not specified what punishment Paul was given. This, however, is said to be the last instance of trial by Ordeal of Touch on record.

* * * * *

THE SKULL THAT 'CONVICTED' A MURDERER
(Southwest Virginia)

(Author's note: In past volumes in this series I have written of some of the quaint customs of mountain people regarding murders. In one instance a killer was brought to "justice" 40 years after the deed, when the fingerbone of the victim stuck to his skin. Such a happening, 150 or so years ago, was said to indicate who the guilty party was. Following is another, somewhat similar account which has been told and retold by the mountain people for several generations. The date and exact location of this occurrence are unknown. The authenticity may also be in question, although, as with most such traditions, there usually was some basis in fact upon which the tale was woven.)

 here was a man named Asa Meters. He and his brother had a large farm and a number of sheep. One day while they were out shearing sheep his brother accidently fell on some upturned shears which pierced his heart and killed him. At least that's what Asa told his neighbors.

No one believed him. It was, rather, commonly believed that Asa had murdered his brother to gain his share of their property, for Asa was known to be a "driver," i.e., ambitious. The suspicions grew when they looked at Asa. Blue Ridge folks could "read" a face, and Asa "looked" guilty. It was said that when people looked at Asa's hands, "they saw blood."

Still, no one had witnessed the crime, but the speculation was further fueled when the brother was hastily buried in a field in back of the old farmhouse with not even a decent marker. Some time later, Asa hired a man named Henry Holt to plow the field.

During the plowing he unearthed the brother's skeletal remains. There was, at that time, a prevalent belief that the identity of an unknown murderer could be determined by placing the victim's skull over the suspect's head. It was thought that in so doing, the suspect would be unable to lie.

And so it was that Henry Holt managed to place the skull in Asa's loft, above the fireplace. When Asa stooped to fix the fire, Henry accused him of killing his brother. It was said that Asa, though not answering the question directly, began to shake. Henry said he almost shook himself to death.

In the days that followed, Asa had difficulty eating because, as one writer put it, "the vapor of his brother would grab the food away." Nor could he sleep, since "his brother's ghost would throw itself down on top of him and smother him. He could only sit by the fire and try to beat his brother's ghost with a stick. A gray 'something' hovered over him all the time."

Asa was never brought to trial. It wasn't necessary. Justice was being served, mountain-style.

Islands of Intrigue

(The Chesapeake Bay)

ne may wonder why there are so many legends of ghosts on islands in the Chesapeake Bay. That is because these islands are surrounded, naturally, by water, and there is a time-honored tradition that discarnate spirits from another world do not cross water. How, then, did they get there?

There are two principal islands. One is Tangier, located roughly halfway between Reedville on the mainland and Onancock on the Eastern Shore. The other is Smith Island, a few miles north of Tangier and just across the Maryland state line. Both are sites for the homes of grizzled watermen, and others who like the remote, quaint, and away-from-civilization lifestyle the islands have featured for nearly 400 years.

Both were landed upon by Captain John Smith, during his explorations of the Bay in 1608. He was met then by friendly Indians, and the reputation for hospitality has been carried through to this day, although it may take "strangers" who come for more than a short visit time to "settle in." The long-time inhabitants are, too, a very close knit group. In fact, many are related.

At Tangier, for example, a man named West bought the island from the Indians for "two overcoats." He sold part of his holdings, in 1686, to John Crockett, and his eight sons, who settled here. Many Crocketts remain. Smith Island originally was a "place of exile" for those settlers of Jamestown who had been found in disfavor. However, because of the abundance of fish, game and wildlife, and the richness of the soil, they seemed to have the better of it over their fellow colonists who remained in the hostile environs of

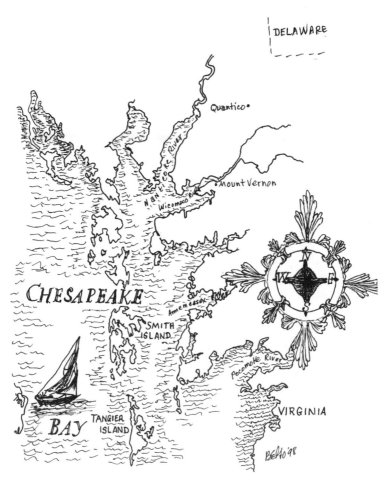

"Islands of Intrigue"

Jamestown.

The main occupation of the islanders is, and has been for centuries, derived from the water. This includes oystering, crabbing and fishing. The watermen are a hardy breed who still speak with an Elizabethan twang which "mainlanders" sometimes find difficult to decipher.

They also are a very superstitious lot, and are reluctant to speak openly about the supernatural. They believe deeply in omens, or, in their words, "tokens." One never paints a boat blue, for instance, because that brings bad luck. One never carries walnuts aboard a vessel because walnut trees grow in cemeteries. Nor does one allow black luggage aboard ship, or work on a Sunday. The whys behind some of these tokens have been lost to memory, but they nevertheless are still strictly, even fiercely, adhered to.

Amid such enduring superstitions, combined with imagination, the isolation, and the long nights and sometimes stormy seas, legends have emerged. Some involve tombstones. Early settlers here built simple frame houses, often within neat picket fences. At Tangier one can still see tombstones in the yards of some of the houses, as the custom was to bury the dead nearby.

One often told tale concerned a Tangier waterman. While fishing on the Bay one evening, the corpse of a man drifted up to his boat. The man pulled the body into his boat and stripped it of its coat, which he fancied for himself. He later went ashore and buried the corpse. Two nights later the vision of the drowned man appeared to him, asking for his coat. When this reoccurred on three successive nights, the harassed waterman threw the coat at the specter and shouted, "Take your damned old coat, I don't want it."

Drownings seem to play on the watermen's psyche. Once when a crew was anchored off the mainland, one of the men went ashore in a skiff to slake his thirst. When he didn't return, the others went to bed. Sometime later, in the darkness, they were awakened by the sounds of the skiff approaching. They then heard the oars being thrown up and someone climbing on board. The handle on the cabin door turned. Two of the crew members went topside to look. There was no one there! They went back to bed, but then heard the same sounds repeated. They heard someone walking across the deck, but, again, on investigation, they found no one. The captain then told them they must be anchored over a drowned man's corpse, so he ordered the boat to be moved. They heard nothing after that.

A similar incident occurred to another crew on a recently bought boat one night. The owner had been warned that the vessel was haunted, but he had scoffed at the suggestion. The crew's first evening out in the Bay, however, cast some doubts. They had anchored for the night and were sitting down below in the cabin when the craft began to roll from side to side. The captain went on deck. It was a calm, clear evening and the sea was as slick as glass. There was not even a hint of a breeze. The motion stopped. But when he went back below, the rolling started up again. This time the captain pulled his bed covers up and shouted that he didn't care who was up there rocking his boat, he had to get some oysters in the morning and he was going to sleep. The mystery remained unsolved.

In the November 1871 issue of "The Southern Magazine," there is reference to an English gentleman who settled in the vicinity of the islands off the Eastern Shore, and who, on a memorable night perhaps in the early 1800s had an extraordinary experience. He was the grandparent of the magazine article's author. This is how it was described:

"He was a thorough Englishman, fond of high living, and noted far and near for his fine horses and his convivial qualities. He often went into the city, and seldom returned before the small hours of the night, and generally lively from the effects of potations imbibed in genial company.

"One night the family were awakened and alarmed by his arrival at home, his horse white with foam and trembling with fatigue, and the old gentleman himself in a state of uncontrollable excitement. As soon as he recovered his breath enough to speak, he eagerly inquired if any of us had seen *a woman in patchwork*. Becoming partially composed, he proceeded to relate the following circumstances:

"'I was just coming along the road thinking no harm of any-body, when just the other side of the bridge, my mare stood stock-still. I tried to urge her forward in vain. She planted her four legs and stood fast. I glanced around to see what was the matter, and I saw by the light of the moon a woman dressed in patchwork; she was tall and slim, and I clearly distinguished the bright colors of the scarf which composed her dress.

"'Each of the innumerable pieces of which it was made up seemed to *glow with a light of its own*; the woman's eyes looked like coals of fire, and her long hair fell over her shoulders in disheveled locks. Suddenly my mare made a bolt to run by her, when the woman in patchwork sprang lightly from the ground and seated herself behind me, and so rode every step of the way home. She jumped down at the gate and disappeared.'

"This was my grandfather's story, and to the day of his death he believed in the reality of the woman in patchwork."

* * * * *

On Deal Island, north of Smith Island in Maryland waters, there is a popular legend about a woman who got her wish — and then didn't want it. When her husband died, she had him buried in the island cemetery, but it was hard for her to let him go. It was said that you could hear her crying late at night, saying, "Oh Lord, send him back to me!" Several weeks later a hurricane swept through the Bay, flooding the island at high tide. The storm unearthed the coffin of the woman's husband and washed it up to her doorstep! When she saw it out the window, she allegedly screamed, "Oh Lord, I don't want him. I didn't mean it. Take him back!"

Islanders also tell of an eerie premonition of death that occurred during a thunderstorm. A young girl's mother had died and she was raised by her grandmother. One day, during a storm, the girl ran in the house and told her grandmother that she had seen her dead mother outside and that she had told her she was going to take her (the child) with her. The next day the grandmother went outside and found the mother's grave open and the coffin visible, apparently uncovered in the downpour. The young girl died within a month.

One of the "most haunted" sites in the Chesapeake Bay is said to be Wading Place Bridge on Smith Island, midway between Rhodes Point and Ewell. It is here that a baby is sometimes heard crying in the marsh, and a mother's wails are heard as "she searches for her lost child." Only the most stout-hearted will dare to venture across the bridge late at night. One who did, and who caused a practical joke to backfire, was a young man who crossed the bridge on a regular basis to see his girl friend.

Some pranksters decided to have some fun with him, so one night one of them sat in the middle of the bridge in a rocking chair, cloaked in a white sheet, and with his pals hiding in the brush, waited for the young man to cross. When he did, the man in the rocking chair began to rock and groan. Instead of running away, however, the young man approached the ghost, assumed a karate position, and declared he was going to come through or over the "ghost." The prankster, fearing bodily harm, jumped up and fled in terror himself, sending the rocking chair over the rail and splashing into the water.

Other legends abound on the islands. There are stories of spectral dogs that portend death; of headless horsemen and even headless horses; of a woman who, centuries ago, was murdered by her husband who cut off her head and ever since, she returns on the anniversary of her demise to walk in the area of the old "coffin house" on Smith Island. There are tales of pirates who still stand guard over buried treasures they hid in the 1700s; and of the spirits of slaves who long ago helped their masters to bury riches and then were killed in the process so they would never reveal the hiding place.

One can hear of such things today by taking one of the summer cruise boats to Tangier or Smith Island. The sagas are still told in the colorful old-English dialect of the watermen.

But a visitor should remember — never to take along any black luggage!

Stir Not the Bones!

(Author's note: In past editions in this continuing series on Virginia ghosts, I have written, rather extensively, about cases where the bones of people long deceased have either been improperly buried, or were disturbed from their resting places. There was the lady with the tortoise shell comb, for example, in "The Ghosts of Richmond" (1985); "An Obsession Named Melanie," in "The Ghosts of Tidewater" (1990); and "The Corpse Who Demanded to Be Reburied," in "The Ghosts of Virginia, Volume II" (1994). Such cases, apparently, are not all that uncommon, and, it seems, one of the reasons for ghostly returns to earth are to make sure that a person's mortal remains are, in fact, left alone.

And, so, here are three more instances, two strikingly similar, where voices from the beyond made their presences — and their demands — clearly known. The first was originally published in George Holbert Tucker's fine book, "Virginia Supernatural Tales," and the second in Doris Kuebler Leitner's booklet, "Ghost Stories of Olde Towne, Portsmouth, Virginia." These episodes also have been the subject of various newspaper articles over the years. The third is based on an interview.)

BURIED IN A FRUIT JAR
(Campbell County)

The late L. Lee Barnes of Sedgefield Farm near New London in Campbell County was an amateur genealogist who loved to trace his family tree — a tree which included some very distinguished Virginians. One, Captain Thomas Lee, founded Leesville in the county. One day Barnes was out in his family's graveyard, gathering information from the old

tombstones, when he discovered the marker for Mrs. William Lee, the wife of one of his ancestors. But he could find no site for her husband, which puzzled him. So he decided, against his wife's strenuous objections, to dig next to Mrs. Lee's grave.

There, he found some bones and a short length of tightly tied hair. He believed this to be William Lee's queue — the 18th century style of gathering a man's long hair at the nape of the neck. Barnes then gathered the bones, placed them in a large fruit jar, and set it on the mantel shelf in his living room, again, much to the dismay of his angry wife.

Several days later, Barnes and his wife were sitting around the stove in their living room, when both were startled to see a "stately elderly woman, wearing a high white lace cap and black dress and cloak," peering through a window at them. The woman then disappeared "into thin air." He went outside to look, but found no trace of the woman.

Then, strange things began to happen at the front door of Sedgefield Farm. The old brass knocker would rap loudly three times in succession, but there was never anyone there. This continued for several days. Mrs. Barnes felt the appearance of the mystery woman and the rappings were somehow connected with Lee's bones in the fruit jar.

Next, Barnes had a vivid and quite scary nightmare. He dreamed he had awakened in his darkened bedroom and saw the "stately elderly woman," surrounded by an eerie light, walk through the bedroom door and stand at the foot of his bed. She then raised an accusing finger, shook it at him, and announced in a threatening voice, "Put it back where you got it!" She then vaporized.

As Tucker wrote, "Barnes awoke in a cold sweat." He told his wife of the dream and first thing the next morning, he went out and dug a hole next to Mrs. Lee's grave, and reburied the bones he had found. Once that was done, the strange phenomena ceased.

* * * * *

BEST TO LEAVE WELL ENOUGH ALONE
(Portsmouth)

few years ago, a young couple, who have asked to remain anonymous, were restoring their 18th century home in Portsmouth. While working in the yard, they uncovered an old, unmarked grave. The husband had started a collection of relics he had found in the yard and decided to keep several of the bones, although his wife objected. (Sound familiar? Read on!)

A few days later, they were sitting by a large bay window which overlooks their rear garden, when, all of a sudden, both saw an old, white-haired lady staring at them through the glass. Stunned, they ran outside, but there was no one there. They couldn't figure out how the woman had gotten there. The yard is surrounded by a eight-foot-high solid brick wall, and the only entrance is through a gate which they kept locked. They couldn't bring themselves to believe that an elderly woman could have scaled that wall.

The next night, the woman appeared again, standing in the middle of the garden. The wife turned on outside floodlights and

ran outside to find — nothing. Several nights later, the apparitional woman appeared once more, this time at the foot of the couple's bed. She pointed a bony finger at them and announced, in a shrill voice, "You put my bones back!" She then vanished.

At daybreak the next morning, the husband returned the bones where he had found them. They never saw the old woman again.

* * * * *

DARE NOT DISTURB AN INDIAN MOUND
(Sedalia)

(Author's note: Warren Ayres is no stranger to ghostly activity. Warren is from Sedalia, Virginia, between Bedford and Big Island. I met him at the October 1996 Garlic Festival, held annually at the Rebec Winery in Amherst County. One of Warren's neighbors, for example, told him of sighting the fleeting form of a woman dressed in a long flowing white gown one night. The man said the woman disappeared in thick brush and woods right before his eyes. Warren has had his own psychic encounter.

"A few years ago," he says, "I was going upstairs in my house when I saw what appeared to be a blood stain on the stairs. I had no idea of how it got there or where it came from. I went in the kitchen to get some paper towels, and when I returned it was gone! That was about 18 years ago, I guess."

Warren then told me the following account of what might be considered an Indian curse:)

I'm not going to name the man involved. He's a very private man. Keeps to himself mostly. I hardly ever see him. He has signs posted on his land. One says 'no arrowhead hunting. If I catch you, I'll shoot you.' You see, there was an old Indian mound on his land and people would come over and look for arrowheads.

"Well, about two years ago, he built a lake on his property and he bulldozed the mound. It is now either an integral part of the dam or its underwater. I'm not sure. Whatever, he disturbed that old Indian burial ground, and they say that brings bad luck. It was about 20 to 30 feet long and about six to eight feet high.

"I can tell you this. In the past two years: his girl friend left him; he had a heart attack; a storm blew the roof off his house; and he's been taken to court because his lake covered up some land owned by other people. I guess you could say a terrible string of things has happened to him ever since he moved that mound."

CHAPTER 64

The Miser's Curse

(Author's note: As I have often said in the past, one of the great pleasures of doing a series of books like this — is the research. I love delving into old archives, and poring through, as Poe said, many a volume of forgotten lore. Obviously, the more I have written about Virginia ghosts, the more difficult it becomes to find something not previously discovered. Thus, it was with great joy that, while scanning through dozens of old books at Jack Hamilton's rare book shop in Williamsburg one rainy day in November 1996, that I came across a chapter title called "The Miser's Curse." The sub-title was "A Veritable Ghost Story." I became excited.

It was in a bound and tattered volume of Harper's Magazines covering the first few months of 1857. It was in the April issue. I eagerly turned to the page and was delighted to find it was in the geographical realm that would qualify for inclusion in this series, although the exact location, and certain other details, were not disclosed. Although the type in these old magazines is small enough (perhaps six point) to justify a magnifying glass, I nevertheless perused the material on the spot. I found it absorbing. The author is anonymous. I felt he, or she, did an excellent job of writing. I include it here with only slight excerption and editing for clarification. Enjoy.)

Disclaim it as we may, the night side of nature has a wild and mysterious attraction for every human soul. That mystic realm which lies beyond the present life, into which we must all plunge at some future period, must ever possess a thrilling interest for the imagination and the heart.

"The story I am about to relate is one of facts which transpired years ago (dating back from 1857), but there are many yet living who can bear witness to the truth of the following incidents.

"In a small, poorly-furnished room a miser lay dying. He had been a hard, grasping man of the world, a trader in the miseries and wants of others, and by such means he had accumulated wealth which he hoarded with all the greed of his nature. But once in his life had he been known to act with liberality toward any human being, and terrible results to the favored one flowed from that act of paternal pride.

"Look at the miserable wreck that pants and struggles for breath on that bed. He is old, wasted, repulsive, and mean; but even such as he is, he was once loved by a gentle and good woman; but that was in his youth when his step was elastic and free, while his face retained the impress of humanity and had not hardened into what it now is.

"Fortunately for herself, his wife died in the morning of life, leaving three children to his care. The youngest ones, a girl and boy, were left to do pretty much as they pleased, while the father gave all the heart nature had bestowed upon him to his eldest son — a handsome, high-spirited lad, who grew in willfulness as years crept on.

"William Herbert (the oldest son) soon learned to consider himself all-important to his father; the only smiles that were ever seen upon his face illumined it at his approach, and the only words of affection that fell from his lips were addressed to this beloved son. Even his daughter he treated with silent sternness, and repulsed her efforts to win a recognition of her right to a place in his cold heart.

"Theirs was a curious household . . a faithful Negress presided over it as housekeeper after the decease of her mistress. The strictest economy prevailed in every department, and although her master was known to have accumulated wealth, no evidences of it were ever seen. Even in the expenditures of the darling son, the same parsimony was observed. To him, Herbert was niggardly, under the pretext that a liberal allowance would tempt him to indulge in dissipated and extravagant habits.

"As they (the children) advanced to maturity, the father kept the elder son in bounds by promising that when he settled in life, he would act most liberally toward him. But, at the same time, he gave him to understand that he would tolerate no inferior marriage; he must choose a wife from the ranks of the wealthy, and then he would see what he would do for him.

"Tired of the strict dependence in which he was kept, William Herbert, early in life, sought a bride possessing the requisite qualifications to please his father. A young girl from a neighboring county visited his native town, who possessed in her own right a handsome, unencumbered property. He sought her acquaintance, found her sufficiently attractive to suit his own taste, and soon succeeded in winning her consent to be his wife.

"The elder Herbert was delighted with the proposed match, and when his son reminded him of his oft-repeated promise to give him a portion of his fortune when he settled, he at once consented to double the wealth of the bride, thus placing his well-beloved son on an equality with her.

"The marriage took place, but not before William Herbert had taken every precaution to secure absolutely in his own power, the property bestowed by his father. It was a marvel among the lawyers who drew the deeds that such a man as the miser should have opened his purse to such an extent; but he firmly believed that the training his son had received would prevent him from using his wealth with a lavish hand.

"In bitterness of heart, he soon saw his error; the check secured, the younger Herbert soon displayed his natural tastes; they were lavished to profusion, and the money he had never been taught to value justly was expended with recklessness. He purchased a beautiful villa in the vicinity of the town, and furnished it extravagantly. All the appointments of the establishment were luxurious and elegant, and the newly-wedded couple commenced a style of housekeeping corresponding with them.

"The young wife was thoughtless, fond of pleasure, and strongly attached to her husband; the two agreed perfectly in their tastes, and but for the violent displeasure of the elder Herbert, their life would have been without a cloud. He often darkened the sunshine in which they lived by his presence beneath their roof, when sneers, reproaches, and bitter jibes, ever formed the staple of his conversation.

"Sometimes his temper would be aroused to a pitch of fury by the wasteful extravagance he beheld, and he would often anathematize himself audibly for having been so great a fool as to place any portion of his hard-earned wealth at the disposal of such a spendthrift as his son.

"Violent scenes were at length of frequent occurrence, and William finally spoke boldly to his father and told him that his house was his own, and he intended to act as he pleased in it; that he would receive him as a guest so long as he chose to treat himself and his wife with the respect he considered due to them, but he would no longer tolerate insult under his own roof.

"The father listened with repressed fury; but when the son ceased speaking, his passion broke forth in words of bitter vehemence.

"He ended with — 'Your roof indeed; was it not bought with *my* money, for you never earned a penny in your worthless life, and if all this foolish wastefulness goes on, how long will it be yours, do you think? Boy, you know that hard as men think me, I have always loved you; but from this hour you are to me as though you do not exist. I never will darken your threshold again, and if you come to the direst poverty, as I know you must, not another penny of mine shall you ever receive. . . I shake the dust from my feet, and bid you never again to greet me as your father. I am no longer such to you, for henceforth I am your bitter and uncompromising enemy.

"'I leave with you what you may smile at — the miser's curse — but it will fall, fall, fall!' And as he repeated the ominous word, he stamped his feet violently upon the floor, and in a species of blind frenzy left the house never again to reenter it.

"From that day Herbert (the father) was harder and more grinding in his dealings than before. The only soft feeling his heart had ever known became a source of bitterness, and a sort of maniacal hatred of his undutiful son took possession of him. He watched his (son's) extravagant career with malicious eagerness, and gloated over the evidences which came, year after year, that his prophecies were slowly fulfilling themselves.

"With no habits of business, and a careless disregard of expenses, William Herbert soon found that even his ample resources did not save him from embarrassments. The fortune he thought inexhaustible wasted slowly away . . . until his utter ruin was consummated. No mercy was shown; he was stripped of everything, and thrown helpless and penniless upon the world with a wife and four young children dependent upon him. Then the father wrote:

"'Where is your roof now, William Herbert? Come not, undutiful ingrate, to appeal to me in behalf of those you have impoverished by your mad and unprincipled wastefulness. Beg, starve, steal, but from me you gain nothing. . . Go now where you belong, among the wretched and the outcast, and take with you the renewal of the miser's curse!'

"To the miserable, broken-down man this was the last bitter drop that caused his cup of anguish to overflow. The knowledge that his own father . . . now gloated over his unhappy condition, overcame the last remnant of fortitude, and he sank into a brain fever which threatened to destroy him. The tender care of his wife saved his life, but the few resources left to the ruined family were exhausted by his long illness, and Herbert arose from his couch to face a world with which he was utterly unfitted to wrestle.

". . . Oh! the struggle of poverty is dire enough to those born to it; but to the gently nurtured, accustomed to the careless case of wealth, how much more bitter it is, who shall tell?

". . . Two more children were added to the suffering family during these terrible years — heirs of want and suffering; and bitter were the tears of self-reproach shed over their helplessness by the destitute parents, when they thought of what might have been, in contrast with the miserable reality before them.

"Herbert made more than one effort to soften his father. He vainly appealed to that affection which had once existed, but alas! it was now turned to the most cruel enmity. His appeals were rejected with such bitter, stinging contempt — such overwhelming abuse, that he soon ceased to make them, and resigned himself to the lot he had incurred by his own recklessness.

"At length the miser sickened; day by day he grew worse; he became aware of his own danger, and summoned a lawyer to make his will. Every legal technicality was brought in play to exclude his eldest son or (his son's) children from ever succeeding to the smallest fraction of his estate. The property was bequeathed to his younger children and their heirs, on the sole condition that they would never share the smallest portion of it with their discarded brother.

"Herbert heard of the old man's dying condition. . . The heart of the son yearned to behold once more the father who had loved him in his boyish days, and he went slowly toward the shabby old house in which his family dwelt. Twelve years had rolled away since he last stood beneath its roof. (The old housekeeper told him it was useless, but the younger Herbert persisted in seeing his father one last time.) 'I must see him . . . let the result to myself be what it may.'

"The dying man lay apparently in a light slumber . . . He

rushed impetuously toward the bed, threw himself beside it, and thus kneeling he grasped the hand that lay upon the coverlet, already cold with the dews of approaching death. At that touch the spirit of the departing one struggled back to life; he who seemed scarcely breathing but a moment before was suddenly endued with terrible vitality. He started up in the bed, his glazing eyes glaring with evil passion, and his lips writhing with the efforts to utter the torrent of anger that surged within him.

"He wrenched his hand from his son, and regarded him with an expression that half paralyzed him. William could only stammer —

"'Pardon — pardon — remove the curse, O father! Let it not

The Miser's Deathbed Curse

cling to me through my whole life.'

"The lips of the dying man moved, but for many moments they had no power to produce a sound. At length the iron will mastered even the benumbing influence of the stern conqueror, and a strange, unearthly voice, which sounded as that of some demon seeking utterance through his tongue, shrieked forth —

"'You! you! how dare you approach me? Hence! I say; hence! before I spurn you from my sight!' and he attempted to spring from his bed. . . With raised finger, he continued — 'Hear my last words, William Herbert, and know that they are the utterances of as deadly a hate as ever sprang up between man and man. I have no pardon for you; and if my resentment can manifest itself beyond the grave, I will come back to you and make your life a bitterness to you. I have little faith in parsons or their cant; but I believe there is a demon — I have known him, I have felt his influence — and if he will give me the power to torment you, I will surrender myself to him body and soul. Now go, and take with you the renewed curse of him you would not suffer to die in peace.'

"Exhausted by the effort, he sank back, and by the time his head touched the pillow he was dead.

"Horror-struck at the result of his effort at conciliation, Herbert left the house bewildered and trembling. As he walked through the streets toward his own abode, it seemed to him that a form flitted beside him, breathed coldly upon him, and even touched his person with icy fingers, but when he turned toward it, nothing was there.

(William Herbert then went home and told his wife.) "'Hope for nothing for us, Mary, for an evil spell is upon us and we may never escape from the miserable doom of poverty and suffering. The old man was inexorable, and my presence only exasperated him into an excess of fury that hastened his death.

". . . For many hours Herbert could not sleep, for the same weird consciousness of a *presence* that was strange and inimical to him made itself felt, though it was invisible. . . After long effort he slept, and in his sleep that awful death-scene was enacted again and again. When he awoke he felt even more jaded and worn out than before slumber had fallen on him.

". . . He learned that the funeral would take place on the second day from that, for the miser had a lively horror of being buried alive, and had requested that his body should be kept until the third day.

"The evening of the burial was cold, gloomy and depressing. Herbert walked mechanically in the procession, looking self-absorbed, and slightly excited. . . Those who closely observed him thought he was trembling upon the verge of insanity, and the story of the last awful interview between the father and son was whispered among them.

"The two brothers stood side by side at the head of the grave, and when the coffin was lowered, the elder one was observed to lean over and peer into it with an expression that seemed to indicate an intense fear that the dead might again rise to mock him. He evidently listened eagerly when the clods rattled upon the coffin; and when the attendants were pressing down the earth into the full grave, he suddenly jumped upon it, and aided in stamping it down, while he muttered,

"'Bury him deep — fasten him in, so he can not come back to torment me as he threatened!'

"Scandalized at such conduct, his friends endeavored to draw him away, but with a ghastly smile he resisted them, as he said,

"'I tell you I *must* see that he is well buried, *for he has been with me ever since the breath left his body.* I cannot see him, but I can feel his presence and it suffocates me. Oh, men! pack down the clods well — pack them — pack them till they are as hard as the heart that rests beneath them.'

"'Poor fellow, he is mad. He must be taken care of!' was said by many; but Herbert quietly replied,

"'No, I am not mad; I am only haunted by a demon into whom the spirit of my father has passed.'

(Later, Herbert returned to his home.) " . . . The hours waned away and the fire burned low upon the hearth. The two (Herbert and his wife) had sunk into moody silence, when suddenly Herbert started and exclaimed.

"'What — what was that, Mary?'

"'I saw nothing. Oh William! you startled me so that I am all unnerved.'

"'No — I can see nothing either, but I hear — oh, I hear deep, agonizing breathing close to my ear. It is as if a weight is pressing upon the breast of a suffocating man, and a giant hand seemed to clutch my feet. Oh, my God! what can this be?'

"His wife arose pallid and trembling, for she too heard the sounds he described, though she did not feel the numbing pressure upon her feet. In a voice strained with agony, Herbert said,

"'You refused to believe me, Mary, when I told you that the old man haunted me; now you hear for yourself — Hark!'

"This exclamation was caused by a crash which came from the next room. It seemed as if some heavy article of furniture had fallen and broken in pieces. This was followed by an uproar which sounded as if the fragments were endued with life, and were carrying on a brisk warfare against each other.

"The children were in that apartment, and the mother seized the candle and rushed to see what had happened. The room was found in its usual condition, but its young occupants were all awake and frightened at the tumult around them. As the light streamed into the apartment, the noise shifted to the attic; by this time Herbert had recovered sufficient self-control to follow his wife. They quieted the fears of the children as well as they could, and when they again slept, the two ascended to the upper rooms and examined them.

"The strange noises had partially died away while they were soothing the fears of the children, but as the two mounted the staircase, they again commenced; every nook was examined, but as they entered one room the sounds invariably flitted before them to the next.

"In this terrible watch passed the greatest portion of the night, and when they retired, a perfect chorus of raps was kept up around the bed.

"The horror of those hours left their impress forever upon the unhappy man. He arose with hair partially blanched, and an expression of bewildered anguish upon his features which never again left them.

"It was many years before spiritualism came in vogue, and although hundreds heard these noises, no explanation was offered. The common opinion was, that the miser had indeed sold himself to the Evil One for the power to torment his unhappy son.

"It was an established *fact*, that William Herbert *never remained three nights in any house without having, on the third one, the same inferno enacted beneath its roof.*

"Many years after his father's death, the writer saw him in (another) city, whither he had come at the invitation of his brother, on his way to take possession of a farm belonging to the wife of the latter which had been offered him as an asylum for his premature old age. His wife was with him, a pale emaciated woman, who looked as if a weight of sorrow brooded ever upon her heart.

"Before they came, Mrs. John Herbert (William Herbert's brother's wife) stipulated that they should not remain in her house over the third night, but William unfortunately was attacked with illness, and two weeks elapsed before he was sufficiently recovered to proceed to his new home. The usual consequences followed, and for 18 months it was impossible to sleep in peace in their home.

"The noises gradually subsided, but the evil spirit seemed to be omnipresent; for while they still made night terrible there, letters were received from the new home saying that even to the secluded spot they had sought, the mysterious sounds had followed them, and to his dying hour William Herbert was haunted by the spirit of his father."

Recollections of a 'Psychic' Family

(Roanoke and other sites)

s it possible for an entire family to be psychically sensitive? One begins to wonder after talking to Mary Vaught of Lafayette, Virginia, near Roanoke. She and her brothers and sisters seemingly are able to recite ghostly incident after incident, all different, depending upon to whom you are talking. And that can add up to a lot of incidents, because at one time there were 15 children in the family — 10 girls and five boys! Strange things just seem to happen to members of this family.

The psychic inheritance might stem from Mary's late mother, Annie Hope Tillet, of Leesburg. She was born in 1912. She married Ralph Isenberg. Annie, according to her children, was a true psychic. "She used to tell me when I was real little that you should never be afraid of a spirit," says Alma Heixenbaugh, one of Mary Vaught's sisters.

Alma says she grew up in southern Maryland and the house the family lived in for awhile, near the Mary Surratt House in Clinton, was haunted. "There was a lot of tragedy there," Alma notes. "This occurred not only to us but to previous occupants. My brother had polio, and wore leg braces which gave off a metallic click when he walked. He died in the house. For years afterward, we could still hear that distinctive click at night, as if he were still walking around."

At one point, the family almost moved into the Mary Surratt

House. (Mary Surratt, readers of past volumes in this series will remember, was convicted of conspiracy in the assassination plot to kill President Abraham Lincoln. She was, in 1865, the first woman ever hanged in the United States, though she protested her innocence up to the last minute. There have been reports of her ghost appearing in Clinton, and at other sites.) Alma says the family could have rented the house, decades ago, for $25 a month, but decided not to move in because, at the time, the building had neither electricity or indoor plumbing.

Alma and Mary's sister, Ruby, however, did visit the house one day and had a chilling experience. "She definitely felt a strong presence the minute she entered the place," Alma recalls. "She said her hair stood straight up on end."

Alma and Mary's sister, Norma, and their mother both had psychic premonitions of their deaths. "Norma lived about 70 miles away in Hollywood, Maryland," Alma says. "She called one day in January 1997, and sounded perfectly normal to me. She wanted us to drive over to see her, but we were doing something else. So she said if we didn't come we would never see her alive again. She called about 2:30 in the afternoon. She died that day at 3 o'clock."

Alma says that when she was six years old, "my mother told me that she would die when I was 15. She said that everybody had a time to die and she knew when hers was. And she did. She died when I was 15. She had come home from the hospital for Thanksgiving, and she told us, 'you'd better give me my Christmas presents now, because I won't be around for Christmas.' She died that night."

Annie was buried at Arlington National Cemetery. Her husband, Ralph Isenberg had once been a guard at the Tomb of the Unknown Soldier, and they had met there. Alma says one day she and her sister, Beverley, went to the grave site for a visit. "She used to yell at us all the time about eating crabapples when we were little," Alma says. "Well, there was a crabapple tree near her grave. It was a quiet day and there was no wind. Suddenly, a crabapple fell off that tree next to us. Beverley and I just looked at each other and smiled. Then we looked up at the tree, and there was one leaf that just kept shaking. It was like an omen, like mom knew we were there."

Alma had another psychic revelation in March 1996. She dreamed one night of seeing a man riding a horse. "He was riding toward my brother and mother, but I couldn't see his face," she says. Her father died shortly after the dream.

Mary Vaught has had psychic impressions, too. The strongest occurred when she and her husband, Carter, and their children, moved into a house at 1232 Kerns Avenue in Roanoke in 1963. "I could sense the house was haunted," Mary says. "I got sick right after we moved in, and we went to one doctor after another, but they couldn't determine what was making me sick. I think it was the house.

"We used to hear the doorknob turning at night, and then something coming up the stairs. We all heard it. We would hear moans. One time our son, Carter Vaught, Jr., said something unseen 'pushed' him into a closet and then locked the door. At first, my husband was a skeptic, but in time he came to believe. He said one night he was sitting on the bed in our bedroom upstairs playing the guitar at about six in the evening. The children were all outside playing. He said he heard someone coming up the stairs. He knew it wasn't any one of us. Then he saw the doorknob to the room turning and the door starting to open. He said he got off the bed, went over to the door, and raised the guitar over his head. When the door opened, he swung the guitar down to bash whoever it was over the head. But he said the guitar went right through it. There was no one there."

On another occasion, Mary's daughter, Marylyn, was in her bed one night when she saw a vision of an old farmer in "old timey clothes." He stood at the end of her bed. She hid under the covers and when she finally peeked out, the apparition was gone.

"A lot of things happened in that house," Mary says. "Another time I couldn't get the front door open, and a neighbor came over to help me. There was no one in the house, but we both heard someone running up the stairs and the door slamming. She grabbed a baseball bat and we looked all over but we didn't find anything." Mary says that no one could live in the house for more than a few months before moving out. "We finally had to get out of that house, and as soon as we did, I wasn't sick anymore."

But her encounters weren't limited to the home on Kerns Street. Once she was sitting on a porch at another house in Dry Hollow, near Salem. "The moon was real bright that night, and everything was so quiet and still," she says. "The next thing I knew, I looked up and saw a man with a khaki shirt and khaki pants, and he walked right towards me. I said, 'who are you? Get out of here!' And when my husband turned on the lights, he had vanished. I know the bedroom we slept in would get icy cold at times, even in the summer. And sometimes you could smell roses, I mean a real strong scent, like you were in a funeral home or something.

"That old hollow was really haunted. You could knock on the door of just about any house there and people would tell you a hair raising story or two," Mary says. "There is a legend that a young couple jumped off the trestle at the end of the hollow because they couldn't get married since they were too young. People said you could still see their spirits there on certain nights."

Apparently, the psychic sensitivities of the family are being passed on, generation to generation. Annie Tillet Isenberg seems to have given them to her children. And now, says Alma Heixenbaugh, her daughter may have inherited the "second sight." Alma says when her daughter was 13, she envisioned Alma having an auto accident — the day before she had one!

CHAPTER 66

Skull & Crossbones

Odds and Ends of Psychic Activity in Virginia

MOUNTAIN FOLK BELIEFS

* A century ago folks in the mountains of the western part of the state had some strange customs and superstitions. Here are a few:

— Three blows struck by an invisible hand upon the door signifies that death is near the hearer, or some member of his or her family.

— Other omens of death included: doors that open "of themselves;" the howling of a dog; three "barks" of a red fox; and a wild bird flying in the house and perching there.

* There was a strong belief among the mountain people that ghosts, or, in their words, "hants," could not cross water. This is still held to be true today in some remote areas. Here are a couple of examples dating to the mid-19th century.

— A young woman, riding double on horseback with her father, saw a "tall white form" rise beside the horse. Her father did not see it, and the horse did not react. She said the specter moved along beside them until a running stream was reached, where it vanished upon its brink.

— A young man, riding by "Crackwhip Furnace," then abandoned, said his horse was attacked one evening by an "invisible adversary." The animal snorted and reared in terror. Finally, it sprang forward and dashed down a hill into a brook. The man said whatever it was that had beset them, it could not follow across flowing water, "but a shriek that shook his heart swept by him as he fled."

* There also was a strong belief that spirits could return to mete

out justice which hadn't been served in courts. Consider the following examples:

— Before the Civil War, in what is now part of West Virginia, a land owner murdered one of his Negro women, with "aggravated circumstances of cruelty." The crime was investigated, but while everyone in the area knew he had committed it, they couldn't prove it and nothing was done. It was then that a "white dog" appeared on the estate. A number of slaves and others saw it and believed it to be a specter, because it would vanish before their eyes. It was said that the "goblin brute" hounded the murderer night and day, until he "pined away," confessed, and then died.

— Two poor women suddenly came into money, for which they gave an "improbable account." They apparently had murdered a man, and it was passed along that his ghost returned and passed along the garden fence between sunset and dark upon the hill where the women's cottage stood. According to what was told, one woman was soon "literally frightened to death," while her younger companion "lived longer and suffered more." She "wasted away till nothing of her was left but a little pile of bones."

* * * * *

THE CROAKING BULLFROG

During the Depression years, in the late 1930s, as part of the Works Progress Administration's writers' project, black writers interviewed a number of still-surviving former slaves, and the sons and daughters of former slaves, recording oral histories. The following humorous incident was told by the Reverend W. P. Jacobs of Phoebus, Virginia. He had been born in 1852, and then was about 85 years old.

"Many slaves were smart. Whites called the slaves superstitious. Yet more whites were superstitious than slaves. The slaves used superstition to fool the white man. No slave in those terrible days staked anything on chance in the open.

"There was one Negro on our plantation that even the overseer feared. He had a red flannel jacket which he could make talk. He would hang the jacket on a nail, say something, squeeze it, and the jacket would groan, moan and carry on. If anyone else touched it, the jacket didn't move. The solution was this: the Negro had a huge bullfrog sewed in his jacket so that the frog could breathe.

When others touched it, the frog sat still; when the Negro touched it, he stuck a pin in the frog and the frog yelled and jumped. The ignorant overseer couldn't see through that and gave the slave very few orders."

* * * * *

QUAINT CUSTOMS

rom the book, "The Magic and Folk Beliefs of the Southern Negro, come the following curiosities:

— In some parts of the south, all cups, pans and buckets were emptied after a funeral because "the spirit" will remain on the premises if encouraged by free access to food and water.

— At one time, in Norfolk, after a death in the house, the position of the door knobs was changed, so that the ghost may not find its way in. In other areas, a new addition was made to the house to "fool the ghost," especially if the dead man had been wicked.

— In some regions when a man died, coffee and bread were placed under the house of the deceased "to prevent his ghost from returning and haunting the living."

— There once was a practice where molasses was placed at the foot of a grave and a pone of bread at the head, so that "the dead person can sop his way to the promised land."

— At one time there was a ritual known as "cooking for the dead." Dirt would be taken from the person's grave and set in a saucer. Then a favorite dish would be cooked, preferably by two cooks, such as turnip greens. A table for three would be set, and the two cooks would start to eat. They would watch the third plate. "Unseen hands will manipulate the knife and fork, greens will be taken from the dish all the time, but the chair will remain vacant. All will be well, but should you speak while your invisible guest is with you, the wind will blow, the dogs bark, the chickens cackle, and thunder and lightning appear to frighten you!"

* * * * *

AFRO-AMERICAN FOLKLORE

rom the annals of Afro-American folklore on file at the Hampton Institute in Hampton, Virginia:

"Once upon a time was a family of people who were different from all the people around them. They had very nice stock around them, a large orchard, all kinds of poultry, and a beautiful flower yard. When one of the family died, they that remained buried the one that was dead. When all of them died but one, he became very lonely and died very soon. There was not anyone to bury him, so he lay on his bed and decayed. After his death, the house was said to be haunted, and no one could go inside it. The next year after the last one of this family died, the fruit trees bore a tremendous quantity of fruit, but no one came to get it.

"When people rode along the road which was near the house, they were often tempted to take some of the fruit, someone would speak to them and frighten them, so that they would forget the fruit. One day an old man who was a thief came by the house and saw all the fruit and the poultry, and a large number of eggs lying under the flowers. He asked the people around why they did not get some of those things that were wasting there. The people answered by telling him if he could get any of them, he might have them. 'Very well,' replied the old man, 'I will have some of those things before I sleep tonight.'

"So he laid his coat that had his arms down just a little ways from the house, and stopped there until night came. As soon as it was a little dark, the man arose and went inside the orchard, and tied eight hens which were up a large apple tree to roost. When he had tied the eight, he discovered a light somewhere, he did not know where. He looked down on the ground, and there were two large dogs with lamps on their heads, which were giving him a good light.

"When he saw this, he became so frightened that he turned the hens loose and fell backwards out of the tree. The dogs jumped after him just as soon as he got to the ground. The man jumped up and began to run as fast as he could, with the dogs right behind him. His home was about four miles, and he ran every step of it. When he got to his house, he fell in the door speechless, and lay speechless for a long time. When he came to his senses, he told his wife and family about what had happened to him.

"After that, there was not a man in the community that was any more honest than he was. He had been a rogue all his life up to this time. After this happened he always worked for what he got."

* * * * *

WHO'S COUNTING?

ccording to a report in the book, "Ghosts Along the Cumberland," by William Lynwood Montell, there are more ghosts of men than women — at a four to three ratio.

* * * * *

A TIMELY WARNING

avid Sillaman of Virginia Beach told the author that his granddaughter, Kristina, saw an apparition of a departed relative one day as she walked out of school. It told her not to get on the school bus. She didn't. The bus was involved in a fatal crash that afternoon.

* * * * *

AN UNWANTED SHOVE

atsy Carter of Wakefield, Virginia, tells of a legend at Warrique Plantation in Southampton County. In the early 1800s, one of two things happened: either a bridegroom or a member of the wedding party fell down the stairs and was killed; or a jealous person, in a pique, pushed someone down the stairs. Ever since, a number of people have complained of feeling a "force" at the top of the staircase trying to shove them downward. "I have felt this sensation," Patsy says, "and I can assure you it is very real and very unpleasant."

* * * * *

STRANGE DEATH RITES

he following is offered as an interesting sidebar. It comes from a book titled, "The Great Hereafter, or Glimpses of the Coming World." It was written by Madison C. Peters, D.D., and published in 1897. Peters included a section on "Curious Facts Concerning Funeral Rites." Whether or not any of these practices are continued today, is not known. Here are some excerpts:

* "The Greenlanders bury with a child a dog, to guide it in the other world, saying 'a dog can find his way anywhere'."

* "The Norseman had horse and armor interred in his grave, that he might ride to Valhalla in full panoply."

* "The music continuously kept up at the Irish wakes used to be for the purpose of warding off evil spirits."

* "The Mexicans gave slips of paper to the dead, as passports to take them safely by the cliffs, serpents, and crocodiles."

* "The natives of Dahomey kill a slave from time to time, that he may carry to the departed news from the living."

* "The Fijians strangled wives, slaves, and even friends of the dead, that his spirit might not be unattended."

* "Certain tribes in Guinea throw their dead into the sea, thinking thus to rid themselves of both body and ghost."

* "Some tribes of Mexicans bury their children by the wayside, that their souls may enter into the persons passing by."

* "The Brandenburg peasants empty after it (the body) a pail of hot water, to prevent the spirit's return."

* "The Chinese scatter paper counterfeits of money on the way to the grave, that the evil spirits following the corpse may, by delaying to gather them, remain in ignorance of the locality of the grave."

* "The Egyptians turn the corpse round several times before coming to the grave, to make it giddy, in order that the ghost may be unable to find its way back to torment the living."

* * * * *

SOME QUAINT VIRGINIA FUNERAL CUSTOMS

In some areas of the Shenandoah Valley the church bell would be tolled when someone died. It was a way of announcing a death in the area. The bell would be tolled six times for a woman and eight for a man. Then there would be one stroke of the bell for each year of the person's age.

A popular ritual 100 or so years ago was known as "Waking the Dead," or a wake. One or two couples would sit up with the deceased through the night. One reason for this was to "protect the body from cats and rats," since there was an old superstition that these animals were attracted to a dead body and would gnaw at it. In the days before embalming, the body was not put in a casket right away. Instead, it was laid out on what was known as a "cooling board." Often a family ironing board served this purpose.

In the old days, before modern cemeteries, most burials were in church yards or in family burial plots. A hearse was never used and there were no carriages to form a funeral procession. Everyone walked. A minister and the family physician led the pall bearers, followed by family members. If the deceased was a man, the men in the family walked first; if a woman, the women led the procession.

* * * * *

WHY SOME BELIEVE IN GHOSTS

The following was excerpted from an article published in the Southern Literary Messenger in November 1839. The writer, though unnamed, was from Williamsburg, and the highly respected journal was edited and published in Richmond.

". . . The reason that ghosts are more universally believed in than any other supernatural essence, is — 1st, That it is very natural to suppose that those with whom we have lived in terms of love or friendship will not desert us, if possible, even in death. 2nd, on account of this feeling, and the tendency which I have supposed above, it is more natural for men to attribute effects, whose cause is unknown, to the spirits of the dead, than to imagine other beings in order to account for them. 3rd, As these circumstances are common to all mankind, this belief has therefore been universal."

CHAPTER 67

The 'Non-Ghost' That United a Couple in Love

(Author's note: Okay, extend me a little literary license here. The following account is extracted, excerpted and edited, from an 1880 issue of Harper's New Monthly Magazine. The author is anonymous. The exact location is not specified, although it is indicated to have occurred in a Southern port city, and quite well may have been Norfolk. The time is also unknown, although an educated guess would be a few years before or after the Civil War. Only the first names of the principals have been disclosed for reasons unexplained. As best I can ascertain, the article is based on an actual occurrence.

Now, accepting the above, I have chosen to include it in this volume because of its: unusual tone and character; the explicit and exquisite writing style; and the compelling nature of the story. It also reminded me a lot of Edgar Allan Poe's classic — "The Tell-Tale Heart." The major participants involved are these: Esther, a young lady who was early accustomed to a high society lifestyle which has had to be cut back due to family financial losses; Linton, her life-long neighbor and best friend, who has long sought Esther's love; Winny, Esther's long-time close girl friend who has maintained her position in high society; and the tragic figure of a young man named Captain Santerre.

nd then there was Esther's family home. The author of the article described it this way: "The house, an old discolored mass of bricks, monopolized the whole square, for it stood in the center of a perfect wilderness of greenery. Tall forest trees grew there, straight magnolias towering above roof and chimney . . . all shading a wilderness of rose bushes. Thick vines threw their embracing arms from bough to bough, dropping twisted loops of giant tendrils almost to the ground . . . Even at noonday there brooded shadow and mystery about the place."

There also had been persistent rumors that the house was haunted; that a ghost resided in a chamber in the garret which had been locked for years after servants had reported hearing strange sounds there.

For some time, Esther has not been herself. She is pale, has lost weight, and seems to be depressed all the time. Linton believes that her sadness is linked to the horrible and unexpected death of Santerre. A dashing naval officer, he had only been known to the family for a relatively short time. Both Esther and Winny had crushes on him, but he was apparently not yet ready to make any sort of commitment to either young lady.

On a dare-bet with Esther's two brothers, Santerre said that he could spring over the stone balustrade of the piazza on the west front of the family home, leading out from one of the bedrooms, and that he could clear the iron fence that separates the garden from the yard, and reach the ground in safety.

He didn't make it. It isn't specified exactly how Santerre died, but it is intimated that he may have fallen short in his leap and become impaled on a spike of the iron fence. However it happened, it was an awful shocking experience. He had been brought into one of the bedrooms where, blood-soaked, he clung to life for six days, gasping for every breath, and then expired. Linton had felt that Esther had been secretly in love with the Captain, and he with her, and this perhaps explained her sullen moodiness.

The author's narrative begins as Linton is visiting Esther at the house, trying to get her to tell him what is wrong.)

" 'Esther,' " Linton said, 'what is troubling you? . . . You have known me, boy and man, from childhood; can not you trust me?'

" 'Yes, yes,' she eagerly cried; 'it is not the trust that is wanting. If only I could, if only I dared. I have tried in vain to be self-reliant, to be sensible if possible, and I have failed so entirely — so entirely.' . . . Her eyes filled with tears and her voice trembled . . . 'I know that you are kind and brave, manly and tender-hearted, and I need help so much! My brain feels giving way. I have been *so* skeptical, *so* determined in my disbelief, and *it* has been so fearful, so horrible, so unaccountable. Why should it have been forced upon me? . . .

"'Leave me now,' she said. 'I may not be disturbed tonight. Sometimes, but very rarely, I am allowed to rest without hinderance — when it is stormy, or when the night is dark and wild; and whatever it is, it seems to shun the conflict of the elements. There is a storm brooding now, and I may escape tonight. Come to me tomorrow evening, and if I can, I will tell you everything. Indeed, I must, for I cannot bear it alone. . .'

"'As you please,' he replied. 'You are the best judge of how far I am to be relied upon in any emergency. Give or withhold your confidence, it will make no difference. I shall always, I think, be the same to you.

"'Always the same,' she said. 'Always the truest, the kindest, the most unselfish friend that any woman was ever blessed with. I cannot tell you why I shrink from confiding to you this story, for a fearful story it is.'

(The next evening Linton arrives at the house.)

"'Esther, what have you to reveal to me? It can be nothing but for which an easy solution can be found. Your imagination has been excited, and has exaggerated whatever it is into an alarming matter. I wish to hear all about it now — this instant. I cannot see you so distressed, and feign indifference.'

"'You shall hear,' she said; 'but promise not to interrupt me. Listen to the very, very end, I entreat you, and then give me some explanation that may satisfy me, or I shall die, I believe.'

(Esther then recounted how she had been in Europe at the time of Captain Santerre's death. Esther's mother had become ill there and died, and her grandmother had been "struck with paralysis." Esther returned home and was visited by her friend, Winny.)

"'Winny came from the plantation to see me. She was as gay and thoughtless and noisy as ever, (and) inquired why had we resolved to live again in such a gloomy, dreary old prison-house, and what rooms I had determined to immure myself in. I told her . . . the back ones, for the sake of the westerly view . . . and the comfort of the little piazza that led out of the chamber windows.'

"'I should not like to sleep in either of them,' Winny said lightly. 'Captain Santerre, when he was picked up apparently lifeless, was taken into one of those rooms, and there laid upon the couch . . . He gave no sign of life except the loud sobbing, struggling of the breath to escape, and the hurrying beat, beat of his heart. It could be heard even outside of the house, sounding like nothing human. If I were you, Essie, I would change my rooms: you might hear him some night, and you would not easily forget it all.'

(Esther continues) "'This conversation occurred about a week after our return (from Europe). It was then late in the winter. I was very busy for some time getting the house rearranged comfortably . . . I had never remembered Winny's careless and cruel words, or her description of Captain Santerre's death, and could feel no nervousness living in the changed rooms where so sad a tragedy had been enacted. . .

"'And now, Linton, I come — oh, so reluctantly! — to the cause of my distress, or terror, I should say, for terror and horror worse than death have I borne for weeks. I know that I am sane, and that my bodily health is good. I disbelieve entirely, as I have always asserted, in the existence of any phenomena contrary to the laws of nature. I am not a weak or a fanciful woman, or even a superstitious one, and that I have great control over myself I have shown by bearing for six weeks all the suffering that I will relate to you, and well as by trying in every way my mind could suggest to elucidate the mystery. I have failed. And now I want your help, and am more than relieved that you have persuaded me to rest part of my burden upon your shoulders. God grant that your investigations may lead to the elucidation of the mystery!

"'One night after Mrs. Prynne's (the housekeeper) departure, I awoke suddenly with a confused feeling of fright — wide awake, with every sense alive, as we are when aroused in the dead of night by the unexpected cry of fire or murder. I sat up in bed, listening intently in the deep silence around me, when there smote upon my ear a faint, oppressed, and smothered breathing, low and distinct. Quick as light Winny's careless speech came to me.

"'I pushed my hair back, and waited, motionless; and then, regularly, steadily, commencing softly, as if half suppressed, then momently increasing in volume and agony they came — those awful sounds. Gasp after gasp. They filled the room. They labored like a soul in mortal agony, ever growing louder and louder, stronger and stronger, and between the suffocating sobs came the bewildering beat, beat, beat of the crushed and lacerated heart.

"'The room, the air, the walls from which they re-echoed, everything around me, above me, below me, resounded with the ghastly tumult, and was burdened with the horrible regularity of the struggling breath that came fluttering and sobbing and writhing in the still night like a tortured spirit in torment, like an agonized body broken upon the wheel. I sat up in my bed, motionless, pulseless, breathless, but my senses ever keenly alive. I *knew* that I was not dreaming, and that my imagination had not conjured up that scene, that there was no deception in the sounds I heard, and I forced myself to remain calm.

"'For three-quarters of an hour it lasted, commencing low, then rising, and lastly culminating into a tumult of tones that forced me to crush my hands into my ears, and then it died away as it had commenced, and I strained my ears to hear the last of the faint, faraway sobs that had ceased.

"'The next morning I awoke late, for I had dropped asleep near day-dawn from exhaustion, and my first thought, under the brightness of the summer sun streaming in the windows, was entire disbelief in the possibility of the night's occurrence. It was a feverish dream, and nothing more, and at the time, could I have summoned courage to have sprung out of bed, the nightmare would have been dispelled. All day I busily occupied myself, and allowed but scant time for reflection upon supernatural phenomena. . .

"'In this healthy mood I went up to my chamber, said my prayers, went to bed, and dropped quietly to sleep almost immediately. . . Linton, in the dead of night, at the same hour, again I awoke, for my ear as suddenly caught that first faint struggling gasp. I did not wait one moment, but sprang out of bed, lit my candle, and then I stood still and waited. It was not for long. The gasps, the struggles, the stertorous heaving of the laboring chest, again filled all space, while the terrible monotone of the beat, beat, beat of the anguished heart never varied half a second.

"'This was no freak of the imagination, no delusion of the senses, but an awful reality. Still, it could not be what I dared not think of. I quieted my nerves, and went mechanically around my chamber and sitting room. I stepped out into the calm of the sweet-smelling summer night, out on the piazza — that piazza from which he had sprung; but I shrank back, for the horror grew louder, the struggles stronger. I wandered into the hall . . . I returned to my rooms, never for a moment losing those sounds, that had only become fainter as I went farther along the passage, and as I neared my chamber filled the dark space, and beat the air with a regularity that was maddening.

"'I did not faint, Linton. I did not feel like fainting. I could only die once of horror; but why did not either insensibility or death come? On the contrary, every nerve was strong. I did not, I could not, I would not, believe! . . . I peered into the obscurity of the garden, for my ears were so filled with the ghastly horror that I did not know where to seek it. It was all around me, but it came louder and more shudderingly from that piazza, and I shrank back into a corner of the sofa. . .

"'In my sudden passion I called to him — to it — to whatever the horror might be that was blasting my life. I could no longer endure the quiescence that accorded to such sounds their aggravated terror.

"'Speak to me, Captain Santerre,' I cried aloud. 'I am alone and suffering. Through what power are you here, and why this ghastly presentment to me alone of a past agony? If aught of the manliness is left that was yours in life, cease this horrible travesty of vitality. Come to me, if come you must, in a more seemly shape.' My brain was throbbing, and my wild address, as you may suppose, died on the air; but the tumult was again fading away, and then came silence — still, dead silence, like the calm of exhaustion. Hardly a breath could be heard.

"'The first night that I was disturbed, Linton, was the second of August. It is now the middle of September; so for six weeks I have lived with this nightly terror near me. Do you wonder that my cheeks are pale and my eyes hollow?'

"Linton had listened with surprise at first, then with a kind of puzzled amusement, and lastly with infinite compassion. All the tenderness of his love, and love controlled almost beyond repression for years, was thrilling his nerves and throbbing at his heart. . . Mingling, too, with this feeling rose a suspicion, gathering force as it grew, that there was an added horror she had not alluded to in her narration, nor could he ask any explanation; but he knew that the scenes she had described were the death-bed scenes of the man she had once loved, perhaps still mourned, and the only solution he could at that moment confusedly grasp at was that a dormant sympathy had been reawakened in her heart by returning to the neighborhood of the surroundings of the terrible tragedy which had closed Santerre's life, and had conjured up the nightly scenes she had borne with such secrecy and courage, and had blown the embers of an almost forgotten fancy into flame.

"'I cannot doubt that I have absolutely heard for the last six weeks all I have related to you, Esther said. 'Still, I do not believe in the possibility of its being of a supernatural nature. What have I done to him,' (suddenly bursting into hysterical sobs) 'that he should come to me nightly to rend my heart with this awful agony.'

(Linton then asked Esther if the sounds had come last night, during which there had been a terrible storm.)

"'I was spared it all,' she said. 'In the turmoil of wind and rain, and the swaying and crashing of the old trees, I dreaded the added sounds I had every reason to expect. None came, thank God! Not a groan, not a sob. Can it all be over? And if it is, what has it been?'

(Linton then leaves, promising to return to spend the night with Esther on the piazza to hear for himself the sounds which have haunted her. He returns. It is three a.m. the next morning.)

"'I know, Linton, what you are beginning to doubt,' she commenced, when her voice sank away to a faint whisper, as a low, suppressed, gasping sob breathed lightly into the still air of the summer night, and then another, and another — struggling, gasping, heaving, sobbing sighs, as if the soul beating against its earthly bars strove and fought and writhed to be free, and yet suppressed, restraining the sounds that they might not penetrate too far. Muffled as they were, they filled all the space around. Above, below, wherever the ear met them, their fullness swelled upon the tension; and now, added to the anguish of the struggling soul, came with mechanical regularity the beat, beat, beat of the throbbing heart, agonized beyond endurance. . . Even her vivid description of her fearful experience had not prepared him for what he now heard.

"'Essie, my darling,' he said, 'I do not wonder at the delusion you have labored under. I can well imagine your feelings during this terrible trial. Winny's foolish speech, and the wonderful similarity of the sounds we hear to her description of the scenes of that awful death-bed, may well have deceived you. Your terrors were quite natural, my poor girl; but can not you imagine even now what has caused them?'

"'No,' she answered. 'What are they? From where do they come? Listen, they are dying away — fainter and fainter.'

"'They will be gone entirely in a few moments, Esther; quite as soon as Mr. Winstoun's little steamboat has rounded the tongue of land and steamed out to sea. Your ghost, my dearest, is a modern ghost. The sobs that struggled through the air were the steam-throbs of her engine, mellowed by the distance; the agonized and oppressed heart beats, the beat of her paddle wheels. The silence of night, the echo of the woods between us and the ocean, the situation of the house, and the strange peculiarities of the laws which govern acoustics have all combined to produce this delusion. When to these causes were added the mysticism of night, and the strong influence of the previous thoughts which had for a considerable time affected your mind, it is not strange that your senses prepared as a medium for such impressions should have succumbed to the result.'

" 'But the disturbances have occurred with such frightful regularity,' she said. 'They commence and die at exactly the same hour.'

" 'Because the steamer makes her nightly trips at the same hour. When she leaves the plantation wharf she is farthest from us. As she touches the edge of the wood of water oaks, we catch the first pant of her engines and beat of her wheels. The sounds culminate as she nears the point, and as she rounds it and makes for the open sea they die away till they are lost in the distance.'

" 'And last night?' she asked. 'Why did I not hear it?'

" 'Last night was too stormy for any small vessel to leave port . . . Your not hearing her during the storm helped me to my solution of the mystery.'

" 'But why should I never have heard it until the second of August, the anniversary of the very night of his death?'

" 'The corresponding date is the only strange part of the whole affair. It has been simply a coincidence,' he said. 'Mr. Winstoun had before then used the outside ocean steamer for transit and freight . . . She ceased running the first of August until business should revive in the fall, and so he was compelled to use his own little private steamer. . . Bring me the night glass, that you may see her before she steams out of sight.' She brought it silently, and fixing the focus, he showed her the faint light and vapor of the little vessel beating and throbbing against wind and tide.

" 'And now,' he said, after a long pause, 'can not you let all other illusions die away with this one? I have seen and felt the depressing influence of that more important specter which has stood between us like a wall of ice, and I dared not before tonight venture in his presence to put my fate to the test; but may not a living, loving devotion that has stood the wear of time, coldness, and, worse, indifference, be worth the shadow of a fancy or a memory that I think was only called into being after the object had ceased to exist? It was Santerre's terrible death, in the prime of youth, strength, and health, added to the knowledge of his secret love for you, that has held your fancy, more than filled your heart, for so long. You have given a great deal in return, as the suffering of the last six weeks proves. Is not a warm human love an equivalent for this phantom romance?'

"The fading dream of her girlish romance, more of brain than heart, vanished before the light of his strong human love, and as the last star of night melted into the dawning day, she laid her weary head upon his breast with a long sigh of relief and — consent.

"'I must leave you now, Esther, but I lay upon you my first command, which is, to rest as quietly as you can. I will not seek you before this evening at our usual hour of meeting; and, Essie, before I go, make me a promise that as long as you live you will never join in any disparagement of ghosts. *I* shall sympathize with them, believe in them, even adore them forever. Long live the ghosts of the nineteenth century!' "

Some Ghosts That Weren't

(Statewide)

(Author's note: Imagination can sometimes play strange tricks on the mind. And when imagination is jolted with stark fear, the result can be terrifying. Thus is the case with the following true accounts; incidents in which the witnesses believed they were being haunted by supernatural forces, when in reality there was, at the end, a perfectly natural explanation. But, in the interim, put yourself in the shoes of those who had the experiences. Who can say if you, or I, might not have acted similarly, and been scared to death in the process?

The first of these accounts was reported in "The Southern Literary Messenger" in March 1851.)

THE 'GHOST' IN THE GARRET

youth, about 14 years of age, was sent to pass some weeks of his summer holidays with a great aunt, who lived in one of the old counties of the Old Dominion. The venerable lady occupied one of those great mansion houses, memorials of the colonial aristocracy of Virginia, built of imported bricks, full of staircases and passages, and with rooms enough to accommodate half a dozen families, and scores of individual guests, when congregated for some high festival.

"But at this time it was almost deserted. The old lady and her grand-nephew were the only white persons within its walls. She occupied a bedroom on the first floor; our hero slept in the story next to the garret; and the servants were all in the basement. During the day, his time passed merrily enough. Horses, dogs and guns — boating and fishing — filled up the hours with sports, in which he was supported by as many of the Africans, great and little, as he thought fit to enlist in his service.

"But the nights hung heavily. His aunt always went to bed at an early hour. The few books in her library were soon exhausted; and the short evenings of summer seemed to his sleepless eyes to be stretched out interminably. Now and then a gossip with some old Negroes, who had grown gray in the family, beguiled him with snatches of the history of the former occupants of the hall; and these narratives, as might be anticipated, were plentifully sprinkled with incidents of the superstitious character, in which such old crones delight.

"One night, he had lain in bed a long time, courting in vain a relief from ennui in sleep. He had listened, till he was tired, to the ticking of the antique clock, to the whistling of the wind about the clusters of chimneys, and the echoes that repeated and prolonged every sound in the interior of the house, through its vast and empty spaces. The latter class of noises had entirely ceased; and the profound stillness that pervaded the mansion was broken only by the monotonous voice, which told him how slowly the weary minutes were passing by.

"He had thought over more than one tradition of the olden time, as it had been related to him, with its concomitants of a supernatural description; until, in spite of his better reason and his fixed disbelief of such things, he found himself growing nervous and uncomfortable. He began to fancy that he saw strange things in the uncertain moonlight, and was almost afraid to look at them steadily enough to undeceive himself.

"Suddenly, he heard, right over his head in the garret, a dull knocking sound, which traveled back and forth, now in this direction and now in that, with a succession of thumps. Anon he thought he could distinguish something like a stifled voice; and this impression was confirmed when the knocking got opposite the door of the garret, whence it came down the stairway and through the passage, unobstructed, to his room.

"A wild, unearthly cry, uttered as if by a person choked or muffled, and expressive of painful suffering, smote upon his ear. He started up in bed; and at this instant the sound began to descend the stairs. At first, it came down two or three steps with successive thumps — then it seemed to roll over and over, with a confused noise of struggling and scratching — and so on, with an alternation of these sounds until it reached the floor of the passage. Here the dull knocking was resumed as it had been first heard in the garret, rambling hither and thither, at one time approaching the chamber door, till the poor boy strained his eyes in instant expectation of witnessing the entry of some horrible shape.

"But it passed by and at last arrived at the head of the next flight of stairs, where it recommenced the descent after the manner already described. At intervals rose the same stifled wailing, so full of mortal terror and agony, that it almost froze the marrow in his bones. When he was assured by the sound that the traveler had arrived at the floor below him, he mustered courage, and by a great effort jumped out of bed, huddled on his clothes, and hurried to the head of the stairs, armed with an old sword that hung in his bedroom, and which had probably seen service in the Revolution or the old French (and Indian) war. But he had no mind to encounter his mysterious enemy at close quarters, and contented himself with following its progress at a safe distance, and peeping over the balusters in the hope of catching sight of it.

"In this, however, he succeeded only so far, as to get one glimpse, as it passed a window, of something with an enormous and shapeless head; and the slow chase was kept up, till he found himself at the head of the steps leading down to the basement, while his ghostly disturber was at the foot, thumping and scratching at the kitchen door, and uttering the same indescribable cries as at first.

"Two or three of the servants had been aroused by the din, and were crouched together in the furthest corner, trembling with fear, and in momentary expectation of suffering death, or something still more dreadful. At last the latch of the door gave way to the repeated assaults of the unwelcome visitor, and he rolled into the middle of the floor, in the full blaze of the fire light, and under the very eyes of the appalled domestics.

"The mystery was at an end — the ghost exposed — and an explosion of frantic mirth succeeded to the breathless terror which oppressed them.

"An old gray tom cat, as it turned out, in his rambles through the house, had chanced to find in the garret a large gourd, in which the housemaids kept grease for domestic uses. Into the opening of the gourd Tom had worked his head with some difficulty, and without duly considering how he was to get it out again. When he attempted to do this, he found himself tightly grasped by the ears and jaws, and secured in a cell which became every instant more intolerable.

"Hence his struggles to escape — hence his unearthly and smothered cries — and hence the extraordinary varieties of locomotion, by which he accomplished his long journey from the top of the house to the bottom. Our hero drew from the issue of this adventure a confirmed resolution against a belief in the supernatural; and detailed the particulars next morning, with great unction, to his good old aunt, who had slept comfortably through the whole of the uproar."

* * * * *

WHAT'S GOOD FOR THE GOOSE . . .

St. Luke's Church, four miles east of Smithfield, has been described as an "ancient and beautiful Gothic edifice." It was built in 1632, and is the oldest brick Protestant church in America. According to local legend, inhabitants of the area during the Revolutionary War buried the county records and the vestry books in an old trunk when they heard of an intended raid by British troops under Tarleton. Unfortunately, after the war when the trunk was dug up, many of the records crumbled to pieces.

The church was not used and remained in neglect from 1830 until the 1890s when it was restored. There is reason enough to suspect a haunting story or two involving St. Luke's Church. Buried, for example, in the adjoining graveyard, are the remains of many Civil War casualties, and there have been a few residents who claim they have heard moans and cries emanating from the plots late at night. The reports are largely unsubstantiated, however.

The one legend that has survived was told by Mrs. H. D. DeShiell, who wrote a book on the history of Smithfield. Exactly when this episode occurred is not known, although it probably dates to the 19th century when the church was in sad disrepair, virtually in ruins.

Nevertheless, it still offered a semblance of shelter on the storm-tossed night a horseback rider approached it. No sooner had he tied his horse and propped himself up against a wall in a dry corner of the church, when something in the graveyard caught his eye. He described it as a "white, fluttering" sensation. Whatever it was, blurred by the rain and diminished in the darkness, it

Some Ghosts that Weren't

appeared to be trying to escape an open grave site. Whatever it was, the rider had seen enough. He and his steed galloped away toward town at thoroughbred speed.

The mystery was solved soon afterward, however, with a logical explanation. Either the frightened rider, or someone else, came back in the light of day to investigate. What they found was a rather large goose, which had fallen into the open grave and couldn't quite manage an escape on its own, thus explaining the frantic fluttering.

* * * * *

THE 'DAID' MAN WHO CAME BACK

he following is based on an interview held during the Works Progress Administration's writers' project in the late 1930s and early 1940s. This particular experience was told by Arch Mefford to James Hylton on the outskirts of Wise, Virginia, July 7, 1941.

A man had left to berry pick one day and about 20 years ago down at Tacoma not far from Coeburn. He was a man by the name of Lem Hall, and well knowed round Coeburn then. Two fellows, one was a Hartsock I think, waylayed him and knocked him in the head and took his wad of money and left him for dead.

"But he (came to) long afterwards and got up and then made it to a house a little ways down the hillside. He got better and left the country area right then, and everybody thought he had died out in the hills, and (they) hunted all over for him. But they never did find him, 'course, and thought he'd fell in the water and washed down.

"Anyhow, they all thought he's daid, and some time later they's having a big meeting down in the meader and somebody spoke up and said a word or two that ought to be said about pore old Lem Hall. And then they got to talking about him right much. The preacher knowed him and started to talking right in the meeting there about him, and the first thing you knowed, they was preaching about I don't know what all about poor old Lem. I recollect that they shouted and sung and preached about how awful it was to be called away from earth in that manner.

"Well, Lem had a dog and it was missing, and people thought iffen they'd find it they'd find the body of Lem, but they were never able to find it and that is they why they'd all started preaching about him that night at the meeting.

"Well, that got everybody to thinking and talking about him and the next morning they's all in for a big fooling. Lem had got himself cleaned and washed-up a mite and lit outten the country and got himself a job somewhere over in Scott County, working at a road job and saved up a mite of money.

"He'd heard about them thinking him daid and allowed as how he'd fool them once and for all, so he just up and walked off his job there the next morning after the meeting, he's walking on the streets of Coeburn and went on up to Tacoma a mile or so off, and it liked to have skeered everybody to death, too. They'd all

396

been riled up at the meeting the night before about him, and then to see him on the very street seemed too much for them.

"The two fellows that had hit him in the haid and robbed him, lit out and haven't been heard of since, though there is an indictment waiting on them when they do show up iffen ever they does."

* * * * *

A 4-LEGGED GHOST

In the book, "John Jay Janney's Virginia — An American Farm Lad's Life in the Early 19th Century," one gains an unusual insight into what life was like in the commonwealth in the 1800s. Following is a rather humorous incident which occurred when Janney was a youth:

"Some localities were believed to be haunted. There was a deep, heavily-timbered ravine just on the east line of my grandfather's farm, which the 'big road' crossed. Many of the neighbors were afraid to cross it on a dark night (and it) was known through the neighborhood as the 'haunted hollow.' We never learned the origin of the title, and never heard of but one ghost in it.

"There was a grog shop half a mile beyond it, at which some of the farm hands would gather on Saturday evenings. Joe McGeth, who worked for my grandfather, was one of them and he would sometimes get quite tipsy. He had a little feist (dog) which followed him everywhere, and one evening when Joe had become quite drunk, the boys caught his dog and tied all the white rags they could find around him, so that he looked like a big bundle of rags.

"Just as Joe reached the edge of the hollow, he heard something behind him, and looking back, saw the dog. With a wild 'hellow,' he broke into his best gait and kept up his yelling. The folks in the kitchen heard him coming. He came with a yell, tramping on the porch, and as they opened the door, Joe fell headlong on the floor. Just as they raised him to his feet, his dog came panting in, and then the shouts of laughter brought Joe to his senses. That was the only ghost ever really seen or heard in the hollow."

* * * * *

A DESCENT INTO HELL

he following two episodes are taken from the March 1851 issue of "The Southern Literary Messenger."

"A laborer, on his way homeward about nightfall, was passing along the outskirts of a little village, when his ear was assailed by repeated groans, which seemed to issue out of the very ground beneath his feet. Looking about him, and listening, he presently discovered that they proceeded from an old well, which had been abandoned, and was half filled with rubbish. Approaching the edge of it, he called aloud, but received no answer, except the same groans, which were uttered at intervals, with a hollow reverberation, that appeared to die away in subterranean passages. To see anything below the surface was impossible; and the man set off at once to announce this strange occurrence, and seek assistance from the nearest houses.

"The alarm spread rapidly; and, in a little while, a busy crowd was collected at the spot, with torches, ropes, and other implements, for the purpose of solving the mystery, and releasing the unknown sufferer. A windlass and bucket were hastily procured, and rigged up; and one, more adventurous than his neighbors, volunteered to descend.

"They let him down about 20 feet, until he reached the bottom, which he declared to be completely covered by a large barrel, upon which he found firm footing. At this time, the noise had ceased and the newcomers were disposed to question the truth of what had been told them. But those, who had first reached the place, stoutly and angrily reasserted the reality of what they had heard. The first explorer had been drawn up almost to the top, when the groans were renewed, to the discomfiture of the skeptics, and the dismay of some of the bystanders.

"Dark hints were conveyed in smothered whispers from one to another. A few were observed to steal out of the circle, and silently move off towards their homes. None showed any particular inclination to repeat the descent in their own persons. But, at last, two or three, more resolute than the rest, determined, "at all hazards and to the last extremity," to know what was beneath the barrel. A pair of shears was sent for, such as are used for hoisting heavy packages into warehouses. Another descent was made, and, in spite of groans that might have shaken the nerves of Pilgrim himself, the shears were securely hitched on either side of the barrel. Several pair of strong arms were applied to the windlass, but all their efforts proved fruitless for a time. it seemed as if the barrel had been anchored to the rock-fast foundations of the earth.

"At last, however, it yielded a little; and with a slow, interrupted motion, and a harsh, scraping sound, an empty barrel, with no heading, was detached from its fastenings, and then brought up rapidly to the top.

"Once more, a daring fellow went down, armed to the teeth, after giving repeated injunctions to his assistants to turn very slowly, and hold on hard. He encountered at the bottom a formidable animal indeed, at least in such a situation.

"It was no other than a cow, jammed into the lowest part of the well, with her branching horns pointing directly to the sky above. The poor beast, indulging a natural taste, had thrust her head into an empty salt barrel. Her horns had stuck fast in the sides; and retreating blindly, in her efforts to escape, she had backed down the dry well, dragging the barrel after her, which fitted so closely to the walls of the pit, as to break the force of her fall.

"With some difficulty, the poor creature was extricated from her sad plight, without injury."

* * * * *

THE PRESENCE BEHIND THE PULPIT

 he following is also excerpted from the March 1851 issue of "The Southern Literary Messenger."

". . . He was a lawyer of respectability in this state (Virginia), and was riding alone one summer evening to attend a court. The clouds, which had been threatening for some hours, shut out the expiring gleams of daylight by suddenly folding together their dark and heavy skirts, and began to let fall those great drops of rain which precede a thunder-storm.

"The road was lonely; for it lay chiefly through forest land, and where it skirted a plantation, it was generally at some distance from the mansion. The traveler was thus obliged to keep on his course, long after the increasing violence of the storm had made him long for some shelter, however humble. In vain did he endeavor, by the aid of the lightning that flashed every instant around him, to descry some house; in vain did he hope, in the moments of darkness which intervened, to discover the faint twinkle of light from some log cabin or Negro quarter.

"Meantime, the elements seemed to lash themselves into greater fury; the lightning blazed incessantly, the thunder crashed into his ears, and the falling limbs of trees contributed to the danger and embarrassment of his situation. His horse became terrified; now he stood still and trembled, resisting every attempt to urge him on; and now obeying a sudden and frantic impulse, he would spring forward with a force that menaced destruction both to his rider and himself.

"After some miles had been passed in this way — an experience which no man can well appreciate, who has not endured it — the traveler was overjoyed to find himself in the neighborhood of a house. It was one of the old glebe churches, deserted and partly in ruins; but the walls and roof were still sufficiently good to afford some protection, and of this he gladly availed himself. Dismounting at the door, he led in and tied his horse, and took his seat in one of the pews, until the abatement of the storm should allow him to proceed.

"The place, the hour, the scene, were calculated to excite impressions of awe; and his first feelings of satisfaction naturally gave way to thoughts of a serious and solemn character. Thus occupied, he sat for some minutes, taking advantage of the fitful light, which momently illumined the church, to survey its interior.

"At last his eyes rest on the pulpit, and he sees — no! it is impossible — yes, he *does see* a figure all in white, its face pale and ghastly, but its eyes gleaming with the fire of an incarnate fiend! Now it stretches itself upward, tall and erect, its long skinny arm pointing to Heaven! Now it leans over the sacred desk, gesticulating and gibbering, with wild and devilish grimaces, that seem to mock those, to whom they are addressed, with threats of hellish torture!

"Is there anyone else in the church? Not a soul is visible. There is our lawyer alone, with that strange and fearful preacher — no inattentive observer, we may be sure, of the pantomime, which is but half revealed to him; it is only pantomime, for the roar of the elements drowns every other sound, and no voice falls upon his ear. What are his thoughts? It would be hard to say.

"Let the man of firmest nerves imagine himself, fatigued and exhausted by such exposure and toil, placed in a situation so unusual, and witnessing a spectacle so terribly like the legends of infernal malice and blasphemy, and let him pronounce, if he can, that his courage and self-possession would be equal to the trial.

"But to return — for some time the presence of the sole spectator seemed to be unnoticed by the occupant of the pulpit. But at last, during one long, vivid flash, their eyes met, and — oh! the agony of that moment! — he saw that he was discovered! Instantly, the figure descended from the pulpit, and approached him with rapid strides. It was all over with his manhood now — he thought of nothing but flight — of taking refuge in that very storm, from which he had but recently escaped.

"He rushed toward his horse — but the animal had broken bridle and was gone! Without stopping to look round, our hero gained the road, and set off at full speed; for he heard close behind him the yells and screams of his pursuer! It was a race for life — aye, and for what besides life, he dare not think; but he strained every nerve to outstrip the fiend who held him in chase.

"Alas! alas! his hour was come! Breathless, alike from exertion and from fear, his foot slipped, and he fell prostrate, while his enemy, with a shriek of triumphant hate, leaped upon him, and fastened her claws into his face and throat! He was incapable of resistance, for he had fainted.

"Fortunately, at this very juncture, a number of other persons came to the rescue, whose approach was quickened by the cries which they had heard. They extricated the insensible man from the hands of the MANIAC, and took measures for his restoration and her security. The unhappy woman had escaped that day from the custody of her friends, and hid herself in the woods. The vicinity of the old church was a favorite haunt of hers, and the storm drove her within its walls.

"Her disordered mind, excited by the sounds and sights of the tempest, sought a vent for its tumult in imaginary declamation from the pulpit, till the sight of a human face and form gave her feelings another direction.

"With what motive, she first approached the intruder, of course, could never be ascertained; but the confession of weakness which his flight implied, and the maddening stimulus of the pursuit, would have sufficed to change an indifferent, or even a kindly purpose, into one of bitterness and fury.

"Such is the explanation of this singular and painful adventure; an explanation, however, which, in the impressions left upon the mind, does approximate nearly to the effect of tragic and supernatural fictions."

CHAPTER 69

Some Humorous Ghosts That Weren't

HOW A SLAVE GOT HIS PIG

The following is excerpted from an old Virginia family history written in 1910. The event described likely happened in the antebellum days preceding the Civil War.

There was, at the time, a wealthy plantation owner. He had a number of pigs. One of his slaves loved pork, and contrived a plan to steal one of the pigs. He killed one and hid it in the family cemetery. He planned to go back at night and retrieve it. But he quickly had to improvise when a neighbor came over to view a new tombstone that had been placed in the graveyard. Upon seeing the slain swine, she immediately went to the Master and informed him.

After dinner, Judge Frank Christian, the proprietor, and his son, Johnny, walked out to the cemetery to try and solve the puzzle. But they saw no pig. Instead, there was a loud, mournful yell. Johnny asked his father what it was. He was told it probably was an owl. As they neared the graves, there was a second and more loud and distinct groan. This was no owl! And then amidst the tombs there came a third "deafening and agonizing cry" from the very site of the new headstone.

It "struck resistless terror to Johnny's heart and, answering it with a cry almost as painful, he took to his heels and soon found himself (in spite of darkness and obstructions), safe in his father's home! And the painful truth was that Judge Christian was only a little way behind his son in the race homeward."

Then, from the graveyard, came a gleeful giggle. The slave had slipped onto the grounds before the father and son had arrived. He had hidden the pig in some brush, and squatted down beside it. When Johnny and his father came, he began wailing.

And that night he ate roasted pig!

* * * * *

A 'HAUNT' THAT WAS HILARIOUS
(Stafford)

(Author's note: The following is excerpted from the October 1921 issue of "The Confederate Veteran," a magazine for southern survivors of the Civil War. It was related by a man named Jim Warden, who had served as a scout during the war. It is humorous enough to tell on its own, but it also contains one of those amazing and inexplicable coincidences which seem to occur occasionally, but nevertheless confound the mind.)

I had been on scout duty, and my command was operating in the vicinity where the town of Stafford is now located. My father's home was about 10 miles west of Stafford, and I took occasion to visit the family one night and get a good square meal, though it was risky business. I hitched my horse back of the house in a thicket, and when the family retired for the night, mother gave me a large white cotton blanket, as the nights were kind of frosty, you know, and I came down to this old graveyard as a safe place to sleep.

"Well, I found a nice grassy bed right between two graves, whose large flat marble slabs had toppled over, and I lay down and had just gone into a dreamy snooze when I heard the clatter of horse's hooves, and, looking toward the entrance, where once there had been an old gate, what was my terror when I distinguished the outline of a horseman riding directly toward where I lay. Great Scott! I pulled my revolver and quietly watched the intruder on my dreams. Then as he approached to about 20 feet, he bent over and seemed to be looking for me, and there he sat on his horse, bending this way and that. I was confident he was trying to find my hiding place, for it was very dark.

"Then an idea seized me, and, wrapping the ample white blanket about me, I sat up. The horse gave a snort. I raised up with the white blanket fluttering about me and stepped up on one of the mounds. The stranger saw it. He gave one wild, despairing yell, and out of the cemetery he rushed in a mad gallop, and I lay down convulsed.

"But listen: there is more. About 10 years ago I was riding past the same old graveyard, in company with a man who was reared not a thousand miles from this spot, when this companion said: 'Warden, do you believe in ghosts?'

"'No,' said I. 'Do you?'

"'You bet I do, Warden, and so would you if you had been with me once during the times of the war.'

"'Why,' said I, 'what about it?'

"He stopped right along about here, filled his pipe, and said in a deep, solemn voice: 'Warden, I always feel skeery when I come by this old graveyard, and I feel like something was crawling up my spine, and I kind of hate to tell it, but you and I were old scouts in 1861 and 1862. Well, sir, listen: One night I was out on scout duty near here and I lost my spur, and the lazy old nag I was mounted on was so slow that when I came to the gate yonder I rode in to get me a good sprout that I knew was growing out of the old neglected stumps. Well, Warden, I was trying to break one off at the root and didn't want to dismount, when suddenly my old horse gave an unearthly snort, and as I turned to look, Holy Moses!, there arose out of one of those long graves a ghost 10 feet high, flapping his wings and starting for me. Great Heavens, Warden! I'm scared when I think of it, and the sight of that ghost has haunted me all these years ever since.'

"And then I laughed and laughed until my sides fairly ached, and then I laughed some more. It was just too funny, and you are the very man I wanted to hear it. I told my companion all about it and detailed every incident until he was thoroughly convinced, and then he laughed. But the evil spell that had haunted him for all these long years had been broken . . ."

* * * * *

NOT SEEING CAN BE BELIEVING
(King and Queen County)

(Author's note: The power of suggestion can sometimes be a frightening thing, as witnessed in the following experience. It is taken from a piece written by William Garnett in his book, "Tidewater Tales,," published in 1927. He tells of a character named "Charlie," who was a slick salesman in his day. The episode began one night early in the century at a country store in King and Queen County.)

fter making his sale at the store, Charlie waited around for someone to give him a ride. He apparently had no means of conveyance of his own. It was very dark and raining hard. After awhile an old Negro known as "Zack," stopped in the store. Zack was talked into taking Charlie in his buggy, but Zack was only going part way. So Charlie quickly concocted a plan that would take him all the way to his destination.

As they rode off, Charlie asked Zack if he believed in ghosts. Zack answered: "I hardly know what I believe on that subject. I've seen strange sights in my life, but then I don't say that any of these was ghosts." He then was asked if he was afraid of ghosts, and he replied, "I can't say that I is exactly that, but, still, I ain't looking for them night or day."

Charlie said the reason he was asking was because he had lost a very dear friend recently, and he would like to stop by the graveyard where he was buried — which was on their way — because he wanted "to have a talk" with his departed friend.

"Is he dead?" Zack asked, his eyes wide open.

"Oh! yes, and has been buried several weeks."

"W-W-Well." Zack stammered, "how you going to talk to him if he is dead and buried?"

Charlie told Zack that was why he had asked him if he was afraid of ghosts. "You see," he said, "I have a great power over these poor wanderers of the dark and stormy night, and it helps me to call them up and soothe them with a friendly talk."

Zack looked at Charlie as if he were an "escaped lunatic." Just then, they came upon a church, and Charlie drove the buggy right up to the cemetery gate next to it. Zack sat "as quiet as a statue, freezing with fright." Charlie told him he saw his friend. "Be perfectly quiet," he told Zack. "Your horse is safe and so are you if you keep perfectly quiet. One sound, and all is lost." He then called out to a grave site in the pitch blackness: "Harvey, Harvey, come up Harvey! That is right. Come right along Harvey . . . A little higher, just a little higher. There you are, come to me, Harvey!"

As Garnett wrote, "There was a rush and a rattle and a bang and a tearing of old clothes, and the quickest disappearance from that buggy ever seen before. Zack went as hard as his old feet could carry him through the woods in a straight line for his home. Charlie stood and watched and laughed until he was sore. He got in that buggy and went on to Courtney's Store in short order. He then sent the horse and buggy back to the old man and fully remunerated him for the use of the horse and buggy; but Zack says 'nothing in this world would pay him for that ghost coming out of that grave that night and for all the skin he scratched off himself running through the woods.'"

* * * * *

THE CORPSE THAT ATE A POTATO

There is an old Negro folk tale, centered in Floyd County, Virginia, concerning the death of one of the elder members of a family that lived in a log cabin in a rural area. The deceased was in a coffin in the main room of the cabin. Members of the family were "sitting up with the dead." They had put some potatoes on the fire to roast, but, as it was late at night, they had fallen asleep.

By chance, two men came upon the little cabin, perhaps drawn by the smoke from the chimney. They peered through one of the windows, and immediately concocted a macabre idea. They slipped into the cabin and stole the potatoes. Before they left, however, they set the head and shoulders of the dead man up in the casket, pried his mouth open, and put one of the potatoes in it. Then they went outside and looked again through the window, waiting to see what happened when the others woke up.

The first one who awakened, stretched, then looked back toward the body. He let out a yell, said, "he' done come to and eat up all my potatoes. Now he sits with one in his mouth," then lit out of the house as fast as his legs would carry him. The others followed in close pursuit.

The last one out, however, caught his overall suspenders on the door latch, which had a hook on it, and fearing that he had been grabbed by the corpse, fainted dead away. It was quite some time before any of the others went back to check on him.

CHAPTER 70

The Most Fearful Ghost That Wasn't

(Near Richmond)

(Author's note: There is a story behind this next story. Back in 1984, when I was doing research for the book, "The Ghosts of Richmond," published in 1985, I came across a most curious writing. It was a very old magazine article titled, "Night in a Haunted House." It was a very scary piece, and very well written. For a long-forgotten reason, even though the article involved a house in the Richmond-Petersburg area, I did not use it.

As the years passed, and I began writing about ghost legends all over the state, from time to time I would think of the article, but by then it had gotten lost in the mounds of files I had collected. Once I even made a determined effort to locate it, which resulted only in frustration and a mess in my storage room. But it was *that* kind of write-up — one that stuck with you; memorable.

Cut to the present: In doing research for this book, I spent several days in the College of William and Mary Library poring over state and county histories, family collections, volumes on area folklore, and what have you. I also checked the indexes for a number of old magazines, including Harpers, Scribners, Lippincotts, the Virginia Literary Journal, and on and on. Then I went through 150 year old editions of The Southern Literary Messenger, that sophisticated and highly respected journal that was edited and published in Richmond. It was, at one time in the 1830s, distinguished by the editorial presence of none other than Edgar Allan Poe, my personal favorite author. In fact, one of my biggest thrills was sitting in Poe's Southern Literary Messenger chair, and at his desk in 1993 when the Today Show people came down to film me for a Halloween TV clip. (They didn't show the segment in Poe's chair. Oh, well!)

Anyway, I had gone through the bound volumes of this magazine, looking under the index headings of "Ghost," and "Haunted House." Later, I decided to fan through them again, this time checking the entire index. It was a labor of love anyway, because sprinkled among the pages were some of Poe's original works — short stories and poems.

And then, I came to the June 1855 issue. In the index I found "Night in a Haunted House." THERE IT WAS! I couldn't believe it. I let out what must have sounded like a cross between an Indian war whoop and the Rebel Yell, which drew some raised eyebrows from students and other researchers. I didn't care!

And so, here it is. Since it was published in 1855, and since there was no name attributed to it, I assume it was not written by Poe, and published post humously (Poe died in 1849) because the author did not have Poe's vocabulary (nor for that matter did anyone else). However, it presents, I believe, a strong case for anyone who has thought about spending a night in a haunted house — to think twice about it. As I said, it was one of the most chilling pieces I have ever read. If such things tend to keep you awake at night, I would recommend reading this in the daytime. While the author is anonymous, I am led to believe that this is an actual experience. I present it excerpted, but otherwise as it was written. Enjoy!)

A NIGHT IN A HAUNTED HOUSE

ithin a stone's throw of the line of the Richmond and Petersburg railroad, and not more than half a mile from James River, stand the blackened and roofless walls of a large brick building. Its position on a naked and barren hill renders it visible in some directions for several miles; and from various parts of Richmond, especially from the southern windows of the Capitol, it still forms a conspicuous object in the distant landscape. If the reader is not a resident of that vicinity, but has passed along the railroad between Richmond and Petersburg, before the fire occurred by which the wood work of the building was a few months since destroyed, he may have been struck by the lone and desolate appearance of the house; and if his question was asked of one in any degree familiar with neighborhood traditions, he was informed, among other particulars that the place had long had the reputation of being haunted.

"Indeed, its situation alone might well raise evil surmises in minds of a superstitious turn. No other house stood near it; no pale or hedge enclosed it; no tree or shrub or flower grew in its vicinity; nothing but the bare and sterile earth, over which a few consumptive cows and lean broken-down horses turned out to die, wandered about in quest of such subsistence as the place afforded. Its unsheltered site exposed it to every wind that blows, especially to the north wind, which, sweeping across the river from the hills on the Richmond side, raved and roared about the old mansion in such a way as to put timorous misgivings into the heart of any chance tenant who happened to occupy it. If he was right who said that superstition 'Can yells of demons in the zephyr hear,' then certainly superstition might have heard a whole legion of demons yelling in the winds that howled round the old haunted house.

"It was built by a man of wealth and standing in the days of our grandfathers. Why he selected so singular a site, I have never been able to learn . . . Perhaps he was ambitious to cover the barren hill with groves and gardens, and make the desert heath blossom like the rose. If such was his plan, however, the fates were against it; for whether the strange sights and sounds that gave the house its evil reputation made it an unpleasant residence to him, or whatever else was the cause, it is certain he abandoned it before any sort of out-of-door improvement had been made.

"After his departure, the place fell from time to time to various tenants, who were attracted by the low rate of rent. None, however, remained long; for it was remarked that misfortune seemed to brood over the house; that sickness and death were alarmingly frequent within its walls; and that whether its stately halls and panelled chambers were haunted by preternatural visitants or not, they certainly were singularly often the scenes of the heaviest afflictions that human life is heir to.

"It is now many years since I paid the old house a visit. My curiosity was excited by the current tales in regard to it; for I always had rather a taste for superstitious marvels. I found it a large and stately building, finished within in the old aristocratic style of Virginia . . . At the time of my visit, it had been but a few weeks abandoned, and several pieces of furniture of small value were still left in some of the rooms. In one of the principal chambers I observed an old black-walnut cupboard, which may have been used as a wardrobe, a stick-backed chair without the top-board, and a black hair sofa . . . On seeing the old sofa the thought occurred to me that as the weather was warm and no covering required, it might be made a tolerable couch for the night, if I had courage enough to despise the popular stories about the place, and defy the powers of evil that were supposed to hold their revels there. The thought I confess was a little startling, but I considered myself quite a philosopher for my years (then about 19), and was vain enough to think such idle superstitions as shook the souls of the weak and credulous were far below that serene region in which my thoughts were accustomed to soar.

"In short, I resolved to pass the night in the haunted house, and thus put to proof my courage and philosophy. Accordingly I returned to Richmond; and after nightfall, having wrapped up a candle in a newspaper, and put a book and match-box in one coat pocket, and a loaded pistol in the other, set forth without communicating my purpose to any one. It may raise a smile to think I should arm myself against ghosts with a pocket pistol, and I might have been puzzled to give a reason for the precaution; but I felt that my courage could somehow be firmer, and less liable to surprise by any sudden assault, if I had such a staunch and trusty supporter at hand in case of need.

"It was a clear, moonlight night in midsummer, and the walk, though long, was not unpleasant. The lonely old building looked particularly grim by moonlight, and I felt an uneasy misgiving as I approached it. But I had gone too far to think of retreating. An old white horse that in the moon's uncertain light had a pale and ghostly appearance, stood a few rods from the front porch. . . He seemed, I thought, to be worn out with years and privation, and evidently not destined to much longer sojourn in this world of sorrow. . .

"The front door was open, just as I had left it that morning. I paused on the threshold an instant, and then bracing my nerves with a long, deep breath, entered and stood a few feet within the hall. All seemed deserted, and still as a churchyard at midnight. The moon shining through the casements showed me the staircase leading to the room I had elected, and I commenced ascending. Every step resounded through the great empty house with a prolonged reverberation that was almost appalling. . . I lost no time in lighting the candle by means of a match, and then looked carefully round to see that no lurking thing of evil lay hidden in any of the recesses. All was empty and still, and no enemy near. . . I then reclined upon the sofa; propping up my head with a cushion . . . Finally, I drew the book from my pocket; and resolving to give imagination the least possible leisure for idle vagacies, tried to immerse all my thoughts in reading.

"The volume I had brought was Pliny's Epistles. I had some recollection of a story told by him about a haunted house, in which a sage old Greek had ventured to pass the night; and fancying a resemblance between him and myself in more points than one, I had a curiosity to learn the issue of his adventure. The letter I was in search of was soon found; but I quickly began to suspect that the choice of that story for my evening's entertainment was not very judicious, and that the disparity between the force of will and reason shown by the old philosopher, and that I could call up at need, was somewhat broader than I had imagined. The story is indeed a striking one, and impressively told. I shuddered as I read, lest a specter like that described, of the old man, squalid and emaciated, with his long neglected beard, and clanking his iron fetters as he walked, should visit me in my lonely room.

"Several times I almost started at what seemed the sound of human footsteps in the adjoining apartment. I listened attentively, and thought the noises, though strangely loud for such a cause, were produced by the multitude of rats with which the old house abounded. They scampered about in every direction, squeaking and gibbering in such a way as to deepen the vague feeling of terror which, in spite of all my philosophy, I found was fast creeping over me. . . To judge from the commotion among them, famine had begun its work, and was inciting a predatory cannibal war among themselves. The sounds of fierce struggling, and the shrieks of pain, sometimes so startling and loud as to make me doubt the real nature of the combatants, appeared to indicate when a death grapple had commenced; and deepened the effect which night and solitude, and the ghost story I had been reading, had already produced on my imagination.

". . . Suddenly, there issued from the next room the most demoniac yell I ever heard, which made me bound quite up from the sofa on which I was lying. Again the frightful sound arose; but accompanied this time with certain sputtering noises and lengthened wailing cadences, which I had heard too often to find a difficulty in recognizing. 'They are only cats, after all,' I mentally exclaimed; 'but, bless my soul! how much like devils in conflict their voices sound.' Taking the candle from its stick, I advanced to the next room, though with some trepidation; for old tales of the alliance of cats with the infernal powers officiously forced themselves upon my memory at the instant. On entering the room, immediately two of these animals, one grey and white, the other as black as a demon, rushed out of the opposite door, and down the staircase.

"Returning to my room, I readjusted the candle and lay down again. It was now nearly one o'clock . . . I extinguished the candle and tried to compose myself to sleep. . . How long I slept I cannot tell, but probably only a short time, when I was waked by a heavy pressure on the chest. The moonlight was sufficient to show me the cause of the disturbance. The large black cat I had chased out of the adjoining room had returned; and seated on my breast, was gazing intently into my face with his great glassy eyes. I gave him a smart blow with my clenched hand, on which he bounded away and disappeared. I then rose and bolted the door; after which I returned to the sofa and lay down again . . .

"It was quite evident, that nothing strange or unnatural had happened to me during the evening. Still, if my imagination could be excited by such trivial causes, then certainly I was not the man to undertake such philosophic knight-errantry as attacking popular superstitions and expelling ghosts from haunted houses. If anything should occur during the night of such a nature as to baffle all my attempts to explain it, it was impossible to say how far my nervous system might be deranged, or my reason disordered, by phantoms of my own creation.

"On the whole, it might be better to abandon the enterprise, and late as it was, return to Richmond to pass the night. But then, on the other hand, I was ashamed to confess even to myself that I was afraid of my own imagination, as children fear the dark, and as to ghosts, my reason, I flattered myself, was so well fortified against them, that even if one should actually appear wrapped in its winding sheet, and gliding through the room in the stealthy noiseless way which seems the approved mode among them, I should still have sense enough to despise the specter as a mere dreaming fancy, or some other illusion quite as unreal. I concluded therefore to stay the night out, come what might; for I was determined not to yield to apprehensions which even a schoolboy ought to be ashamed of.

"Feeling more secure with the door bolted, I soon sunk to sleep again; during which I had a dream that took its complexion in some degree from my present situation. I found myself in an old deserted castle, which seemed to belong to days of feudal antiquity. It was surrounded and in part overshadowed by a dark grove of gigantic oaks, that added gloom and awe to the solitude of the place. The wind which moaned sullenly through the trees dashed the shutters against the sides of the building, and made the old broken doors creak, and the walls shake, as it swept through the long empty halls. . . I wandered about from one apartment to another, till I came to a square aperture cut out of the floor, from which was seen the upper portion of a ladder communicating with the darkness below. . . I gazed intently into the vaulted recess that opened before me.

"Something like a human figure indistinctly seen in the dim obscurity of the place arrested my attention. I looked again; and my eye becoming accustomed to the darkness, I was enabled to discern an object from which I recoiled in horror. It was the body of a man suspended by a rope, and so near me that if he had been alive, I might have felt his breath upon my face. His strained, staring eye-balls, his clenched and grinning teeth, and his distorted features, livid and swollen with the blood forced back from the heart by the cord around his neck, were frightful indications of his last agony.

"I hastily ascended the ladder on which I stood, and was hurrying away from the place, when my dream was suddenly dispersed, and I started awake and trembling at some dreadful sound. Something I had heard to alarm me, I could not mistake in that; but what it was, I was at an utter loss to conjecture. The cats in the next room occurred to me; but I was fully convinced that in this case they were not the cause of the disturbance. I listened attentively; but all was still, except the commotion among the rats, which still continued, though much abated, and the sighing and whistling of the wind, that had risen while I slept.

"I was beginning to doubt whether it was not all a mere dreaming illusion, when a sound, which I at once recognized as what had made me start in terror from sleep, burst upon the silence and re-echoed through the house. It seemed a hollow, maniac laughter, choked and throttled by sudden strangulation. A second time it resounded from the next room, and a moment after appeared to float upon the air within the building. All my philosophy vanished in an instant, for such unearthly sounds could scarcely be imagined to proceed from a thing of this world.

"I lay trembling with terror, and covered with a cold sweat; but what was my horror when, a few minutes after, the hideous sounds were heard in the *very room* I occupied. Starting half erect from the sofa, I saw by the light of the setting moon, which now shone broadly in at the western window, what seemed an enormous spectral head, with horns and great glaring eyes, peering from above the old cupboard in the corner.

"With a suppressed shriek I fell back upon the sofa; on which the phantom spread its wings, and gliding out of the nearest window, again sent forth a peal of fiendish laughter, as if in derision.

"It was an owl, the great horned owl of Virginia.

"I was now too much agitated to sleep again. These repeated alarms had disordered my imagination so far that it had become a prey to all sorts of fancies; and the reason which by daylight derided superstitious tales failed me at my utmost need. . . It is true, nothing had occurred during the night which might not be easily explained on natural principles. Cats and owls are apt to haunt deserted buildings, especially when peopled with rats as this house was. But still, the concurrence of so many startling incidents was singular; and might have been designed by some preternatural power to punish that proud conceit of my own reason which led me into the present undertaking.

"It is surprising what an effect thoughts of this kind, which came thronging into my brain, had upon my excited imagination . . . In this state I remained a considerable time, my mind tossed to and fro, in the contest between fear and reason, and my disturbed fancy incessantly conjuring up fresh sources of alarm. Meanwhile the question of returning to Richmond was again suggested. But the moon was now set, and a cloud which had for some time been gathering had overcast the sky and rendered the night intensely dark. I thought I should probably be unable to find my way back to the city before daylight.

". . . I therefore lay quiet on the sofa, composing my thoughts as well as I could, but not daring to dispel the darkness by lighting my short end of candle, lest it should burn out before day, and leave me without the possibility of a light, whatever emergency might call for one. There could not, I thought, be more than an hour or two of darkness remaining, and that time I hoped to pass without farther disturbance. But in this I was destined to a signal disappointment.

"The house had now become comparatively quiet. The rats no longer ranged about with the same restless energy, or fought with the same fury, as before. Except an occasional squeak, or a slight scrambling noise, they were now silent and still. The darkness, it seemed, was too thick and impenetrable, to allow even them, imps of the night as they were, to roam about with freedom. The pattering of the rain, which had begun to fall, was almost the only sound audible. I was beginning to feel the soothing influence of this continued quiet, and my imaginations were gradually assuming a less excited cast.

"But an indistinct noise of what sounded like irregular tottering footsteps at length reached my ear. I listened with a beating heart and an undefined dread, fearing the sounds were the precursor of something terrible. Nor did my apprehension deceive me. A noise as of violent struggling ensued, followed by a dreadful groan which seemed to roll upon my ear out of the pithy darkness in which my room was shrouded. And such a groan, so long, deep and agonizing, surely never fell on mortal ears before. It was such as might have come from one of the lost spirits of Dante's Inferno — so much of hopeless convulsive anguish seemed poured out in the sound.

"Then followed a heavy stamping and struggling, as of hoofs on the floor, and again and again those awful groans resounded through the house. At length the sounds grew fainter, appearing to come far and farther away from the depths below; as if the condemned spirit my terrified imagination supposed it to be, had been seized by his jailor demon, and borne struggling downward to the dark prison which which he had escaped.

"All the time I lay half-mad with terror. Indeed I think I must have been for a time in a high delirium; for I lost all distinct consciousness of my situation, and fancied myself begirt by such horrible phantoms, as only an insane imagination could have presented. Devils grinned in my face, and yelled blasphemies in my ear; sheeted ghosts glided by gazing at me with their dead rayless eyes; and cold clammy corpses laid their lifeless faces against mine, and sought to fold me in their embraces. How my reason escaped an utter wreck I can scarcely conceive; but surely no one ever approached nearer the gulf of raving madness, without falling into it, than I then did.

"At last I began to recover consciousness, and I found that the day was perceptibly dawning. My courage in some degree revived; and I ventured to hope I might after all survive that dreadful night. Still, my limbs were twiching convulsively with nervous excitement, and I feared to move, or look around, lest some frightful specter should blast my view. I remained therefore lying on the sofa, trembling and anxious, till it grew light enough to distinguish surrounding objects clearly. I then summoned courage to look around my room, almost expecting some strange and terrible sight would meet my glance. Everything, however, appeared just as I had left it when the candle was extinguished the night before.

"At length I rose and opened the door, glancing fearfully into the next room as I passed through the passage. But nothing was to be seen that could help to explain the mystery. I then descended the stairs, and reaching the front door, was about to sally forth, too glad to escape from such a pandemonium; when I was startled and shocked to find the old white horse of the night before lying dead on the porch steps, with his head and forefeet resting on the flooring of the porch, which in some places was smeared with blood and foam. I gazed at him a moment, with a feeling of pity, not unmoved with terror, and then forcing my way with some difficulty (for his body left but a narrow passage), I hurried from the fatal house.

"My mind was still so much disturbed by the deep agitations it had recently suffered, that for a time I never thought of connecting the frightful sounds of the previous night with the death of the poor old horse. But while walking across Mayo's bridge on my way to the city, the truth flashed upon me at once. He had been seized with one of those painful disorders — perhaps intestinal worms gnawing his vitals and causing intolerable anguish. In his distress, he remembered having seen me enter the haunted house; and with that instinct which drives domestic animals to seek relief from men, he endeavored to make his way up the porch staircase he had seen me ascend. But his strength failed, and he sunk on the steps; and the dreadful sounds which had driven me almost to madness were the groans and convulsions of his dying agony. How I came to think the noise proceeded from my own room, I cannot well explain. Perhaps terror, combined with the startling loudness of the reverberation through the old empty house in the dead of night, may have suffered to produce the illusion.

"I returned to the city, not a little humbled and crest-fallen, and reached my place of abode before the family had risen. The night's adventures, I kept a secret from everyone; for I had no mind to encounter the ridicule which my ambitious design and ignoble failures merited; but they taught me such a lesson that I have never since ventured to play the philosophic hero, or indulged the conceit of a mission to attack and exterminate popular superstitions. . .

"If the reader is disposed to sneer at the timidity displayed under the circumstances I have recounted, permit me to suggest that he can scarcely anticipate how he would himself act in a like situation, unless his strength of nerve has been fairly proved by some similar trial. In ordinary conjunctures my courage, I flatter myself, may compare with that of other men. But the imagination, when fully roused, is an agent of fearful power; and my own experience recommends it as a safe and wise maxim, never to subject it, without necessity, to dangerous experiments, in which it may escape beyond the control of the judgment, and lay reason prostrate in the dust."

The Lost Legends of Bathurst

(Essex County)

(Author's note: I stopped off in Fredericksburg in December 1996, after a book signing at Tyson's Corner, to visit my friend (and customer) Bill Beck, who runs one of the finest antique and rare book shops in the state. While rummaging through his spacious section on Virginiana, I came across and old and long out-of-print booklet titled "Essex County, Virginia — Its Historic Homes, Landmarks and Traditions." It had first been published in 1940.

I had written about houses in the area before, most notably, Elmwood, Blandfield, the McCall House, Kinloch, Brooke's Bank, Linden, now a bed and breakfast inn, 10 miles north of Tappahannock, and Bladensfield, which tragically had burned down only a few weeks earlier. I had also reported on the spectral manifestations at Mt. Airy, near Warsaw, a few miles east of Tappahannock. And I had often heard about the spectral form of a 'blue lady,' who has been periodically sighted over the years at St. Margaret's School for Girls, although I have never been able to pin down a detailed description of just who she was or why she appears.

In reading the booklet, I learned more about the colorful history of Essex County. I had never realized that Tappahannock, for example, is older than Richmond, Fredericksburg, or Williamsburg. Old Rappahannock County was formed in 1656 from Lancaster County, and it was divided into Richmond and Essex Counties in 1692.

Captain John Smith first landed here in 1608, although he was driven back to his ship by the local Indians. Tappahannock, by the way, is an Indian name meaning "on the rise and fall of water. In the early 1600s, Jacob Hobbs established a waterhouse and trading post here, and the area was thus then known as "Hobbs His Hole."

In the introduction of the booklet, which was edited and published by the Woman's Club of Essex County, I learned that in 1728 the local court ordered payment for a "substantial prison, and a stable, and for a ducking stool to be erected on the end of the wharf at Tappahannock Town," presumably for suspected witches. It also stated that "both men and women were often lashed at the whipping post as court punishment." There also is a still-existing Debtors' Prison in the county.

In thumbing through the pages I ran across some more curious facts. Of Bellevue, a house situated on the Rappahannock River, this was said: "When the Yankee gunboats came up the river on their way to Fredericksburg during the War Between the States, this beautiful place was selected for bombardment and the house was injured by shells which penetrated the roof and crashed through the stairway breaking the floor joints. Unexploded cannon balls which were driven into the river bank were afterwards dug out and placed along the walk to the river where many of them remained until recent times.

"During this bombardment the master of the house, Edmund Macon Ware, lay dying. It is a cherished memory of the family that the house was saved from annihilation by the gallantry of a Negro slave, Randall Segar, who in the midst of the falling shells ran back and forth across the lawn waving a white shirt as a flag of truce till the firing stopped."

And, of another house, I read: "There is a tradition that Tuscarora was once a landing place for pirates; the hiding place of rich treasure was supposed to be under the big cedars that skirted the river. It is interesting to know that on Tuscarora more Indian arrows, hatchets, and pounding mills have been found than on any other place along the river in the lower part of Essex County."

The old Bestland Meeting House once stood where a cemetery is now located. It was a frame structure, unplastered, and without heat, which prompted this comment in the booklet: "A log fire was kept burning in the church yard to which those who became uncomfortably cold during services might resort."

Reading further, I found this: "It is said that in one of the Upper Essex Churches (originally founded in the 1770s), a member was turned out of church because she purchased a piano for her daughter, and that one of the young women was 'churched'

Bathurst

because she wore a red dress to church. These things were considered too frivolous and gay for members of the Church of God."

Of Brooke's Bank, circa 1731, is this passage: "On three sides of each chimney a series of diamonds was worked with glazed brick to discourage any witches from coming down into the house. In case any spirits slipped through, the doors were paneled in the double Cross, or the Cross and open Bible design, and had Holy Lord hinges on them to protect all Brookes."

In a section of the booklet on "Other Places and Things of Note" is a piece on "The Mad Stone." It reads: "About 55 years ago a colored man, Walter Lee of Westmoreland County, was bitten by a mad dog on the upper part of his arm. He was rushed to

420

Tappahannock where a Dr. Jeffries applied a mad stone to the bite. Lee kept the mad stone on his arm for 24 hours and he went away apparently healed. On December 1, 1953, this same Walter Lee, who still bears the mark of the dog bite on his arm, made an affidavit which is on file in the clerk's office to the effect that he had received treatment by use of the mad stone.

"The mad stone is quite old. It was first noted in the old Richmond Enquirer of 1805. One of these notices said, 'The subscriber offers for sale the Chinese snake stone, formerly the property of Mrs. Tabb of Matthews County so famous throughout Virginia for its efficiency in extracting venom from the bite of a snake or mad dog.' The article went on to say that the price of the stone was $2,000.

"One would probably expect to see an actual 'rock' formation, but the stone is actually a small polished piece of porous substance resembling petrified wood or iron wood which we are told was to be found in the stomach of a deer. Before the Pasteur treatment was discovered there were many mad stones in Virginia and even doctors admitted they might have some chemical content which drew poison out of dog and snake bites."

REFERENCES TO HAUNTINGS

Also in the booklet, I found, to my delight, three references to ghostly activity in the old houses of Essex County — none of which I had covered previously. At Mount Clement, for example, built about 1750, there was this intriguing note: "Many stories have arisen of the spirits that haunt the place. Periwinkle and ivy cover the old cemetery but the walls surrounding it loom up in the loneliness and gloom. . . It is interesting to note that all the deeds (for sale of the house) contain a clause reserving the burying ground, with the right of 'ingress, egress and regress'."

Vauter's Church, 18 miles north of Tappahannock, was built in 1731. It featured a pulpit in the rear of the church "reached by a stairway. . . The first Bible was originally chained to the pulpit." Of the supernatural, this was added: "It is said that at night the old aisles know again the footsteps of some restless spirit 'returned to the scene of its purest, earthly memories'."

Unfortunately, after a number of hours in the Essex County Library, which surprisingly has a large and impressive selection of books on Virginia history — and after several calls to area historians, I was unable to track down further information about the ghosts at Mount Clement or at Vauter's Church.

I was a little luckier on learning more about the legends surrounding the third house reported to be haunted — Bathurst.

According to a Virginia Landmarks Commission archaeology report written in 1973, "Historically, Bathurst is one of the most important sites along the Rappahannock. It is noted on all the early maps of Virginia." There is some conflict as to when the house was built. One account says an architect from the University of Virginia, "who came to see Bathurst, said that by 1692 (supposed date of the house) there were few houses in Virginia built like it, and that some of the materials were made in England. Leading from the front porch steps for about 15 or 20 feet was a flagstone walk, the stones of which could only be found near Liverpool, England."

In the book, "Settlers, Southerners, Americans: The History of Essex County, Virginia, 1608-1984," however, it says that Bathurst was situated on a plantation site which Francis Meriwether occupied in the 1690s, "was built sometime after 1740. The plantation was perched on the southside of Piscataway Creek, approximately two-thirds of a mile from the mouth."

In the booklet on Essex County old homes, it says that "Francis Meriwether, the son of Nicholas Meriwether of Jamestown Island, built Bathurst. The name of the manor obviously stems from his wife. "He married Lady Mary Bathurst whose father, Lancelot Bathurst, was High Sheriff of New Kent County." Meriwether was the first clerk of the newly formed Essex Court. It is stated here that he died in 1712. If so, how could he have built a house that didn't exist until "sometime after 1740?" Perhaps there was a predecessor house at the site.

Whatever. It is known that Bathurst was put up for sale in 1793, and the advertisement then used offers a descriptive insight into what the house was like. It read: "For Sale on Credit . . . That valuable tract of land in Essex County called 'Bathurst,' containing 700 acres, lying on waters of the Piscataway Creek about two miles below Tappahannock.

"There is a commodious dwelling house, containing four rooms below and four rooms above stairs, with kitchen, laundry, dairy, meat house, stable, etc; a large barn nearby central of the plantation, with a comfortable house for an overseer and quarters for Negroes convenient thereto, a grainery situated directly on the bank of the Piscataway where there is sufficient depth of water to admit a vessel of 2,000 bushels to approach and receive her load within 15 or 20 feet of the door of the said grainery."

Eight rooms "allowed the gentlemen of Bathurst privacy and refinement in their domestic lives. . . The gentlemen of Bathurst ranked among the county's and colony's most eminent men." The house also featured a "secret passage" to the Piscataway Creek, "closed by a small three by three foot panel of beautiful handi-work."

The archaeological report says "The house was bought in 1938 with the intention of dismantling it and moving it to another sec-tion of the state, (Charlottesville) but the building was found to be in too advanced a state of decay, and it was pulled down." (All sal-vagable materials were sent to Charlottesville for use in the home being built there.) The old brick chimneys stood as silent sentinels for several years, then they were torn down and used to build another house.

There is a tantalizing footnote in the booklet: "Perhaps no other place in Essex County has gathered so great a number of stories and traditions of romance and tragedy." At least one of these leg-ends has been preserved, with the help of Mrs. Neill Ware, wife of the present owner of the property. It involves Francis Meriwether and Mary Bathurst, and took place around 1670. Here is what Mrs. Ware found out:

ary was a member of the Bathurst family of England, which since has attained the high-est distinction. . . She was espoused to an officer of the army. To the marriage of these parties, there was parental objection, and the lovers proposed to go to Scotland (from England), where parental consent was not required. The officer, Francis Meriwether, and Miss Mary made arrangements to meet at a certain point on the coast near the home of the latter, and then to take shipping to Scotland.

"The route led across and along the river. This trip was made in a small vessel or open boat, but before the destined point was reached, where she was to be joined by Meriwether, a storm arose and the boat was driven out to sea — and was taken up by a vessel bound for Virginia and to the Rappahannock River.

". . . So Miss Mary and her attendant were brought to the Rappahannock River to a trader whose house was where the pre-sent Bathurst house is located on Piscataway Creek. It turned out this trader's wife had been a servant in the Bathurst family. She (Mary) did write to her lover by this vessel which had to make a trip to the West Indies before returning to England. The vessel was lost, and the letter did not reach Meriwether. The attendant of Miss Mary had returned in this vessel and was also lost.

"He (Meriwether) was aware that the boat in which Miss Mary had embarked had been driven to sea, and after long and anxious inquiry, as nothing could be ascertained about the boat or the lady, he concluded she had been lost.

"He threw up his commission in the army and came to Virginia, reaching there about the time a threatened attack was contemplated on the colony by the Indians of the upper Rappahannock. As Meriwether was an officer at home, he was put in command of an expedition and sent up the Rappahannock. They came up the river as far as what is known as 'Lowry's Point,' and there fixed their headquarters.

"It was the custom of the Indians from the uplands to come down the river to the famous fishing grounds in this neighborhood in the fall of the year, and it was supposed that the hostile Indians would select this period, unite their forces, and march down to the settlements. Hence, the force under Meriwether was directed to take post at this place and send out parties to watch the Indians.

"One of these reconnaissance parties, in going up Piscataway Creek, saw smoke ascending from some structure which they knew was not a wigwam. This party, under command of Meriwether, landed and found it was a house, and upon entering, found it was the home of a white family who had fled at their approach. The soldiers were sent off to search for the family, leaving Meriwether at the house.

"While alone in his thoughts, he drew from his breast a picture of his lost love, passionately kissing it. . . A door suddenly opened *and Mary stood before him!* For an instant she paused, then with a glad cry sprang into his arms. They returned to England and were married.

"In a few years they came back to Virginia." They settled at Bathurst.

There is yet another colorful legend associated with the house, although the details of this one, like the old house itself, have been stripped away with the sands of time. The date of this event is not known, although it likely may have occurred sometime during the first half of the 19th century. One of the residents of Bathurst then was described as "the lovely daughter of the house." She apparently had two suitors who fought, figuratively and literally, for her affection.

The competition got out of hand, and one of the suitors "was shot and buried beneath an old pear tree." It is believed that his blood stains on the floor of the house could not be washed away, and he returned, in spirit form, to continue to pursue the love he had so ardently sought in life.

The Dark Secret of Kinloch

(Essex County)

uthor George Bagley once wrote, "The homes of Virginia are ruins now, not like the ivied walls and towers of European lands; but ruins nevertheless. The houses indeed are still there, little changed, it may be, as to the outside, but the light, the life, the charm are forever gone."

He could well have been speaking of Kinloch, a brooding mansion north of Elmwood in Essex County. In 1924, Virginia Showell, in her book, "Essex Sketches," wrote of the approach to the house: "There is a road that is seldom traveled. The stranger, once off the main highway, will feel that he has left the world of cities and towns and even traffic. If the trip is toward evening, a rosy cheeked girl driving home the cows will stop to gaze at the unusual sight of an automobile, and the tinkling of the cowbells will be the only sound to break the stillness.

"The little cabins are few and far between, and it is with a start of surprise, when after five miles of lonely country roads, a sudden turn discloses a stately brick mansion, surrounded by a whole colony of outbuildings, also of brick. Though the lawn in front is overgrown and neglected, within its 13 acres are Norway spruces 75 feet high, Irish and English yews, chestnuts, pecans, silver maples, Georgia maples, firs, and many other rare trees that remain of the 300 varieties, arranged by a landscape gardener in 1850.

"Around the closed and shuttered house seems to hang a spell, somewhat like that which rested on the Sleeping Beauty's palace. It stands a monument of dignified reproach to a generation that has outgrown it, and the outbuildings and little cabins in the rear are protestants, less stately but equally pathetic."

Author Showell described winding iron stairways leading to

the front porch, "whose pillars are of Corinthian marble, as is also the facade of the doorway which opens into a central hall 60 feet long."

The mansion was built for Richard Baylor, a wealthy land owner, starting in 1845, and was completed four years later. Money seemed to be no problem in the construction and furnishing. As Mrs. Showell said, "He dreamed a dream of his descendants living there, generation after generation, somewhat after the manner of the English estates, and little thought that time and an altered social condition would result in its present desertion."

The walls, for example, are two and a half feet thick. The winding stairway that leads from the main floor to the second story is of solid mahogany. The huge rooms include double parlors, library, and dining room, plus several bedrooms. In the vast basement are "all kinds of storerooms, wine closets, pantries, and an enormous kitchen with a flagstone floor and big fireplace."

Mrs. Showell seemed especially enchanted by the attic area. "They contain many things which recall former occupants. The visitor notices among the scattered papers on the floor, pardons issued by the Federal government to distinguished members of the Baylor family, old almanacs and Confederate bills."

It was said that from the observatory above the house, five counties could be seen on a clear day — King George, Westmoreland, Richmond, Caroline, and Essex. In the middle and second half of the 19th century, the house and grounds were virtually entirely self sustaining. Showell: "It would be hard to imagine life in greater ease and abundance. Every fruit and vegetable which the climate could produce, were to be found in the orchard and six-acre vegetable garden. The choice wheat and corn were prepared in the brick watermill, (still standing in 1924), and hogs were fattened for the kind of hams which have made Virginia internationally famous." There were cows for milk, and chickens for eggs and broilers. And there were servants to tend to every need: cooks, laundresses, waitresses, maids, and field hands. Aunt Lucinda, for instance, was "a high priestess in cooking meats, and Aunt Jane had peculiar skill in cakes and pastries."

Consequently, Kinloch, in its time, was a central point for high style social life in the area. Showell: "The isolation of Kinloch was not felt in the days when guests arrived by the dozen, bringing maids and horses for a two week's stay. For the young people, there were trips to Richmond and Norfolk in the winter, to enjoy a round of balls and parties, and every debutante had her summer at

Kinloch

'The White.' There were fox hunts, card parties, balls, and interchange of visits at neighboring estates."

But changing times passed the mansion by. "Those were days of peace and contentment too ideal to last." The remoteness of the house, and the tremendous upkeep it demanded, led to its eventual desertion. In 1903, the last residents moved out. Twenty years later, "Weeds and sturdy saplings of native growth have obtruded on the stately lawn and formal garden; the brick paths leading to the many outbuildings are almost hidden; and only a few hardy flowers remain. . . The iron dog stands sentinel alone."

It is not recorded, but perhaps another reason for the abandonment was the ghost of Kinloch. 'He' is said to have roamed about the rambling mansion long after the mortals departed. There is some controversy about why the ghost appears, and how he left the present world. But there is no debate over who the spirit was. He was a young student who came to Kinloch to tutor one of the Baylor children. According to one version, he became depressed over poor grades at a state university. The more common rendition, however, is that he fell in love with his student's sister, but was spurned.

Mrs. Showell writes, "After a prolonged struggle with his hopeless passion, he had retired to his room one night and locking the door, had shot out his scanty supply of brains, the supposed blood stains being still visible on the floor of this much-avoided room.

Margaret DuPont Lee, who wrote about the episode in her 1930 book, "Virginia Ghosts," says the young tutor "became much depressed, notwithstanding the best effort of the family to cheer him and make life pleasant. He would accept no invitations, go nowhere. One morning the maid informed Mr. Baylor she could not get into the tutor's room. A ladder from outside revealed the fact the young man had cut his throat."

In either case, he reappeared in his room long after his burial. One who encountered his spiritual presence was Kate Fontaine of Hanover County. She was in the guest room that had formerly been 'his' room one night in 1866. She had retired and was reading a book when she heard, as Mrs. Lee described it, "a deep sigh, followed at an interval by another. Arising, she looked under the bed, thinking a dog might be there. A third sigh interrupting her reading; she went across the hall, telling the experience to Miss Baylor, who at once invited her guest to pass the night with her. Next day the room's history was revealed.

Others also attested to the tutor's reappearance. It was recorded that, "He appears periodically, a slender, tall young man, strolling in the rose-garden at evening, towards the iron fence of the cemetery."

CHAPTER 73

Ethereal Sights and Sounds at Elmwood

(Essex County)

f there are any ghosts in the house today, I don't know anything about them," says Mrs. Helene Garnett, mistress of Elmwood, near Tappahannock in Essex County. She should know. Her late husband, who was a direct descendant of the mansion's builder, dating to pre-Revolutionary War days, inherited Elmwood in 1943, and Mrs. Garnett has lived there ever since. Her husband died about 17 years ago.

"Oh, I've read the books and I've heard the stories, but I'm pretty much a down-to-earth person. I don't particularly believe in all that. I have never heard or seen anything of the ordinary," she says.

But there was a time, swear many long-time county residents, when the great house was indeed haunted by multiple spirits ranging from the fun-loving and jolly, to one who screamed in agony from a horrible accident which befell him more than a century and a half ago.

In fact, there was a time in the 1930s, following the publication in a Fredericksburg newspaper of the ghosts at Elmwood, when the manor, then abandoned, became the focal point of curiosity seekers for miles around. "People came here from all over after that article was published," says Mrs. Garnett. "They would sit on the kitchen steps at midnight waiting for something to happen."

They were drawn like moths to a flame by descriptions of the house such as: 'it is isolated from modernity, and no scenic setting could be built more suited to the tales of haunted houses;" and "a sense of isolation without peace, remoteness without tranquility, pervades the air. The silence is oppressive! A weird influence permeates the abandoned structure."

To these solemn accounts, written in the 1930s, were added reports from neighbors and others that strange sounds could be heard emanating from the house late at night; strange because the house had then been deserted for more than 65 years!

Elmwood was built in the mid 1700s by Muscoe Garnett for his son, James Mercer Garnett. The estate comprised 1,000 acres, and the huge house was described as one of the finest in the colony. Made of brick, it stretched an incredible 100 feet across the front flanked by twin chimneys and adorned with 20 windows, 10 on each floor. The main hall is 20 feet wide, leading to cross halls, each 10 feet wide and 20 feet long. Hall woodwork is elegant black walnut, hand-carved and in natural finish. At the cross hall entrances there are arches that have been called the finest work of colonial architects.

In the blue room is a rose colored marble mantel, and above it a cornice of soft white and blue, touched with silver. A Victorian book shelf is filled with periodicals and books in French, English, German and Latin. A carved rosewood sofa is at one end of the room and there are chairs of the same soft tint, upholstered in sapphire velvet. By the door stands an old spinet.

Carved woodwork distinguishes the enormous drawing room with paneled walls a delicate ivory color. Like the doors, the wainscot and baseboard are the soft color of the natural black walnut wood. The mantel, ashes-of-roses in color, is made of the finest marble. In the library, paneled with curly maple, are built-in book shelves of maple and mahogany.

The Virginia Landmarks Register says, "The wealth and influence of the Garnett family in the 18th century is illustrated by Elmwood, one of the most ambitious of Virginia's colonial mansions. . . The house is set off by a largely intact formal garden and a park, all situated on a ridge overlooking the Rappahannock River valley."

In the days of James Mercer Garnett, it was said to be a most hospitable home, often filled with visitors. Many a gay party and dance were held at Elmwood. The house was remodeled in 1850 by the third Muscoe Garnett, who removed the old stairway and added a tower. It was occupied at different times by both Confederate and Federal troops during the Civil War. Then in 1870, the family moved out, and Elmwood stood vacant for the next 70

Elmwood

or more years.

It was during this brooding period that the many ghostly manifestations surfaced. Although the house was empty, the furniture and many antiques and other items remained in it and were watched over by a succession of caretakers. It was these custodians, neighbors, and others who occasionally passed by during the long decades between 1870 and the 1940s, who said the house was haunted.

The spinet was often heard being played by unseen hands, always late at night, and generally when there was a full moon. And then there was the revelry. The sounds of great parties, laughter and singing, echoed from the house and swept all the way to the caretakers' cottage. Yet, lantern-lit investigations revealed no human source for the nocturnal merry making. Inside, as the caretakers dusted and cleaned periodically, doors would open and shut mysteriously, and although Elmwood was heavily carpeted, loud footsteps would echo along the halls and in certain rooms.

Even more unnerving to those who kept up the interior of the house during its days of vacancy, was the scary neatness of the "Doctor". He had been a friend of the Garnett family who had come to visit for a "few days" sometime late in the 18th century. He stayed more than 50 years! He was accepted as a member of the household, and was known as an entertaining man of "cheerful yesterdays and confident tomorrows". He also was a meticulous tidier who wouldn't allow servants in his room to clean. He kept it spotless himself.

A century after his death caretakers still were afraid to enter his room. He was believed by some to have "come back" to walk softly about at night placing things as he wanted them to be, changing them around when the mood struck him, dusting off the furniture, and leaving the room immaculate, and once again silent, by dawn.

Perhaps the strangest of all phenomena at Elmwood occurred in the mid-1800s, before the Civil War. It was described by Virginia Showell in her 1924 book, "Essex sketches," and by others. It was during these antebellum days that Mrs. Muscoe Russell Garnett threw a glittering series of parties and dances. It has been suggested that one of the reasons for her hostessing such activities was to get her bachelor son married off. It was during one of the fancy soirees, allegedly in 1852, that a most extraordinary ghostly manifestation occurred. Mrs. Garnett had invited a number of guests from the neighborhood. They were gathered in the ballroom listening to a young lady playing the harpsichord.

Suddenly she stopped playing, but the instrument went right on. The keys continued to rise and fall, but the music changed. Instead of the contemporary melodies she had been playing, the strands of a minuet, from an earlier day, were heard. Then everyone turned their heads to the hall stairway. There, descending hand in hand, was a young couple, dressed in full colonial costume. One writer said it was a couple "long since dead, dressed in the quaint costume of their day." There were audible gasps among the guests. No one recognized the couple.

The man and woman then entered the ballroom, and as others backed up to make room for them, they danced the entire length of the room without so much as glancing at anyone. They then seemed to "float" down the back steps and went outside, continuing to dance along the walk in the moonlight, until they absolutely vanished from sight. When they did, the music ceased.

Young Muscoe Garnett, as astonished as everyone else at the spectacle just beheld, chased after them. He raced through the boxwoods and said he heard a "rustling sound" coming from the old family cemetery. But he could find no trace of them.

Sometime later, at another Elmwood party, the mysterious couple reappeared and repeated their graceful waltz across the ballroom. This time, however, Muscoe ran down the steps and locked the door. But it didn't matter. The couple went *through* the door. By the time the stunned Muscoe managed to unlock the door and run outside, they again had vaporized.

He sat, perplexed, before a long mirror. Then he noticed, in the reflected background, the face of a beautiful young girl. It appeared to be a startling likeness of the phantom woman he had just seen! It was, however, a guest of some friends who had been invited to the party. She said that many years ago her mother had visited in the area and fallen in love with a local young man, but her father had disapproved and had taken her north. Muscoe Garnett later married this young woman.

But the identities of the gay couple who danced the minuet were never learned.

And, finally, there were the spine-chilling shrieks which pierced Elmwood's grounds on nights when storms of wind, thunder and lightning "bent the pine trees and lashed the house." Neighbors and caretakers told of the screams rising above the roar of the storm; shattering cries of agony. And those aware of the history of the house believed they knew the cause. One of the young Garnetts was crushed with his horse by a huge falling tree one night as he rode homeward in a terrible storm. His battered body was found the next morning.

But once the house became occupied again in the 1940s by members of the Garnett family, ending 70-odd years of eerie emptiness, the ghostly sounds ceased. It is as if to say the Elmwood ghosts, outraged at their abandonment for seven decades, could finally rest in peace once they knew their home was back again in friendly hands.

CHAPTER 74

Blithe Spirits at Berry Plain

(Dogue)

never feel alone in this house."
Joan Poland is speaking of her ghostly "friends" at her home, Berry Plain, in Dogue, Virginia, King George County. It is near the birthplace of James Madison, fourth President of the United States. "When we bought the house in 1994, we were told the oldest part dated to 1780," Joan says. "But we have verified through court records, that it actually was built in the 1720s."

Located only a few hundred yards from the Rappahannock River, Berry Plain, in its earliest days, was an ordinary, or tavern; a stopover eating place for travellers. In 1730, when a ferry service began across the river, the house also became an overnight hotel.

Sometime later in the 18th century, Elizabeth Washington, a sister of Lawrence, who was a cousin of George Washington, married a man named Thomas Berry, and they lived here, hence the name. The granddaughter of Fielding Lewis, a hero of the Revolutionary War, also lived here. Berry's grandson sold the house in 1845 to John Fayette Dickinson, and that family resided in the house for more than 100 years, selling it in 1959. Dr. Gary Hussion, a practicing orthodontist in Stafford County, bought Berry Plain in 1986, and sold it to Tom and Joan Poland eight years later.

Joan believes the house contains multiple spirits, each dating to a particular section and era. Additions were made in 1780, 1845, and 1949. Today, there are 12 rooms and an English basement. Joan says the house survived during the depression years in part though the sale of boxwoods to John D. Rockefeller, Jr., for use in the restoration of Colonial Williamsburg. Both Dr. Hussion and the Polands have restored and maintained the house and grounds with a loving care. Apparently, the resident spirits have approved.

Dr. Hussion says that he learned about the ghosts before he moved in. One of the previous tenants told him he slept with a baseball bat because of the "rats, snakes, and ghosts!" He said he rarely slept without hearing the sounds of a "heavy tread" of boots clomping up the stairway. He never discovered any mortal source for the intrusions.

"I would have to say that, being a scientific person, I was a non-believer before I bought Berry Plain," Dr. Hussion says. "But after experiencing all the strange occurrences, I became quite certain that there was 'something' there. How do you explain it? I have no idea."

When the doctor first moved in, the house was in disrepair. Thirty-four windows were missing. Sometimes he would be alone in the house, spending the night before going duck hunting. "Virtually every night I was awakened by footsteps going up the stairs and coming into the bedroom I was in," he says. "It was like something was coming right up to you, but you couldn't see anything, even in bright moonlight.

Dr. Hussion says he wasn't the only one to experience the nightly excursions. Some workmen stayed in the house while doing some repairs. They, too, heard the footsteps. One man finally left after a few days, saying he couldn't handle it.

Dr. Hussion's wife, Faye, experienced encounters as well. "The first introduction I had was one night while I was asleep in the upstairs bedroom, I felt something tugging on the covers at my knees," she recalls. "I wasn't sure what it was at first because I was half asleep. But then there were two strong tugs, and I knew I was awake. I wasn't imagining it. But I never saw anything."

Faye says that on another occasion when she was alone in the house, she noticed the swing on the back porch was swinging on its own. There was no wind. The place was closed up except for a big wooden door which opened to the porch. She then heard and felt "a sensation." The door opened wide enough "for someone to pass through," and then gently closed. She saw no one.

Then one night Faye was sitting on a sofa in the English basement in front of a fireplace. She and Gary were reading. Gary got up to stoke the fire, and because of the heat, Faye moved to the other end of the couch. There, out of the corner of her eye, she could see into the kitchen area and the stairway which went up the hallway.

"Suddenly, I felt a movement," she says. "I looked up and there on the stairway I saw a a film or apparition. It was like a smoky

Berry Plain in Dogue, Virginia

film. It was moving up the stairs. I said to Gary, there's something on the stairs, and he said he saw it, too. Then it disappeared."

This was the Hussion's only sighting, although the doctor said a farmhand once told him that he had seen an apparition on the stairs. There was also a report of the vision of a "wispy lady in white," at the little cemetery adjacent to the house. There are three or four headstones here, one for a small child.

The Polands have experienced similar "activities." "The first night we were here, we chose to sleep in the bedroom in the oldest section," Joan notes. "The ghost made its appearance that night. It pulled the covers off our bed. I was so tired, I didn't think about a ghost, and I just said, 'get out of here'!" Joan adds that this has happened several times, and that the bed gets bumped on occasion. "It's a perceptible bump. You can really feel it."

There have been several other occurrences. One day Joan found a small swatch of mysterious cloth on a stair. It appeared to be of another era. She plans to have it dated. Joan had some women over once. On the stairway is a corner cabinet. It has a sturdy door which Tom says you have to pull on it to get it to open. Three of the women, at different times, said that as they passed the cabinet, the door was open. Each closed it, but it seemed to keep opening.

"Sometimes we smell the strong scent of ham or tobacco in the house, and we have smelled potatoes frying out by the old slave quarters in the back," Joan says. "We never could determine the cause of these odors."

And then there is the portrait. Joan bought the painting of a woman in black at an antique store and hung it in the house. One day in July 1996, Joan was vacuuming in the dining room, which is in the oldest part of the house. "I looked up and saw a woman 'float' past me. That's the only way I can describe it," Joan says. "She was wearing a black dress of a bygone era. I really didn't see her face. And then she just vanished. I was scared to death. I ran out of the house. Tom was in the field, and when I reached him, even though it was in the middle of summer, I had goosebumps all over me. And then I thought about the woman in black in the portrait, and I said 'that's who I saw'!"

There are even more manifestations. Joan says she and Tom sometimes hear a skirt rustling. "It's like the swishing of taffeta. We heard this right after we bought the portrait." The Poland's cat, Maggie, may see something at times, also. Joan says the cat sometimes "follows" something with its eyes, as if someone was walking across the room. There was also an incident involving Joan's daughter, Mary. One night she and her husband spent the night in the house. Her husband had been reading a magazine before going to sleep. Mary was awakened in the middle of the night — by the distinct sounds of someone riffling through the pages of the magazine. Her husband was sound asleep.

The variation of manifestions — ranging from the sighting of a woman dressed in black, to the heavy tread of booted feet on the stairs — has convinced Joan that there may be more than one spirit in residence. "I think there may be two or three, or even several, and each seems to make itself known in a different section of the house, one in the oldest area, one in the 1845 addition, and so on," she says. "We have noticed that as the house renovation has been completed, that the phenomena has slowed down somewhat. Perhaps they like what has been done to Berry Plain, that it has been well kept up."

Just who are the spectres? Joan and Tom are not sure, although she feels the vision of the woman wearing a black dress may be the woman in the portrait. But what about the heavy tread that is heard going up the stairs? Research on the house may have provided a clue. The Polands learned that when the house was a tavern, in the early 18th century, that a young man had been killed there. In old records, there is a graphic description of how his body had then been brutally descecrated. Perhaps it is he who has returned, ascending the stairs late at night in pursuit of his enemies of long ago.

CHAPTER 75

The Concerned Phantom
of Ferry Farm

(Fredericksburg)

(Author's note: In my book "The Ghosts of Fredericksburg and Nearby Environs," published in 1991, I included a chapter head, "Some Ghosts that Should Have Been." It included a number of sites where one might suspect a spectral return, but none had been reported. One such place was Ferry Farm, across the Rappahannock River from Fredericksburg in Stafford County. This was the boyhood home of George Washington. He lived there from the age of six to the age of 11, when his father died. Here is what I wrote:

One might think a sighting would be made at Ferry Farm — site of the cherry tree and silver dollar legends. He (Washington) spent his youthful formative years here, although, out of necessity, he was asked to shoulder some man-sized responsibilities at a relatively early age, following his father's death and his older brother's illness.

"'I would love to have a ghost here,' says Bob Siegrist, executive director of Ferry Farm today. 'There is one thing about this place, though, and there may be an explanation for it, but I don't know what that would be. And many people have made the identical comments and observations, and I have to agree with them, because I have felt the same sensation. There is an atmosphere of peace and quiet here that seems to permeate. I've had workmen say, it's so peaceful and quiet here. Many visitors have said the same thing. Once an eight-year-old schoolboy came up to me and said, 'Mr. Siegrist, it's really peaceful here.' It affects me the same way. There are days when I walk around the farm, that I don't want to go back inside. It's just a feeling you get. I don't know if that has anything to do with George Washington or with psychic phenomena, but someday I would like to have a psychic expert walk around the place and see what he or she sensed'."

Interesting, yes. Ghostly, no.

In doing some further research, I learned some more. In Washington Irving's classic, four-volume biography of Washington, he described the house where young George lived in Ferry Farm as being "similar in style to the one at Bridges Creek, and stood on a rising ground overlooking a meadow which bordered the Rappahannock. . . the meadow was his playground, and the scene of his early athletic sports; but this home, like that in which he was born, has disappeared; the site is only to be traced by fragments of bricks, china, and earthenware." Washington moved here in 1738.

In the book, "Virginia — A Guide to the Old Dominion," written during the depression years as part of a Works Progress Administration project, it says: "If George Washington ever threw a Spanish silver dollar across a river or ever cut down a cherry tree, Ferry Farm was the scene of his skill and cunning."

I hadn't really thought anything about the area for six years, when, one morning in March 1997, out of the blue, I got a call from a lady named Laura Agee from Prattville, Alabama. She had been reading my book on Fredericksburg when she came upon what I had written about Ferry Farm, and then decided to call and tell me that there was a ghost there after all — not one of Washington or his era, however.

"We lived in an house in a sub-division there at 25 Jefferson Street," she said. The house had been built in the 1940s. "My mother had recurrent dreams about a Civil War Union soldier there whose head had been shot off. We think he was buried under the house. My mother said the soldier appeared to her a number of times and communicated with her by writing in old fashioned script. He told her his name was Jones, and he was from Ohio, and he wanted her to get in touch with his family. He appeared to her as being very young — either in his late teens or early twenties. His appearance was so real to her, that she moved out of her bedroom into another room, because we believed a Union soldier had been buried beneath the house under her room. She was very upset about the experience, and didn't tell us about it until years later after we were grown."

Laura said she felt she and other members of her family possessed psychic sensitivity. "My father had a chilling experience once near Dumfries," she recalls. "During a severe storm he took refuge in an abandoned house. While he was on the ground level, he said he kept hearing moaning and groaning and the sound of chains rattling upstairs. He walked up the steps and said he saw, huddled in a corner, the apparitional vision of a bunch of slaves linked together in chains. He said he got out of there as fast as he could.

"Anyway, I thought you might be interested in my mother's experience at Ferry Farm. You can call her. She now lives in Roanoke."

I called her mother, Mrs. Ann Motley. "Oh, yes," she says, "I will never forget it. It was a person, definitely dressed in the uniform of a Union soldier. It scared me to death." Mrs. Motley says the man appeared to her twice, and it was so real she is not sure if it was a dream or not. "It was so vivid. He appeared in my bedroom. He was silhouetted against a very bright light. He either had no face, or it was hidden in the shadows. I never saw his face. He told me he wanted me to know all about him, but I was scared. I told him I didn't want to know.

"He communicated with me through some sort of thought transference. He would write things down on a piece of paper in the most beautiful old handwriting. He said that he had been killed by a cannonball which tore off his head. (The bloody battle of Fredericksburg took place in December 1862). He then let it be known that his name was 'Jones Murray.' I asked him where he was from and he communicated 'Ohio'."

Mrs. Motley sensed that the soldier wanted her to get in touch with his family, perhaps to let them know what had happened to him, where he was, and that he was "okay." "I thought about trying to find out about him," she says, "but he had given me two surnames. I didn't know if his last name was Jones or Murray, so I don't know how I could have found anything out.

"I do know that it was all very real and I was very frightened, so after he appeared to me the second time, I moved my bed into another room. I never saw him again after that."

The encounters occurred sometime in the 1950s. The family moved out of the house a few years later. "I went back to visit a neighbor there about five or six years ago," Mrs. Motley continues. "She told me some strange things had been happening in the house. The lady that was then living there asked my neighbor if I had died. She told my neighbor that someone, or something, kept opening up the doors in the house to let their cats and dogs in and out, and the woman wondered if I had died and my spirit had come back. She said none of her family opened and closed the doors. Stuck windows would also seem to open by themselves on occasion. I was afraid to tell her about my encounters with the soldier."

Mrs. Motley's daughter, Laura, says that a number of people have lived in the house at 25 Jefferson Street over the years, and that many of the families mysteriously moved out shortly afterwards. Some of them wouldn't talk about it.

Perhaps the youthful Union soldier still materializes, trying to find someone who will get in touch with his family, or descendants, in Ohio.)

CHAPTER 76

The Spectral Return(s) of James Monroe

here are perhaps only a few people in the long history of the country — probably less than a single handful, if that — who could write a more impressive and powerful resume than James Monroe, a native of Westmoreland County, and fifth President of the United States. It has been said that Westmoreland is "distinguished above all other counties in Virginia as the birthplace of genius," including such notables as George Washington, Richard Henry Lee, Francis Lightfoot Lee, and Robert E. Lee, among others.

It also has been written that Monroe progressed to "more high public offices, elective and appointive, than have ever been bestowed on any other American, before or since." A college student at William and Mary at age 16, he became a Revolutionary War hero in 1777 at the Battle of Trenton. He was 19. Five years later he was chosen to the Virginia Assembly, then to the Confederation Congress of the U.S. He became: a United States senator; a minister to France during Washington's administration; governor of Virginia (four times); Secretary of State and Secretary of War during James Madison's administration; and, in 1817, President. He fathered the Monroe Doctrine, and was instrumental in America's purchases of the Louisiana Territory and Florida.

In 1780, Monroe began studying law under the man-genius who was to become his lifelong friend and ardent supporter — Thomas Jefferson of Albermarle County. (Forty-five years later, in 1825, Monroe served on the board of visitors of the University of Virginia with Jefferson and Madison.)

In 1786, Monroe settled in Fredericksburg and took up the practice of law in offices at 908 Charles Street. He was there only three years, but aside from his legal work he also managed to be chosen to the city council, became a vestry man of St. George's Church, and served as a trustee of the Fredericksburg Academy. He was, to say the least, a most energetic man.

The site where Monroe began his professional career is today a shrine, encompassing his law office, a museum and a memorial library. Here, for a nominal fee, one can see the magnificent Louis XVI furniture bought in France in the 1790s and later used in the White House. The desk is the one on which he signed his historic message to Congress in 1823, a portion of which became known as the Monroe Doctrine. Here, too, are: the statesman's green cut velvet suit with heavily embroidered waistcoat, and sword and sash, worn at the Court of Napoleon; duelling pistols heavily inlaid with silver; his Revolutionary War gun; his wife's exquisite jewelry and court gowns; the dispatch box in which he carried the Louisiana Purchase papers and many other fascinating mementoes. On one wall hangs the priceless portrait of Monroe painted in the White House by Rembrandt Peale. Thousands of books and historical manuscripts and documents are amassed in the library, a haven for Monroe scholars. Outside, a splendid bust of the Virginian by Margaret French Cresson overlooks the walled, old-fashioned garden, where, upon special occasions, Mrs. Monroe's julep is served.

Unquestionably, the man most responsible for the painstaking preservation of this shrine-museum was a rather eccentric character-about-town named Laurence G. Hoes (pronounced Hoos). He was the great, great, great grandson of James Monroe. He has been described, alternately, as highly imaginative, gruff, gregarious, demonstrative, demanding, determined, blustery, irritating and commanding. Apparently, there was little middle ground with Hoes, townspeople either liked him, ignored him, or, in the words of one resident, "hated his guts."

Whatever, Hoes is credited with almost single-handedly saving the Monroe building from being demolished earlier in this century. He and his mother bought it in 1927. She died in 1933, but for more than 50 years, Laurence Hoes devoted his life not only to preserving Monroe's law offices in Fredericksburg, but to faithfully perpetuating the fifth President's memory and long list of notable achievements.

He coaxed, cajoled and commanded distant relatives and others to donate "Monroeabilia" to the museum. The quest became an

Statue of James Monroe in Fredericksburg.

all-consuming passion. That he was able to keep things going through the great depression and World War II is a tribute to his determination and endurance.

It therefore seems justly fitting that Hoes should be the one person to have experienced an extraordinary psychic event at the site in the late 1960s, about 10 years before he died.

It was told one blustery, rainy January day by Mrs. Lee Langston Harrison, the museum curator. She had collected it from some of the long-time guides at the building, some of whom have worked there for more than 40 years, and are reluctant, to this day, to repeat it. Here is what Mrs. Harrison said:

"Mr. Hoes was walking to the museum one winter's day. We think it was in the late 1960s. He was walking down Charles Street, and when he got adjacent to the Masonic Cemetery, which is next door, he saw two men standing at the front door of the museum. Apparently, he became excited at the thought of two prospective paying customers during the slow off season, because he shouted at them to go on into the building.

"The men, both tall, appeared to be having a lively animated discussion, possibly an argument, and when Mr. Hoes shouted, they both turned to face him. It was then that he noticed their dress. They were in 18th century attire, each with silk knee britches, silk stockings, knee buckles, low quarter shoes fashioned with buckles, embroidered waistcoats and long jackets! Mr. Hoes then realized that the two men, still engaged in their heated discussion with occasional raised voices, looked strangely familiar. The taller one had distinctly red hair, and the other brown hair."

It was at this instant, Mrs. Harrison believes, that the revelation struck Hoes. He was looking squarely at James Monroe and Thomas Jefferson!

As Hoes neared the entrance, the two men turned to him again, and the one with brown hair — allegedly Monroe — waved at him. Then the two turned back toward the closed front door and

James Monroe Law Office in Fredericksburg

Crack in the door of the James Monroe Law Office in Fredericksburg.

walked through it! Breathless, Hoes reached the door seconds later, but he couldn't open the door. It appeared to be stuck. He pounded on it and shouted for the guides inside to open it. When they finally did, Hoes screamed at them, asking where the two men had gone.

They told him that no one had come in. They hadn't seen anyone. Hoes became agitated. He thought they were playing a joke on him; that they had seen the "visitors," but weren't telling him. He ranted at them. At this point, the guides, seeing how excited and serious Hoes was, joined him in room-to-room search of the building. It yielded no sign of the two gentlemen.

So far as Mrs. Harrison can determine, neither Hoes nor any of the guides ever saw or heard of any such incident afterwards. Hoes died in 1978. He was not a drinking man. How then, does one explain his incredible experience on that cold wintry day? In the psychic realm there is a phenomenon called a "time warp," in which a person or persons in the present somehow is given a view of something that may have occurred in the distant past.

There have been reports of such happenings although they are extremely rare, psychic experts say. One apparently took place early on Sunday morning in 1971 near the old colonial-era church on Jamestown Island when a troop of men, women and children, clad in "settler-style" clothing marched past two tourist-witnesses. The difference here was the tourists said the group appeared to be talking and laughing, but they heard no sounds. Hoes adamantly declared he heard his two "visions" arguing, at times in loud voices.

Could the time-warp theory possibly explain Hoes' experience? Did Jefferson ever visit his former law student at Monroe's Fredericksburg law office? And if they went inside, where did they go and why didn't anyone else see them? Did Hoes have a sensitivity the others in the building didn't? Intriguing questions, yes, but it is likely they never will be answered. Any hope of an explanation undoubtedly went to the grave with Laurence Hoes.

And finally, there is a curious footnote to this ghostly episode. Today, at the James Monroe museum, there is a long and wide crack in the warped front door. Guides who have worked there for 30 and 40 years or more swear that the crack appeared the same day Hoes saw the apparent apparitions of two of Virginia's most famous sons!

* * * * *

THE PHANTOM ROCKER AT ASH LAWN

Thomas Jefferson had Monticello, his magnificent manor home atop a hill overlooking his beloved Charlottesville. And he certainly had enough interests to occupy his time — from farming to architecture to wine making to absorbing himself in his impressive library, and on and on. One thing The Man was lacking to a degree, however, in the semi-seclusion of his Albemarle retreat, was the spirited stimulation of conversations with his intellectual contemporaries.

In fact, Jefferson sought to develop "a society to our taste" in the vicinity of Monticello; a dream that eventually helped lead his friend and presidential successor, James Madison, to residence at Montpelier in Orange County. He also encouraged another close friend and long-time statesman associate, James Monroe, to move to a site only two and a half miles from Monticello.

There, at a 535-acre tobacco farm first known as Highland, Jefferson sent his own gardeners to plant orchards even before Monroe moved in. The tract was on the east side of Carter's Mountain, a few miles southeast of the town of Charlottesville. Monroe and his wife, Elizabeth Kortright of New York, moved there in November 1799, and changed the name of the house from Highland to Ash Lawn. It was to be their home, off and on, except for the eight years Monroe lived in the White House, for the next 26 years.

By plantation and manor standards, it was not impressive. The original portion of the house, in fact, was called a "simple cottage." It was modest because the future president was in debt at the time of its construction. Still, he called it his "castle cabin," and he undoubtedly relished his long conversations and leisurely dinners over Madeira wine with his illustrious neighbor. The "cabin" eventually was enlarged in 1860 with the addition of a two-story porticoed section. More recently, the philanthropist Jay Winston Johns bequeathed Ash Lawn in 1974 to his alma mater, the College of William and Mary in Williamsburg, Virginia. It has been faithfully restored and today is open to the public as a museum commemorating Monroe's Albemarle County residency.

There is a specific ghostly phenomenon associated with the house, but guides and hostesses at the site are reluctant to discuss it. It involves an antique rocking chair in one of the small rooms. This chair allegedly rocks away all on its own, on occasion, with no one in it. Members of the Joseph Massey family, former owners, have reported seeing the chair in action a number of times, although there is some confusion as to just which members experienced the rocking.

Margaret DuPont Lee, in her 1930 book, "Virginia Ghosts," says it was Joseph Massey who told her about the incident. The parapsychology expert Hans Holzer wrote in his 1991 book, "America's Haunted Houses," that it was a Mrs. J. Massey who saw the spectacle. Perhaps both did. The Massey family did own the home at one time. They said they had seen the chair rocking by itself, and either (or both of them) said their brother John also saw it. (They both must have had a brother named John.) Both said they had no qualms talking about it, and that it appeared as if someone were sitting in the chair at the time. The chair would continue to rock until one or the other of the Masseys touched it. Then it stopped.

Who is the mystery rocker? There was at least one mention, in an article written by reporter Mary Beth Donahue of the Charlottesville Daily Progress some years ago, of a "pretty girl" who draped her long hair over the back of the rocking chair to dry it by the fire. According to Donahue's source, the girl's hair "caught fire and she was burned to death." Allegedly, it is she who can be heard crying on cold nights, although the reporter did note that "more level-headed observers contend it is the resident peacocks making the crying noises."

Holzer conjectures that it might be a spirit so attached to his former home and refuge from the affairs of state that "he" still liked to sit in it, rock, and think things over.

Whether or not it was Monroe who rocked in the chair, Ash Lawn is well worth a side trip from Monticello, and the nearby historic Michie Tavern. There are summer music festivals, and at Christmas time, madrigals are sung and the home can be toured by candlelight. But alas, the puzzling mystery of the rocker likely will never be solved. On a recent visit to the house the chair mentioned by the Masseys was nowhere to be seen, and the hostess could offer no explanation as to where it had gone. Perhaps it rocks unseen somewhere in a dusty attic or in storage where the phantom rocker can contemplate the affairs of the world without being disturbed by curious tourists.

* * * * *

EXTRAORDINARY CIRCUMSTANCES
REGARDING THE REBURIAL OF JAMES MONROE

There is a rather bizarre footnote to the Monroe "incidents" that may or may not have a bearing on his alleged ghostly appearances in Virginia. It involves the reinterment of the President's remains — 27 years after he had originally been buried!

How did this come about? Monroe died on July 4, 1831, when he was 73 years old, continuing an extraordinary chain of coincidences which had begun five years earlier when both John Adams, the second President, and Thomas Jefferson, the third President, had passed away on July 4, 1826. Monroe died in New York City, far from his Virginia roots. His wife had died earlier, and beset with ill health and financial troubles, Monroe, in 1830, had reluctantly agreed to move from his beloved Loudoun County estate at Oak Hill to the home of his youngest daughter, Maria, in New York.

Although, at the time, some Virginians felt he should have been brought back to Virginia for burial, there was no vocal outcry, so his family had him laid to rest in the Second Street Cemetery in New York on July 7, 1931. And there his body remained for the next 27 years.

In 1858 — the 100th anniversary of Monroe's birth — a Virginian in New York suggested erecting a monument at the gravesite. When this was made known to Virginians, then-Governor Henry Wise initiated plans to have the President's remains removed from New York to his home state. Monroe's family consented, and the plans were put into action.

Why had Virginia waited so long to claim the body? Good question. The only answer recorded was the response of Governor Wise's son, O. Jennings Wise. He said: "James Monroe's head was bowed down to the grave, partly by a series of personal animosities and political acerbates, which chased him even to the tomb. Was it not, then, appropriate, exceedingly proper, that every memory of dissent, every voice of dissonance, and every discordant tone, should be allowed to die away, and be obliterated from the minds of men, before Virginia proceeded, in the fullness of time, to pay the merited honor to the remains of her illustrious dead?"

Curiously, a book was published in 1858 documenting, in explicit, and sometimes excruciating detail, on the reburial. It was titled, "Removal of the Remains of James Monroe." There is an interesting quote in the book that reads: "Providence, as it were, seemed, at this particular juncture, to have caused his resurrection — to have called up the spirit of 76 — the spirit of patriotism and of union, which had rested with his body and hallowed his grave . . . Though dead he still speaketh."

And so the proceedings began. And what elaborate proceedings! There was more pomp and ceremony for this occasion than there had been during Monroe's funeral in 1831. When the body was exhumed, it was taken to a church in New York, where 10,000 people passed by the coffin. Thousands more lined the streets on Broadway and other avenues as the hearse passed enroute to the ship, "Jamestown," for passage to Virginia. When the ship landed in Norfolk, officials marched through the streets of the city and treated those who had accompanied the body to mint juleps.

When the steamer docked in Richmond it was written that "the wharves were gathered with thousands of persons, white and black, of every condition in life; carriages, omnibuses and baggage wagons, drawn up in long lines . . . while on the hill to the north were assembled thousands of ladies and children, all dressed in holiday attire." One observer noted, "On no previous occasion has such a vast throng of humanity been visible on Main Street."

There were scores of speeches, proclamations, declarations and testimonials — at the grave site in New York, at the church in New York, at the wharf, in Norfolk, in Richmond, and at the grave site in Hollywood Cemetery in Richmond. And there were parades. The procession was accompanied from New York to Virginia by the Seventh New York Regiment, more than 500 men strong. There were marching bands, drums and whistles, and church bells that peeled throughout.

Finally, on July 5, 1858, the body of James Monroe was laid to rest on a hill in the southwest corner of Hollywood Cemetery, overlooking, with a commanding view, the James River and the city of Richmond. The mahogany coffin was studded with silver stars.

Even then there was an ominous sidelight to all the pageantry. The body of a man was found floating in Gillie's Creek, near the James River close to Richmond. It was 23-year-old Laurens Hamilton, the grandson of Alexander Hamilton, and a member of the Seventh New York Regiment which had escorted Monroe's body to Virginia. In the book written about the occasion, it states, "At what time and how the distressing casualty resulting in his death occurred, it is impossible to say." It was assumed that he had fallen overboard during the voyage up the James. "The noise of his fall in the water and his cries for help, if he uttered any, were drowned by the cheering and rattling drums."

Of this sad incident, a New York newspaper headlined, "What Shadows We Are, and What Shadows We Pursue." This was followed by this comment: "This evening they (the Seventh Regiment) are expected to return (to New York) to follow one of their own number to the place appointed for all living. They left us thus to bury the dead — and thus they come back to bury the dead. A funeral there (Richmond), and a funeral here!"

Monroe's burial assured the success of Hollywood. The young cemetery, then only about ten years in existence, had been struggling for recognition, acceptance, and survival. Monroe's interment gave the cemetery lasting prestige, as well as a prime tourist attraction. In fact, for the next 75 years of so, Richmonders and tourists alike came to Hollywood for tours, sightseeing, and picnics. It became a favored showplace.

After President Monroe was buried, there was some thought given to making an attempt to have the remains of both Thomas Jefferson and James Madison transplanted to Hollywood to rest along side their long- time friend and compatriot, but apparently this never got past the idea stage.

And, finally, there was the controversy over the Monroe monument erected over his grave site in Richmond. It is a 12-foot-tall metallic structure, put up in late 1859, that was said to have been inspired by the delicate iron grills found around many statues in European cathedrals.

According to the Virginia Landmarks Register, Monroe's tomb, "the centerpiece of John Norman's romantically landscaped Hollywood Cemetery, is a tour de force of both Gothic Revival design and artistry in cast iron . . . The scheme recalls that of Henry VII's tomb in Westminster Abbey, also enclosed by a metal screen but lacking a dome. The tomb was designed by Albert Lybrock, an Alsatian architect who settled in Richmond in 1862."

Despite this account, however, many found the structure obtrusive, and critics dubbed it "the Bird Cage."

Amidst all of this — the movement of his body 27 years after the fact, the circus-like atmosphere of his reburial, the unfortunate death of young Laurens Hamilton, and the erection of the much-talked-about monument — one might suspect Monroe's ghost would have reason to reappear here. It has not. Perhaps he achieved lasting peace once he was laid to rest, finally, in his beloved Virginia.

Tomb of James Monroe in Hollywood Cemetery, Richmond.

CHAPTER 77

Bouquets of Psychic Roses

o roses, above all other flowers, somehow have a special psychic significance?

Perhaps so.

Other flowers have occasionally manifested in the realms of ghost lore. In Bland County, for example, there is an account of the curious reappearance of daffodils at a site called the "Old Crabtree Place," near Ceres. It was here 200 or so years ago that maurauding Indians massacred the pioneer family of Jared Sluss.

In a history of Bland County, it is written that the site is "marked and identified each spring by a field of pure, white-scented daffodils, which were planted by the tender and loving hands of Mrs. Christin Sluss. Although the field where the daffodils grow has been cultivated many, many times, the appearance of the daffodils each spring represents a living memorial to a noble family whose struggles, death and noble deeds made our rich heritage possible."

The strange reappearance of violets occur at a house of tragedy in Gloucester County. It was here, at Church Hill, that a young woman named Elizabeth Throckmorton lapsed into a deep coma while pining for her lost lover. She was presumed dead and buried alive in a plot beyond the garden. The evening of her burial a disgruntled butler dug up her grave in an attempt to steal her jewelry. One ring would not slip off her finger. He severed the finger, and in so doing the shock revived the young woman. Upon seeing this the frightened butler ran into the woods and was never seen again.

Elizabeth somehow managed to climb out of the grave, crawl through the garden in a fresh snow, up the front porch steps, and scratch at the door. Her father, inside before a fire in deep grief, either didn't hear the scratchings, or dismissed it as being the family dog, and didn't answer.

The next morning they found Elizabeth frozen to death. She has, over the years, reappeared in ghostly form. The most telling phenomenon concerns the violets which grow in lush profusion near the steps to Church Hill. They are said to be finer and more beautiful here than those in any other parts of the grounds. The legend is they are watered by the tears of a dying girl seeking shelter from the season's first snow.

At historic Carter's Grove near Williamsburg there is a reoccurring mystery surrounding carnations in the "Refusal Room." This is where it is alleged that two young women turned down proposals of marriage offered by none other than George Washington and Thomas Jefferson.

Whenever white carnations are placed in this room, they are mysteriously ripped to shreds late at night and found scattered about the next morning. No one is in the house at night. Other flowers in the house remain untouched.

Could it thus be the spirit of one of the two famous spurned lovers, unable to contain his rage over rejection? Some say it more likely may be the return of one of the women who refused. One account says that when Mary Cary watched the triumphant Continental Army enter the area after the Yorktown surrender in 1781, commanded by General Washington, she was so overcome by chagrin that she fainted dead away in her husband's arms.

So it is speculated that it may be her spirit which sometimes slips into the house late at night to tear the carnations in a fit of anger at what might have been had she accepted Washington's original bouquet and proposal offer more than two centuries ago.

But these seem to be isolated cases. Roses seem to dominate psychic activity around the commonwealth. One of the most common announcements of ghosts comes forth in the manifestation of the sweet scent of an attar of roses — when there are no flowers in the house. This has been observed at such reputedly haunted places as Haw Branch in Amelia County and at various other sites.

* * * * *

THE ENIGMA OF THE YELLOW ROSES

 ld Quarters Number One is a famous house at Fort Monroe. In it, a lot of psychic activity has occurred over the years. Thirty-odd years ago Mrs. Bayly Unger lived here. She says whatever it was in the house apparently didn't like yellow roses.

"I put flowers in a vase on a hall table. And every time I had yellow roses in that vase — and I mean fresh yellow roses — the next morning when I came to the table I would find all the petals strewn about the floor. It didn't happen with any other color roses, or any other flower, just the yellow roses. The stems and the leaves would still be in the vase, but the petals were all over the floor, as if someone had ripped them out!"

* * * * *

THE REAPPEARING ROSES

 ohn O'Brien is a truck driver who lives in a trailer near Callao in Northumberland County. There may be evil spirits who live with him, because a lot of poltergeist "things" happen in the trailer. Objects get flung about by unseen hands. Photographs get ripped up by invisible fingers. John's girlfriend has even been physically assaulted by an unknown entity.

A few years ago John's daughter, Marlene, brought two red roses to the trailer. She put them in a vase. After a few days they wilted, and John took them out to throw them away. He forgot, however, and drove up to Maryland when he realized he still had them with him. He took them to a dumpster and threw them in it. When he got back home — and no one had been in the trailer in his absence — there were the two red roses still in the vase! There was a note taped beside them saying, "This one is for you."

"Well, I took the roses out again," John says. "Peggy (his girl-friend) and I went up to the Moose Club and I threw them in the bushes. I told some of the fellows inside about the roses, and they wanted to see them, so we went outside and looked for them, but we couldn't find them anywhere. Would you believe it, when we got home that night, there were the two roses in that vase just as fresh as the day they were bought. And there was another note attached to them that said something like 'Keep your sanity'."

* * * * *

THE REAPPEARING ROSE

One of the great families of Albemarle County was founded in the Green Mountain area by John Coles, an Irish immigrant who came to the Virginia colony probably sometime in the late 1730s. He prospered as a merchant in Richmond, moved west with the pioneers, bought 3,000 acres in the southern part of the county, and built a frame hunting lodge on the slopes of the mountain. He called this modest house Enniscorthy after his Irish ancestral home.

Enniscorthy II was built in 1784, and, as one author phrased it, "became the gathering place for such noted Virginians as Jefferson, Madison, Monroe and Patrick Henry." It was at this site that Jefferson had sent his wife and daughters for safety when Colonel Tarleton was approaching Monticello during the Revolutionary War.

Surrounded by fields, mills, slave cabins and acres of great trees, shrubs and plants, Enniscorthy II, a "great rambling house," was the long established home for the Coles family for more than 50 years. Elizabeth Langhorne, a Coles descendent, has written that at the time, "one did not doubt that it (the house) would last forever."

Then on a cold wintry day, the last Monday of December 1839, a strong gale was blowing from the northwest. As Mrs. Langhorne described it, "From some hearth or chimney a shower of sparks had risen; flames had caught and gone roaring with the wind against the gable end of the house. Once started, no effort availed, the whole house went. Only the portraits and some furniture were saved.

"Also devoured by the intense fire were every last shrub and plant which had so picturesquely ringed the house, including a prized rose bush. Nothing was left. Everything had been burned to the bare ground."

From these ashen ruins, Enniscorthy III, a two story brick house arose in 1850. It stands proud today. Mrs. Langhorne says that soon after the new home was erected, a photograph was taken of it.

In the picture the prized rosebush that burned in 1839 appears!
"I can't explain it," she says. "But I have seen the photograph.
It is there. There's no mistaking it."

* * * * *

DOLLEY MADISON SAVES THE ROSE GARDEN

he indefatigible Dolley Madison, wife of James Madison, the fourth President of the United States, was so charismatic and effervescent in life, that some believe her spirit has lingered on in Washington, D.C. There have been reports, for example, that a ghostly Dolley has been glimpsed on occasion at the Octagon House, a few blocks from the White House, at 1799 New York Avenue. The Madisons lived here for a few months in the early 1800s while the White House was being renovated.

An apparition appearing in the exact likeness of Mrs. Madison has also been seen at a house on the corner of Madison and H Streets where she spent her last days. According to the National Directory of Haunted Places, "On moonlit nights her ghost is seen rocking on the porch. Her ghost was so famous, that gentlemen leaving the nearby Washington Club late at night would habitually tip their hats to Mrs. Madison's specter."

Dolley is credited with starting the famous rose garden at the White House during her husband's administration. There is a persistent legend — recorded by such well-known "ghost writers" as Dr. Hans Holzer and Suzy Smith among others — that a century later, when Woodrow Wilson was President, his second wife, Elizabeth Bolling Wilson, directed gardeners to dig up the rose garden.

As the workmen approached the garden they said the apparition of a short, attractive woman appeared "in her 19th century fashions and furbelows," and scolded them unmercifully. Frightened, they refused to begin shovelling. It is said when word got back to Mrs. Wilson, she abandoned her plan. The famous White House rose garden was saved!

THE CASE OF THE RELUCTANT ROSE

You may have seen White Marsh in the movies, and not realized it. This magnificent, white-porticoed mansion, described as the "epitome of Southern plantations," and known as the "Queen of Tidewater," has, in fact, been the setting for a number of major films over the years.

And no wonder. At first sight, even today, one might well expect a Southern belle in hoop-skirted gown, escorted by a tall gentleman resplendent in an ivory-colored suit and wide-brimmed hat, to appear on the front steps. White Marsh has that effect on first-time visitors.

Situated strategically back from the Ware River in Gloucester County, the house stands amid a grant of land originally made in the 1640s. There are conflicting reports about exactly when the Georgian Colonial mansion was built by Major Lewis Burwell; some say about 1735, others about 1750. In time, the estate passed to Evelina Mathilda Prosser, who married John Tabb, son of Phillip Tabb of Toddsbury.

There were then 3,000 acres in the White Marsh plantation, worked by from 300 to 500 slaves. It is believed about 1,500 slaves are buried in a graveyard near the peach orchard. Despite all the splendor, however, Evelina, known as "Mother Tabb," was not happy here. She had lost two of her children in infancy, and wanted to move to Norfolk or Williamsburg to enjoy a gayer social life. Mr. Tabb did not want to move, and he told his wife if she would make herself content at White Marsh, he would create the finest garden in Virginia for her. It was then that the terraced gardens were built, and many rare and fine trees were planted in the park.

Sometime after the Tabbs died, descendents reported seeing a vision of Evelina in the house. She would enter a certain bedroom, open the lowest drawer of a bureau and remove all the infant clothes inside it. Ever so carefully, she would take each article, shake it, refold it and place it back in the bureau. She then would quietly slip out of the room and dematerialize.

Years later a Mr. and Mrs. Hughes from New York moved into White Marsh. The pride of the garden had always been the proliferation of magnificent rose bushes. One day in May they were full of buds and on the second terrace was an especially luxuriant bush on which Mrs. Hughes found a full-blown rose with rich, creamy petals.

As she reached out to pluck it, a most extraordinary thing happened. The bush began swaying violently as if whipped by a strong wind. Mrs. Hughes looked around in dismay. There was not even a hint of a breeze stirring. She tried again, and again the bush trembled as if being shaken by spectral hands. Perturbed, she grabbed the stem firmly, but the rose was snatched from her hand and it began swaying again. At this point, the shutters of the house began banging sharply.

She fled to the house in terror and told her husband about it. He confidently approached the bush, but the same thing happened once more. A prudent man, he left it alone, fearing if he did pick the rose something disagreeable might happen. The incident spread through the county and many visitors came to see the reluctant bush.

Servants contended it was the hand of Mother Tabb which had intervened. They said that had been her favorite rose and she allowed no one to snip it. Mrs. Hughes eventually grew nervous over the phenomenon, and she ordered that the bush be destroyed.

Soon after, as she was making her rounds of the garden one morning, she found the rosebush gone, roots and all.

She asked the gardener if he had dug it up as she had commanded.

He told her, "No!"

* * * * *

THE LADY WITH THE ROSE IN HER HAIR

(Author's note: The following incredible account is excerpted and paraphrased from an article initially written by Eddie Harrell, and published in Fate Magazine in 1960. It is included here with the permission of Fate Magazine. The experience begins in September 1908, when Harrell was a student. His parents, Charles and Laura Harrell then moved into a large three-story house across from the city park in Norfolk. The house had been built sometime in the late 1800s. Eddie was away at school most of the time, but when home his room was on the top floor off the hall. Servants occupied a large room in the rear.)

ctive psychic phenomena seemed to surface almost instantly after the Harrells moved in. The servants almost immediately asked if they could move to another room. They were at first reluctant to give a reason. Eventually they told the family they heard unexplained noises. This included whispered conversations from unseen entities and the sounds of furniture being moved about. They said they felt the presence of a "third person" in their room. Because they were obviously disturbed, the Harrells allowed them to move into another room.

Eddie came home from school over the Christmas holidays. On New Year's Eve, he awoke in the middle of the night and found the ceiling light on. Strange. He had turned it off before retiring. As he sat up in bed, he said he was amazed to discover a woman standing in the window alcove of his room. She seemed to be looking out onto the street below. He described her as being "tall, slender, and dressed entirely in white, which contrasted strongly with the mass of black hair dressed high on her head." He then noticed that she had a single red rose tucked into her hair. Still, Eddie could not make out any distinct features.

Intrigued, he spoke, asking her who she was and why she was there. As he did, the room was suddenly cloaked in darkness and the lady had disappeared. He leaped out of bed and turned the lights on. There was no one in the room. He mentioned the incident to his father the next day, but he dismissed it, and Eddie left soon after to go back to school.

The following Easter, he returned home for a visit. On Easter morning he and his family were having breakfast in the parlor with friends, when one of them, a Miss Ocie Johnson of Portsmouth, looked somewhat astonished and asked, "Who was that?" She said she had seen someone pass by the hall door and go upstairs. Eddie told her it must have been one of the servants, but she said no. It was a young woman dressed entirely in white, with lace capelet sleeves and a long train," Ocie insisted. Eddie said he felt his knees weaken.

That evening, he went to his room upstairs and nodded off while reading. When he opened his eyes he saw the figure of the woman again. She appeared exactly as Ocie Johnson had said, except she hadn't mentioned the single red rose in her hair. Eddie said the woman seemed "opaque and solid." He couldn't see through her. Nevertheless, he said he was nearly paralyzed with fright. Finally, he managed to ask again who she was and why she was there.

As he did, he said the figure appeared to dematerialize slowly before his eyes. He gradually was able to see the window sash through her white dress. Her black hair, with the red rose in it, dissolved in the light of the room. Once she had disappeared, Eddie said he heard a loud whisper next to his ear. A voice said, "Wait." He encountered nothing further out of the ordinary during this visit.

The following Christmas he came home again, and the house was full of relatives and friends. One night his mother asked him to sleep in another room — the former servants' room — because his cousin was to sleep in his. In the middle of the night he awoke and every light in the room was on. The mystery woman in white stood in a far corner, partly screened by a lace curtain. When he got out of bed, the lights extinguished and the woman disappeared.

The next morning at breakfast, his cousin told of an unusual dream she had the previous night. She said it must have been a dream, but she was sure that she had been awake, and it was more like a vision. She said the lights in her room were on although she was certain she had turned them off. She said she could see through the transparent partitions between her room and Eddie's, and that she observed him sitting in a chair reading a book, "while behind him stood a tall woman in white, with a red rose in her hair, and she was looking over his shoulder. The red rose fell from her hair onto the floor by the chair. At this, Eddie said his heart was racing. After breakfast Eddie's father called him aside and they went upstairs to the room where Eddie had slept.

There was a red rose, "as fresh as if it had just been cut," on the floor beside the chair!

That, however, was the last known manifestation of the ghostly lady. Eddie's father died the next year and the family moved to Washington, D.C.

Who was the woman in white and why was she there? Had she suffered a tragic and traumatic death in the house? Was she searching for a long lost lover? The answers probably will never be known.

Haft a century later, Eddie wrote that he still had the red rose in a glass bowl. "The petals," he said, "still hold a strange freshness, seemingly a kind of petrified wax."

THE REAPPEARANCE OF THE PINK ROSE PETALS

(Author's note: At the 1997 Newport News Fall Festival, which is annually held the first weekend in October, I was signing books when an attractive, well-dressed lady approached and said she had an experience I wouldn't believe. I told her others had said the same thing to me, and I was always appreciative to hear what they had to say. Her name is Mary Kinstler and she lives in Newport News. Here is what she told me:)

hen I was 12 years old, my grandmother died in Roanoke. Her name was Mary Moody. I was named after her. I was always very close to her. We had a special relationship. I think she knew she was going to die, because a few days before she had given me her watch, which I had long admired. She said she wouldn't need it where she was going. My grandfather had died a year earlier and I believe she died grieving for him.

"At the church where the funeral service was held, as I looked down into the open casket, there were five small pink sweetheart roses in a little bouquet. There was one for each of her grandchildren. She had always loved pink roses. Grandmother was buried wearing a beautiful pearl gray dressing gown.

"Thirteen years later, I was in the hospital. A few months earlier I had had a very difficult birth delivery, and there were complications afterwards. I had cancer and it was serious. They were going to operate on me and they weren't sure if I would survive. I was in an isolated room and only my husband could visit me. There were no flowers allowed in the room. A priest was summoned.

"Shortly before they were to take me to the operating room, a vision of my grandmother appeared to me, wearing the same pearl gray gown she had been buried in. I was wide awake. It was not a dream. She smiled at me and said, 'don't worry. You will live to see your children's children.' And then the vision vanished.

"Nurses and attendants came into the room. As they were lifting me from my hospital bed to a gurney, three pink rose petals fluttered to the floor. As I said, there were no flowers in the room.

A nurse shouted, "where the hell did they come from."

"That incident occurred more than 20 years ago, and my grandmother's prophecy proved to be correct. I survived the operation and there has been no reccurrence of the cancer. The doctors can't explain it.

"I believe the three pink rose petals represented symbols of my three children. And I am convinced, as my grandmother told me, I will live to see my children's children."

Author L.B. Taylor, Jr., and illustrator Brenda Goens.

About the Author

L. B. Taylor, Jr. — a Scorpio — is a native Virginian. He was born in Lynchburg and has a BS degree in journalism from Florida State University. He wrote about America's space programs for 16 years, for NASA and aerospace contractors, before moving to Williamsburg, Virginia, in 1974, as public affairs director for BASF Corporation. He retired in 1993. Taylor is the author of more than 300 national magazine articles and over 30 non-fiction books. His research for the book "Haunted Houses," published by Simon and Schuster in 1983, stimulated his interest in area psychic phenomena and led to the publication of five regional Virginia ghost books, four covering the entire commonwealth, and one on Civil War Ghosts of Virginia.

(Personally autographed copies of: "The Ghosts of Williamsburg" - 84 pages, illustrated, $7; "The Ghosts of Richmond" - 172 pages, illustrated, $10; "The Ghosts of Tidewater" - 232 pages, illustrated, $12; "The Ghosts of

Fredericksburg" - 177 pages, illustrated, $10; and "The Ghosts of Charlottesville and Lynchburg' - 188 pages, illustrated, $10; ($40 for all five); and "The Ghosts of Virginia" (Volume I) - 400 pages, illustrated, $14; "The Ghosts of Virginia" (Volume II) - 400 pages, illustrated, $14; Civil War Ghosts of Virginia, $12; "The Ghosts of Virginia" (Volume III) - 450 pages, illustrated, $15; are available from L. B. Taylor, Jr., 108 Elizabeth Meriwether, Williamsburg, VA, 23185 (757-253-2636). Please add $3 for postage And handling, $4 for multiple book orders. Also, please specify to whom you wish the book(s) signed.)

L. B. Taylor, Jr., is available (depending upon his schedule) to speak on the subject of Virginia ghosts to civic, social, fraternal, business, school, library and other groups. Call or write about dates and details.

If you have a ghostly or unusual psychic encounter you would like to share with L. B. Taylor, Jr., (for possible future publication), please call or write the author.

OTHER BOOKS BY L. B. TAYLOR, JR.

PIECES OF EIGHT: Recovering the Riches of a Lost
Spanish Treasure Fleet

THAT OTHERS MAY LIVE (Air Force Rescue & Recovery Service)

LIFTOFF: The Story of America's Spaceport

FOR ALL MANKIND

GIFTS FROM SPACE (Spinoff Benefits from Space Research)

CHEMISTRY CAREERS

SPACE SHUTTLE

RESCUE (True Stories of Teenage Heroism)

THE DRAFT

SHOPLIFTING

THE NUCLEAR ARMS RACE

SPACE: BATTLEGROUND OF THE FUTURE

THE NEW RIGHT

THE GHOSTS OF WILLIAMSBURG

SPOTLIGHT ON ... (Four Teenage Idols)

EMERGENCY SQUADS

SOUTHEAST AFRICA

DRIVING HIGH (Effects of Alcohol and Drugs on Driving)

CHEMICAL AND BIOLOGICAL WARFARE

HAUNTED HOUSES

THE GHOSTS OF RICHMOND

THE COMMERCIALIZATION OF SPACE

ELECTRONIC SURVEILLANCE

HOSTAGE

THE GHOSTS OF TIDEWATER

THE GHOSTS OF FREDERICKSBURG

THE GHOSTS OF CHARLOTTESVILLE AND LYNCHBURG

THE GHOSTS OF VIRGINIA - VOLUME I

THE GHOSTS OF VIRGINIA - VOLUME II

CIVIL WAR GHOSTS OF VIRGINIA

THE GHOSTS OF VIRGINIA - VOLUME III